RULING
PEASANTS

◆ ◆ ◆

RULING
PEASANTS

Village and State in Late Imperial Russia

◆ ◆ ◆

Corinne Gaudin

Northern Illinois University Press *DeKalb*

© 2007 by Northern Illinois University Press
Published by the Northern Illinois University Press, DeKalb, Illinois 60115
Manufactured in the United States using acid-free paper
All Rights Reserved
Design by Julia Fauci

Library of Congress Cataloging-in-Publication Data
Gaudin, Corinne.
Ruling peasants : village and state in late Imperial Russia / Corinne Gaudin.
    p.   cm.
Includes bibliographical references and index.
ISBN-13: 978-0-87580-370-8 (clothbound : alk. paper)
ISBN-10: 0-87580-370-9 (clothbound : alk. paper)
1. Land reform—Russia—History—19th century. 2. Village communities—Russia—
History—19th century. 3. Land tenure—Russia—History—19th century. 4. Peasantry—
Russia—History—19th century. 5. Russia—Social conditions—1801–1917.
6. Russia—Rural conditions. I. Title.
HD1333.R9G38 2007
320.8′4094709034—dc22
2006026554

contents

✦ ✦ ✦

TABLES

♦ ♦ ♦

ACKNOWLEDGMENTS

◆ ◆ ◆

"In the village there are always enemies." "There is no one to complain to." These two phrases, which I heard repeatedly from elderly peasant women in the 1990s while walking through villages of Riazan province, could serve as epithets to this book about earlier generations of Russian villagers. When I began this project, I expected to find a reforming state in confrontation with a resisting peasantry, the anticipated story fitting quite well within a "roots of revolution" framework. Within a few months in the local archives, however, research questions began to unravel as I realized that they were riddled with unexplored assumptions. How much unity was present in the peasant community? In fact, what was this "community"? What did it mean that villagers were so assiduously complaining against each other to state officials? Was there even such a thing as customary law? Could one speak of "weapons of the weak" when more often than not peasants sought to appropriate the weapons of the strong against village rivals? Such a retreat to first-level questions is by no means surprising, and not only because it is always part of the research process. Historians of rural societies everywhere have been paying more attention in recent years to the contradictory and contingent ways peasants were connected to state and authority. They have effectively questioned earlier assumptions about rural societies bound by mentalities and social structures that impeded change. They have been showing how peasant communities were forged as much in their active engagement with the state as in their resistance against it. This book is part of that rethinking.

The first of the many debts that I have incurred over the years it took to complete this book is owed to archivists of a generation now retired and underappreciated. When I first arrived to work in provincial archives, I was primed to see the heads of reading rooms as gatekeepers rather than guides. Fortunately, people like Galina Ivanovna Khodikova in Tambov and Iraida Gavrilovna Zhuravleva in Riazan adjusted to the changed political climate more quickly than I did. They provided guidance whose value I did not grasp at the time, opening avenues I had not considered. By the time I realized how precious had been their help and advice, they were retired, replaced by a new generation of overworked, underpaid, and underappreciated archive workers, a group to whom I could transmit my thanks in person. I have benefited from the aid of *sotrudniki* of the archives of Moscow province (TsIAM), of Tver province (GATO), and of St. Petersburg's RGIA, and most particularly that provided by Galina Alekseevna Ippolitova in St. Petersburg and Andrei Nikolaevich Mel'nik in Riazan. I also thank the staff of the extraordinary Russian National and Russian State libraries in St. Petersburg and Moscow and the Helsinki University Library's Slavic Collection.

I am especially grateful to colleagues who read and commented on various incarnations of the manuscript: Stephen Frank, who also generously shared ideas and research materials; Christine Worobec, whose keen eye spotted flaws of writing and logic; and Scott Seregny, who provided meticulous and copious comments until health problems prevented him from doing more. His cheerful intellect is sorely missed. Colleagues here at the University of Ottawa—Eda Kranakis, Sylvie Perrier, Paul Lachance, Don Davis—kindly commented on parts of the manuscript and provided comparative insights. Pat Gentile took precious time away from her own research to read the final draft. I would also like to thank the anonymous reviewer, and the no longer anonymous David Macey: one could not hope for a more generously engaged critic. When the project was still in embryonic form, Ron Suny and Geoff Eley offered valuable criticism and encouragement. I am deeply indebted to Bill Rosenberg, who taught me the most about *le métier d'historien*. Finally, this book would never have been finished without the intellectual comradery, incisive critique, patience, impatience, and moral support of Amy Nelson, Kouky Fianu, and Norbert Desautels. I can also say the same about my mother, Colette Gaudin. As a modest apology—for this research took me away at precisely the wrong moment—I dedicate this book to her, her courage, and her passion to always understand more.

Research for the book was conducted thanks to grants from the Social Science Research Council and the American Council of Learned Societies with funds provided from the National Endowment for the Humanities, the International Research and Exchanges Board, and the University of Ottawa. The American Association for the Advancement of Slavic Studies, publisher of *Slavic Review,* has kindly authorized me to incorporate into chapter 5 parts of my article "'No Place to Lay my Head': Marginalization and the Right to Land during the Stolypin Reforms," no. 4 (1998).

Transliteration of Russian terms follows the Library of Congress system, except that the soft sign is dropped from frequently used terms (volost', Riazan', Tver'). Translation of Russian administrative terminology follows most common practice, with one exception. Historians have variously rendered the term *volost'* (prerevolutionary Russia's smallest administrative unit) as canton, township, and county. Each of these is a false cognate whose definitions have varied depending on the country and century. Why would a reader necessarily draw the appropriate analogy with early nineteenth-century France when seeing "canton"? This term for me will always connote something large and Swiss. Each of the other options can lead to similarly absurd associations. Volost is therefore not translated.

Ruling Peasants

◆ ◆ ◆

introduction

✦ ✦ ✦

In 1910, a correspondent for the capital's major liberal newspaper, the *Sankt Peterburgskie vedomosti* (St. Petersburg News), traveling in the western province of Poltava, published a vignette that for him characterized all that was wrong with Russia's system of rural administration. Driving along one of the province's dusty roads, he expressed surprise to see his "typically lazy" driver suddenly pull off the road, sit up to attention, take off his hat, and bow furiously at a passing dilapidated carriage in which sat a man dressed in a peasant overcoat. "The *volost'* scribe himself," the driver explained. "A real scoundrel, but without him we are as if without a head."[1] The St. Petersburg correspondent's surprise was likely feigned for rhetorical effect. Few other rural personages had been so consistently vilified in the "sketches from the countryside" that had been popular since the 1870s. The dishonest scribe *(pisar')* had become the emblem not only of the shortcomings of rural administration, but also of the image of the closed village. Reform-minded bureaucrats, reactionary nostalgists of strong patriarchal authority, neo-populist agronomists, and liberal publicists all deplored the depredations of the corrupt minority of village strongmen who allegedly maintained their hold over village institutions to the detriment of the honest majority. With a curious and near universal unanimity, political rivals who agreed on little else concurred in their diagnosis of the principal maladies afflicting rural society.[2] Backwardness, ignorance, and helplessness bred scoundrel scribes, unscrupulous barroom lawyers, and abusive village elders who conspired to block outside efforts to introduce either order or enlightenment to the village. After decades of government efforts to bring order and justice to the countryside, educated Russians remained convinced that peasants—and the wrong sort at that—in fact ruled the countryside.

The apparently intractable "peasant question," as publicists called it, preoccupied Russian statesmen as no other. At the time of Russia's first census, in 1897, three-quarters of the empire's inhabitants lived primarily off small-scale agriculture. Eighty-six percent of the population was still legally classified in the peasant estate, the vast majority of urban workers attached to their commune of origin through passport registrations and tax obligations. Agriculture accounted for over 80 percent of exports, and small-scale farming supplied the country with over three-quarters of its marketed grain. Peasants provided the army with the bulk of its soldiers (80% in 1915) and government coffers with a significant—if unknown—

proportion of its revenues.[3] And Russia was a peasant empire not only in its economic and demographic profile. Under the last two tsars, the simple Russian peasant was at the center of the monarchy's legitimizing myths as never before. Both Alexander III and especially Nicholas II emphasized the mystical and loving bond between tsar and people. The idea that the "thousands of invisible threads" stretching from the tsar's heart to the poorest peasant cottage was the source of the nation's strength and unity was reproduced in countless official ceremonies, pamphlets, and monuments.[4] The empire's stability, as well as the government's ability to fulfill its economic, military, and foreign policy ambitions seemed to depend on the peasant's willingness to produce, market, pay taxes, and fight.

In the face of difficulties in explaining the apparent impermeability of village culture, educated Russians continued to resort to the cliché of "two Russias": one urban, educated, European, civilized, the other illiterate, backward, and resistant to progress. The cultural gap between "the bast-shoes and the frock-coat" that caused so much anxiety was no doubt exaggerated, arguably no greater than that which existed between educated elites of western European countries and their respective peasantries.[5] That it appeared to be so was in part due to the particular features of Russia's administrative system. In 1861 the drafters of the Emancipation legislation had lacked the human and economic resources necessary to establish a centralized system of local administration to perform the tasks previously ascribed to serf-owners. The Emancipation legislation therefore reinforced village collective institutions, allowing the government to administer the countryside through elected peasant officials. In most of European Russia, land was allotted as the property of the land commune (zemel'noe obshchestvo), and the assembly of heads of household regulated its usage. The village society (sel'skoe obshchestvo) was responsible for apportioning and collecting taxes and redemption dues, for controlling movement in and out of the village, and for the general maintenance of good order. Lay peasant courts (the volost' courts) were charged with the conduct of local justice. Each of these institutions, which confined over three-quarters of the population to estate-specific laws and administrative structures, had been vaguely conceived as temporary concessions to practical exigencies that would fall by the wayside as peasants were remade from serfs to citizens. Although the tsarist bureaucracy would spend the next half century debating the modalities (and even the desirability) of this transition, the core local institutions created in 1861 were to remain in place until the 1917 revolution.

That the Russian government ruled the countryside through intermediary peasant corporate bodies was neither unusual nor necessarily unwise; such systems had at one time characterized all of Europe's anciens régimes. Communal institutions of self-administration were not incompatible with strong centralizing states, and "strong communal organizations did not mean less domination, but more" as village officials were coopted by governments to do their policing and tax collecting for them.[6]

What was more unusual in Russia was that old regime institutions had to serve the ambitions of an increasingly *dirigiste* state concerned with economic modernization. In the final quarter of the nineteenth century, the tsarist government embarked on a series of administrative and agrarian reforms explicitly predicated on overcoming the resistance of an ostensibly cohesive, self-regulating, and impenetrable village. A succession of new officials, decrees, laws, ministerial instructions, and legal rulings sought to constrain local autonomies and transform village institutions of self-administration into reliable executors of state policies. State concerns extended beyond the traditional arenas of tax collection and policing to embrace activities traditionally regulated at the local level. How villagers were to till and redistribute their land, how they were to settle internal disputes, how they were to conceive of property rights, or how they were to implement welfare provisions all became the objects of growing state intervention. How the village community responded to new legislation and administrative practices and how these responses in turn affected the state's reforms are the subjects of this book.

State intervention dramatically changed the rules of village politics. Contrary to the prevailing assumptions of that time, the village was not closed. In the 1890s, peasants came into contact with state agents, laws, and institutions to a degree they had never before experienced. As the government established new offices, new courts, and new laws for the countryside, villagers made immediate and massive use of them. They flooded local authorities with complaints, appeals, and petitions against their neighbors, their communes, and their elders. This study of the practices of village institutions from the "counter-reforms" of the 1880s through the period of the Stolypin agrarian reforms is intended to shine a spotlight on these daily administrative encounters between peasants and local officials. More precisely, I analyze the practice of those village institutions that were at the center of state-peasant dialogue: the village assembly and its elected officials, the peasant—*volost'*—court, and the land commune. The purpose is to uncover the peasant experience of authority at its most quotidian, prosaic, and local level in order to understand villagers' changing expectations of what the state was supposed to do for them, and how successive reform efforts recast the rules of internal village politics. Intravillage politics offered officials ample opportunity to intervene in village affairs. Why these interventions rarely succeeded in advancing the state's agenda is one of the questions of this book.

◆ ◆ ◆

At first sight, the story of state-peasant relations in late Imperial Russia is a relatively straightforward one of confrontation between a reforming state and a resisting peasantry. A rich historiography on bureaucracy and state reforms has shown that a fundamental weakness of the tsarist state was its inability to penetrate the countryside and overcome peasant "particularism." Late Imperial Russia remained "undergoverned" with far fewer police and civil servants per capita than western European states of the same period. This quantitative weakness was compounded by debilitating ministerial rivalries, carefully maintained by tsars intent on conserving their powers of arbitration, that resulted in lack of coordination in drafting or implementing state policies. Meanwhile, specialized ministries lacked bureaucratic structures extending into the provinces and districts. They were forced to rely on ostensibly all-powerful governors who themselves did not have subordinate staff in the countryside. The only all-estate organs of local government—the elected zemstvos responsible for local welfare—were dominated by the nobility, and perceived by peasants as just another government agency whose powers of taxation they resented. But most important, historians have emphasized that a state so intent on reforming society was unable to reform itself. As the adherents of autocratic authority hostile to calls for greater rule of law were able to block, dilute, or undermine measures that promised to involve society in its own transformation, peasants were excluded from meaningful public participation in political life.[7] Amidst these myriad shortcomings of the state, what the peasantry did and thought seems almost superfluous. And indeed, in most works on the state, the object of administration is relegated to the background and the image of the peasantry remains that projected by tsarist officials. The "unadministrable and unteachable village" appears closed and united in an impenetrable subculture.[8]

The assumptions about the closed village have been reinforced by works on rural society that have paid close attention to the internal, integrating norms of village life and to peasant resistance. That peasants were rational actors on the historical stage and that they manipulated, negotiated, and subverted government legislation no longer needs to be demonstrated. Village communities and land communes were largely able to adapt to the challenges of industrialization, growing out-migration, greater literacy, and increased contacts with the outside in ways that preserved their tax base, their modes of land tenure, and the authority of elders. Works on rural schools, the army, and the peasant experience in the city have shown how villagers "peasantized" the very institutions that were supposed to transform them. Peasants maintained their own conceptions of crime that fit poorly with state priorities and that left them increasingly frustrated at authorities' unwillingness to address their concerns.[9] And when peasants rebelled in 1905 and 1917, they did so as communities, village assemblies disciplining the rebellion by organizing the seizure of noble estates.[10] Historians have neither idealized peasant society nor ignored dissension and cleavages. But the goal of most research has been, in the words of Moshe Lewin, to try to understand the cultural and social mechanisms of village life "that allowed it to surmount internal strife and defend itself, as long as feasible, against external powers."[11] It is solidarity and continuity that have been privileged as having explanatory value. Historians have restored agency to the Russian peasant, but at the cost of marginalizing the state, whose initiatives have been studied primarily in order to understand the ways in which they were diluted, absorbed, and deflected by the recalcitrant village.

What is largely missing in the story of state-peasant relations is an understanding of the real, day-to-day encounters between administrators and peasants at the village level in periods of relative political stability. There seems to be an implicit—if unexplored—assumption that such an undertaking would not fundamentally alter our understanding of rural society. This is in part due to the great shadow that the 1917 revolution has cast over the study of the last decades of tsarist rule. Rebellion has been privileged as an object of study on the assumption that it reveals what is otherwise hidden, that the politics of rebellion are moments when the "public transcript" of deception and prevarication is swept away by long-hidden peasant dreams finally bursting forth into the open. The revolutions of 1905–1906 and 1917 have been described as dramatic "moments of truth" when peasants demonstrated their attachment to the redistributional land commune, their solidarity against outsiders, and their willingness and capacity to reject the tsarist state.[12] It has been assumed rather than demonstrated that between episodes of rebellion, peasant activism retreated into manipulation, subversion, collective foot-dragging, and other manifestations of passive resistance.

The problems with this assumption are threefold. The first is that the politics of accommodation rarely follow the same rules as the politics of rebellion. Recent work on state formation and state reform in contexts as diverse as postcolonial Latin America and early modern Europe have shown, by bridging social and institutional history, the dangers of cleaving too closely to dichotomies of dominating and dominated, resistance and acceptance. As historian Florencia Mallon has remarked, "as soon as the traces of independent initiative are systematically investigated and local power relations are taken into account, the solidarity and unity of the subaltern presence . . . begins to come apart."[13] Peasants—in Russia as elsewhere—were complicit in the system of rural governance. They served as village elders, judges, and police deputies. The political stability of the empire depended not only on rule over peasants, but also on rule with them.[14]

The second problem in assuming that rebellion was but the open expression of passive resistance is that the growing proximity of state institutions and laws in the post-Emancipation period created openings for their strategic appropriation in internal village power struggles. There is little evidence that peasants sought to restrict behavior that would invite involvement by outside authorities. On the contrary, villagers called upon state officials in ever-increasing numbers. Even a cursory look at the local administrative archives of the post-Emancipation period reveals a level of exchange between peasants and officials that belies the image of the closed village. If in the 1840s, the village and volost courts of Tambov province had been processing some 1,400 cases annually, in the early twentieth century, this number surpassed 130,000.[15] In some regions of the empire, as many as one-quarter of the cases decided by peasant judges were being appealed to land captains, the state-appointed official closest to the village. On the eve of World War I, each of the empire's two thousand land captains had to process on average three times as many administrative and judicial complaints as two decades earlier. And the bulk of these petitions were about internal village affairs: they consisted of complaints against village elders, appeals against decisions of the village assembly, disputes between neighbors, and conflicts within families. Periods of consensus or solidarity were the exception; factiousness was the rule.

The third problem in presuming continuity between the politics of accommodation and the politics of rebellion is that it fails to take into account shifting horizons of political expectation.[16] When the dreams of "black repartition"—of a redistribution of land from private owners to the peasantry—receded from the realm of the possible back to the realm of dreams, peasants played by the rules of the game. When villagers fought over land, they never mentioned the phrase so prevalent in 1905 and 1917 in conflicts with private landowners, that "land belongs to God." Instead, they spoke of "property" and of rights deriving from redemption payments. When petitioners argued about the ties and obligations that defined their local community, they never spoke of "commune" *(obshchina, mir)*, but of the official categories of "village society" and "land society." And in the process of engaging with authorities, in the process of fighting among themselves in terms defined from above, peasants and their communities were transformed. Key concepts such as "custom," "commune," and "property" did not exist out of time and place but were forged in the process of dialogue between rulers and ruled. One cannot presume an egalitarian mentality rooted in the need to ensure subsistence and in the exigencies of open-field agriculture.[17] Notions of rights and fairness were grounded in lived experience and in the repeated, quotidian exposure to law, courts, and officials. One of the points of this book is to show how the state's policies contributed to forging a certain kind of peasantry with historically constituted notions of property rights, community, and justice.

The purpose here is not to overturn the existing historiography, but to complement it. The story of resistance and of the resilience of the peasant commune is only half the story. The other half is about collaboration, and about the transformations that took place at the intersection of intra- and extra-village authority. If we privilege the first half of the story to the detriment of the second, we are left with little understanding of how rule was accomplished. We risk overemphasizing continuities and overlooking the fundamental transformations that were occurring in rural Russia. We also are in danger of underestimating the importance of conflict and cleavages in village society, overestimating solidarity, and ultimately overdetermining revolution.

But if, as I argue, the image of the "two Russias" did not come from peasant rejection of state institutions, then what would explain its extraordinary persistence? The answer lies in large part in the changing dynamics of the dialogue between peasants and state. State intervention in the late imperial period did fundamentally transform the Russian countryside. But the village experienced simultaneously too much and too little reform. The government, in its attempt to regularize administration in order to direct change in the countryside, opened up new opportunities for villagers to appeal to and use state institutions, raising peasant expectations of what the state could do for them. At the same time, the state's reformist ambitions constrained the practice of local officials in ways that undermined the paternal modes of governing it put forth as the cornerstone of its legitimacy. The regime's continued attachment to ideals of autocratic authority, and its concomitant distrust of bureaucracy and rule by law, meant that it stepped back from establishing a normative and institutional framework within which new types of conflicts could be argued. Local administrative practice poorly expressed the government's expectations; peasants no longer knew which language to use to appeal to the authorities. The result increasingly was a dialogue at cross-purposes, undermining former modes of manipulation, negotiation, and accommodation that had given rural administration much of its systemic flexibility. Administrators were left with few effective means to address the rise of tensions in the countryside, weakening the regime's ability to confront the challenges of agrarian reform and World War I. The weakness of the tsarist bureaucracy lay less in the effectiveness of peasant collective resistance than in the bureaucracy's own inability to communicate clearly with its rural subjects.

❖ ❖ ❖

The story I wish to tell begins in the late 1880s. It was then, with the "counter-reforms," that the Russian government tried to give itself the tools necessary to mold rural society and that the peasants began encountering state officials on a regular basis. It is in this period also that—to paraphrase Peter Waldron's blunt formulation—the political ethos of the Russian state became most confused.[18] Some of the consequences of this confusion are examined in the opening chapter, which outlines the shifting ideological, legal, and institutional context within which peasant self-administration was embedded. The *dirigiste* aspirations of the tsarist state were constrained by a paradox familiar to all of Europe's old regimes, that of modernizing and rationalizing administration without undermining the ideological underpinnings of absolutism. In Russia, this dilemma took on greater acuity after the 1880s for two simple reasons. The first was the deep attachment of the last two tsars to the ideals of paternal rule; the second was the qualitative shift in the level of the government's direct intervention in the countryside. The first task of defending the prerogatives of autocracy rested on a logic of rule by mercy, whereby personalized authority—unmediated by institutions—resided above regulations, above procedural rules, above law. The second task rested on a logic of rule by a bureaucracy able to enter the village and consistently implement the government's regulations. As long as the second goal remained subordinate and state intervention more reactive than proactive, conciliation of these two conceptions of administrative authority posed minimal problems.[19] Reforms from the late 1880s onward, however, tried to achieve both goals simultaneously. Policies sought alternatively to protect rural society from the corrupting pressures of change, and to encourage the integration of peasants into civil society. They aimed to preserve paternal administrative discretion, all while seeking uniformity in local administrative practices. The result was what one could call a sedimentary bureaucracy, to adapt the image coined by Alfred Rieber.[20] The successive superimpositions of bits and pieces of contradictory legislation meant that increased state presence rarely translated into increased ability to communicate reformers' expectations and priorities.

Such confusions and contradictions did not remain locked up in the upper echelons of bureaucracy merely paralyzing the state's ability to reform itself. They reverberated throughout the administrative system, greatly affecting the practice of the government's principal local agents and through them the elected peasant elders, judges, and scribes. The most important layer of rural administration was the office of land captain (*zemskii nachal'nik*). Created in 1889 to revive a paternalist and tutelary conception of administrative authority, the land captain was to solve the perennial problem of under-administration of the countryside all while protecting the collective interests of the commune against predatory private interests. Chapter 2 explores the central role land captains played in framing state-peasant relations up to 1917. The land captains were often the only non-peasant officials with whom peasants ever dealt, and much of the communication between government and peasants took place through the complaints and appeals filed in their offices. They were the tangible manifestation of the increase of state intrusion in the village, shaping peasants' experience and expectations of authority. But how successful were these new officials in transmitting the state's priorities? Did they manage to bolster the authority of peasant officials so that the latter became partners in rule? How did their presence affect the way village factions fought local battles? The answers to these questions point to the enormous difficulty land captains had in fulfilling their conflicting mandates. Their very presence opened the door to strategic behaviors that they could ill control, leading many captains to conclude that peasants were indeed an unruly lot, and peasants to conclude that captains were arbitrary and hardly a source of paternal justice.

The next two chapters delve more deeply into the village by examining the two key institutions of peasant self-government: the volost court and the village assembly. It is here that we get to the questions at the crux of this book, namely, how peasants, in the process of engaging the state, evolved conceptions of custom, property, and community. The volost court dealt with most internal village disputes. Reformed in 1889, these lay tribunals were designed to be accessible, cheap, free of formal requirements, and close to the population. Not only were peasant judges permitted to follow "custom" in regulating inheritance, but they were enjoined to rule "according to conscience" and "internal conviction" and to try to bring about peaceful settlements in civil cases. The courts were extraordinarily popular and the rise of peasant litigation was unprecedented, far outpacing population growth. By 1905, volost courts in forty-three provinces were processing over 3 million cases annually, which represented approximately two-thirds of all of European Russia's judicial business.[21] Litigation rates were comparable to the very busiest of western Europe's local courts. Chapter 3 explores some of the reasons for, and consequences of, this rising court use. Ostensibly, the willingness of villagers to eschew informal and extra-judicial dispute resolution signaled that state authorities had succeeded in their goal of penetrating the countryside. But were peasants satisfied with the court encounter? Why and how did they use the volost courts, and how did village attitudes toward justice intersect with state priorities? Finally, how well did the rural legal system fulfill its primary function of resolving conflicts? The courts worked relatively well as long as cases stayed at the local level. Increasingly, however, they did not: over one-quarter of land disputes were appealed to higher administrative venues, giving authorities an extraordinary opportunity to guide the work of the volost courts and to mold peasant understanding of property relations. Little use was made of this opportunity. Peasant willingness to call on outside authorities as arbitrators of internal quarrels, instead of facilitating juridification of local conflicts and finalizing disputes fed a crisis of raised expectations. The government created a demand for adjudication that it could not (or would not) meet.

The second key village institution was the assembly of heads of household *(skhod)*. While historians have recognized the dual function of the assembly, which under varying circumstances could serve as an instrument of government administration and as an enforcer of communal cohesion, it is the second function that has been privileged as the norm. The ideal type *skhod* embodied collective ideals, enforced conformity through unanimous decisions, and sought to preserve local autonomy and self-rule. Any deviation from this purported traditional base (evidence of dissension, of voting, of peasant unwillingness to participate) has been successively attributed to the emancipation, migration, the influence of urban culture, the rise of a money economy, demographic changes, land reform, or revolution.[22] The only way to make sense of repeated discoveries of the purported decline of the assembly is to analyze it—as David Sabean has suggested for villages of early modern Germany—not as an expression of bounded community, but as a forum "in which alternative strategies, misunderstandings, conflicting goals and values are threshed out."[23] In fact, unanimous decision making was never anything more than an unattainable ideal. Village solidarity was fragile at best, and at most times absent. Whether the assembly was dealing with taxes, land redistribution, or banishment, its actions cannot be deduced from a priori assumptions about peasant culture. The fluid boundaries of community were continuously being renegotiated in relation to state laws and demands. In the face of external pressures, the assembly reacted by redrawing the boundaries between insiders and outsiders in ways that excluded rather than integrated. In the process of "threshing out" the balance between obligations and rights, villagers increasingly conceptualized rights to land tenure within a framework imposed from above. The irony is that the very success of state efforts to define the terms with which peasants argued over land and communal membership would complicate the implementation of agrarian reform launched in 1906.

The final chapter of the book serves as a case study of how the pieces of the administrative puzzle (courts, assemblies, land captains, concepts of law and custom) functioned together on one issue that the government cared deeply about, namely property reform. When Prime Minister Petr Stolypin launched his ambitious modernizing projects in 1906, he had envisaged the elimination of estate-based institutions. If peasants were to receive the right to request property titles to their share of communal land, to enclose their parcels, and to separate from the commune, reformers then reasoned that the state needed to administer peasants as citizens and proprietors subject to the general laws of the empire. But the failure of the administrative and legal reforms to obtain requisite support in the new legislative bodies—the State Duma and State Council—would mean that institutions created in order to bolster peasant collectivism would be given a central role in overseeing its dismantlement. Historians of the Stolypin agrarian reform have looked for its repercussions and for peasant reactions primarily in police and land reform committee archives, largely neglecting the much more numerous peasant petitions, assembly resolutions, and letters of complaint filed with the volost courts, the land captains, and the district congresses.[24] How did local officials respond to the inevitable problems and tensions accompanying such an ambitious effort to transform land tenure? This question goes to the crux of the question of the reforms' viability. No matter how careful, balanced, and flexible the conception of the new policy may have been—and this remains a debated issue among historians—that conception was translated for villagers by the words and actions of local administrators.[25] I argue that the vocabulary of land possession that had emerged in the post-Emancipation decades intersected poorly with the new legislation and the meanings ascribed to these concepts by administrators. Disputants made references to claim rights, "property" rights, law, and custom that not only defied the logic of the new agrarian legislation, but revealed conflicting notions of "fairness" that greatly exacerbated internal village divisions. Meanwhile, the old community-based institutions and mechanisms of dispute resolution were increasingly incapacitated, unable to address new types of conflicts. The reforms thus exacerbated a problem that had marked—albeit in a more muted form—Russian rural administration since the 1890s: they created a whole host of new grievances, but not the institutional or legal framework to address them.

✦ ✦ ✦

The geographical focus of this study is primarily on the central agricultural and industrial provinces of European Russia. While much of the local material comes from the contiguous central provinces of Riazan, Moscow, and to a lesser extent Tver (with comparative data from other provinces), this is not a local or even a regional study. None of the provinces discussed here is "typical," but then no province or locality ever is. These provinces did have in common the predominance of open-field agriculture conducted under the aegis of the redistributional commune, and all were deeply affected by industrialization. Large pockets in each of these provinces saw near universal, seasonal, male out-migration to the rapidly growing cities. Some regions in southeastern Moscow and western Tver were dominated by rural industries, while peasants of northern Riazan survived primarily thanks to cottage industry. Villages conveniently located near a hub of the rapidly expanding railway network were able to compensate for poor soil by developing commercialized dairy farming or truck gardening. Only southern Riazan, within Russia's black earth zone, could still be described as "traditional" by the turn of the century. There, three-field grain agriculture predominated, and virtually the only source of local earnings was to labor on private estates.

But even these modest generalizations overstate the homogeneity of the regions under study. As Russian historian Pavel Zyrianov has rightly noted, no two Russian villages were alike. Even neighboring communities could have highly different demographic and economic profiles, patterns of landholdings, levels of tax burden, literacy, or out-migration. Each of these factors could influence how local peasant institutions functioned. Rural historians almost everywhere have become much more attuned over the past few decades to the "micro-variability" within what once appeared to be relatively homogenous peasant societies.[26] The purpose here is not to dilute this variability into some non-existent statistical or ethnographic average, but to uncover the range of peasant responses to state authority and outline the patterns according to which local institutional authority was conjugated. The conclusions drawn here do not extend to areas with significant proportions of non-Russian peasants—governed by different legal and administrative codes—but to the "Great Russian" provinces of the center of the empire, precisely the provinces central to the government's thinking about the apparently intractable problem of ruling peasants.

IDEOLOGIES OF AUTHORITY AND INSTITUTIONAL SETTINGS

I

♦ ♦ ♦

"Issued from unrelated committees with no links between them and at times obeying conflicting impulses, Russian legislation necessarily remains fragmented, incoherent . . . . The old laws subsist alongside the new ones with which they do not fit . . . . [Russia] resembles those castles built at various epochs, where one sees the most different styles side by side, or again those old houses, redone little by little and piece by piece, which never have the unity or the convenience of residences erected according to one plan and in one sweep."[1]

In his 1897 study of the Russian Empire, French journalist and traveler Anatole Leroy-Beaulieu was picking up on a theme common among observers of the tsarist bureaucracy. Commentators both outside and within Russia noted the coexistence of conflicting laws, overlapping and rival jurisdictions, and the government's inability to impose a uniform vision in the application of legislation. These critiques were sometimes followed by a corollary. Leroy-Beaulieu thus mused: "We can ask ourselves whether, under an absolutist regime, the defects of administration have for the future of the country almost as many advantages as disadvantages." According to this optimistic speculation, the incoherencies of the central bureaucracy were diluted as one went down the administrative ladder. Precisely because of Russia's "undergovernment," of the inefficiencies of local bureaucracy, and of the general "impotence of a legally omnipotent administration," peasants were somewhat sheltered from the rivalries and caprices of the center.[2] Russia's top bureaucrats were understandably less sanguine, though no less aware that the autocracy's powers did not measure up to its ambitions. The minister of internal affairs, P. A. Valuev, spoke in the 1860s of the "complete absence of ruling government." Forty years later Sergei Witte, finance minister from 1892 to 1903, disparaged a bureaucracy "omnipotent in the extent of its authority, but . . . incapable of any vital activity."[3]

Much of the historical research of the twentieth century has confirmed the aptness of Leroy-Beaulieu's first observation. In the fifty-three years between Emancipation and World War I, the tsarist government was continually studying rural society and administration, and tinkering with isolated pieces of existing legislation. A bewildering succession of committees and commissions examined the possibility of overhauling the system of local administration throughout this period, although only twice (in 1889 with the land captain reform and in 1906 with the Stolypin agrarian reform) did these efforts lead to significant recasting of even part of that system. Each tinkering produced legislation that fit poorly with the rest of the system. Each wave of reform brought to the village new officials imbued with values, ideologies of authority, and assumptions about peasant society that deeply affected the ways they approached their duties. But each wave was constrained by values, practices, laws, and institutions that had emerged from previous reforms. These successive superimpositions ensured that increased state presence did not always translate into increased ability to communicate priorities and effectively implement policies.

Leroy-Beaulieu's corollary has remained largely unexplored. Were peasants in fact sheltered from the contradictions of existing legislation, from political wrangling among ministries, from alternating ideological *mots-d'ordres* coming from St. Petersburg? The answer to this question lies in part in the accumulated legislative minutia that translated the government's visions of rule and authority into practice. British historian Derek Sayer has rightly cautioned that when discussing "the state" and the impact of its "hegemonic projects," one must not only examine overarching pronouncements but also determine how cohesive projects remained in the process of implementation.[4] This caution is particularly applicable to post-Emancipation Russia where each main period of legislative activity (1861, 1889, 1906) would leave its mark on the subsequent round of reforms, constraining their scope and creating incoherencies that deeply affected the way peasants were to live and to receive these reforms. Such incoherencies were in fact amplified as reforms entered the village, and much of what has been identified as peasant "particularism" was forged in the necessity of navigating the sometimes conflicting and imperfectly applied central policies from a position of relative powerlessness. This chapter will focus on the government side of the peasant-state relationship, outlining the system as established in legislation and the shifting visions of what this legislation was supposed to accomplish. The following chapters will examine how the system worked in practice.

Rural Administration under
the Emancipation Statute

The system of rural administration established for former serfs in 1861 and extended to state peasants in 1866 largely segregated Russia's peasantry from the empire's general administrative and judicial system. This outcome had not been intended by the majority of the members of the Editing Commissions responsible for drafting the General Statute Concerning the Rights of Peasants Emerging from Serfdom. Drawn largely from the ranks of reform-minded bureaucrats, these officials saw an "all-estate" *(vsesoslovnyi)* society as both a desirable sign of modernity and a means toward more effective governing. Firm believers in the state's ability to direct social change through legislation, they aspired to regularize and rationalize bureaucracy so as to make it a more effective instrument of rule and to transform peasants into citizens.[5] The legislators nevertheless reinforced peasant corporate bodies as a temporary expedient: reformers feared both the alleged civic immaturity of former serfs, as well as their vulnerability to former owners who had hitherto held judicial, police, and administrative powers on their domains. The state also lacked the financial and human resources to administer the countryside directly. The Emancipation statute therefore opted for indirect rule of the countryside, devolving administrative duties upon institutions of peasant self-administration, all the while envisioning the gradual evolution of former serfs into full citizens subject to the empire's general laws.[6] Little would come of these evolutionary hopes, and two temporary principles established in 1861 would continue to define rural administration until 1917. The first was that the countryside would be ruled through peasant intermediaries, and the second was that rural institutions should serve to protect the "rural way of life *(byt)*."

The primary mediating institution between newly freed peasants and the tsarist state was the village society *(sel'skoe obshchestvo)*. The legislation did not so much sanction existing traditions of land use as create a standardized institutional framework that regrouped state, serf, and crown peasants into a single estate of "free rural inhabitants." The *sel'skoe obshchestvo* was defined as an economic and fiscal unit "for the protection of the peasant way of life and the fulfillment of obligations to the government."[7] The village societies of the twenty-nine central provinces of "Great Russia" were automatically classified as redistributional *(v obshchinnom pol'zovanii):* arable land allotted to peasants was communal property. Individual households held temporary user rights to shares, the number of which could change according to criteria established by the assembly of household heads *(skhod)*.[8] The assembly was mandated to make decisions relating to collective land ownership and use, notably regarding the periodic redistribution of land among households. The assembly also had the right to refuse or accept new members, and to banish individuals for harmful and depraved *(porochnoe)* behavior. It was to elect and pay for village officials: police deputies *(desiatskie)*, tax collectors, and especially—every three years—the village elder *(starosta)* responsible for calling and running the assembly and implementing its decisions. The village society thus had little to do with the land commune *(obshchina)* of Slavophile and populist conceptions; the term *obshchina* was not even mentioned in the legislation, nor was it used by peasants.

While the village society was given substantial authority to regulate village social and economic life, it was not to be an autonomous body, and the General Statute defined its powers to ensure the fulfillment of state fiscal needs. If the assembly overstepped its official jurisdiction the resolution *(prigovor)* would be void, while the elder and any responsible participants could be fined or disciplined.[9] The assembly was required not only to set taxes for communal expenses (many of these obligatory), but in repartitional communes it also apportioned state tax obligations that were levied on the community as a whole. Through the system of collective responsibility *(krugovaia poruka)* for taxes and redemption payments, the village society had considerable power over its members, who could leave the commune or give up their share of allotment land only if they paid up all debts and taxes. In the event that a household accumulated arrears, the village society was supposed to either reallocate taxes among the village's households, or take measures for their collection (by selling off some of the delinquent's movable property, hiring him out, or in extreme cases removing his allotment altogether.)[10] Communal membership, in short, was compulsory: land tenure coupled with fiscal and administrative obligations.

The General Statute and related legislation left the door open for evolution out of the communal land system. With a vote of two-thirds of its members, a redistributional commune could transfer to hereditary land tenure *(podvornoe vladenie),* in which case each household became individually responsible for its share of the redemption debt (collective responsibility still applying to all other taxes). Legislators, fearing that peasant inexperience would lead to excessive land sales and impoverishment, set temporary restrictions on disposal of allotment land. Mortgages on land were forbidden until the end of redemption payments (scheduled over forty-nine years). Sales were forbidden for nine years. After that period, and until full payment of the redemption debt, redistributional communes could sell land with permission of provincial authorities, while households in hereditary communes could sell if the purchaser discharged any remaining land debt. A household could retire its redemption debt early, in which case its land became "personal property" *(lichnoe sobstvennost')* free of restrictions on sale and mortgage. It then had the right to leave the land commune and demand consolidation of its lands in a single plot.[11] While only a minority of peasants was able to make use of these provisions before they were rescinded in the 1890s, the regulations on redemption reflected the evolutionary intent of the 1860s legislation.

Unlike the village society, the volost did not seek to unite peasants with common economic interests. As a territorial unit gathering several villages within a radius of twelve kilometers and with a population of between

300 and 2,000 male souls, the volost was designated as the local administrative and judicial instance. It also had an assembly, composed of one elector for every ten households, charged with discussing affairs pertinent to the volost's general welfare. In practice, however, the assembly's role was largely limited to electing an elder *(starshina)*, hiring a scribe *(pisar')*, and approving volost expenditures. The elder's duties included a wide array of administrative tasks, such as supervising tax collection, implementing court decisions, providing authorities with information and statistics, and reporting to police any disorder or unauthorized absences. Both the village and the volost elders were empowered to impose sentences of less than one ruble or two days of arrest for minor offenses.[12] In short, the elders were responsible for ensuring the welfare and good order of their villages and volosts. The new system involved peasant officials in every aspect of local governing.

The final peasant institution set up following the Emancipation was the volost court, composed of three to twelve lay judges elected by the assembly from among the volost's inhabitants for one-year terms. This court was to adjudicate misdemeanors between peasants (such as petty theft, assault, disorderly conduct, insult), and civil disputes involving property valued at no more than one hundred rubles. Judges were "allowed to rule on the basis of local customs" in cases of inheritance, and in other civil disputes if there was no written agreement or contract. Although contemporaries—and later historians—often blamed the volost court as key to perpetuating the peasant isolation, the court also was designed as a transitional institution. The Editing Commissions had feared that general courts, reformed along western lines in 1864, would be overwhelmed by petty litigation if they were opened to millions of uneducated and inexperienced peasants. Legislators also believed that villagers were not ready for a statutory law ill-suited to the special needs of peasant life. Allowing a limited scope for custom meant that volost court decisions could not be appealed on substance: the reformers deemed it absurd to permit the appeal of decisions based on custom—by its very nature embedded in local circumstances—to courts designed to follow the civil code.[13] For criminal matters, the reformers did not even bother to draw up a new rural criminal code. Until the publication of a new code, judges were to follow the procedural and sentencing guidelines set out in the Rural Judicial Code *(Sel'skii sudebnyi ustav)* that had applied to state peasants since 1839.[14] This entire system of rural justice was conceived as a necessary concession that could fall by the wayside as peasants were drawn into the general judicial system.

The Emancipation legislation did not delineate the modalities of transition out of a separate peasant administrative system. The goal was to permit change rather than to direct it. Legislators were confident that peasants, once no longer stunted by restricting institutions, would grow into civilized adulthood. The new laws aimed merely to provide the legislative framework within which what was conceived as inevitable modernizing transformations could occur. But despite some significant adjustments in jurisdiction and organization undertaken in the following decades, the core elements of the rural administrative system remained essentially unchanged until the revolution. What did undergo alteration were the structures that articulated local units with the general system of administration as the government increasingly feared that it had lost control over the countryside and sought more proactive policies to make the transition from a "system of rule *with* peasants [to] one of rule *over* them."[15]

SHORTCOMINGS AND CRITIQUES OF INDIRECT RULE

The system as it had emerged from Emancipation quickly came under fire by critics from across the political spectrum. As Francis Wcislo has aptly noted, there existed a fundamental contradiction in peasant institutions "charged to foster peasant civil life while simultaneously overseeing the most traditional fiscal and police concerns of the state."[16] For some critics there was not enough fostering into civil society, for others too little order. Liberals regretted that the Great Reforms had not gone far enough in breaking down estate distinctions and in extending civil laws and individual rights into the village. Conservatives, on the other hand, felt that the Great Reforms had gone too far in breaking down natural social hierarchies and had introduced foreign, formal, cumbersome procedures into the countryside. Neither of these visions was able to shape the legislative process until 1889 when Alexander III decisively sided with the conservative minority bent on reintroducing principles of rule consonant with autocratic ideals. But on concrete issues, ideological opponents were surprisingly in accord; they largely agreed on the diagnosis of rural maladies, if not on the remedy. Underlying political differences was a growing consensus by the 1870s that peasants were unable to rule themselves for their own common good and that state institutions were powerless to shape peasant society in any meaningful way.

The first broad category of criticism was aimed at the very structure of the new local institutions. Publicists and ethnographers of liberal, Slavophile, and populist bent alike condemned the *sel'skoe obshchestvo* (village society) as an artificial unit that did not necessarily include households united by common land usage. In order to facilitate the implementation of the provisions of the Emancipation settlement, the General Statute had specified that whenever possible village societies should be formed from the households of a single former owner. Since several landowners could each own parts of a village, especially in the south and central black earth regions where large settlements predominated, this meant that villages could be divided into several *sel'skie obshchestva*. On the other hand, the provision that estates or villages of less than twenty male souls should be united with other neighboring estates could give rise to administrative units that gathered several small villages without common economic interests, a situation more often found among state peasants, and in northern and some central industrial provinces (see table 1-1). Further adding to the lack of congruence between administrative and socioeconomic units, peasants of a single owner had not necessarily belonged to a single land commune. They might also have been variously tied by land usage, for instance using arable land separately, but sharing woods or pasture. Peasants without common land ties could after Emancipation thus find themselves in a single village society, the only administrative and fiscal unit recognized by the new legislation.[17]

Several practical problems arose from such arrangements. If a separate land commune wanted to redistribute its allotment land, it needed (at least on paper) to obtain approval of two-thirds of the household heads of the entire village society. Households without arable land in common could find themselves unhappily grouped into a single fiscal unit under the regime of collective responsibility, so that a poorly endowed land commune was responsible for arrears of its land-rich neighbor. It was not unknown for peasants in a populous but poorly endowed land commune to use their numerical weight in the assembly to absorb the land of a smaller neighbor.[18] On the other hand, villages divided into several village societies found it difficult to address problems affecting the entire settlement. Large villages with several assemblies and several village elders found it cumbersome to coordinate work or collect funds for projects of general interest such as road repair, maintenance of wells or drainage ditches, or the construction of schools, churches, and rural hospitals.

Peasant practice partially compensated for the legislation's shortcomings. According to ethnographic reports of the 1870s and 1880s, some villages elected two sets of officials: the official *starosta,* and unofficial "field elders" responsible for regulating agricultural work and relations. Individual groups of peasants united by land usage could act separately in unsanctioned assemblies *(selennie* and *chastnye skhody),* gathering in the larger assembly only once or twice a year for the apportionment of taxes and the election of an elder. Sometimes, the full assembly functioned as an appeal instance, gathering when members of a constituent land commune were unable to come to an agreement. Other complex village societies formally requested separation, accounting for the gradual increase in many provinces in the number of village societies.[19]

In 1884 the Governing Senate began to legalize peasant practice by recognizing the right of partial (land) assemblies to conduct their own land redistributions *(peredely).* The land commune later gained jurisdiction over acceptance of new members and over household divisions. And an 1899 law finally recognized the smaller assemblies for fiscal purposes (distribution of tax burden and application of collective responsibility provisions).[20] Social measures, however, remained the exclusive preserve of the village society, and the legal adjustments did not extend to cover the

TABLE 1-1

NUMBER OF SETTLEMENTS, VILLAGE SOCIETIES, AND LAND COMMUNES

IN SELECTED PROVINCES (1880s)

PROVINCE	villages	village societies	land communes
Riazan	3,362	4,848	5,402
Tambov	3,365	3,627	3,970
Moscow	5,114	3,594	5,700
Tver	10,809	4,042	11,392
Vladimir	6,252	4,159	5,303
Novgorod	9,631	4,890	6,263

Sources: Numbers for villages and village societies come from "Sel'skoe obshchestvo," Entsiklope-dicheskii slovar' (St. Petersburg, 1893), 57: 282–83. For the number of land communes in Riazan (1882–1887): A. Selivanov, Svod dannykh ob ekonomicheskom polozhenii krest'ian Riazanskoi gubernii (Riazan, 1892). Tambov (1880–1885): Kuchumova, 331. Tver (1882–1891): "Tverskaia guberniia," Entsiklopedicheskii slovar', 64: 713. Vladimir and Novgorod (1885): Statistika pozemel'noi sobstven-nosti i nasel'ennikh mest Evropeiskoi Rossii (St. Petersburg, 1881), 2: 194; and 7: 4. Moscow: Moskovskoe gubernskoe zemstvo, Sbornik statisticheskikh svedenii po Moskovskoi gubernii (Moscow, 1879), vol. 4, pt. 1: 6, and, vol. 3, "Svodnaia tablitsa," n.p.

problems of villages divided into separate village societies. For most observers the fact that assemblies had to act outside of official regulations to accomplish certain essential tasks bespoke the inadequacy of the regulations. The village society, critics concluded, was tailored to state fiscal concerns rather than to peasant social or economic needs, thus reducing its importance as a genuine peasant institution.[21]

Even sharper criticism was reserved for the volost, denounced as an artificial creation of legislators, a geographic invention randomly gathering village societies with no preexisting economic or social ties. The volost was burdened with such a wide array of police and fiscal duties, critics argued, that it could hardly be expected to respond to the peasant population's needs. Nor could it serve the interests of the state, which lacked regular bureaucratic structures extending to the local level. Critics objected to the hypocrisy of designating the volost as an institution of peasant "self-administration" when the proliferation of government authorities who needed to communicate with the countryside produced streams of conflicting demands that turned the elders into petty officials (chinovniki). Given the high demands and the low pay, critics added, the "best" peasants (understood to mean literate, sober, and respectful of authority) refused to serve, while individuals attracted by opportunities for embezzlement bribed the assemblies to get elected. Not only did this leave honest villagers defenseless against unscrupulous local bosses and undermine any nascent respect for legality and procedure, but it hardly served the demands of bureaucratic efficiency.[22]

Volost and communal budgets were frequently cited as evidence of bureaucratization of peasant institutions. On this point, critics were quite correct. The bulk of local tax levies *(mirskie sbory)* was spent on mandatory administrative expenses: salaries of elders, judges, and scribes, upkeep of volost buildings, purchases of paper and ink. In addition, the General Statute required peasant administrative bodies to repair roads, supervise local military recruitment, provide postal horses, accompany and guard prisoners in transit through the locality. Altogether, in 1881 these obligations consumed approximately 87 percent of volost budgets. More reliable 1891 figures show 86 percent of volost and 49 percent of village expenditures tied to obligatory administrative, police, and social duties. Even expenses designated as voluntary—construction of schools, hospitals, and churches, and the salaries of teachers and priests—were in fact often imposed by the authorities. Only spending related to agricultural tasks such as renting supplementary land or hiring herdsmen (22% of village societies' expenses) can truly be labeled voluntary.[23] For peasants, possession of allotment land was intimately associated with the burdens of village taxes, labor obligations, and administrative duties.

The system of local taxation came under fire on three counts: as burdensome, as unfair, and as economically irrational. Liberal critics pointed to the numerous general police, administrative, and social functions devolved onto peasant institutions, so that in reality peasant self-administration was neither peasant nor self-administrative. Since local taxes were levied on allotment land, only peasants paid the costs of what amounted to general administrative expenses and of services that benefited the entire local population. Taxes in kind (or more precisely in service) were also levied on the village communities. Peasants alone were beholden to provide labor for road and bridge repair, fire fighting, and police work. Critics argued not only that these levies were justifiably resented as unfair, but that the diversification of the rural economy rendered them irrational. With the rise of out-migration and cottage industry, the construction of rural factories, and with an increasing number of nonpeasants living in the countryside, the assessment of allotment land alone corresponded less and less to a household's capacities of payment, or to the actual needs and makeup of the rural population.

The most consistent critique of peasant administration as chaotic and disorderly, however, was rooted in a common perception of villagers' civic immaturity. Rural observers, ethnographers, and government commissions all insisted upon the prevalence of illiteracy among peasant officials, the universal custom of drinking at the assembly, and the pervasiveness of bribery and corruption. Reporting on the results of an 1880 inspection tour of Tambov province, Senator S. A. Mordvinov summarized what was rapidly becoming the prevailing wisdom regarding peasant institutions.

> Peasant self-administration, established as the cornerstone of welfare in the villages . . . has virtually ceased to exist. The village and volost assemblies . . . have lost all credit in [the] eyes of the people. Decent peasants do not show up at the assembly, or are brought there against their will. Not one matter is decided objectively, since there are no assemblies where persuasion with vodka by the interested parties does not occur. Very frequently . . . assembly decisions are drawn up in advance by the scribe and, on his instructions, are signed by the illiterate delegates who do not attend. Village and volost elders, who almost without exceptions are illiterate, play a secondary role. Peasants are indifferent toward elections, believing that even if a good person were elected, the office would corrupt him.[24]

There was striking unanimity in analyses of the ills befalling peasant administration. Accounts of general peasant indifference to endemic corruption and embezzlement of local resources by village officials cut across the political spectrum, and blame was laid at the door of the cunning *miroed* (literally "commune-eater"). The term *miroed,* as used by commentators in the 1870s and 1880s, referred to wealthy peasants who allegedly controlled communal resources thanks to the illiteracy, ignorance, and helplessness of their fellow villagers. In the words of S. Sashkov, writing in the Slavophile journal *Delo* in 1881, these new-style predators had caught the village in "a spider's web" of debt servitude. Another analyst, writing in one of Russia's foremost progressive journals, echoed: "Everything has been given up into the hands of the volost elders, the scribes . . . the kulaks, the commune-eaters." As a result, "the peasantry cannot through its own strength affect the slightest useful change."[25] Even populists, long accused of idealizing the commune and overestimating its solidarity, were alarmed by evidence of increasing economic differentiation and the apparent control of village institutions by the wealthiest villagers.[26]

By the early 1880s, concern over the *kulak-miroed* had reached near panic levels, permeating all government discussions of rural reform. Senatorial inspections of village administration conducted in 1880 and 1881, which did much to establish the official agenda of debate for the coming decade, juxtaposed the village's genuine collective interest to the *miroed's* exploitative self-interest. "The peasant . . . has not found protection against oppression by the strong," explained Senator Mordvinov, so that peasant self-administration had been perverted beyond recognition.[27] Likewise, when the Kakhanov Commission—formed in 1881 to draft a proposal for local administrative reform—solicited reports from provincial zemstvos, the *miroed* had pride of place. I. Iu. Skalon, a reformist official in the Ministry of Internal Affairs (MVD) and later governor of Viatka, stressed that the reports pointed to one overarching problem: the emergence since Emancipation of a new village type "who gnaws at and undermines the commune *(mir)*, striving to subordinate its [general] interests to his own personal ones." With the spread of a money economy, argued Skalon, the village had divided into two unequal, antagonistic groups: the well-to-do and their poorer neighbors, the exploiters and the exploited, the clever manipulators of the village assembly and the cowed, silent majority.[28] Commentators of all political stripes agreed that the honest tiller had neither the strength nor the knowledge to protect himself against the strong and clever.

How had such a deplorable situation come about? Again, the answers betray a remarkable consensus, as they were built upon analysis of very real problems in the system of rural administration. The Great Reforms had left authority over peasant institutions fragmented, far from the village, overburdened, and correspondingly weak.

The system that was to guide peasants in their transition from serf to citizen suffered from numerous shortcomings, notably in the areas of supervision and appeal. Administrative supervision had first been entrusted to the peace arbitrator *(mirovoi posrednik)*, charged with overseeing the dismantlement of serf estates and mediating settlements between peasants and landowners. The arbitrators were also supposed to ensure the proper collection of taxes and redemption payments, verify that peasant assemblies did not overstep their official jurisdiction, and investigate complaints against peasant officials. These latter obligations, however, tended in practice to be neglected. After the task of drafting land charters was completed in 1864, the office became something of a sinecure for nobles with ties to the district marshals of nobility who nominated them. In 1868 Russia's governors were virtually unanimous in condemning the arbitrators for indifference, passivity, and general ineffectiveness in fulfilling instructions. Government worries over mounting arrears prompted the MVD to call for replacing the arbiters with "strong and effective executors" in the countryside.[29] The office of peace arbitrator had few defenders when it was abolished in 1874.

The district bureaus for peasant affairs, which replaced the arbitrators, did little to improve the situation. The arbitrators' administrative obligations were simply transferred to the new bodies with the exception of tax collection, which was handed over to the police. Precincts were abolished and jurisdictions extended to an entire district *(uezd)* with populations ranging from 100,000 to 300,000. Of the bureau's five members, only the permanent member did not simultaneously hold another position. Responsible for investigating all land cases, the permanent members were rapidly overburdened and correspondingly slow. Many boards and permanent members were soon tarred with the same reputation for indifference and passivity as their predecessors.[30] This reputation was not entirely ill-deserved. There is little evidence that Riazan district boards, for instance,

TABLE 1-2

RURAL ADMINISTRATIVE STRUCTURE (1861–1917)

	1861–1874	1874–1889	1889–1917
		Governing Senate	
Ministry		Ministry of Internal Affairs (MVD), Land Section (*zemskii otdel*)	
Province		Provincial board for peasant affairs	
District (*uezd*)	District congress of peace arbitrators	District board for peasant affairs	District congress of land captains
Precinct (*uchastok*)	Peace arbitrators		Land captains
Volost		volost administration	
Village		village assembly (*skhod*)	

ever examined the substance of peasant complaints. Hearings focused narrowly on formal and procedural requirements (such matters as verifying whether the elder had overstepped his jurisdiction, or whether an assembly resolution had passed with the requisite number of votes). Local investigations were invariably entrusted to the volost elder, and assembly decisions were rarely overturned. Boards rarely gave peasants motives for their rulings. Peasant complaints to the provincial board that "the district board did not take our complaint and we don't know why" were more than ingenuous protestations but betrayed a legitimate frustration with authorities who were far from the village, both geographically and figuratively.[31] In the words of Senator M. E. Kovolevskii, the boards were reduced to "strictly formal, paper relations" with villagers.[32] The shortcomings of the district boards and peasant complaints against them played no small part in feeding the growing perception in government circles that peasants were clamoring for a strong hand, for an authoritative official who could dispense rapid punishment and just protection.

The justices of the peace (*mirovye sud"ia*) also proved to be a disappointment. Established with the 1864 judicial reforms, they perhaps best embodied the evolutionary hopes of the Emancipation legislation. Charged with judging minor crimes not subject to the volost courts, these justices also adjudicated peasant disputes over property valued between 100 and 500 rubles and over nonallotment land, as well as disputes normally under the purview of the volost court if one of the litigants was not a peasant. The peace courts were to serve as a bridge between popular and official conceptions of justice, between the volost and the general courts, between custom and written law, and thus were designed to teach peasants about law. To encourage accessibility, formalities were to be minimal, and judges were to encourage peaceful settlements. Only if mediation failed were judges to rule according to "conscience" or to statute.[33] One problem was that the position of justice of the peace did not require special judicial training, so that many judges were ill prepared to render decisions that would withstand scrutiny by judicial appellate instances. As verdicts were overturned, justices had to pay ever closer attention to judicial statutes and legal precedent, which in turn considerably slowed down work and encouraged precisely the type of formalism the courts had been designed to avoid. Overworked and underfunded, the peace courts accumulated large backlogs of cases, and even the most dedicated justices found it impossible to juggle their dual mandate of encouraging respect for the law while remaining a simple and accessible court of mediation.[34]

By the late 1870s the Ministry of Internal Affairs was convinced that the Great Reforms had neither resolved Russia's problems of rural underadministration nor provided the government with an effective agent in the countryside. Divisions within the bureaucracy over the proper solution, however, would delay reforms until 1889. On the one hand, an important reformist tradition within the bureaucracy sought to extend government authority and efficiency through the uniform application and enforcement of law. This entailed moving forward along the lines sketched out in the evolutionary provisions of the various statutes that made up the Emancipation legislation. A majority of the zemstvos submitting proposals on the state of local institutions, as well as the 1881 Kakhanov Commission, asserted that the rural population had become too diverse for the further maintenance of estate institutions to be effective. The discretionary powers granted to the police and the district boards, reformers added, left the village at the mercy of arbitrary outside intervention, thereby fostering a feeling of helplessness among the peasantry.[35] The proliferation of government officials with jurisdiction in the countryside only compounded the problem, as peasants did not know where to turn for redress against abuse. According to this analysis, it was the existence of a separate peasant administration, with ill-defined social and property relations that stunted the development of a healthy understanding and respect for legality and allowed the *miroed* to flourish. The solution proposed was for the volost to become an all-estate, territorial unit that could regulate relations between rural residents regardless of legal ascription. Reformers also advocated the elimination of the separate peasant courts, as only the universal application of legal codes could prevent the *miroed's* manipulation of "custom" that kept the village beyond the reach of administrators. This vision did not entail less tutelage for the peasantry, but it was to be tutelage through rationalized bureaucratic structure and law, the goal of which was to draw an allegedly ignorant and immature peasant into civil society.[36]

Conservatives, on the other hand, argued that peasants were clamoring not for more foreign-inspired laws and procedures, but for justice that was rapid, morally grounded, and corresponded to their patriarchal way of life and deeply embedded customs. Peasants were clearly not ready for the responsibilities of self-administration, and the peasant assembly had demonstrated its incapability of making decisions for the common good. The Simbirsk zemstvo commission, presided over by A. D. Pazukhin—who would soon join the MVD and play a central role in drafting the 1889 land captain legislation—argued that "without proper guidance, peasant officials frequently fall under the most pernicious influence, and are incapable of maintaining the authority that has been invested in them."[37] Lack of proper supervision *(nadzor)* was to blame for the disintegration of rural society, as no strong authority existed in the countryside that could protect the weak majority from the new-style schemers and predators and thus ensure decisions made for the general good.

Calls for the reaffirmation of autocratic principles emphasized the paternalistic, personal, and moral nature of government authority. In this view, most forcefully put forth after 1882 by Pazukhin, rural administration as established in the 1860s was foreign and harmful to the Russian peasantry because it undermined the moral bonds that tied the estates to each other and to the state. Furthermore, it undermined "custom" as the expression of an organic, historically constituted internal sense of justice. Government supervision was too distant from the village, too fragmented, and too legalistic to provide effective guidance and protection for a peasant society besieged by the corrosive onslaught of monetary relations and urban values.[38] What the countryside needed, Pazukhin would argue when given a chance to translate his vision into concrete proposals, was a strong, local official who was a direct representative of the tsar, an official who embodied personal rather than institutional authority, who would rule not according to abstract theory and procedure but according to concrete needs of the ever changing conditions of life.

The different assessments represented two conflicting concepts of governing, as well as conflicting conceptions of the proper nature of authority. But both sides advocated proactive policies, assuming that peasants were demanding intervention and protection. As David Macey has argued, neither remained "content to confine law to the essentially passive function of reflecting . . . reality and permitting future change."[39] While it was the vision of paternalist authority that would ostensibly gain the upper hand in the 1890s with the creation of the office of land captain, adherents of government through law would continue to play key roles within the bureaucracy in ways that would constrain, shape, and ultimately undermine the effectiveness of the new local representative of the tsar's mercy.

Autocratic Authority Refurbished— ## The Land Captain Statute of 1889

In the mid-1880s, the adherents of a restoration of strong paternalist authority in the countryside found crucial support from Minister of Internal Affairs Dmitrii Tolstoi (1882–1889) and especially from the new tsar, Alexander III.[40] The 1889 legislation creating the office of land captain (*zemskii nachal'nik*) was but part of a broader shift in the monarchy's conception of its role and its projected self-image. Alexander III, and later Nicholas II, sought to reaffirm the affinity between the tsar and the peasantry. As Richard Wortman has shown, this project was no mere conservative reaction but represented a dynamic of change, a proactive effort to build a new form of national unity between government and governed.[41] And this effort went beyond ceremonial expressions of the familial ties that bound the father-tsar to his peasant-children and the traditional practice of direct petitioning of the monarch. The ideals had to be made real, and the land captains were a way of bringing benevolent paternal protection and justice into the countryside. As Tolstoi had explained in 1887, the land captain was to be "a conduit manifesting the tsar's authority before the population." The new officials were to resolve problems of institutional weakness in a way consonant with the ideal that the monarch remained the father-tsar, a source of justice and mercy. Thus Tolstoi emphasized that the "new order of supervision *(nadzor)* [by the MVD] is alive, a stranger to formalism, free of written documents *(bezpis'mennym)*, or to put it more precisely, is defined by an unbureaucratic approach."[42] Land captains in effect represented the institutionalization of the ideal of extra-institutional authority.

Accordingly, the 1889 Land Captain Statute emphasized supervision of peasant institutions and guardianship *(popechitel'stvo)* of the peasants' moral and economic well-being. These concerns and the general spirit of the new institution were neatly summarized in the preamble of the 1889 law:

> With constant concern for the welfare of Our fatherland, we have turned Our attention to the difficulties encountered among rural inhabitants of the Empire. One of the main reasons for this unfortunate situation resides in the lack of a firm government authority close to the people that would combine guardianship over rural residents with care for the conduct of peasant affairs and with the obligation to protect the welfare, order, safety and rights of individuals in rural areas.[43]

The legislation established from sixty to seventy land captain precincts *(uchastki)* in each province, and the key requirement for the new officials was that they possess "comprehensive familiarity with the needs and life *(byt)* of the population." Few precise regulations restricted their activities, as paternal concern for their charges and detailed knowledge of local conditions were considered the best guide to decisions made in the interests of the village as a whole. The land captains in essence were to extend the protective cloak of the tsar's benevolent paternal authority over the least of his rural subjects. They were expected to open the village to beneficial outside influence, their wide discretionary powers enabling them to identify and protect village collective interests.

Hereditary nobles were deemed to possess both the local knowledge and the selfless dedication born of the service tradition necessary to undertake the mission of restoring moral, social, and economic order in the countryside. Priority in appointments was given, therefore, to local landowners with either higher education or previous experience in rural administration. Only if there lacked candidates from the nobility could the MVD name non-nobles to the post.[44] The Land Captain Statute should not be seen, however, as an attempt to shore up the landowning nobility's declining political power. Tolstoi had written in his recommendations to Alexander III: "All local institutions should be state institutions, linked with central government authority."[45] The conservative nobility, increasingly touchy about real or perceived threats to its prestige or autonomy, did not mistake these statist ambitions.[46] The new legislation used and reinforced estate structures but represented a renewed state effort to gain effective control over the countryside.

On paper the power of the land captain was enormous. He could review any village or volost resolution and recommend its cancellation to the newly created district congress of land captains *(uezdnyi s"ezd)*, not only if he found it illegal (for instance, if the village assembly overstepped its jurisdiction, or if a resolution was passed with less than half of householders present), but also if he deemed it harmful to village interests. The land captain also reviewed all resolutions regarding collection of taxes and use of communal funds. He heard complaints against elected peasant officials and could fine them up to five rubles or impose seven days arrest and recommend their removal from office to the district congress (article 62 of the Land Captain Statute). A land captain could also fine or arrest ordinary peasants for not fulfilling "lawful orders" (article 61). In addition, this official picked peasant judges and volost elders from among the candidates elected by the volost assembly. He was responsible for deciding whether a woman could receive a passport without her husband's permission, and he also played an important role in the distribution of loans and in obtaining permission for migration. Finally, article 39 charged captains with protecting villagers' economic and moral well-being, a charge that could range from instituting welfare measures, organizing fire fighting, and ensuring cleanliness of streets, to protecting widows and orphans.[47] There was hardly any area of village life that did not potentially fall within the land captains' jurisdiction.

Finally, the land captain was given a central role in the administration of local justice as the government decisively abandoned the principle of separation of administrative and judicial responsibilities that underlay the Great Reforms. Whereas judges for the volost court had previously been elected directly by the assembly, now the land captain selected four judges from among eight candidates put forward by the village societies. Appeals of volost court decisions were now allowed, the land captain charged with reviewing which cases merited being heard by the district congress. This responsibility was particularly important in light of the abolition of the justices of the peace, which greatly enlarged volost court jurisdiction. The limit on civil suits tripled to three hundred rubles, while all limits were lifted for inheritance of allotment land and related property. The reformed courts also took over inheritance of non-allotment land valued at less than five hundred rubles. This last measure perhaps best embodies the spirit of the 1889 reforms and its rejection of the evolutionary aspirations of the 1860s, as estate ascription became more important than form of landownership in determining whether individuals would be subject to the general courts under the civil code or to the separate peasant courts. Peasants could no longer "graduate" to the general courts simply because they had acquired landed property.

Most criminal cases previously heard by the justices of the peace were divided between the volost court and land captains. The bulk of petty crimes, including theft of goods up to a value of fifty rubles, fell to the peasant judges, while land captains heard cases of primary interest to local landowners such as trespass, agricultural labor contracts, and illegal cutting of forests (porubka). In addition, captains ruled on civil cases among peasants and non-peasants involving property valued at less than three hundred rubles.[48] Under these new "temporary" regulations—which would remain in place throughout most of the empire until the revolution—peasants were almost entirely cut off from the general courts (unless they committed a major crime) that had trials by jury, rights to representation, and adversarial principles of adjudication.

The 1889 administrative and court reforms were but part of a broader government effort to protect the integrity of the commune by attacking what were deemed to be its most harmful attributes. From the late 1880s, the government had passed a series of measures aimed at bolstering the authority of the assembly and of household heads so that the land commune could better cushion against economic disruption and social instability. In 1886 the government moved to limit household partitions, as it feared that smaller nuclear households with few adult workers were less resilient to economic downturns. Henceforth, partitions had to be approved by two-thirds of the assembly.[49] In 1893, general communal redistributions of arable land were limited to minimum intervals of twelve years in an effort to reduce field fragmentation and stabilize tenure. Partial redistributions *(skidki-nakidki)*, allowing the commune at any time to remove land from a household that had lost members or accumulated arrears in order to reassign it to another, were severely restricted so as to prevent wealthy peasants from taking advantage of others' misfortunes and seizing control of an inordinate amount of allotment land. Finally, in the same year, the government erased the distinction between redeemed and unredeemed allotment land. Neither could be mortgaged, nor could allotment land be sold to a non-peasant. Any sale of land by an entire commune required provincial board approval and additional permissions from the Ministries of Internal Affairs and Finance for land worth more than five hundred rubles. According to the majority of the State Council (the body responsible for advising the tsar and drafting legislation), the concept of land as commodity was foreign to Russia. In addition, peasants—by allegedly undertaking too many land sales that led to impoverishment—had shown that they were incapable of using their rights responsibly. For these reasons, the State Council also revoked the 1861 provision whereby peasants who had paid off their redemption debt could claim title to their land and even consolidate it in a single plot without communal approval. The intent of the framers of the Emancipation settlement, concluded the State Council, had been to designate allotment land as a special fund "for the preservation of the peasant way of life."[50] A phrase designed in 1861 to explain temporary restrictions during a fixed period of transition was thus elevated to first principle.

Ostensibly, all these measures further segregated peasant society, but in fact they brought state officials more directly into village life. And herein lay a fundamental contradiction in the land captain reform. The underlying assumption of the legislators had been that traditional patriarchal authority embodied in organic, historically constituted custom had been weakened by foreign legal principles, by impersonal administrative structures, by parasites spawned by the growth of monetary relations, by city morals. In theory, therefore, it would suffice for land captains to protect peasants from nefarious outside economic, cultural, and political influences for custom to restore itself. Yet another underlying assumption of the 1889 reforms was that peasants—backwards, illiterate, helpless, infantile even—had been unable to protect their own customs and institutions. The restoration of a "genuine" peasant culture thus first required reform of rural reality as it existed. In practice, this left land captains with little practical guidance for their actions. On the one hand, the preservation of historically constituted custom demanded that land captains not intervene unduly in village affairs. On the other hand, when they found that peasant society did not conform to their conceptions, land captains were to reform rural society as it actually existed.[51] In many ways the MVD was asking for the impossible.

Land captains realized long before the MVD the practical impossibility of simultaneously promoting and preventing change. In 1891, for instance, the MVD amended the instructions issued by the Riazan provincial board following the latter's first inspection of its new officials. No, the MVD wrote, communes could not be compelled to allot land to illegitimate children, as this was to be decided by the assembly according to custom. Nor should captains apply the rule preventing communes from removing land from absentees "too formally," because this would block the commune's ability to use its resources most effectively. Again, such issues were best left to "custom." The MVD also demanded that captains not "tie the volost courts to the letter of the law": for instance, the decision as to whether absence from the village excluded a relative from inheritance of a household plot had to be settled according to custom. Thus the MVD continued through five more items, each time emphasizing the importance of respecting custom.[52] A land captain receiving such instructions might understandably be puzzled. How was he to defend the weak and protect the commune against manipulation if what the commune decided was declared "custom" and therefore out of his purview? Especially since he had received but a few months earlier an MVD circular reminding him of the dangers of excessive assembly autonomy and of his obligation not to remain a mere spectator to abuse. From the start, there emerged a disjunction between the MVD's practice and its publicly professed ideology of authority that left captains shaking their heads in dismay at the "endless circulars" raining down from "self-loving officials" sitting far from the village in "bureaucratic Petersburg."[53]

If land captains did not have the freedom of action they had expected, it was also because the 1889 reforms did not do away with the legal and administrative context within which they had to operate. In many ways, the new officials were ill suited to their bureaucratic times. Numerous St. Petersburg officials disliked the new legislation, deeming it a revival of archaic conceptions of governing that undermined efforts to achieve rational delineation of administrative and judicial powers. Alexander III had signed the MVD's proposal into law in spite of majority opposition within the State Council. Even as conservatives gained the upper hand within the highest circles of the St. Petersburg bureaucracy, the reform spirit of the 1860s found refuge until the turn of the century in the Senate, the Ministry of Justice, and to a certain extent even the State Council, all bodies with a say in how the land captain legislation was to be implemented.[54]

The Governing Senate played an especially important role in shaping the 1889 institutions. William Wagner has shown that the Senate, through its cassation practice, was instrumental in transforming inheritance and family law even in the absence of significant legislative changes.[55] A similar, if more subtle, evolution can be seen in the realm of administrative regulation. The Senate's principal mandate was to "defend the exact meaning of the law and [ensure] its uniform application throughout all judicial instances of the Empire."[56] While the First Department was charged with administrative supervision—resolving conflicts of jurisdiction, hearing complaints against illegal actions by officials—the civil and criminal cassation departments served as a final court of appeal in the judicial system. The Second Department, established in 1884, had jurisdiction over decisions rendered by peasant administration. Its rulings were binding for the lower instances, and only the tsar could overturn a Senate decree.

According to the letter of the 1889 legislation, the Senate had little discretion to review decisions of the new rural institutions without MVD approval. Tolstoi had deliberately sidelined the Senate, arguing that it was overburdened, slow, and lacked the practical information necessary to make decisions free of "formalism."[57] In theory, only three types of cases could be submitted directly to the Senate for cassation. First, appeals against provincial board decisions on land organization were sent to the Second Department. All other provincial board administrative decisions were final; any complaints about their legality had to be forwarded through the MVD, which decided first the merits of the case. Second, the Senate could reopen decisions on criminal cases that were founded on false testimony, or in which new circumstances were discovered. Otherwise, a provincial board's judicial decision that was taken in "clear deviation from the true meaning *(istinogo mysla)* of the law" could be forwarded to the Senate only through the Ministry of Justice, but again "in conjunction" *(po snoshenii)* with the Ministry of Internal Affairs. Finally, article 127 of the Land Captain Statute allowed for direct submission of administrative rulings to the Senate when a provincial board found that district boards or land captains had overstepped their jurisdiction, had exceeded their authority, or had rendered a decision that constituted "a clear breach of the law."[58] For the vast majority of local administrative rulings, the MVD was the gatekeeper controlling access to the Senate.

In spite of all these restrictions, the Senate played a decisive role in circumscribing land captain autonomy through its cassation rulings. The MVD itself quickly recognized the need to involve the empire's highest administrative court in implementing the 1889 reform. The first years of the land captains' activities were marked by considerable confusion, and not a few cases of egregious abuse of power. The Senate's judicial expertise was necessary to untangle complex issues of procedure and jurisdiction, and to define the limits of "law" and "custom." And in spite of the ministry's scorn for "formalism," a code word for excessive deference to legal procedure, it needed Senate decrees to ensure consistency of administrative practices throughout the empire. As long as provincial boards acted as final judicial and administrative courts of appeal, their decisions in practice (if not in law) set precedents for lower instances. But nothing guaranteed uniformity between provinces. As critics pointed out, Russia now had as many senates as there were provincial boards, a situation that threatened to undermine the utility of land captains as reliable executors of state priorities.[59] The Senate had been reorganized in the 1860s specifically to deal with such problems of "fragmented cassation." Although the MVD could impose some uniformity in local administrative practice by issuing "official explanations," these did not have the binding character of a Senate decree.

As early as 1892, the MVD lost some of its control over triage of appeals against provincial board decisions. Armed with its mandate to ensure uniform application of laws, the Senate determined that provincial boards could not reject appeals against their rulings on the grounds that these were officially classified as "final."[60] And once a case arrived before the Senate, the minister of the interior could not always control the outcome. Any case touching upon its jurisdiction had to be forwarded to the ministry for a recommendation, and the minister or his deputy had the right to participate in deliberations. But if the Senate disagreed with the ministerial conclusions at the department level, the case was forwarded to the General Assembly, where the ministry had only one vote. If the required majority decision (usually three-quarters) could not be reached, the case was handed to the minister of justice who issued a recommendation. Finally, if this opinion did not garner the necessary majority, a special commission of the State Council decided the case. While only 330 cases, or 0.15 percent of the Second Department's caseload, were forwarded to the General Assembly in the twenty-five years between 1884 and 1909, and a mere 29 cases reached the State Council, these widely published rulings were binding in future decisions at all levels of the administration.[61]

The crucial role played by the Senate is best illustrated by its gradual erosion of the powers embodied in article 61 of the Land Captain Statute, which allowed land captains to punish peasants for "non-execution of a lawful order." From the beginning, there was uncertainty over the expression "lawful order." Did this refer to any order that the land captain might deem wise to give as long as it was not illegal—allowing, for instance, a land captain to decree that peasants doff their hats to officials, that they replace straw roofs with tin (as a fire-prevention measure), or that they never be seen drunk in public? Or did the phrase refer only to fulfillment of orders prescribed by law? The first interpretation was preferred by those who emphasized the land captain's role as guardian of peasant economic and moral well-being, the second by those who valued his role as conduit for state law.

In the early 1890s, a series of key Senate rulings limited the land captains' discretionary powers: zemskie nachal'niki (land captains) could not arrest the author of a groundless complaint against village leaders—this should be dealt with under the article regarding insult to officials. Land captains could not fine participants of a village assembly for removing land from an entitled villager—the decision could only be overturned in the process of review of assembly resolutions. Nor could they fine villages for not contributing to grain stores, as such situations were covered in the tax code. Peasants who refused to repair roads or plant trees could not be arrested under article 61 but had to be judged according to article 29 of the Regulations on Punishment. In 1896, one Gerasimova appealed a fine levied for "groundless complaint" against a volost elder by a captain intent on discouraging litigiousness. The case was finally decided in the State Council, which confirmed—over MVD objections—the principle that land captains could only give orders that enforced obligations already set out in existing positive law. The decision specified that it was the law that defined the rights of each Russian citizen, and the 1889 statute on land captains had in no way restricted the rights of peasants—as free rural inhabitants—set out in 1861. Since the law represented the "solemn expression of the Autocrat's will," land captains could fulfill their mandate to become a "firm government authority [vlast'] only if their orders strictly followed existing laws." In practice, this meant that captains could no longer issue local decrees. The narrow definition of "lawful order" also meant that most punishable offenses were covered in existing law codes and that they were to be handled under judicial, not administrative, procedure. Over the next seven years, the Senate overturned fully 83 percent of appeals on this issue.[62] By the time article 61 was repealed in 1906, it had become virtually inoperative.

Senate rulings played a similar, if more modest role, in narrowing the circumstances under which a land captain could discipline assemblies or overturn a village resolution if he deemed it detrimental to the interests of the village society. Land captains could not overturn a resolution simply because it was harmful to one member of the village, but only if it deprived him or her of a right. Nor, after 1900, could a captain overturn an elder's election merely because he considered the candidate unreliable; an election could be annulled only if the candidate did not meet formal requirements (namely, age and residence requirements, and the absence of a criminal record). An 1897 ruling forbade land captains from canceling a resolution once it had been implemented. This last case concerned a resolution from 1891 leasing out communal land for ten years at an abnormally low price. The local captain in 1896 had annulled the agreement on the grounds that the renter had exploited the commune's dire need in a year of harvest failure and famine.[63] Such rulings were most demoralizing precisely for those zemskie nachal'niki who most sincerely believed in their paternal mission of protecting the common good of childlike peasants against private monied interests.

Conservative commentators raged against Senate rulings for shackling land captains in debilitating regulations. Critics were quite correct to see in these developments a deviation from the original conception of the land captain as the incarnation of autocratic authority, where a paternal figure with local knowledge and broad powers would dispense justice that was prompt, strict, moral, and merciful.[64] High officials in the MVD were not so quick to recognize the contradiction. While the ministry publicly trumpeted the triumph over bureaucratic and legal formalism, it continued to issue reams of instructions, guidelines, and explanations that increasingly constrained the land captains' freedom of action. From the outset, there existed an inbuilt tension between the calls for strong, local, flexible, paternal authority, and the need for reliable executors of state policy. The resulting dissonance not only caused frustration among land captains, but practical problems as well, for any effort to better guide the local officials' work undermined the flexibility at the core of the institution. The MVD would not confront this contradiction until the turn of the century, and even then it would do so with remarkable timidity.

CONTRADICTIONS OF THE LATE IMPERIAL BUREAUCRATIC ORDER

The first explicit complaints from within the bureaucracy that the land captains were not particularly efficient representatives of state authority came from somewhat unexpected quarters. Many provincial governors had initially voiced considerable enthusiasm for the reforms, expecting the captains to be reliable executors who would allow provincial authority to extend into the districts. But the land captains came to office at a difficult time. Most had been at their posts less than a year when they were called upon to help deal with the consequences of the catastrophic harvest failure of 1891. In addition to their regular duties, captains were called upon to fulfill an astonishingly broad range of extraordinary tasks. Given the scale of the emergency, the land captains were bound to disappoint.

The avalanche of requests, orders, and directives issued in 1891 provide a measure of the governors' excessively high expectations for the new officials. Riazan governor D. P. Kladishchev, for instance, requested that land captains identify households in need of tax extensions, that they help zemstvos verify that aid was being used by the truly needy, that they *personally* (emphasis in original) check that fields sown with loaned seed were properly plowed, that they issue travel certificates to impoverished villagers so that these persons could benefit from lower rail fares. Land captains were simply unable to keep up with the succession of urgent requests, and numerous orders had to be repeated: the governor requested three times that land captains report on the state of grain reserves in each village, twice that they collect data on the economic conditions of communes in their precinct, and no less than four times that they identify households in extreme need.[65] On 30 May the governor had asked for detailed information on shortages of seed for winter fields: within seven days, land captains were to identify communes that lacked seed along with the corresponding number of *desiatina* (roughly equivalent to a hectare) and of individuals affected by shortages. One week later, the governor extended the deadline to the end of the month after realizing that the data he had received had not been based on personal inspection, but on declarations by elders. He concluded with a moral plea: "I do not doubt that land captains, whom the law has charged with guardianship over the peasant population and with care for its well-being, will attend to this matter with heartfelt solicitude." Apparently, such gentle reminders of duty were insufficient to bring forth the required information: in September the governor was suggesting that since the sowing of winter fields was completed, it would be "a *good moment* to suggest to gentlemen land captains to *speed up* the collection of data according to the May 30 circular [emphases in original]."[66] Under the circumstances, the governor's almost delirious praise for land captains in the 1890 provincial annual report—written in 1891 and already discussing the harvest failures—might appear surprising. But annual reports were written for the tsar, and they were hardly the place to highlight shortcomings either in the state of provincial administration or in his majesty's pet projects.[67]

The governors could do little more than cajole land captains into action, and there was little they could do to improve the staff. Their powers of appointment were limited to a veto of candidates put forth by the district marshals of nobility. The provincial boards responsible for supervising the captains—and who could recommend disciplinary action—were overworked and understaffed. In any case, disciplinary action and removal from office depended on an MVD reluctant to weaken the authority of land captains in the eyes of the population.[68] In 1896, Tula Governor V. K. Shlippe—who firmly agreed that captains should be master of their precinct as fathers in their family—noted ruefully in his annual report that the MVD removed officials "only for the most serious crimes." He further deplored that too many captains were careless, without energy, and fulfilled their obligations superficially, concluding that "their work has borne no fruit, but since it does not cross the border into illegality *(prestupnosti)*, the situation is tolerable."[69] Faint praise indeed.

By the second half of the 1890s there were officials in the MVD ready to listen to such misgivings. The 1889 legislation had been tailored to the assumption that good men mattered more than good laws, that generalists would respond more effectively than functional specialists to both state and peasant needs. Yet chronic difficulties in attracting and retaining good candidates, a point belabored in annual governors' reports, undermined some of the MVD's confidence in its agents. In 1902 the MVD admitted in a report to the State Council that less than half of the empire's 2,300 land captains were adequately qualified for the post.[70] Because the land captains were called upon to execute ever more specialized tasks, their shortcomings were particularly worrisome. Land captains had to be statisticians, not only during the famine of 1891, but also in the following years as they reviewed requests for extensions on tax payments, a Herculean task requiring surveys detailing the value of household property, the area and fertility of its landholdings, its income and expenses. The 1893 law on land redistributions demanded closer involvement in agriculture and an understanding of landholding arrangements. In 1899, the captains also became fiscal agents, taking over from the police responsibility for collecting taxes. And with the growing body of Senate rulings and MVD explanations, the *zemskie nachal'niki* needed ever more detailed judicial knowledge. The ministry continued its attempts to impose some uniformity and control over local administrative practices by issuing circulars and explanations, and by requiring that reports be submitted on standard forms. In 1898 it explicitly recognized the need to sacrifice some local flexibility by drafting the first official instructions to guide the land captains' work—instructions issued, however, only in 1905.

But a more important contributor to changing attitudes toward rural administration was a renewed concern within the top levels of Russia's bureaucracy over the link between administrative structure and economic development. The famine of 1891 and the commune's inability to mitigate its effects fed the debate over the compatibility of communal landholding with the goal of improving agricultural productivity. The government was especially concerned with chronic tax arrears and continued periodic crop failures that seemed to threaten both the empire's fiscal health and its industrial ambitions. The debate centered around two related key questions: whether the system of rural taxation was effective and whether communal land repartitions *(peredely)* were a barrier to improving agricultural productivity.

Even as the government was strengthening communal land tenure in the 1890s, attacks against the commune were becoming more widespread within the government, among agronomists, and in the pages of Russia's "thick" journals. Critics of the commune blamed the periodic redistribution of strips for low agricultural productivity, assuming that households insecure in their holdings lacked incentive to fertilize and improve their land. Redistributions, in conjunction with population growth, were also presumed to aggravate problems of field fragmentation. Open fields, interstripping, and collective grazing of cattle on stubble after harvest—which prevented fencing and forced obligatory crop rotations—were said to prevent agricultural experimentation by the industrious and enlightened few, submitting them to the will of a majority bound by tradition.[71] The 1893 law limiting redistributions to a minimum of twelve-year intervals had been intended as a partial response to these problems. The goal was to give peasants greater security in their holdings and thus stronger incentive to improve their parcels. But a sizable minority of the State Council criticized this measure as inadequate. I. I. Vorontsov-Dashkov, minister of the imperial court, launched a particularly scathing attack on the commune, methodically targeting the social, moral, economic, and political arguments put forth by its supporters. He argued that the collectivism of the redistributional commune fed not solidarity and mutual aid, but "predatory instincts" since peasants continually eyed their neighbors' parcels, or worse, the lands of private landowners. "Thus has the socialist instinct found ground in the *mir*," concluded Vorontsov.[72] A growing minority of officials agreed that the commune stunted agricultural progress and undermined political stability.

The system of collective responsibility *(krugovaia poruka)* for redemption payments and taxes, one of the rationales for establishing the village societies in 1861, also came under fire as ineffective and even counterproductive. The requirement that migrants obtain passports from their commune might have ensured that wages made their way back to the village, but clearly it did not prevent the accumulation of arrears. A massive survey conducted by the Ministry of Finance from 1887 to 1893 provided a wealth of concrete data to support these views. Village assemblies almost never resorted to redistribution of arrears among households unless pressured by police. Indeed, historian A. M. Anfimov has found that in 1900, only 139 communes (of the 62,084 to which the legislation applied) passed resolutions to apply *krugovaia poruka*.[73] The commune rarely granted tax relief for households in temporary difficulty, nor did it provide tax-free allotments to orphans or the elderly. Local inspectors reported tax delinquents even among wealthy peasants who waited as long as possible to settle accounts for fear of having to pay the arrears of their poorer neighbors. Key Ministry of Finance officials concluded that collective responsibility had in fact become a major cause of tax arrears.[74] By the turn of the century Sergei Witte, as finance minister from 1892 to 1903, became the most ardent and effective critic of the regulations on collective responsibility, arguing that they were a disincentive to agricultural production as peasants feared that any surplus could be removed to cover the tax payments of their less productive neighbors.

By the late 1890s, Witte was advocating the incorporation of the peasantry into an all-estate system of government. Neither genuine social stability nor economic progress would be possible until the peasant was secure in his property and civil rights, argued Witte. Both the arbitrariness of local officials and the insecurity of land possession characteristic of communal agriculture stifled individual initiative and stunted the development of legal consciousness. Witte's criticisms found fullest expression in the reports of the Special Conference on the Needs of Agriculture, an interministerial commission—appointed by Nicholas II in 1902—whose work over the next two years laid the foundations for much of the agrarian reform legislation of 1906. Many of the conference's provincial committees emphasized the deleterious effects of the constraints of communal agriculture and periodic repartitioning of land. The majority of the committees argued that customary law theoretically governing volost court rulings and regulating land usage was outdated as it was predicated on a society uniform in its needs, outlook, and lifestyle that no longer existed.[75] The implications of these criticisms were straightforward and farreaching: the resolution of the agricultural problem would entail decisive abandonment of principles of indirect rule through corporate bodies.

Even before the government embarked on agrarian reform in 1906, it took several important steps to loosen the authority of village societies over their constituent households. Collective responsibility for taxes was lifted in February 1903, and in November 1905 the government cancelled all redemption debts outstanding after January 1907. These decrees removed much of the rationale for communal interference in household affairs, a development recognized with the decree of 5 October 1906 ("The Repeal of Certain Restrictions on the Rights of Rural Inhabitants").[76] A household no longer had to obtain village assembly approval before partitioning. Restrictions on peasant movement were eased: the commune could no longer prevent the departure of one of its members because passports could be issued without consent of a head of household. The assembly lost the right to force indigent peasants to hire out and remit their wages to the commune to cover arrears; migrant workers could be registered in their place of residence and work, rather than in their communes of origin as had previously been the case. The decree thus began untangling the administrative functions of the village society from the agricultural functions of the land society, and the liberal press praised it as a first step toward a return to the principles of 1861.

The 5 October decree also restricted the tutelary role of the land captain, who lost the right to fine and arrest peasants without formal procedure. Captains could no longer overturn a village resolution if it would lead to a "clear loss to the village society," or even if it violated the rights of some members of the commune. Henceforth, a village resolution could be reviewed and overturned only if a member of the village society appealed it, or if it was illegal.[77] The decree eliminated those powers that most clearly reflected the assumption that the captain knew best what was good for peasants.

The limitations on the land captains' powers fell far short of bureaucratization, however.[78] The MVD did make an effort to improve the officials' qualifications and accountability, but the measures taken are striking for their modesty. In 1903, for instance, the ministry proposed to create training courses for candidates that would conclude with an exam. Although the minister, V. K. Pleve (1902–1904), would defend his proposal to the State Council on the grounds that the peasantry had outgrown "its recent patriarchal way of life and this completely changed the situation of the office of land captain," it did not mean that the ministry was ready to submit nobles to obligatory formal training. When exams and courses were established in 1907 and 1908, they were required only of ministerial appointees, individuals named for lack of local candidates who did not meet the property or education qualifications. It is doubtful that the eight-week (120-hour) course sufficed to prepare an inexperienced candidate for his post. Noble land captains received not even that, their training left in the hands of already overworked provincial boards. The measure was a far cry from professionalization of the office.[79]

A particularly critical 1905 inspection, conducted by the head of the MVD's Land Section *(zemskii otdel)*, V. I. Gurko, seemed to signal more far-reaching changes. Published in the Land Section's public journal *(Izvestiia zemskogo otdela)*, the report deplored that each local official acted according to his own criteria *(po-svoemu)*. The result was that rules could vary greatly over time, as well as from one district to the next. Gurko concluded that the peasantry's general lack of respect for law and authority was exacerbated by the land captain's arbitrary use of discretionary powers.[80] But such scathing critique translated into few practical measures. In August of 1905 the MVD finally issued its Instruction to Land Captains *(Nakaz zemskim nachal'nikam)*. In the justificatory circular accompanying the release of the Instruction, Minister B. A. Bulygin (1905) acknowledged—although largely to deny its significance—the fundamental contradictions of the 1889 reforms. On the one hand, he reiterated that the primary objective of the 1889 institutions was to create a local authority close to the population and knowledgeable about its needs. Such closeness implied a certain degree of discretionary power allowing land captains to respond to constantly changing circumstances that fell outside the realm of exact regulation. On the other hand, land captains embodied government authority and therefore were obliged to "tailor their activities to the general order and goals of government activity, without replacing them with their own judgment, be it well-intentioned." Bulygin still praised the utility of discretionary powers, as long as officials remained within the general framework of the law, and as long as they satisfied the obligation of consistency and exactitude *(opredelennost')*.[81] The Instruction was designed to guide land captains to better balance these twin goals of discretion and consistency.

The Instruction introduced few concrete changes. For instance, while the land captain could present a question to the village assembly for consideration, he could not tell villagers how to vote and he had to leave before voting began. The MVD also established a system of frequent and regular inspections by central authorities to complement the existing lackadaisical review by overworked and indulgent provincial authorities. Moreover, the land captains were to inspect volost and village officials every two to three years. Otherwise, the Instruction merely reiterated that a land captain had to make a sustained effort to be close to the rural population, rely less on peasant officials, and investigate complaints personally. It also exhorted captains not to rely on haphazardly collected information, but to compile systematic data on virtually every aspect of life in their precincts: population, households, stores, markets, churches, taxes, arrears and their causes, types of land, sown area, average harvests, and even debts incurred for the purchase of horses.[82] The Instruction thus imposed more tasks, more controls, more regulations but did not provide more land captains, more training, or more money. Tact, local knowledge, and dedication remained the attributes of the ideal land captain. "Lack of supervision *(nadzor)*," "excessive formalism," and "insufficient closeness to the population" would remain leit-motifs of MVD inspectors' criticisms of *zemskie nachal'niki* until 1917.

The revolution of 1905–1906 for a time shifted the political balance in favor of more far-reaching reform. The agrarian disorders demonstrated the inability of the existing system to maintain order. The communes had not served as a bulwark against social instability but instead had served as the primary units for the organization and disciplining of the rebellion. As peasant assemblies voted and proceeded to seize noble lands and crops, it became clear that the land captains had not succeeded in convincing peasants that their economic well-being did not depend on increasing the size of their allotment. The *zemskie nachal'niki* more often than not had ig-nominiously fled the countryside in the face of the peasant uprisings.

Some high officials seemed little surprised by the inability of land cap-tains to contain discontent. Sergei Witte, in a memorandum to Nicholas II, sneered at the "miserable role" of "striking" land captains.[83] By Decem-ber 1905, as rebellion spread in the countryside, Gurko sent an angry cir-cular informing governors that the high-handed and indifferent behavior of "most" land captains was one reason for the widespread peasant disor-ders, and that provincial authorities should take the most energetic meas-ures to remove unsatisfactory officials. But there was little governors could do. Removing unsatisfactory land captains, when it was "rare" (in Gurko's assessment) to find one with close and trusting contact with the peasant population, was clearly impossible. There simply would have been too few officials left. In fact, when the MVD in the following months began re-ceiving an unusually high number of requests from land captains to be re-lieved from office, the ministry condemned these as reprehensible. Gover-nors were to inform captains that it was now more than ever important to place the obligations of service above personal interests, and that requests for departure would not be granted, while poor performance would lead to disciplinary measures.[84] In spite of the ministry's rather panicked threats, it could do little to prevent passive resistance by land captains re-luctant to face the wrath of rebelling peasants. The inadequacy of local of-ficials' behavior only underscored that it was impossible to continue tai-loring an entire institution to a few extraordinary individuals. Abolition of the office of land captain was among the many proposals that the new prime minister, Petr Stolypin (1906–1911), would present before the newly elected State Duma after 1906.

It was all the more important that the government find reliable and ef-ficient instruments of the central bureaucracy given the challenges of im-plementing the agrarian reforms decreed on 9 November 1906. The decree and subsequent legislation, globally referred to as the Stolypin agrarian re-forms, dramatically loosened the commune's power over its members by giving individual households the right to take out land titles on their share of communal holdings. This right brought with it several important changes. Allotment land titled as personal property (a process referred to as *ukreplenie*) could be sold, whereas previously, abandoned land could only escheat to the commune. A householder could also request that his individual strips be consolidated into a single parcel, a request the commune was obliged to satisfy if it was filed at the time of a general repartition. At other times, enclosure would be granted if the district congress deemed that it was not "inconvenient or impossible" for the commune. Titled land was no longer the common property of the entire household, but the personal property of its head. When the decree was voted into law by the State Duma on 14 June 1910, the scope of the reforms was extended: communes not having undertaken a general repartition since land was originally allotted after Emancipation would automatically be converted to hereditary tenure, and half of a commune's households could force village-wide consolidation.[85]

The stated rationale behind the land reforms was to free enterprising and innovative peasants from the collective traditionalism of communal agriculture, but the government also sought to prevent excessive disruptions and landlessness. The agrarian reforms bore the mark of continued concern for peasant immaturity and vulnerability. Titled land retained its special legal status as "allotment" land, in other words, land allotted to peasants at Emancipation. It was therefore categorized as "personal" and not as "private" property, a designation that limited rights of disposal. Peasants who took out title could not sell to a non-peasant and could mortgage only to the Peasant Land Bank. No purchaser could accumulate more than six shares of allotment land.[86] The preservation of the special status of allotment land meant that without reform of village and volost administration, the local tax burden would continue to fall on holders of allotment land. Without legal reforms, the new peasant proprietors would remain subject to the volost court and its right to rule according to "custom," even though in most villages of central Russia "personal property" was a new category of tenure about which there hardly could be any custom. Without changes to village administration, the new forms of tenure posed again the problem of defining the relationship between the village society and the land commune whose functions had increasingly merged over the previous decades.

The reformers were perfectly cognizant of these problems, and Stolypin had conceived of the agrarian reforms as part of a package of projects intended to dismantle estate-based legal and administrative structures and to rule peasants as citizen smallholders. In a much quoted 1906 speech, Stolypin explained to the Duma:

> Our fatherland, reformed by the will of the Monarch, must become a state ruled by law, since, until the written law defines the obligations and protects the rights of individual Russian citizens, then those rights and obligations will depend on the interpretations and whims of private persons . . . That is why the government has made it its main task to [draft] a whole series of legislative bills that will establish firm norms for the newly forming state life of Russia.[87]

This emphasis on rule of law *(pravovoe gosudarstvo)* left little place for ideals of personal, discretionary authority, or for estate segregation. Nor did it leave much place for the ill-defined overlap of functions that had hitherto characterized village and land societies. As Stolypin explained in 1907: "As long as the peasant is poor and without personal property, as long as he is in the commune's clutches, he remains a slave and no written law can give him the benefits of civil freedom . . . [and] the government cannot reach out to him."[88] Political, cultural, and economic renewal were to go hand in hand.

Historians have heatedly debated whether the primary goal of reform was the destruction of the commune, the improvement of agricultural productivity, or the creation of a political base of support for autocracy. These goals cannot be disentangled, however. Various officials within the high administration emphasized one or the other of the constituent goals at different times. In addition, individualization of land tenure and property reform was conceived to unleash individual initiative and agronomic improvement, thereby creating a new class of peasant proprietors that would be drawn into citizenship and thus "strengthen the base" of state power *(gosudarstvennost')*.[89] This was an instrumental conception of property as transformative and an essential step to integrating peasants into civil society. Administrative reform was central to actualizing this transformation of peasants into citizen proprietors.

Among the bills brought before the State Duma in the years of Stolypin's premiership was the proposed overhaul of village societies and volosts into all-estate institutions encompassing all property owners within their territory. The distinction between allotment and non-allotment land would be erased as local taxes would be levied on the basis of property values, thereby eliminating the functional overlap between village societies and land communes. The office of land captain was to be abolished. In its stead, precinct commandants would receive authority over all inhabitants of the area, but without judicial powers. Finally, volost courts were to be replaced by justices of the peace subordinated to the general courts and with jurisdiction for all minor cases regardless of the estate to which litigants belonged. Together, these proposed changes would have dismantled the system of indirect rule through corporate institutions.

Even before Stolypin's assassination in 1911, however, the new State Council—reorganized since 1906 into an upper legislative chamber dominated by the conservative nobility—had rejected all but one of these proposals.[90] The only project to emerge from the legislative process, albeit diluted beyond recognition, concerned the volost courts. The court's jurisdiction was reduced (limits on civil suits were lowered from three hundred to one hundred rubles) while salaries were to be increased and paid for by the central government to shield judges from the influence of local peddlers. The land captain lost his supervisory role, the task of hearing appeals now falling to an upper village court presided over by a justice of the peace. But the volost court remained an exclusively peasant institution insulated from the general civil and criminal codes. In rejecting the Ministry of Justice's more ambitious project, the State Council committee on judicial reform spoke in language reminiscent of the 1880s:

> The conditions of toil in the countryside and life itself within the commune, with its own interests by no means similar to the interests of urban dwellers, have left their stamp on the Russian peasantry and have sharply isolated it in its moral and legal consciousness. . . . Breaking the centuries-old layers of the peasant legal order at its roots with artificial norms, even if theoretically correct, would be an inappropriate measure, unwise and not agreeing with the true needs of peasants' daily life.[91]

This was language—with its emphasis on peasant isolation and special needs—that Stolypin's conservative successors at the head of the MVD could understand. N. A. Maklakov (minister from 1912 to 1915) was determined to protect autocracy's prerogatives and was deeply hostile to the idea that law could trump administrative discretion. This was hardly the man to revive Stolypin's stalled projects. Even the modest court reform had been implemented in only ten western and southern provinces— deemed readiest by virtue of the predominance there of hereditary land tenure—by the beginning of the First World War.

The failure of these reform efforts had important practical consequences, as existing rural institutions retained a vital role in the countryside, and the central ministries had no alternative but to continue to rely on them. It was the village society and its assembly that voted on land titling and consolidation, the volost courts that resolved disputes over allotment land (whether in personal ownership or not), and the volost administration with its elected elder that registered, notarized, transferred instructions, and remained the government's primary conduit of information about the countryside. Land captains were given a central role in implementation of the agrarian reforms. Charged with teaching peasants about the new laws, they also heard appeals of assembly refusals to grant titles and were responsible for local investigations when disputes arose over consolidation or land reorganization. District congresses and provincial boards continued to hear appeals of volost court, village assembly, and land captain decisions. The 1906 reformers had envisioned centrally established judicial and administrative structures that would frame and transcend local and estate specificities. Instead, administrative bodies were drawn into the immense task of micromanaging the inevitable disputes that would emerge from the reform process. The consequence of this, which will be examined in the final chapter of this book, is that the government had created new rights but neither the legal nor institutional framework necessary to regulate them.

◆ ◆ ◆

In the post-Emancipation decades, Russia's system of rural government consisted of several superimposed administrative cultures and practices— peasant, bureaucratic, and paternalistic—that posed particular problems for the coherent application of reforms. As Richard Robbins has argued: "The Ministry of Internal Affairs never made an unambiguous, final choice between the goals of a rationalized, bureaucratic hierarchy and a vital, independent local authority."[92] Instead, the goals were pursued sometimes in alternation, sometimes simultaneously. While this may not have been a problem in theory, it became so in practice, especially as the government's aspirations for proactive intervention in the countryside grew. The land captains, called upon to exercise local initiative in the name of better control, had to function within a bureaucratic culture that restricted their autonomy. Their mission was to defend traditional hierarchies, to preserve moral traditions and customs, yet they first had to change rural society in order to do so. The MVD was asking the impossible from its agents. As the next chapter will show, the difficulties that land captains faced in translating their dual mission into practice ensured that they were bound to be found wanting by administrative superiors, leaving the most dedicated among them frustrated and disillusioned, and peasants rather confused about the *nachal'nik's* proper role.

Likewise, the reformers of the Stolypin period had to contend with the consequences of earlier state reform efforts. As the 1860s had been a formative period for many officials who rose to positions of power in the following decades, so was 1889 a formative period for a new generation of officials.[93] The institutions established or reformed in 1889, and the values underlying them, gained their own momentum and permanency. Institutions specifically designed to reinforce the collective structures of rural society were called into service to oversee the dismantling of those structures. As we shall see in the following chapters, the late imperial reforms would be complicated by the extent to which the reforms of the 1890s had in fact succeeded in shaping peasant understandings of law, custom, authority, commune, property, and state power.

LAND CAPTAINS, PEASANT OFFICIALS, AND THE EXPERIENCE OF LOCAL AUTHORITY

In the course of 1890 and 1891, land captains were introduced with great ceremony in twenty-eight provinces of European Russia.[1] Governors, in their inaugural speeches to the new officials, enjoined them to be firm and strict, but not severe; they were to be feared, but loved. Land captains were also told to be tactful: the rural population had lost the habit of submitting to authority and the situation required lenience for illegal actions that did not arise from evil intentions. Further, governors encouraged the land captains to inspire trust, so that peasants would go to them for advice instead of to the first self-styled advocate they could find at the local tavern. On arrival in his precinct, the new land captain was to tour villages and present himself to assemblies as the new "father-chief" (*otets-nachal'nik*). He was to call a church service to pray for the health of the tsar and then remind peasants of the evils of drink, litigiousness, and kulaks, as well as the dangers of abandoning the church, losing respect for elders, and falling under the dangerous influence of urban culture. Governors assured noble land captains that they were "the empire's first estate *(soslovie)*" but also reminded them that their task would be easy only if they remembered they were the "instrument of government power."[2] In short, the ceremonies of investiture embodied in symbolic form the main components of paternal authority, with its emphasis on the moral harmony of relations both among peasants and between *sosloviia*. The *zemskii nachal'nik* was to be the father-protector of the weak, the scourge of the kulak, and the local embodiment of the tsar's mercy.

But the land captains' mission went beyond protection; they were also to open the village to beneficial outside influence. As the governor of Iaroslavl explained to the newly appointed captains of his province,

> The bad behavior of volost and village elders paralyzes district administra-
> tion, finance, police, and zemstvo . . . . Under your supervision, guidance,
> and strict legal relations with peasant officials, they will turn into true collab-
> orators . . . . Under your guidance, the *skhod* should become a proper general
> assembly . . . . If you can become an authority *(vlast')* who can discuss all af-
> fairs with peasants, understand peasant institutions, then the peasantry will
> trust government authority, associating firmness with the defense of the
> weak against the strong.[3]

The successful land captain, concluded the governor, would not only improve the moral, physical, and economic well-being of peasants but also
"quiet the voices of those who see salvation against disorder in an all-estate
rural administration." In short, the *zemskie nachal'niki* were presented as
the answer to Russia's economic, moral, and even political difficulties.
Peasants would become partners in rule, gratefully bound through the
land captain to tsar and state.

A number of obstacles would limit the land captains' ability to mold rural society and bring government-mandated order to village institutions.
Some of these obstacles, as already seen, were bureaucratic, as land captains had to function within the context of sometimes incongruous administrative and legal frameworks. The new officials were also overwhelmed by the extent of their responsibilities and constrained by their
lack of preparation. But the task of turning peasant officials into "true collaborators" posed the greatest challenges. Land captains understood well
that success depended on the very institutions and peasant officials they
were supposed to control and supervise: the peasant assemblies, the volost
and village elders, and the scribes and judges. This dependence quickly led
to a major quandary. Peasant officials were the designated villains in the
prevailing image of the closed village; but then "litigiousness" was seen as
a symptom of the breakdown of patriarchal authority. If land captains
dealt severely with elders and scribes, they might encourage frivolous
complaints against them. This would only undermine the authority of the
intermediary officials without whom the captains could do very little. On
the other hand, if land captains upheld the authority of elders and scribes,
they might encourage the very abuses of power they were supposed to
eradicate. Nothing in their arsenal of special powers and punitive tools
would successfully help the land captains to overcome this dilemma.
Caught between their twin fears of litigiousness and corruption, land captains were hampered in their ability to co-opt peasant officials.

Land captains were nevertheless one of the few points of contact between village and state, and their presence in village politics did much to
forge the dynamics of peasant-state relations in the last decades of the
Russian Empire. They were at the core of villagers' experience of authority.
As expected, they expanded opportunities for peasants to appeal to outside officials, bringing the state and its preoccupations more deeply into

the heart of the village. Charged with preserving peasant customs, land captains in fact accelerated the introduction of new terms of reference and new procedures, thereby opening the village to state bureaucracy and facilitating peasants' use of state power in internal battles. But in spite of all their efforts to command, land captains were to become simply one more player in the web of village politics. As peasants competed for their favor, most overworked *nachal'niki* had neither the time nor the local knowledge necessary to untangle the hidden webs of local rivalries that often underlay village disputes. Instead, these new government representatives tailored their activities to the mission of guiding and defending the "ignorant" and "helpless" peasant, reading the situations they encountered through the prism of their assumptions about peasant culture. But these readings were highly personal, and therefore highly variable. Land captains ultimately reinforced peasants' conceptions of authority as personal, but in ways that had little to do with the ideals of tutelary authority they represented.

THE LAND CAPTAIN AT WORK

Many of the first reports from Russia's governors on the introduction of land captains were highly enthusiastic; the new officials seemed to be everything the framers of the 1889 legislation had hoped for. Vladimir's Governor I. M. Sudienko, as a former member of the MVD's Special Commission that had approved the early drafts of the legislation, was understandably passionate in his praise of the new officials in his 1890 annual report, but his assessment echoed that of many of his colleagues.[4] According to Sudienko, the land captains, all drawn from the local nobility, had rapidly succeeded in gaining the population's trust precisely by being close to their charges and avoiding bureaucratic formalism. The report assured that the immoral and costly custom of drinking at the assembly had vanished, so that arrears were now being paid up and order was returning to village affairs. The corrupt judges of the old volost court had been replaced by sober, trusted, and conscientious peasants, and respect for courts was being restored. In short, concluded Sudienko, villagers understood that in land captains they had a defender against the depredations of village and volost officials.

Few press reports, however, shared the governors' enthusiasm. The liberal press regularly published accounts of abuse as proof that its misgivings over the wisdom of giving local nobles tutelary authority in the countryside had been fully justified. The "thick" journals highlighted incidents of land captains' arbitrary decisions such as imprisoning two-thirds of a village assembly for three days for electing the "wrong" elder, decreeing nighttime curfews to reduce wood theft, or arresting peasant women for wearing hats (deemed to be inappropriate urban coquettishness). Other accounts stressed the new officials' boorish behavior, which could range from yelling and swearing to arresting and beating. Even land captains' propensity to address peasants in the informal "thou" *(ty)*, in a reversal of the much-lauded tendency of the justices of the peace to use the formal "you" *(vy)*, was cited as evidence that they were undermining peasants' fragile sense of self-worth and would bring a halt to cultural progress in the countryside.[5] Critics of the 1889 reforms concluded that the land captains were destroying genuine peasant self-government. As one commentator put it, after 1889 peasant officials and peasant judges "were turned into the silent executors of the land captains' will."[6]

What critics and supporters of the 1889 reforms had in common was the assumption that the land captains transformed village administration virtually overnight. There was much exaggeration in both assessments, which reflected fears and hopes as well as deep political divisions over the proper nature of rural governance. But there was also some truth in both accounts.

There certainly is plenty of evidence that villagers did not breathe a collective sigh of relief upon arrival of the father-*nachal'nik*. Some peasants interpreted the language of paternal authority as a "return to serfdom," and some villages stubbornly refused to elect new volost officials. One Tula land captain, who arrived with a crated piano, was met by a crowd curious to see the "new flogging machine." In contrast to the press's usual praise of technological progress, rumors of flogging machines "that could run on their own" (invented in Germany in some versions) spread through a number of provinces.[7] Such rumors point to some of the problems that lay beneath the oblique references to "early difficulties" found in a few governors' reports. At least one governor broke ranks with his enthusiastic colleagues in these early years and reported that land captains used their powers excessively and arbitrarily with the regrettable consequence of weakening respect for authority among peasants.[8]

The behavior of at least some land captains did little to reassure worried peasants. Several incidents of peasant resistance requiring army intervention were clearly attributable to land captain abuse. The Kharkhov police chief squarely blamed land captain V. A. Protopopov, for example, for villagers' refusal to elect new officials in his precinct. Protopopov had exacerbated peasant fears by refusing to explain the new laws, flaunting his powers, and threatening beatings. A captain in Orel ordered the arrest of one woman per household when villagers refused to repair a dike diverting water to a noble landowner's mill. Even though it was the landowner who had broken the contract with the commune, the governor ordered troops to intervene. Accusing the land captain of "extreme naiveté" and demanding his resignation, the governor also ordered the "exemplary" flogging of ten ringleaders (each receiving 40 to 133 blows), after which, he reported, "peasants voluntarily and without even any order from me repaired the dike within one hour."[9] Even if such open confrontations were atypical and the officials involved were censured by the MVD, they illustrate the potential for abuse of power as well as the atmosphere of mistrust that greeted the new officials.

Conservatives were correct on one point, however, which was that the liberal press tended to sensationalize from the worst examples. After all, not all land captains were inexperienced and ignorant of the law. In Riazan province, three-quarters of the first wave of appointees had previously held positions in rural administration, and nearly half were former justices of the peace. In Tula, one-quarter were former justices, and only six of the fifty-eight appointees lacked prior local administrative experience. It is difficult to know how representative the situations of these two provinces were, as most governors did not provide detailed staff information. But the fact that nearly 40 percent of the first wave of appointees in ten provinces (including Riazan and Tula) held military titles cannot be assumed, as the opposition press often claimed, to reflect lack of administrative experience. Nor does the fact that—because of high turnover—only one-fifth of the land captains in office in 1902 had previous rural administrative experience necessarily reflect the situation of the early 1890s.[10] It had been the MVD's intention to attract precisely the type of candidates who joined the Riazan and Tula land captaincy. The policy seems to have had some success, and in those early years numerous commentators noted that a significant proportion of the appointees were men of experience dedicated to their paternal mission.

While the impact of the 1889 reforms was neither as salutary as its supporters claimed, nor as nefarious as its detractors feared, the arrival of the land captains did bring about real change in village life. Peasants could not avoid the new officials: the land captain was an administrative funnel through which virtually all village problems eventually had to pass. Elections of peasant officials, land redistributions, naming of legal guardians, communal charity measures, court appeals—all had to be examined and could be overturned by the land captain. In Riazan province, captains in their first full year in office examined twice as many cases as the district boards had heard five years earlier, a figure that would again double by 1908.[11] According to one respondent to the Tenishev Ethnographic Bureau, by the mid-1890s villagers were so accustomed to state officials that their visits were no longer momentous and frightening occasions.[12] In addition, the first *zemskie nachal'niki* took office determined to bring order to what they saw as a chaotic situation stemming from ignorance, helplessness, and vodka: they closed illegal taverns, demanded that village resolutions be properly signed and submitted, and removed village elders when they thought that elections had been orchestrated by kulaks. The land captain's presence became a tangible manifestation of growing state intrusion in the village.

In the early 1890s many districts experienced high levels of intervention in communal affairs. Some new land captains undertook a virtual purge of peasant officials, both by supervising elections and by firing undesirable elders. In Vladimir province, elders were being fired at twice the rate of a decade earlier, and peasant officials were five times more likely to be fined or arrested.[13] In the first two and a half years after the introduction of the 1889 law in Saratov province, one-third of all volost elders and scribes were removed from office, along with two-fifths of village elders. Similarly high rates were reported from Smolensk province.

The few fragmentary figures available tracing the arrest or fining of peasant officials (article 62 of the Land Captain Statute) and the overturning of assembly resolutions (article 31) also show a high level of interference. In Saratov, an average of 983 village or volost resolutions (*prigovory*) were overturned yearly, or approximately one for every 2.4 village societies and volosts of the province. Since many assemblies submitted as few as three to five written resolutions a year for review, it can be estimated that land captains were overturning approximately 10 percent of these. In Tula, 35 percent of all peasant officials were punished under article 62 in 1892, and in Saratov the proportion reached nearly 50 percent between 1890 and 1903.[14]

Not all captains were so heavy-handed, however. Data from Orel and Moscow show much lower levels of land captain intervention: 19 percent of all elders and scribes were fined or arrested in Orel in 1892, 14 percent in Moscow province in 1895. Only 4.5 percent of peasant officials were removed from office in Orel, while Moscow captains replaced one in twenty-seven (3.7%). Meanwhile, 483 assembly resolutions were overturned, or approximately one for every eleven communes.[15] Clearly not all villages were experiencing the same level of land captain interference in communal affairs.

Administrative practice varied widely from precinct to precinct, according to the attitude of the individual land captain. For instance, data from forty-two of Riazan's sixty land captains show that 4 percent of all elders were fired in 1899, yet only eight of these captains were responsible for nearly half of the suspensions. Four captains were responsible for 27 percent of all annulled assembly resolutions, while over half of them used their prerogative to overturn resolutions fewer than five times in the course of that year.[16] Even more striking variations were reported in the application of article 61, which allowed captains to detain peasants for up to three days or fine them up to six rubles without judicial procedure. While officials from one Tula district arrested only one peasant in 1892, captains from a neighboring district applied administrative punishment 1,276 times.[17] Similar variations could occur within a precinct when one official was replaced by another. One of the local committees of Witte's 1902 Conference on the Needs of Agriculture illustrated this point by citing the example of a precinct where the land captain arrested or fined peasants without formal procedure approximately 150 times a year. When the captain was replaced, punishments plummeted to three fines a year. When this official in turn left office in 1900, his successor invoked article 61 nearly 900 times, while his neighboring colleague used this prerogative not at all.[18]

Foremost among the reasons for such regional and temporal variation was the wide divergence in style, level of dedication, and political views of the individuals who served. As V. V. Tenishev concluded, on the basis of materials collected by the famous ethnographic bureau of the same name, it was difficult to make any generalizations about the nature of land captain–peasant relations, as the powers used by these local officials ranged "from paternalistic responsiveness to well-meaning inactivity, from just energy to unabashed arbitrariness."[19] Russia's governors may have had a fairly clear idea of what authoritative paternalism was supposed to be, but in practice these ideas translated into a wide variety of administrative styles.

It is in fact impossible to draw the portrait of a "typical" land captain. S. T. Semenov, a peasant-*intelligent* who wrote a remarkably illustrative memoir about life in his native village of Moscow province, vividly described the idiosyncrasies of a succession of land captains in his district. The first was an elderly Slavophile who ordered that petitioners appearing before him wear proper "Russian national dress" rather than city-style jackets or frock coats. Semenov considered him well intentioned, nevertheless. Determined to keep abreast of village affairs, the captain met with the elders every two weeks, and peasants never feared going to see him. His two successors, in contrast, were young local nobles who had taken the position simply to supplement their incomes. Perceived as veritable "peasant-haters" (*muzhiknenavistniki*), they liberally distributed fines and arrests, punished peasants for perceived signs of disrespect, and issued absurd or impossible commands. According to Semenov, peasants feared these officials and avoided any position of responsibility that might necessitate closer contact with them—meanwhile consoling themselves by telling land captain jokes that played on their superiors' mannerisms.[20]

Closer to the intended model of the paternal land captain was A. N. Naumov, who served in Samara in the early 1890s. Later to rise to the post of minister of agriculture (1916), Naumov was a strong believer in the constructive role to be played by local nobility. He entered service full of enthusiasm for his mission to defend the "dark, illiterate, confused masses" and aid in their "material well-being and moral development." He derived immense personal satisfaction from working directly with peasants "without dead circulars and bureaucratic interference," even if his responsibilities extended "only" to 38,000 individuals, all of whom he described as "close to me." Convinced of the need to establish trust without intermediaries, Naumov obliged peasants to present requests orally in order to circumvent petitions written by illegal advocates. He also attended village assemblies to prevent presumed abuse by kulaks. He closed illegal taverns, organized practical courses for judges and scribes, successfully encouraged assemblies to dedicate funds to the building of seven churches and ten schools, taught history and civics to schoolchildren over the local zemstvo's objections, and established a library/tea-house (shut down by his successor) where peasants could go to hear the newspaper read aloud. Naumov quite proudly wrote of his ability to tactfully defuse tense situations; he recounted, for instance, how he turned one village's virulent opposition to establishing a plot of communally plowed land (*obshchestvennaia zapashka*)—required by the local zemstvo to pay off the village's famine relief debt—into bemused acquiescence by promising to plow alongside villagers. Yet, in spite of his tendency to intervene directly in rural affairs, Naumov avoided applying administrative punishments, because he wanted the population to trust rather than fear him, and he was confident of having earned that trust.[21]

It is impossible to know whether Naumov's perception of having gained peasant trust was mere self-delusion. Land captains were quick to see in the style of peasant petitioning evidence that villagers were indeed awaiting a strong hand, and that they needed and welcomed protection. Petitions were clothed in rituals of subservience, teary protestations of helplessness and ignorance, and dramatic affirmations of the absolute disaster that would befall the petitioner if not saved by his Excellency. The volost clerk Nikolai Astyrev had in the 1880s expressed disappointment at the ritualistic quality of the interminable complaints filed in his office: "It always turns out, that the offender is guilty of everything, that he is a thief, a swindler and robber . . . and I had to recognize with regret that these 'stories from peasant life' would never give any understanding of that life."[22] That much theater and manipulation was present in peasant petitioning, there can be no doubt.

Nevertheless, it is possible that some peasants were indeed awaiting a strong local representative of the tsar's justice and that the tearful entreaties that so impressed land captains were not just insincere manipulations of the public transcript. A frequent peasant complaint prior to 1889, after all, had been that there was no one to complain to (*nekomu zhalovat'sia*). The inhabitants of one Samara precinct, for example, as described by Sergei Matveev in his account of his years of service as volost elder, certainly seemed to be waiting for "someone to complain to." When the first land captain—a retired lieutenant by the name of Vel'chaninov—arrived, peasants were most impressed. Of regal bearing, with a full beard to the waist, of kindly manner, addressing elders by given name and patronymic, speaking in colorful concrete images that peasants understood and appreciated, the *nachal'nik* was admiringly decreed to be a "real lord" (*barin*). Soon, a long line of petitioners formed outside his office. In a situation of absolute powerlessness, the opportunity to appeal for outside intervention to redress the local imbalances of power would be welcome. As each petitioner entered in turn, he or she made the sign of the cross before the icon, bowed low, and tearfully asked the *nachal'nik* to be a father. But disillusionment quickly set in. Vel'chaninov was of the mind that peasant officials were swindlers, and he was determined to help the weak and defenseless. Vel'chaninov ruled from the heart, issuing spontaneous judgments that were swayed by the last petitioner who had just stepped out of his office. But then, upon hearing the other side's protests, he would reverse his rulings, and the line of petitioners became ever longer. Everything in the precinct rapidly became a frightful muddle. Vel'chaninov concluded that peasants were just a litigious lot who never let him breathe, and disappointed peasants concluded that the "real *barin*" was in fact nothing but an "empty beard."[23]

Aleksandr Novikov, a land captain who served in Tambov in the same period, had no illusions about gaining peasant trust. Although he took up his post with the same ambitions as Naumov, he ended his six years of service a firm opponent of the 1889 institutions. The land captain's enormous powers—"the land captain in his precinct is everything," he wrote—were proportional to his ignorance of the real state of affairs in his precinct. Novikov quickly realized that he could not depend upon village and volost elders to become his eyes and ears, his trusted aides, and his faithful executors. His decisions, he felt, could only be ill-informed and arbitrary. What peasants needed was "education, education, education," and nobles with their "military-style" approach were particularly ill-suited for the task of educating peasants. Perhaps the only contribution a land captain could make was in his cultural role: by treating peasants with respect, addressing petitioners with the formal *vy*, always keeping his door open, and listening patiently, he could provide a positive model to influence the behavior of lower officials.[24]

One could draw many more such contrasting portraits. Land captains could be liberal advocates of the all-estate volost-level zemstvo or members of the reactionary and anti-Semitic Union of Russian People. Some were former army officers quick to resort to corporal punishment; at least one was a former doctor who distributed free medicine. Some assumed that peasants knew and felt "the nobility's moral superiority," while others felt that the *muzhik* hated the squire. Some believed that peasants who petitioned were generally sober, hard-working people in need of defense, while others saw petitioners as litigious troublemakers unwilling to get along with family and neighbors. A few expressed respect, even admiration, for the intelligence and capabilities of the rural inhabitants in their charge; many more felt that peasants were unable to coherently express their needs and desires, which existed only at the level of "instinct."[25] Such variations meant that behavior tolerated by one land captain could provoke arrest by another. While one captain, a fervent believer in the benefits of the land commune, might use his power and influence to encourage peasants to equalize landholdings in general redistributions, his successor could well be convinced of the harmful consequences of repartitions and systematically overturn resolutions on technicalities. If the first encouraged petitions against village leaders as a means of controlling the nefarious actions of kulaks, the second might interpret such petitions as chicanery and a sign of disintegrating respect for patriarchal authority. In short, a land captain's administrative style could bring considerable change in a precinct, while peasants, and especially their elected officials, scrambled to adjust to his approach and his priorities.

This lack of consistency in local administrative practice was compounded by high rates of turnover. Good candidates were hard to find, and even more difficult to retain. In Moscow, for instance, thirty-six of the province's first fifty-five captains had left office within four years. Tula's governor explained the poor quality of his province's administrators by the fact that a quarter of the staff had changed within two and a half years.[26] The governor of Penza in 1894 blamed the economic difficulties of nobles and poor pay for a dearth of good candidates in that province, a complaint that would be repeated over the next twenty years by other governors, and by the MVD in its unsuccessful battles with the Ministry of Finance for more funds.[27]

Land captains' memoirs and their letters to the press suggest that financial considerations did play a role—albeit a secondary one—in driving nobles from the office. Salaries were usually insufficient to maintain the lifestyle to which a provincial noble was accustomed. Naumov had to supplement his monthly 178-ruble salary with the 100 rubles sent by his father. Other captains reported that the budget for administrative expenses barely covered the costs of paying a scribe and supplying paper and heat. Any travel within the precinct or to district congress meetings had to come out of pocket. Even officials who could afford to subsidize their work resented that the government was unwilling to grant them the resources they needed to do their jobs properly.[28]

There were also more deep-seated frustrations, however, that account for land captains' reluctance to turn the office into a career. Land captains complained primarily of overwork stemming from endless paperwork and correspondence. In a letter to the liberal *Iuridicheskaia gazeta,* one correspondent grumbled that he was turning into a "bureaucratic machine" *(chinovnik-machina).* Another, writing to the reactionary *Grazhdanin,* wrote that while nobles had entered service in order to bring "real" rather than "paper" legality to the countryside, paperwork and formalism were paralyzing their effectiveness.[29] V. Ianovich complained that in addition to judicial tasks, which took up half of his time, the "other responsibilities [were] as numerous as prince Vladimir had wives."

> The land captain cannot be everywhere at once. Like hail from early morning to late in the evening [peasants arrive]: "my wife has run away, my husband has thrown me and the children out on the street, the village elder is drunk, they took away my land, my horse has been stolen, they will not issue my passport. . . ." [He must] judge, persuade, punish, search, protect . . . but he is just one person, gentlemen, alone, all alone *(odin-odinochek).*

How, then, could the MVD really expect him, he continued, also to conduct household surveys and evaluate the relative merits of the 1,434 requests for tax extensions? "The land captain in his precinct is nothing," concluded the discouraged Ianovich; the most competent of land captains could not fulfill the tasks demanded of him.[30]

This sense of being "alone, all alone" was exacerbated by a lack of government guidance for dealing with complex legal and administrative affairs. The Land Captain Statute sketched out responsibilities in broad strokes, providing few procedural instructions or legal details. Preparation for taking office was cursory. The few months of apprenticeship with a provincial board were especially insufficient for men without previous administrative experience, who by 1902 constituted 47 percent of the empire's 2,300 land captains. Upon taking office, a land captain would immediately be confronted with important practical and procedural questions. Could peasants who did not attend the village assembly be punished under article 61? Could court decisions be implemented immediately (without waiting for the thirty-day period of appeal) if both sides renounced the right to appeal? Did the land captain's mandate of improving "economic well-being" give him the right to fine a peasant who neglected his land? Some governors, alarmed by the eclecticism of land captains' improvised solutions, organized conferences to harmonize administrative practice in their provinces. Even these conferences could be problematic, as the guidelines drawn up sometimes contradicted the large body of Senate cassation rulings that had been built up since Emancipation. Not infrequently, the MVD had to step in to point out errors of interpretation. Yet the official MVD "explanations" did not always reach local officials. In 1907, for example, inspectors discovered that several district congresses of Smolensk province were still following a long-overruled 1891 provincial board instruction.[31]

The district congresses and the provincial boards were in theory supposed to provide guidance through inspections, yet by all accounts, until the turn of the century, these remained superficial and cursory affairs. Even someone like Naumov, who valued the flexibility granted him and who was relatively well prepared for his duties with a university law degree, decried the perfunctoriness of the inspection process. In his four years of service he was inspected but once, and the entire process took just a few hours. The inspector (a permanent member of the provincial board) examined a few books and visited no volosts. Either the permanent member was overworked, with over fifty precincts to inspect, or he feared that any negative remarks would reduce the land captain's authority. Whatever his concerns, he took no time to answer Naumov's many questions, and the latter regretfully concluded that communication with the highest appeal instance in the province could occur only through "dead circulars."[32]

District congresses were ill-designed to fulfill their supervisory role. They could be hobbled by collegial relations: several land captains reported a reluctance to overturn colleagues' administrative decisions for fear of undermining their authority, expecting the same favor in return. Naumov wrote fondly of the "familial relations" that prevailed at the monthly meetings, while Ianovich described district level inspections as a children's game of "now you will be the father and I will be the mother." By 1905 even the MVD's Land Section chief (V. I. Gurko) agreed, publicly denouncing the district congresses for collusion and complacency.[33]

Yet even without collusion, time constraints undermined the effectiveness of control and verification by the district congresses. All members had other obligations, meeting once a month in sessions lasting two to six days.[34] Only one member was required to study a dossier in advance to prepare the obligatory oral report. Heavy workloads, ranging from five hundred to fifteen hundred cases a year, usually precluded extended discussion, consideration of the details of each case, or direct questioning of litigants and witnesses. Even in the first years, when caseloads were still relatively light, some district congresses were reviewing thirty cases or more a day, meaning that they could spend only an estimated fifteen to twenty minutes on each one. By the time Gurko was accusing land captains of collusion, twenty-five to thirty cases a day was the norm, and some districts heard as many as fifty. In 1910 the newly appointed land captain Vladimir Polivanov was distressed to find that the administrative session of the district congress consisted merely of signing off on two hundred cases, the resolutions having been prepared in advance by the secretary. As one observer noted, district assemblies and provincial boards had no option but to choose between timely hearings and careful hearings. In either case, they risked reprimand by MVD inspectors.[35] Time constraints, compounded by the 1889 legislation's emphasis on the importance of close local knowledge, encouraged the understandable tendency to defer to the most knowledgeable member, usually the land captain from whose precinct a case originated. In sum, district congresses were ill-equipped to provide the guidance and control needed to ensure the uniform application of laws, regulations, and policies that the government wanted.

By the turn of the century, St. Petersburg officials were increasingly worried that excessive land captain autonomy could have grave consequences, eroding peasant respect for authority rather than embodying firm governmental paternal rule. Senate rulings, gubernatorial instructions, and changing attitudes within the MVD, which culminated in the 1905 publication of Instructions to Land Captains, the 5 October 1906 decree, and a regular system of inspections, were all designed to impose greater consistency in local administrative practices. These efforts did lead to a gradual reduction of land captain intervention in village administration. By 1914 the number of peasant officials fined or arrested in Saratov and Vladimir provinces had declined by almost 60 and 45 percent respectively since the early 1890s. By 1915 land captains in Moscow province were annulling half the number of assembly resolutions, and submitting half the number of peasant officials to administrative punishment as in 1895.[36] The number of resolutions overturned in Riazan also went down, from one for every 12.5 village society in 1899, to one for every twenty in 1908. Fragmentary data show similar patterns in other provinces.[37]

The new controls failed to impose uniformity, however, and wide regional variations persisted. In 1908 land captains in Riazan province arrested or fined 1,145 village officials. Of these punishments, 405 came out of Zaraisk district (affecting over half of the district's peasant officials), while only 25 were imposed in the larger neighboring district of Kasimov.[38] The province of Penza as a whole continued to see a high level of land captain interference between 1902 and 1912; an average of 17 percent of the province's volost elders and 11.2 percent of the *starosty* were replaced yearly.[39] A number of local officials simply ignored certain provisions of the 5 October decree. In 1908 several districts in Tver were still reporting arrests and fines of peasants according to the repealed article 61 (article 57 in the 1902 recompilation). As late as 1910, a land captain in Saratov invoked this same article to detain a villager for five days.[40]

Efforts to increase accountability and uniformity could be thwarted by provincial governors and provincial boards hostile to the MVD's new efforts to better control and discipline the land captains. In 1912, for instance, the Saratov marshal of nobility (as a provincial board member) protested the ministry's reproach that his province too infrequently recommended disciplinary action: "A too strictly formal attitude on the part of the provincial board towards the land captains undermines their authority," he explained.[41] Such defiance prevailed in other provinces as well. The MVD in 1911 regretted that the provincial board of Kostroma, for instance, dealt "very leniently (*netrebovatel'no*) toward the land captains." Complaints against them were usually dropped, and inspections were only perfunctorily conducted.[42] The higher echelons of provincial administration could set the tone for a province more consistent with a traditional tutelary concept of rural administration than with the MVD's aspirations to strengthen the efficiency of a centralized bureaucracy.

The ministry's efforts to reign in land captains' idiosyncratic interpretations of their powers was also complicated by the increasing diversity of individuals filling the office after 1905. The ideal envisioned by Pazukhin and Tolstoi, whereby the *zemskii nachal'nik* would be a local landowner deeply concerned and personally knowledgeable about his district, rarely corresponded to the profile of those actually filling the office. Anecdotal evidence suggests that many of the first wave of land captains had resigned out of ideological disillusionment, to be replaced by what Naumov called "bureaucratic varangians." Ianovich was deeply discouraged after the 1893 law made it more difficult for him to promote "fairness" in land repartitions; others despised the "police work" imposed by the 1899 law making them responsible for tax collection as contrary to the ideal of guardianship; some simply experienced "lassitude" in the face of paperwork.[43] In order to overcome a chronic shortage of candidates, the Ministry of Interior in 1904 opened an avenue of appointment by examination for those who did not otherwise meet the property or education criteria. In addition, a wave of resignations had followed the 1905–1906 agrarian disorders. By 1913, the nobility no longer had a monopoly on the office (one-fifth being non-noble), and only 47 percent held office by meeting the minimum property requirement (as compared with 67.5% in 1903).[44] Most importantly, over half did not come from the district in which they served.

High rates of turnover had become an even greater problem than in the 1890s. By 1908, in five provinces of the central black earth region, 25 percent (in Tambov) to over 50 percent (in Saratov) of the land captains had been replaced in the previous two years. A follow-up inspection of Saratov revealed no improvement by 1911. Vacancies were becoming increasingly difficult to fill, and by 1913, 10 percent of the country's precincts had no land captain.[45] Since it was regular procedure to assign temporary responsibility for a vacant precinct to a neighboring official, one-fifth of the precincts were, in effect, doubly underadministered.

Compounding the effects of turnover and vacancies was the dramatic growth of caseloads. By 1911, the average land captain was hearing twice as many administrative cases and three times as many judicial cases as in 1893.[46] Overwork, which had plagued land captains even in the 1890s, became more acute after 1906 when captains were further charged with implementing key provisions of the Stolypin agrarian reform. Some captains began neglecting other obligations, a tendency unwittingly abetted by the bonuses the Ministry of Interior and certain governors offered for completing large numbers of land titles. According to numerous observers, any official who wanted to advance his career after 1906 turned his entire attention to land reform.[47] Yet, there were also dangers in doing so. MVD inspectors also reprimanded local officials for neglecting their other duties to focus on land reform work.[48] While the frenzy of agrarian reform did not seize all local officials, as more conservative land captains opposed the 9 November legislation and others simply shunned the extra work, it became an additional factor contributing to the enormous variety of local administrative practices.

Given the land captains' myriad obligations, which required a detailed understanding of the social, political, and economic life of the one hundred-odd villages under their jurisdiction, it is no surprise that so many of them were judged unsatisfactory by central inspectors. Alternately overworked, indifferent, or insufficiently knowledgeable about local conditions, few land captains supervised, regulated, or molded rural society as effectively as the government hoped or their critics feared. The 1889 reforms did not give the government the reliable agents it wanted for the consistent implementation of state policies.

There was no doubt the *zemskii nachal'nik* could wield considerable local power and influence, and the 1889 reforms did bring state authority into the village. Yet rapid turnover and inadequate controls made it impossible for villagers ever to be certain how that power would be used. The variety of land captain practices could only reinforce peasants' conceptions of authority as arbitrary and personal. Novikov concluded that the 1889 reforms had in fact encouraged an opportunistic understanding of law and authority in the countryside:

> [The captain] is the main reason the peasant does not believe in the law; for him the law is the command of the *nachal'nik*. "You can do everything," the peasant will tell you when you explain the law to him. . . . It is not illegality that peasants avoid, but the anger of the authorities. They do not try to follow the law, but to please the land captain.[49]

From his first days in office, the *zemskii nachal'nik* could not be ignored; it remained to be seen what effect his presence could have on the dynamics of internal village politics.

VOLOST ADMINISTRATION

The actual work of daily administration lay in the volost, or more precisely with the elected elder *(starshina)* and hired scribe *(pisar')*. As early as the 1870s, critics were lamenting that the volost, rather than being the highest organ of peasant self-government, had become the lowest echelon of the bureaucracy. Given the lack of a regular bureaucratic structure extending into the localities, volost officials were the executors for the growing number of administrations that needed to reach into the countryside, and nothing in the 1889 reforms changed this. In addition to the regular provincial authorities, the police, the military, the provincial statistical bureau, the zemstvo, and the treasury, all needed information collected and orders executed. As the land captain Ianovich quipped from his landlocked province in central Russia: "Only the Ministry of Navy does not request something."[50] The volost administration was charged with ensuring the timely collection of taxes and arrears. It issued passports, forwarded requests for emergency loans, and provided data on harvests or seed stores. It was the volost elder who implemented court decisions and questioned villagers when a complaint was filed. Land captains, no matter how dedicated and competent, knew that they had to depend on the volost: only volost officials could prepare the great majority of the reports that land captains had to file, fill the requests for information they had to respond to, and even enact the "urgent" measures they had to implement. In short, the volost administration was a crucial link in the communication between the village and the upper echelons of government. But did volost administrators gain enough autonomy from the village to serve the needs of the bureau-cracy?[51] Were rural officials turned into "true collaborators" as the govern-ment had hoped, or into "silent executors" as liberal critics feared?

The government after 1889 took some measures to raise the status of volost elders. Land captains were charged with instilling in peasants a proper respect for their elected leaders, and to imbue rural officials them-selves with an awareness of the official nature of their own position. A re-current theme of the governors' speeches to the new land captains in 1890 had been the need to teach peasants the proper respect for authority. Accordingly, land captains were not only to ascertain that peasant officials had a general knowledge of their obligations but were also to verify their moral qualities. The 1889 regulations stipulated that volost elders take an oath of office. The legislation also described in some detail the badges of office, which were to have the provincial coat of arms and the officials' position inscribed on the recto, and a portrait of the tsar with the date of the Emancipation proclamation on the verso. The law even specified how these bronze medals were to be worn.[52] Elders were thus marked as repre-sentatives of higher authority.

Judicial practice sought to defend the dignity of rural administrative of-fice. Although the 1889 legislation itself did not specify punishments for insulting an elected official, Senate rulings and MVD instructions did pro-vide for cases involving transgressions against judges and volost elders to be transferred to the general circuit courts, which could impose longer sentences than the volost courts.[53] The fact that the circuit courts, subor-dinate to the Ministry of Justice, did not necessarily do so does not change the reality that it was more intimidating for the offending peasant to travel to the district center than it was to appear before peasant judges at the nearby volost center. The Riazan circuit court convicted peasants for offenses ranging from accusing volost judges of "ruling for vodka," to simply inter-rupting a volost court hearing with drunken and incoherent swearing. Even addressing the volost elder with the informal "thou" (ty), while never suffi-cient to initiate official proceedings, was noted by the circuit judges as a fac-tor in weighing the credibility of an accusation.[54] An elder or judge, at least as long as he was wearing the medal of his office, was entitled to a level of defer-ence that distinguished him from his neighbors.

One purpose for the government's insistence on the importance of def-erence and procedure was educational: a volost that was well run could serve as an advance post in the mission of educating and civilizing the peasantry.[55] Even the physical layout of the volost building mattered. One architectural proposal from 1901 explained that a well-constructed volost building would combat the negligent attitude of both peasants and elected officials toward local administration.[56] Inspectors' reports invari-ably opened with an assessment of buildings. Most of these comments were disapproving descriptions of dirty, small, dark, cold, and dilapidated volost offices. Only occasionally did they describe a large, clean brick building of which they approved. Such locales had portraits of the tsar hanging in the right places, notices of new legislation posted in the entryway, separate holding cells for men and women, and benches and tables for the judges.[57] In short, they had the proper trappings of officialdom, with the potential to inspire order, awe, and respect.

Closer supervision over the selection of peasant officials did bring about at least one important change. While publicists continued to repeat the old accusation that the assemblies elected "the worst peasants," fragmentary evidence suggests that land captains had been able to impose literacy as a criterion for selection. Data collected by the MVD in 1880 showed that nearly 40 percent of volost elders had been illiterate, while illiterate village elders outnumbered literates five to one. Even Moscow province, with the highest literacy rates among peasant officials, had barely more literate than illiterate elders. After the turn of the century, on the other hand, it was rare to find illiterate volost elders. A survey in Tver in 1902 found that although half of the elders had not received any formal schooling, only six were illiterate (as compared with 30% of village elders). A 1911 Riazan survey of 211 volost elders found only 8 who were illiterate and 26 who were classified as "poorly literate" *(malogramotnyi).*[58]

But literacy was not sufficient to make what the MVD deemed to be a "good elder." The MVD's efforts to inculcate in peasant officials a respect for formal status and procedures met with limited success. Informality continued to define local administration. Official procedure made little sense in a context where reputation and personal ties played an important role. Even if a land captain had the inclination, he hardly had the resources to impose more than a cosmetic formality. Inspectors noted with disappointment countless breaches of regulations at all levels. They berated land captains for failing to award medals to elders who had served well. They found that peasants kept under arrest for a few days by the volost court were sometimes allowed out to work during the day, or might even be allowed to go out for a drink at the tavern. Village assemblies neglected to exclude from participation notorious troublemakers or peasants who had been convicted of a crime.[59]

Perhaps the issue that best illustrates the dilemmas that land captains faced in trying to impose a modicum of official formality in rural administration was rural alcohol consumption. Inspectors consistently deplored the prevalence of vodka in the conduct of village and volost affairs. Countless reports spoke of drinks offered before elections by peasants running for the office of volost elder or judge; or alternatively, by peasants trying to dodge the time-consuming and unremunerative jobs of village elder, tax collector, or police deputy *(desiatskii).* Eyewitness accounts described how a round of drinks typically sealed rental and hiring agreements, and how requests for additional land had to be accompanied by an indication of willingness to "thank" the assembly.[60] Many critics feared that the practice of treating to vodka *(ugoshchenie)* had become the fundamental principle of peasant administration and the cause of commune impoverishment. Instead of seeking to lease communal land or income-producing establishments (such as a mill or a trading stand) for the highest price, it was argued, the assembly was interested only in the size of the "treat." In 1913 the Riazan provincial board was still combating the practice of renting land for vodka by instructing land captains to supervise public auctions and to verify that the income was deposited with the volost administration in designated accounts—and this some two decades after the governor had triumphantly declared that vodka no longer played any role in the conduct of village affairs.[61] Land captains reported drinking to be the most tenacious of village ills, and even their most energetic measures had a noticeable impact only until they turned their backs.

One should not exaggerate, however, either the role of alcohol in rural administration or the militancy of land captains in combating it. While some officials such as Naumov and Polivanov made concerted efforts to eradicate public drinking from their precincts by pressing assemblies to close local taverns, most land captains were surprisingly tolerant of behaviors that so fed the anxieties of publicists and bureaucratic reformers. The zemskie nachal'niki were quite aware that drink was a symbol of agreement, indispensable for sealing a deal or indicating satisfaction and reconciliation between parties in a dispute. They also recognized that drinking did not always denote bribery. Since the assembly was often an unwelcome distraction from more pressing tasks, especially if it was called to deal with questions of peripheral concern to most participants (such as family divisions or minor readjustments in land usage among individuals), villagers came to regard alcohol as a form of compensation for time lost.[62] The problem for land captains was to distinguish between legitimate drinking that promoted reconciliation and solidarity—something they were supposed to promote—and illegitimate drinking that signaled corruption. Land captains tended to follow a simple rule: they condemned drinking that took place before an assembly and thus could be presumed to influence the vote and dismissed complaints about drinking that took place afterward, accepting the practice as a customary offer of thanks.[63] They even turned a blind eye to "thanks" that were negotiated at the assembly as part of the price for leasing a piece of communal land. Such leniency is hardly surprising: an effective land captain could only hope for some degree of credibility if he made concessions to established local practices.

But such concessions were unlikely to win a land captain any praise from MVD inspectors who read the failure to control rural drinking as "lack of surveillance" (nadzor) and an inability to be "close to the population." But the alternative, to punish all infractions, was just as likely to draw censure from the land captain's superiors. Frequent arrests of peasant officials or vetoes of assembly resolutions could also be read as superficial administration. The charge most often levied against land captains—not only by liberal critics but after the turn of the century also by MVD officials—was that it was precisely their arbitrary and high-handed methods that kept them aloof from their precincts. Even the MVD's Land Section chief, Gurko, in 1905 deplored the fact that while discretionary powers had been intended only for exceptional circumstances, they were so frequently invoked as to lead to a purely formalistic mode of administration and to the disregard of thorough investigation. Land captains rarely interrogated complainants or petitioners, charged Gurko. They delegated investigations to volost officials, relied on formal written communication rather than direct involvement, and rarely provided the reasoning behind the decisions they made.[64]

Gurko was not entirely wrong in his assessment. Vladimir Polivanov, assigned as land captain to a northern province five years after the publication of the Gurko report, gave a vivid illustration of the marriage between indifference and high-handedness that characterized some captains. When Polivanov asked a more experienced colleague in a neighboring precinct for advice on dealing with village elders who were recalcitrant in collecting taxes, the colleague responded that there was no point trying to reason with the village elders. The only effective means of spurring them on in their work, he said, was to fine them all: "I do not even look at them, the devil take them all!"[65] This was precisely the type of behavior that the MVD had sought since 1905 to correct with inspections, detailed instructions, and reinforced disciplinary measures.[66] Such cavalier methods contradicted the spirit of the 1889 legislation, with its condemnation of formalism and its emphasis on close contact with the population.

Polivanov's account suggests that in spite of the near obsessive care the MVD took in producing statistics on every aspect of land captains' activities, these data do not reveal much about the relation between land captains and their peasant subordinates. Numbers were at the center of contemporaries' assessments of the 1889 reforms. Critics delighted in citing the numbers of resolutions voided or elders arrested to emphasize the extent to which rural "self-administration" was in fact controlled from above. Supporters cited the same numbers to show the extent to which land captains were needed to bring order to the countryside. But such numbers tell only part of the story, and can even be misleading. For instance, the apparently simple task of reporting the number of overturned assembly resolutions did not measure the ways that both land captains and villages had of bypassing the official process. Land captains, on the one hand, sometimes resubmitted resolutions they found objectionable directly to the assembly, without first sending them for review to the district congress as required by law. In addition, they could pressure a village assembly by threatening arrests, or simply by being present during deliberations.[67] Not all of the land captains' actions entered into the written record.

Many assembly resolutions, on the other hand, especially in the smaller villages, were simply not recorded, thus escaping land captain scrutiny altogether. The village rosters from this period only list resolutions on routine questions that required annual attention (notably regarding distributions of tax obligations) or, more sporadically, that required land captain approval (such as general land repartitions). It is rare to find more than three or four recorded resolutions a year. Yet ethnographic evidence indicates that assemblies gathered four to six times a year in large communes, and as often as twice a month in the smaller villages.[68] A good deal of village and communal business was conducted out of sight of the higher authorities.

Further hindering transparency in village affairs was the tendency among land captains to rely passively on exchanges of paperwork, a point much belabored in MVD inspections. Village resolutions or volost court decisions only came to land captains' attention if they were appealed, and elders were noticed primarily when complaints were filed against them. The economic state of communes would be examined only when arrears became problematic. Such reactive behavior is understandable, considering that precincts were typically composed of 30,000 to 50,000 inhabitants and could include as many as a hundred villages. While reactivity is to a certain extent a feature of any administration, the initial raison d'être for the land captains' appointment had been their supposed closeness to the population and familiarity with local life.

One means theoretically available to the land captain to gain greater familiarity with his precinct and to learn more than what found its way to his desk was the regular inspection of volost and village administrations. The Land Section applied pressure after 1905 to ensure that reviews were conducted regularly and were thorough enough to encourage villagers to respect the formal procedures spelled out in the General Statute (especially those regarding assembly participation and signing of resolutions). Inspections could only be as good as the personnel conducting them, however. The province-wide reviews published in the *Izvestiia zemskogo otdela* almost invariably deplored the insufficient and superficial supervision of peasant officials. The MVD deemed that only sixteen of Riazan's sixty land captains had satisfactorily conducted local inspections. Inspections in Tver were found to be so slow and incomplete as to "lose any practical significance whatsoever."[69] The problem was particularly acute for village administrations. Provincial officials cited the great distances, the lack of roads, and the poor condition of those that existed, to justify not completing their tours, which invariably included only the volost centers and not the smaller, more remote villages.

Land captains often complained in addition that local records were so poorly kept that substantive evaluations of them were impossible. The rules governing assembly participation and the insistence on properly kept village accounts, court records, and assembly resolutions were meant not only to minimize corruption and manipulation by *miroedy* but also to give the government greater access to information and more control over the countryside. Yet, records of village resolutions were sometimes "summarized deplorably . . . ungrammatically, in bad handwriting." At worst, records were completely useless, as evidenced by one inspector's complaint that "in many resolutions, the reviewer, upon reading the resolution, was unable to determine what in fact had been resolved." Court records could likewise be impenetrable, "without grounds for decisions, and when they are [noted], they are unintelligible, confused, ungrammatical, and incomprehensible."[70] And this, when records had not otherwise been piled into a corner without any hope of ever being put in order, been stored in the village elder's home to be played with by children, been destroyed by fire, nibbled by mice, or damaged by mold in the rickety and inadequate wooden cottage that usually served as the administration building. Even the most energetic land captains found it difficult to understand the inner workings of a volost office. Polivanov noted the irony of inspections, where the reviewer knew much less than the reviewed and depended on the latter's goodwill to understand local conditions and penetrate the mysteries of poorly kept records.[71]

Even the ever more detailed statistical information that the MVD demanded of land captains on the state of their volosts was deceptive in its apparent precision. These "mountains of tables," compiled by the scribe (sometimes by the elder), were notoriously unreliable. Numerous observers described the process of gleaning statistics "from the ceiling." As Polivanov caricatured the scribe:

> No matter what incredible demand is presented to the volost administration, it never ruffles the experienced volost scribe, decorated with heavy medals around his neck for diligent service. Order him in three days to count the sand of the sea, it will be done. Not only will it be done, but the scribe will present exact information on the type of each individual grain.[72]

In practice, scribes collected their data by questioning inhabitants, allowing respondents to underreport harvests or possessions. Then in following years, they simply took this data and added or subtracted according to the circumstances (whether the year had produced a good harvest, whether there had been a livestock epidemic, for example). In addition to sounding a cautionary note to the historian attempting to use such data—many government statistics and even some compiled by zemstvos[73] were gathered on the basis of volost reports—these improvised work methods underscore the extent to which the volost administration, not the land captain, was the gatekeeper of local information. Volost officials retained considerable leeway to control information and communication from the village to the state bureaucracy.

Contemporaries were quick to read into this state of affairs confirmation of their assumptions about peasant society. But in spite of publicists' obsession with drink, bribery, corruption, and abuse of office, what stands out from inspection reports is the extent of the inertia and inactivity suffusing volost administration. Under the burden of their myriad obligations, most poorly educated and untrained elected officials simply proved unequal to the task. While by no means as universally corrupt, incompetent, or help-less as critics contended, the elders were nevertheless ill-suited to serve as a link in the bureaucratic chain. At any given moment, approximately half of them had been newly elected, and the reviewers therefore consid-ered their ignorance excusable.[74] The remaining elders were evaluated as "good" and "bad" in about equal proportion. A "good" elder, such as a peasant in Tambov who had served for eight years, was described as "liter-ate, [and] he splendidly knows his duties, is energetic, active, intelli-gent."[75] Such positive evaluations were unusual. Even elders who received awards for their service were often praised for no more than knowing their duties and leading a sober way of life.[76] But conspicuous examples of cor-ruption or defiance were also rare. "Passive" was the epithet most often used in official evaluations of peasant officials.

When it came to carrying out volost court decisions, the inertia of volost elders reached such stunning proportions that alarmed authorities launched a campaign to impress upon land captains and elders the impor-tance of this task. Although an "unimplemented decision" did not neces-sarily mean that fines went uncollected or compensation unpaid, it did mean that no one verified to make sure. For the Land Section of the MVD, this demonstration of the "absolute inactivity of peasant officials and in-sufficient supervision by land captains" could only diminish the very meaning of the volost courts and compromise the land captain's author-ity. By 1908 the problem was endemic throughout the empire. In Tver the proportion of non-implemented court decisions ranged between 50 and 90 percent, and in several volosts even reached 100 percent. There was hardly a volost in Tambov that was not found to be delinquent.[77] The campaign to correct the shortcoming gave mitigated results. Inspectors deemed the situation in Riazan satisfactory by 1912, but this was hardly the verdict elsewhere. While the situation had improved in some areas of Tver in 1913, it had worsened in others. Reports from Samara (1911) and Ufa (1912) also testify to the stubborn persistence of this problem.[78]

The inspectors blamed volost officials' poor work habits squarely on the land captains' loose supervision. "Lack of surveillance" (nadzor) and "lack of closeness" was the litany of reproach applied even to those who re-ceived the best evaluations. And this was the case as much in 1914 as it had been in the 1890s, in spite of the retreat from the language of pater-nalism during the period of Stolypin's premiership. Even Gurko's scathing criticism of land captains still assumed that they could establish trust and turn peasant officials into collaborators. The ministry's efforts were proba-bly misplaced, however, as even with the most dedicated and vehement of exhortations the land captains could not vouch for the quality of the work completed by the volost officials. The extent of responsibilities de-volved upon peasant administrators far exceeded the legal and procedural knowledge of elected officials, especially for the majority who served just one three-year term. In spite of the growing mounds of paperwork, reports, and statistics extracted from the countryside, there was little the land captain could do to guarantee the reliability of the information flowing to and from volost offices and ensure the consistent and reliable execution of government policies. Volost officials had not been transformed into local civil servants.

The Volost Scribe

Much of what has been described thus far about the functioning of volost administration could be interpreted through the prism of passive resistance. But where historians would tend to read resistance, contemporaries overwhelmingly saw exploitation by "commune-eaters" *(miroedy)* and their acolytes. Neither characterization quite accurately describes the role that volost officials played in mediating between the village and the state. Certainly, instances of resistance as well as cases of corruption can be found in the archives, but both were exceptional. Villagers rarely exhibited the kind of unity necessary for effective resistance, and peasant officials rarely obtained the kind of autonomy they would have needed for the appropriation of power to the benefit of a few. This, it would seem, should have been good news for land captains bent on transforming volost administrators into trusted collaborators. But few local state officials were ever able to overcome their fears of the dangers of delegating authority to villagers. Herein lay the land captains' greatest dilemma: they needed peasant officials powerful enough to obtain some independence from local pressures, yet powerful officials were by definition to be distrusted. The constant suspicion under which peasant officials had to labor ensured that the benefits of office would remain meager indeed.

The difficulty land captains faced in obtaining reliable information about village life and politics only reinforced the search for villains. And no figure of rural administration was so consistently vilified by educated Russians as the volost scribe, the lowly *pisar'*. Whether the prescription for Russia's peasants was more knowledge and literacy or more paternally protective authority, the image of the volost scribe could be called upon to show what ills would befall the benighted peasant if he faced, without protection or education, an unscrupulous official who held the key to law and bureaucracy. The *pisar'* was the perfect scapegoat, the designated handmaiden of the *miroed*, the real boss in the countryside.

The volost scribe was theoretically a mere recorder of decisions, a modest hired employee of the peasant assembly, yet his potential power was enormous. He was indispensable to the peasantry, for it was he who filled out all the necessary forms to petition for a loan, for tax relief, or for a land title and only he could assure the timely filing of these forms with the appropriate authorities—or if need be, find ways to bypass the law. While elders were elected for three-year terms, the scribe was hired by the assembly and could theoretically serve one or two decades. The scribe's purported long tenure meant that at times he was the only official with knowledge of local administrative affairs. It also meant that he could establish patronage networks, selling his services to the highest bidder. Taking advantage of low levels of literacy among the peasant population, scribes could manipulate documents to the advantage of their clients by making changes in village resolutions, understating the value of buildings assessed for the zemstvo obligatory insurance, or correcting assessments of household eligibility for emergency loans. Above all, the scribe was criticized for being the real judge of the volost courts. As the only individual with any knowledge of the law and rules of procedure, critics argued, he could always persuade judges to rule as he wished.[79] Some observers went so far as to claim that all of St. Petersburg's decrees remained a dead letter if the scribe chose not to implement them. One MVD inspector was hardly surprised to find a volost of Tver province in which the clerk processed requests for land titles so slowly that most petitioners finally withdrew their request.[80] No other village official so bitterly disappointed the hopes of reformers dedicated to bringing order to the countryside.

The image of the all-powerful scribe using his literacy to manipulate the peasantry to his own benefit was largely mythical, however. As with most aspects of village life, it was easy for contemporary observers to see the worst and the aberrant as typical. Far from being a "demoralizing influence," most scribes barely managed to fulfill their manifold obligations. Provincial inspectors identified the same problems with the volost scribes as with other village officials: most were found to be "lazy," "passive," "inactive," and "listless."

The constraints on scribes were enormous, even greater than those faced by elected village officials. Although generally accorded external signs of respect, they were seen by villagers as outsiders (chuzhye). Unlike the volost elder, the scribe was rarely a local peasant, and occasionally not even a peasant. After receiving some sort of formal education, he worked as an assistant for some years before being hired as a full-time clerk in a different volost.[81] A 1912 photograph of a gathering of scribes in Novgorod, published in the journal Niva, shows almost exclusively clean-shaven young or middle-aged men in relatively stylish urban dress. Their position was not unlike that of village teachers, with whom they were frequently compared.

Like schoolteachers, scribes were dependent upon the peasants among whom they had to live for their position and their salary. But at the same time, they had to satisfy the demands of the land captain, who supervised their work and had the right to remove them from office. If native elders had difficulty navigating the conflicting demands placed upon them, the scribes' position as outsiders thrown into the cauldron of village politics was even more tenuous.[82] They were vulnerable to complaints filed with the local land captain. When these were filed by the volost elder, as was not uncommon, scribes had a difficult time defending themselves. Elders were better positioned to control witnesses called to the hearing. They were also the scribes' administrative superior, and land captains tended to give them credence. After all, the scribe was hired by the volost, and if he could not work with the volost's elected officials, then what was the point of entering further into the root causes of a dispute?

This seems to have been the reasoning behind the land captain's decision in the case of the scribe Andrei Koniaev, accused in 1913 by the Derevensk volost elder (Riazan province) of being a drunk. Koniaev admitted that he sometimes got drunk, but no more than anybody else, and he claimed that the elder's complaint stemmed from his desire to put one of his local acolytes in Konaiev's place. This defense seems credible, for the elder did manage to get one of his close allies hired as scribe after Konaiev's departure. But Koniaev obviously had difficulty finding a modus vivendi with local officials. He had earlier been expelled from his post in the neighboring volost of Kirits, after a particularly acrimonious battle with the *starshina* there involving mutual accusations of bribery and forgery. But then, Koniaev was the third scribe in two years to be expelled from office in Kirits for excessive intervention in local affairs.[83]

The difficulties faced by Koniaev may not have been typical, but they do illustrate the scribe's vulnerability. Numerous volost scribes writing to the national or provincial press testified to the difficulties they faced in juggling the conflicting demands placed upon them. If they did not, for instance, acquiesce to help a villager in a boundary dispute or support a particular local faction in its opposition to land reform, accusations of bribery might suddenly appear on the land captain's desk. A scribe who wanted to keep his position, several correspondents concluded, had no choice but to fall into collusion with peasant officials.[84]

Regardless of a land captain's political leanings, he treated the scribe with suspicion, an attitude encouraged both by the press and by governors determined to free the countryside from corrupting political influences. Scribes were constantly under suspicion of "reading the law" to the advantage of the *kulak-miroed*. But they had to strike a delicate balance between their official mandate, which was limited to honest and accurate bookkeeping, and their unofficial mandate, which was to bring order, honesty, and transparency into local affairs. Scribes who intervened during a court hearing could be accused of manipulating the court, but when the court made errors, they could be held responsible. Scribes were reprimanded by provincial inspectors for allowing peasant judges to treat criminal complaints as civil suits or for allowing out-of-court settlements between litigants when these were forbidden. Poorly run volost courts were blamed not only on insufficient supervision by land captains, but also on "insufficient work by the scribe with the court."[85]

Clearly, it was not easy for the *pisar'* to keep his post. His tenure depended on not offending his various superiors and on remaining relatively unnoticed. Contrary to the prevailing image, few volost scribes made a career out of the position. Data collected in early 1914 by the MVD on 437 scribes from Riazan and Tver provinces indicate that their average age was thirty-five years, while fewer than one in five were above the age of forty. The average age of volost elders in Riazan in 1909, on the other hand, was forty-seven. Scribes who remained in the same volost year after year, while elected peasant officials came and went, were the exception. Their average length of service was 4.2 years in Riazan, and 3.8 years in Tver, slightly less than for volost elders. Forty percent of Riazan's scribes had been in office 3 years or less, 66 percent in Tver.[86] According to a Land Section study of scribes' working conditions, most used the skills they had obtained working in the village to move on to better paying and less stressful jobs elsewhere, taking advantage of the growing demand for bookkeepers on the part of the organizations and industries proliferating in the provinces.[87]

The scribe's position became even more tenuous with the revolutionary disorders of 1905–1906. Many villages turned to the scribe to write their demands, threatening to suspend his salary or even to beat him if he did not comply. At the same time, scribes risked fines and arrest by provincial authorities for having agreed to write out illegal resolutions. Caught between village and administration, some simply chose to flee the village.[88] After 1906 scribes who had given voice to the peasant movement were fined or arrested and removed from their positions. Those who remained at their posts found themselves under heightened scrutiny by the land captains. Both the Tver and Riazan governors repeatedly reminded land captains to pay close attention to the past political activities and work histories of the scribes in their districts. In 1915 the MVD Minister Maklakov sent all governors a similar message, reminding them that past "anti-government revolutionary disorders" had thrived precisely in areas where peasant officials had included "unreliable elements."[89]

This vulnerability, the uncertainty of the scribes' position within the hierarchy, and the resentment over the low status of their job became driving forces behind a movement calling for professionalization of the job of volost clerk. Laments on the "mournful" condition of the defenseless volost scribe became a subgenre of its own in writings about rural life after the turn of the century.[90] A growing number of scribes became active correspondents of newspapers and journals, submitting articles in which they described their working conditions. The semi-official *Sel'skii vestnik* in 1902 began publishing calls for government-funded pensions. Scribes also found spokesmen among advocates for the creation of all-estate volosts, who recognized the scribes as the "living nerve of the village" and saw the potential to transform their "nefarious" appropriation of power into a force for progress and legality. The journal *Volostnoi pisar'*, which began publication in 1914, took on the task of giving voice to the "small specks" scattered all over Russia who "in quiet and anonymity pursue their great task." This could be done, it argued, only by attracting better educated, better remunerated, and therefore more dedicated people to the profession; the *pisar'* should be incorporated into government service instead of being hired by the assembly like a mere cowherd. He should be called by the more respectful title of "clerk" *(deloproizvoditel')* and receive a pension.

By 1914, after a decade of discussion, the MVD was finally envisaging some timid reforms along the lines proposed by *Volostnoi pisar'*. The need to replace mobilized clerks forced authorities to take measures consonant with calls for professionalization, and in 1915 the Land Section created a five-month course to prepare candidates to fill the growing number of vacancies.[91] The MVD also began drawing up legislation, echoing a 1914 Duma proposal, to establish a pension fund, although—with characteristic slowness—it was still studying the issue at the end of 1916. Most significantly, the ministry approved on principle the idea of setting minimum salaries for volost elders and clerks, to be paid by central administration. Such changes might have improved the working conditions of volost scribes, especially if the yet unspecified wage levels were high enough to reduce local officials' dependence on volost assemblies. But the MVD was not seeking an overall increase in the wages of clerks. Instead, its goal was to raise the salaries that were "abnormally low" (less than three hundred rubles a year). The ministry even recognized the danger that a centrally paid minimum salary could lower overall wage levels but summarily dismissed the concern on the grounds that the proposed legislation did not prevent volost assemblies from paying supplements from their own funds.[92] Given growing peasant resentment of the obligation to pay general administrative expenses, the ministry's optimism seems unwarranted. It is doubtful, therefore, that the envisaged reforms would have done much to remove the greatest constraints on the *pisar'*, which were overwork, the need to balance the demands of multiple superiors, and the difficulty of navigating unofficial and official mandates in a context of great legal and jurisdictional confusion.

ELECTED PEASANT OFFICIALS—
VILLAGE AND VOLOST ELDERS

Scribes were not the only designated villains in the government's search for explanations of the shortcomings of local administration. The potential for peasant elders to accumulate local power was also a constant source of worry. In the 1890s Novikov had recognized that the elder was the land captain's closest advisor, the person he would naturally turn to when he needed information about local conditions or needed to decide a complaint or appeal. The elder could then easily influence the land captain's attitudes: he was able "[to] paint an affair in any color: to recount how Ivan had sat in jail, but to keep quiet about Peter, to tell that Semen is a well-known swindler, that Nikita is a troublemaker who keeps all his neighbors in fear."[93] But some of the same factors that limited the elders' ability to serve as reliable agents of government authority also constrained their ability to be independent of the village. An elder's authority depended largely on the support he received from his land captain. But in contrast to the situation prevailing before 1889, the representative of state authority was now accessible not only to the village leadership but also to disgruntled village rivals. The presence of the land captain provided villagers the opportunity to use his power in ways that limited the authority of elders.

At first sight, there appear to be important differences between the power and status of volost elders as compared with village elders. It is no surprise that peasants feared the volost elder's potential powers. He had intimate knowledge of his district, along with easy access to the land captain and the rural police. Decisions regarding tax collection or the sale of property to collect arrears, the implementation (or not) of a court decision, or the outcome of an appeal against a village resolution could depend on the elder's actions and what he might say or report to the land captain. An able *starshina* could accumulate power either to obstruct higher authorities or to embezzle fellow peasants. One volost elder in Riazan, for instance, was found by horrified inspectors to have usurped all power in the volost, single-handedly rendering decisions on disputes that belonged in the courts, and acting independently of the land captain.[94] But the volost elders' power had waned from the heyday of the 1880s when their reputation had been forged. Prior to the arrival of land captains, the elders had been virtually the only conduits of information in and out of the village. District boards examining appeals and complaints had invariably entrusted investigations to volost elders and had little choice but to trust the results of those investigations. After 1889 volost elders were no longer guaranteed such monopoly access to outside authorities.

The position of the village elder *(starosta)* was even more precarious. Most observers noted that these elders generally did little more than call the assembly. When asked whether the elders had any particular influence over the assembly, respondents of a Russian Geographic Society survey of the late 1870s unanimously replied "no." Two decades later, despite the elders' expanded duties, respondents to the Tenishev bureau commented that the *starosta* rarely commanded much influence or unusual respect in the village.[95]

The village elder faced important constraints on his authority and independence of action. A peasant could not refuse the office, and most candidates viewed it as a burden and an unwelcome obligation. The *starosta* was responsible for the general good order and well-being of his community, which included watching over the collection of taxes, verifying the proper condition of roads and bridges, reporting to the police all disorders, fires, breaches of contract, and the arrival of beggars. It was also his duty to execute the land captain's and the volost elder's lawful orders and to assist visiting tax inspectors and police officials. It is little wonder that elders grumbled that they had to neglect their own farms to fulfill their official responsibilities.

The relative positions of the village and the volost elder can be gauged by comparing their salaries and the length of their term of service. Peasants rarely served more than one three-year term as *starosta,* and they sometimes went to great lengths to avoid being elected to the office. In some areas, especially in the first decades after Emancipation, villagers rotated the office annually. Although the practice was forbidden after 1889, it was reported to the Tenishev bureau in the 1890s and was discovered during inspections as late as 1914.[96] In contrast, it was quite common for volost elders to serve several terms. Over half of Riazan volost officials in 1911 had been in office for more than three years, and one in six was in his fifth term. In Moscow, only 29 percent of the volost elders in 1916 were serving their first term, and nearly half were at least in their third term (although these figures are probably skewed by the wartime lack of replacement candidates).[97]

The woeful level of remuneration added to peasants' reluctance to serve as village elder. According to 1891 data collected by the Ministry of Finance, village elders received an average salary of 33 rubles a year. Twenty years later, these levels had changed little: many village elders in three central provinces continued to receive a modest 15–30 rubles a year (at a time when a cow cost 40–60 rubles). Only rarely, in the largest and wealthiest villages close to industrial centers, did they receive as much as 45 rubles. Village elders' salaries were far below those of other peasant officials. Even the judges, whose obligations were limited to showing up at most once a week for court sessions, received salaries of 60 rubles, while the president was paid 100 rubles. The volost elders' salaries, meanwhile, did rise. Averaging 180 rubles in 1891, salaries ranged between 250 and 800 rubles two decades later, comparable to remuneration levels of teachers and feldshers.[98] These salaries more than compensated a household for the loss of labor of its head.

The most important constraints on elected village officials, however, affected village and volost elders equally. They were vulnerable not only to fines and arrests by the land captains but also to complaints filed by the numerous government officials who had to deal with the village. Most often it was the police who requested that the land captain take administrative measures against the peasant officials under his supervision. The charges were remarkably similar from year to year and province to province. They consisted of "willful inactivity," such as a refusal to take adequate fire prevention measures or failure to keep roads in good repair. Zemstvo insurance agents and land surveyors filed complaints of obstructionism in evaluating land and building values. Tax inspectors also turned to the land captains when they found elders less than willing to identify households in arrears.

There was one compelling reason for all elected elders to risk sanctions: they had to continue living in the communities in which they served, and aside from their temporarily endowed authority, nothing distinguished them from their neighbors. In the words of one Tenishev bureau respondent: "These officials never forget that their power is temporary, and at the next election, they will turn into simple peasants again."[99] Village leaders could be called to account for their actions long after they had ended their term in office. Caught in a delicate and uncomfortable position between fellow villagers and the land captain's demands, elders frequently chose to do as little as possible.

The elders only very rarely used their right to fine and arrest villagers for minor infractions, and then, by most accounts, they did so only on instructions from a higher official.[100] In Riazan province, for instance, the village elders collectively arrested an average of 1,386 peasants a year between 1910 and 1914. This represented one arrest for every four elders. The number of fines was negligible, amounting to a mere fifty-six a year for the entire province. The elders of Moscow province were similarly timid, with only one in ten each year availing himself of the right to fine or arrest a fellow villager. The volost elders made more frequent use of their disciplinary powers but were hardly profligate in applying administrative sanctions. In Riazan, each volost elder, on average, arrested or fined seven peasants each year; in Moscow, five.[101]

The desire of land captains and provincial authorities for energetic and active elders led to conflicts with volost and village assemblies, which were naturally interested in electing candidates who would not demonstrate any untoward zeal in the collection of arrears. In one case, which was appealed all the way to the Senate, electors from a volost in southern Riazan complained that the land captain had chosen the candidate with the fewest positive votes. (Peasants cast both positive and negative ballots, and every candidate receiving a majority of positive votes was put forward.) The land captain explained that this candidate had previously demonstrated energy in collecting taxes and implementing volost court decisions, while his more popular rival was "weak and disorderly." The Senate reminded the electors that the land captain was free to choose any of the candidates put forth by the assembly, regardless of the number of votes that person had received.[102]

Unfortunately, it is difficult to know how common such conflicts were. Contested elections did not often get appealed. It was sufficient for the land captain to show up at the assembly and explain that he was not beholden to pick the favored candidate for cries of "We don't want him!" to subside.[103] Nevertheless, it is some measure of the assemblies' success in this sphere that officials cited "inactivity" as the most common motive for firing an elder. In classic examples of passive resistance, elders were expelled for poor collection of taxes, slow implementation of orders from higher authorities, or poor supervision of order in the village. In the province of Simbirsk, of the ninety-six volost elders removed from office over the course of four years, thirty-nine were fired for inactivity. The same reason was cited for the removal of fourteen of the forty-four *starosty* between 1890 and 1895 in the Riazan district of Spassk. Another twenty-six were replaced for habitual drunkenness, another form of inactivity, it could be argued. Only four were fired for embezzlement or corruption.[104]

The elders' passivity did on occasion become openly defiant. In one instance, inspectors described a Tambov elder: although literate, "he absolutely does not know his duties and does not want to know. When questioned by the inspector, [the elder] answered with great calm that he knows nothing because that's the scribe's business."[105] One Ksenefontov, elder of Voskresenskoe volost, Tver district, in 1909 told the tax inspector who asked him for help in preparing lists of households in arrears that he had been elected by peasants and therefore was supposed to support them. Since this elder had been already arrested or fined eleven times in less than two years, the land captain removed him from office. It should be noted, however, that Ksenefontov was expelled only after the tax inspector had undertaken an ambitious effort to collect the arrears that were endemic in the volost. He had managed to stay in office since 1903 and had been reelected twice with no objections from the land captain. In addition, the volost assembly went on to elect a replacement who was no better, in turn expelled for similar obstructionism before the year was out.[106]

Even when the assembly was unable to control the outcome of elections, it had other means available to punish or control elders: it could lower the salaries of undesirable officials. Overnight, an elder or a scribe could see his compensation dramatically cut. In a typical 1908 case from Moscow province, one volost elder had his pay reduced from 450 rubles to 150. Only after he appealed to the land captain was he able to force restitution of his previous level of pay. In other volosts, assemblies stubbornly refused to raise salaries in spite of the land captain's repeated interventions.[107] The setting of salaries became a major area of conflict between assemblies and land captains by the turn of the century. MVD officials considered good compensation essential to attract the best peasants into office and to ensure elders some independence from the volost inhabitants and the temptations of bribery. Since 1893 the provincial board, upon recommendation by the land captain, could decree a raise in the scribe's or elder's salaries if the level of compensation set by the assembly was deemed inadequate. While this prerogative had been invoked only rarely in the 1890s, after the turn of the century it was increasingly common for land captains to step in to prevent the assemblies from lowering salaries of volost officials. After several such incidents in the district of Sapozhok (Riazan), for instance, the district congress decided to set a district-wide minimum salary, instructing land captains to apply the measure administratively in all twenty-two volosts if voluntary approval could not be obtained.[108]

A speech by a land captain from Tver illustrates the mix of cajoling and threats that could be used to obtain an assembly's "voluntary" approval. He explained to the gathered assembly:

> For such a salary no one will want to serve. People will run to give up their office or will bear it unwillingly. They will neglect affairs and will fulfill your requests unwillingly and incorrectly. . . . If you raise their salaries, I am convinced that things will be more pleasant for you . . . [If you do not,] it will be worse for you, and even more so since the provincial board will add even more and willy-nilly you will have to pay. That is why I want [to do this] without compulsion, I want to do what is best for you with good will *(po dobromu i khoroshemu)*.[109]

The land captain also added an argument frequently invoked in such conflicts: if the scribe and elder had proper salaries, peasants would no longer have to pay a bribe of twenty kopecks every time they needed something done.

The land captain, unlike many publicists who deplored the endemic corruption of the countryside, most likely understood that peasants preferred to pay an occasional bribe or make an occasional gift of vodka than pay a regular salary. Upon taking office, a captain would immediately be faced with the difficulty of refusing peasant "gifts." Naumov, for instance, was surprised on his first reception day by an old woman who arrived with some eggs: she would not accept the explanation that her case would be examined "even without eggs," and the bemused Naumov finally had to accept them if he was to have the woman's confidence.[110] A salary gave the peasant official a measure of independence, while the bribe/gift contained an element of exchange and obligation. Ivan Kupchinov, who wrote about his experience as volost scribe in an unspecified central Russian province in 1906–1907, had plenty of opportunity to observe the prevalence of "gifts" in the conduct of volost business. An absentee working in the city who needed his passport renewed might include a three-ruble note in the envelope to ensure rapid processing; a villager who wanted a point of legislation explained would offer a few rubles; any request for a copy of a court decision or a village resolution was likewise accompanied by a gift "in thanks." According to Kupchinov, peasant officials saw such payments as "sinless income," legitimate compensation for their ill-paid service. Kupchinov, who avoided accepting such payments, was viewed with suspicion, both by peasants, who feared that it meant he would work against them, and by the volost elder, who feared denunciation.[111]

The fact is that peasants rarely interpreted small illicit payments or offers of vodka as bribery. When the correspondents to the Tenishev bureau were asked to describe peasant attitudes toward bribery *(vziatochnichestvo)*, most responded that peasants considered small payments normal and necessary to ensure rapid processing of paperwork. What villagers did condemn was the misuse or squandering of communal funds *(rastrata)*.[112] While most contemporary commentators assumed that extra payments reflected abuse of power, they could in fact reflect the opposite: a preference by peasants for a system that strengthened ties of obligation. Land captains—with some notable exceptions—were surprisingly tolerant of these practices. They on occasion even reprimanded overly scrupulous scribes for creating tensions and conflict with their volost elders over the issue of accepting payments: "Life is not the same as the law" . . . "You do not understand the peasant milieu" . . . "You have to be more flexible," these rural crusaders were told.[113]

The final recourse available to villagers who wanted control over their elected officials was to file a complaint against them with the land captain. It is impossible to know how often villagers formally filed such complaints, as these figures were almost never reported. Scattered data do suggest, however, that elders and judges were more likely to face a hearing before the land captain because of their fellow peasants than because of government officials. In Moscow in 1891, private individuals were responsible for 75 percent of the 2,008 complaints filed against peasant officials. In Penza in 1898 the proportion was 84 percent, and in the district of Ostashkov (Tver province) 71 percent between 1906 and 1909.[114]

There were three broad types of formal accusation against village officials: complaints that extended individual disputes but in fact had little to do with the official's actions, complaints that stemmed from personal enmity, and accusations that emerged from uncontained village factionalism. The first group was the largest. Such charges were most often strategic last-ditch efforts to win a court case when the regular appeal process had been exhausted. For instance, one Riazan peasant who had worked several years in Moscow filed an administrative complaint with the land captain after losing three court appeals where he failed to reclaim abandoned land in his native village. He claimed that the village elder had abused his position by representing the commune's interests instead of acting as a nonpartisan elected official.[115] Other cases included complaints that the judges or the scribe had been drunk during a court session, that elders had not delivered notices of court hearings, or that an elder who arrived to implement a court decision was rude and insulting.[116] Although at least one land captain encouraged peasants whom he believed had been unjustly treated by the volost court to make such complaints, most of his colleagues showed little patience with this type of appeal, either because they feared undermining the authority of village leaders or because they saw these cases as the inventions of litigious troublemakers.[117]

Even when land captains did seriously investigate complaints of abusive behavior by elected officials, administrative procedures prevented them from providing redress. This is rather surprising, for one of the land captain's most important mandates was to protect peasants from abusive local bosses by dispensing rapid and equitable justice, free from "artificial" procedural rules. Land captains certainly were prompt, usually holding hearings within two weeks after receipt of a complaint. But procedural rules prevented many grievances from being addressed. The focus of an administrative hearing was in fact quite narrow. Even if the office of land captain combined judicial and administrative functions, Senate rulings did not allow these functions to be exercised simultaneously. When petitioners managed to obtain the punishment of an official, land captains were not free to reverse a court decision and could not award compensation for losses incurred through negligence, or even through deliberate ill will.[118] For instance, a woman who was awarded ownership of a cow by the volost court was unable to get the elder to enforce the decision before the cow disappeared. While the land captain reprimanded the elder for his inaction, the plaintiff was denied compensation and was instructed to address the courts. Likewise, excessive delays in distributing seed loans, sending military papers to villagers working in the city, or filing court documents on time could all cost a peasant dearly.[119] Yet, in accordance with Senate rulings, the land captains had to reject requests for compensation as being in the jurisdiction of the general courts, to the great disappointment of petitioners. Few practices so clearly belied the ideals of paternal authority and justice that land captains were supposed to embody.

Village officials were also vulnerable to complaints by their personal enemies. It was not uncommon for a hearing about insult, abuse, or unjust arrest to uncover a web of old conflicts and past mutual accusations of insult. Charges of partiality *(pristrastie)*, of acting out of ill will *(po zlobe)*, revenge, or malice were accompanied by stories of old land disputes or even older court cases.[120] It was not unknown for elders themselves to use their positions to settle old scores, and even if they acted within their jurisdiction, they could find themselves answering before higher authorities. A woman who was fined fifty kopecks for absence from village assembly meetings claimed, for example, that the fine had been imposed only out of animosity and rancor *(revnost')*—a credible charge since absenteeism was chronic and almost never sanctioned.[121] Land captains rarely investigated such charges; almost invariably, they dismissed them out of hand. Investigation would have required time, intimate knowledge of village politics, and a "closeness to the population" that captains had only in the minds of MVD inspectors.

The final type of charge, more complex, included accusations of bribery, favoritism, or general bad conduct. Such complaints occurred unevenly within a province. Most villages and volosts rarely or never figured in the land captains' registers of complaints. One can only presume that such villages managed to avoid outside intervention by keeping their disputes out of official view. Individual villages, however, and sometimes entire volosts, figured prominently on the land captain's docket. This was the case, for instance, of one small commune of thirty-four households within the village of Iasenok, in Riazan's southern district of Riazhsk.

There, the village elder, Volodin, found himself answering charges ranging from bribery, through late-night extortions of vodka, to manipulating the assembly. In 1911 alone he had to make the trip to the land captain's chamber four times to answer for his conduct. Witnesses invariably gave conflicting testimony. After a brawl in the local tavern, some witnesses claimed that the elder had started the fight, others that he was attacked after politely trying to break up a card game, while the tavern keeper asserted that Volodin had been drunk. Several witnesses who testified for the card players vouched for the general good behavior and seriousness of two peasants who had been expelled from the assembly for three years for systematic disorderly behavior.[122] The roots of the tensions in Iasenok were never revealed. Perhaps Volodin simply took his obligations a bit too seriously. In an exceptionally glowing report by provincial inspectors, this volost's officials had been singled out as unusually competent and active in fulfilling their duties.[123] In any case, the land captain must have trusted Volodin, since he repeatedly ruled in his favor.

As far as the commune was concerned, the best elders were those who did the least. But when elected officials showed blatant favoritism, or when their actions regularly excluded one or another of the powerful factions in the village, peasants did not hesitate to appeal to outside authority. Petitioners against the Izhevskoe village elder (Spassk district, Riazan), for example, protested a mysterious "miscellaneous" expense of eighty-nine rubles in the commune's annual accounts because "this money was used for food and drink, and not for all householders but only those who are close to the *starosta*."[124] In another complaint, a woman accused the elder of chasing her away from the assembly with an ax after she protested that money from the sale of communal hay was to be drunk up. Witnesses questioned by the land captain explained, however, that Guriakova had in fact come to the assembly in order to receive her share of vodka. She protested to higher authorities not because she objected to the drinking up of proceeds from the sale, but because she was denied a share of the spoils.[125] It was not corruption to which she objected, but partisanship.

The issues at the root of acrimonious relations in Podvislovo (Riazhsk district) were more clearly exposed. Of the many complaints that came before the land captain over the course of several years, two in particular stand out. In 1910 Ivan Kolesnikov, the village elder, was accused by a group of peasants (including one Fedor Kochkin) of changing the rental period for a piece of communal land from twelve to fifteen years, after the resolution had been signed in the assembly. Since this was the third incident involving Kolesnikov's writing up resolutions "contrary to the assembly's will," and since the majority of the commune's 150 households no longer wanted him to serve as elder, the land captain removed him from office. If the land captain had hoped by his decision to end the practice whereby village leaders granted their acolytes the use of communal property, he was quickly disappointed. Two years later, it was Fedor Kochkin, as the new elder, who found himself accused by Kolesnikov's nephew (among others) of a similar offense. Apparently, on May 6 the assembly had agreed to rent out some land to Kolesnikov, the former elder, but two weeks later a new resolution gave the same land to one Posrochin. The hearing on the matter elicited conflicting testimony. One witness stated that in early May, Kolesnikov had offered two pails of vodka and thirty rubles for the land, and part of the assembly had agreed. Then on 27 May, the rival bidder had offered more, and the *skhod* "changed its mind." Most witnesses claimed that the new resolution had already been drawn up when Kochkin called the second assembly, implying that the elder had received a bribe from Posrochin.[126] No one denied that vodka flowed rather freely through the whole affair.

In such factionalized villages, battles consisted not only of gaining control over communal resources, but also of controlling access to the land captain. In this way, outside authority, with its priorities and considerations, was given a potentially deciding role in village politics. The *zemskii nachal'nik* could become the arbiter of activities that normally remained hidden to the outside. Land captains rarely capitalized on this opportunity, however. The hearing on Podvislovo was quite typical of investigations of peasant complaints and exemplified everything that troubled the MVD inspectors. Podvislovo exhibited virtually all the elements of village life that land captains had been created to eradicate: drink, bribery, favoritism, abuse of office, depredation of communal resources. Yet, the land captain took no notice of the practice of auctioning land off for vodka and made no mention of it in his verdict. He made no attempt to question any witnesses beyond those presented by the disputing sides. He did not go out to the village to question the assembly himself. Instead, he ruled that conflicting testimony left the charges of bribery unproven.

The behavior of Podvislovo's land captain was not at all unusual. In Moscow in 1891, in Orel in 1892, as well as in Tver's Ostoshkov district between 1906 and 1909, well over half of the complaints filed against peasant elected officials were dropped or ruled to be groundless. In 1898 in Penza, the figure was 68 percent.[127] Overwork, lack of time and resources, compounded by a reluctance to undermine the authority of peasant officials on whom they depended, all conspired to result in many captains paying only cursory attention to accusations against village elders.

Complacency is an insufficient explanation of land captains' laissez-faire approach to village politics, however. In their dealings with the peasant officials, even the best land captains tended to adapt to peasant practices. Inspectors' frequent reprimand was that complaints involving peasant officials were too often dropped either because the complainant failed to show up at the hearing, or because of reconciliation *(primirenie)*. Such outcomes were characteristic of volost court practice, where many complaints in fact derived from posturing in a dispute that was settled outside the courtroom, and where reconciliation was the most likely outcome. Under administrative regulations, however, a complaint of bribery or abuse of authority could not be treated as a dispute between individuals that might be subject to reconciliation. Nonetheless, land captains frequently did so. A peasant official's dual position as a villager and as an authority figure made it virtually impossible to separate out personal issues: an elder could always claim that an incident of impropriety had occurred while he was not on duty. If a land captain insisted on pursuing a case in spite of a declared reconciliation, the parties could always count on the testimony of witnesses, who invariably had heard or seen nothing or could claim that the *starosta* had not been wearing his medal of office.[128] A land captain faced with disappearing or reconciled accusers would have needed much energy and dedication—not to mention disregard for local sensibilities—to pursue a complaint that peasants considered resolved.

The most formidable obstacle to the resolution of complaints against village officials was simply that land captains relied heavily on their elders for information about village life. They did not have the inside knowledge necessary to distinguish between valid and invalid complaints. Inspectors were absolutely correct in noting that the land captains' preferred work methods led to superficial resolution of local conflicts. Satisfied with the testimony of witnesses hand-picked by the litigants, the captains allowed villagers control over proceedings and squandered the opportunities for constructive intervention offered by village factionalism. The combination of limited local knowledge and cumbersome procedural regulations made it improbable that a land captain could satisfy legitimate peasant complaints and fulfill his mandate of dispensing rapid paternal justice in defense of the weak. As one peasant from Vladimir explained: "He is right who reaches the land captain first."[129]

◆ ◆ ◆

Serving as land captain was a thankless and difficult job. The MVD wanted administrative generalists, yet captains were called upon to fulfill an ever growing number of specialized tasks. Increasingly hemmed in by precise regulations and Senate rulings, reviled in the opposition press, attacked as the embodiment of arbitrary rule *(proizvol)*, under suspicion even from their administrative superiors, it is little wonder that captains complained about being "surrounded by enemies." They were caught in an impossible situation: achieving the type of uniformity and control the government aspired to was simply impossible. Reprimanded for exhibiting the type of local accommodation that made their work possible and which they believed to be consonant with their mandate, land captains were also brought to task when they made excessive use of their punitive powers. In the first case they were accused of lacking dedication, in the second of lacking tact.

Nevertheless, it is undeniable that the government extended its reach ever further into the countryside in the course of the half-century following Emancipation. Even a cursory comparison of archives from the 1870s with those from the early twentieth century testifies to the proliferation of investigations, reports, and statistics collected on virtually every aspect of rural existence. The state's increased presence, however, rarely translated into an accrued ability to control the terms of its relations with the peasantry. The government's attempts to inject existing rural administration with a respect for formal regulations and established procedure broke down at every level. Whether in his paternalist incarnation, or as an agent of increasing bureaucratic control, the land captain's influence was overestimated by both detractors and supporters. Most *zemskie nachal'niki* proved unable to be more than sporadically interventionist, and they contributed little to the efficacy of state bureaucracy in the countryside. Even if one captain did succeed in transmitting some sense of what the government considered just and moral, rural inhabitants were likely to be subjected to a different vision by his successor and have their conception of authority as personal and arbitrary only reinforced.

This official ineffectiveness did not mean that the peasantry was united in a naturally oppositional subculture, however. Villages may have been difficult to control, but they were not closed. Peasants invited outside intervention in their complaints against their elders, scribes, and judges. The very presence of a state official bolstered by broad powers of punishment, appointment, and arbitration encouraged peasants to compete for his favor. Land captains were rarely able to take advantage of the opportunity offered by the invitation to arbitrate village factional quarrels. Their limited local knowledge made it unlikely that a land captain could respond to legitimate peasant grievances and fulfill his mandate of dispensing rapid paternal justice in defense of the weak. Far from being the local representative of the tsar's mercy, the land captain was but one more player in the web of rural politics, more likely to be ridiculed than respected. Land captains could never overcome the dilemma posed by the fact that their influence depended on the very peasant officials whose powers they most distrusted. Contrary to the government's intention, the powers of intermediary peasant officials were reduced; for elders and scribes, the benefits of delegated authority were meager indeed.[130] The resulting system of administration on the cheap was not particularly corrupt; nor was it particularly efficient. It muddled along well enough to ensure that taxes were collected, but not well enough to meet the demands of an ever more ambitious and *dirigiste* state.

VOLOST COURTS AND THE DILEMMAS OF LEGAL ACCULTURATION

♦ ♦ ♦

Between 1889 and the fall of the tsarist government, an ever growing proportion of peasant disputes was dealt with not by land captains under administrative regulations, but in the courts under judicial procedures. Few contemporaries saw this development in a positive light, however. By the turn of the century, it was commonplace to lament the growing litigiousness of Russia's peasants. Ethnographers and officials described villages as caught up in nets of lawsuits, in which unscrupulous and semi-literate illegal advocates encouraged peasants to sue, petition, and appeal on the flimsiest of grounds. Critics of the volost courts bemoaned the ignorance of the peasant judges, their predilection for vodka, their venality, and their inability to comprehend even simple rules of procedure and jurisdiction. To Russians of the political and intellectual elite, the legal chaos that seemed to reign in the villages had appalling consequences, and the shortcomings of the volost courts exemplified all that was wrong in the countryside. To conservatives, for whom a well-ordered society was defined by spiritual and moral unity, "litigiousness" was a manifestation of moral decay and social disintegration. Liberals, on the other hand, criticized the courts with equal fervor for their role in allegedly perpetuating the isolation and backwardness of benighted villages.[1]

As with most contemporary generalizations about the countryside, statements about villagers' growing tendency toward litigious chicanery must be treated with caution: rural observers had noted peasant litigiousness at least since the eighteenth century. Recent research has confirmed that, even before Emancipation, peasants were skilled legal opportunists, interpreting legislation to their advantage and seeking recourse at all possible

levels of the administrative ladder.[2] But in contrast to many urban preconceptions of the countryside that were either anachronistic or fostered by
the cumulative effect of alarmist anecdotes and political agendas, the anxieties of educated society did in this case have some basis: all statistical evidence points to growing peasant use of volost courts in the post-Emancipation period.

The mere propensity to address local courts, however, in itself says little
either about the reasons why peasants did so or about the nature of their
encounter with the legal system. Did peasants turn to the courts simply
because a breakdown in traditional community patterns of authority had
made informal methods of resolving disputes inviable and left no other alternative? Did peasant "litigiousness" reflect a new sense of entitlement,
a process of legal acculturation, or even a growing confidence in state-
sanctioned judicial institutions? Or were rural inhabitants attempting to
subvert government intentions and whenever possible impose their own
vision of justice against a state-defined version? Each of these interpretations, advanced in contemporary analyses and explored by historians
since, tend to be presented as mutually exclusive alternatives.[3] Yet, growing court use did not necessarily signal the demise of informal modes of
dispute resolution. Nor did the failure of the state to impose its vision of
legality necessarily mean that peasants succeeded in imposing an alternative vision. It is also important to distinguish between civil and criminal
cases: while the latter remained largely embedded in the logic of village
politics, civil disputes were subject to far greater constraints from above.
Peasants used the legal system for a variety of reasons, and court usage
cannot be subsumed under a single overarching logic.

The most significant change introduced by the 1889 judicial reforms
was the right to appeal volost court verdicts on substance. Peasants were
invited to take their quarrels beyond the volost, and they did so in great
numbers. But appeal instances faced the inherent problem of identifying
unwritten local customs in clear enough form so as to provide a basis for
adjudication by outsiders. The government was unwilling to confront, or
even recognize, that this could be a problem. Even as it idealized peasant
custom, it remained wedded to an instrumental conception of law. Therefore, proposals for codification or for allowing rulings according to precedent were dismissed as measures that would constrain administrative discretion (usmotrenie). The paradoxical result was to disempower the
administrative bodies charged with hearing judicial appeals, underscoring
the dilemma of attempting to enforce central policies through locally defined, malleable, and contested concepts of custom. Until the regime col-
lapsed in 1917, St. Petersburg was in a continuous struggle to square this
circle; first, through Senate rulings that increasingly defined, standardized,
and circumscribed norms of custom, and second, by tightening administrative supervision of judicial procedure. But efforts to find the balance between respecting custom and ensuring compliance with regulations were

almost never successful. Judicial chaos was further exacerbated by the inconsistency with which the administrative vision of a good court was applied. Ultimately, the reforms created a demand for adjudication that the appeal instances could not meet.

THE EVOLUTION OF VOLOST COURT ACTIVITY

Most evidence confirms that the impressionistic accounts of publicists and journalists who deplored increasing peasant litigiousness were grounded in actual developments: the volost courts gradually became busier in the half-century after Emancipation. As might be expected, extrajudicial methods of dispute resolution did not disappear overnight; ethnographic studies conducted in the 1860s and 1870s noted that in numerous regions of the empire peasants resorted to the volost courts only when the village elder, the village assembly, or a council of elders had not first managed to resolve a dispute. According to the findings of the 1872 Liuboshchinskii Commission for Reforming the Volost Courts, peasants in 58 percent of 331 volosts told investigating officials that they favored informal methods of dispute resolution.[4] In the 1870s Aleksander Engelgardt reported in his famous *Letters from the Countryside* that Smolensk peasants preferred to settle problems themselves, and that they "feared the courts like fire." Even a summons to appear as a witness would send peasants into depths of despondency and anxiety, as they could never be certain what the judges would do.[5] In a district of Samara, 90 to 95 percent of all mediated disputes were settled outside the volost court. Only six of forty-two Moscow volosts relied exclusively on the recently sanctioned courts.[6] In some regions the new institution was virtually invisible: in one Riazan volost in the early 1870s, the court never even met.[7] According to eyewitness accounts from the 1870s, some villagers simply did not see any use for the new courts. Even as late as the 1890s, one peasant respondent to the Tenishev bureau stated that he could not see why a person would turn to elected judges who had no more competence than any randomly chosen neighbor: "Just because Ivan or Peter is wearing a badge we have to call him 'your Honor,' but when he takes off his badge he's just Ivan or Peter again."[8]

By the 1880s, however, judges and scribes were regularly complaining about their ever increasing workload. In Vladimir province the number of recorded cases increased sixfold between the early 1860s and 1880, while the rural population grew by slightly less than 50 percent over the same period.[9] While some of this increase can be attributed to better bookkeeping, eyewitness accounts also spoke of expanded court use. In the early 1880s in Voronezh, the scribe Nikolai Astyrev estimated that nearly one-third of the households in his volost had appeared before the court in the course of his three years of service.[10]

After the 1889 reform eliminated the justices of the peace and the resulting changes of jurisdiction virtually doubled caseloads overnight,
volost court usage continued to rise. In 1891 the peasant judges of
Vladimir province were hearing four times as many cases as a decade earlier, and by 1912 this number had again more than doubled, reaching
68,000.[11] Some courts of Riazan province, which in the mid-1870s had
been hearing seven or eight cases a year, were processing hundreds of
complaints by the eve of World War I. Courts that had seen an average of
forty-two cases each in 1875 had to process an average of five hundred
complaints in 1914.[12] For the entire province, the number of complaints
filed grew from 45,888 in 1892 (an average of 184 per court) to 67,126 in
1904, representing an increase of 46 percent. By 1913 the caseload had
jumped another 66 percent. Increases in court use far surpassed population growth. Between 1892 and 1914, for example, while the population
of Riazan expanded at a rate of 1.7 percent per year, its average annual
caseload increased by 3.7 percent. A growth rate in court use double or
triple that of population growth was common in other provinces as well
(see table 3-1).[13] Growth was interrupted only by the outbreak of World
War I, when the social disruption caused by mobilization brought a sharp
decline in judicial business throughout Europe.[14]

By the turn of the century, peasants were indeed behaving like a litigious lot. By 1904, 240 cases were generated for every 1,000 households in
Riazan province; in Moscow there were 231, and in Kursk 378 (see table
3-2). In specific regions, rates went even higher. In Ignat'evo volost
(Moscow province), for instance, by 1914 there were 410 cases for every
1,000 households, involving nearly 1,600 individuals out of a population
of 15,000.[15] Considering that approximately 40 percent of volost inhabitants were under the age of eighteen, this meant that nearly one in five
adults came before the judges in that year alone. In the village of Ry-
bushkino (Iagunino volost), 59 of the village's 238 inhabitants, from 45 of
the commune's 76 households (or 60%), appeared in court in 1909.[16] Even
these proportions understate the extent to which the local court had become a familiar institution: litigants could arrive in court with one or two
witnesses—and sometimes as many as six or seven—in tow. By the turn of
the century, the volost courts had become integral to the fabric of village
life and politics, and it would have been a rare villager indeed who had
not had some personal experience with the institution.

Why did peasants take each other to court in ever increasing numbers?
First, it is important to note that it would be surprising not to observe
some increase in court use in the first decades following Emancipation.
Peasants went to court partly because now they could. The pre-Emancipation system of justice had left the serf population largely beyond the reach
of state administration and under landlord tutelage. Even though peasants
had made use of what few laws were at their disposal and were quick to
seize legal opportunities—with petitions as early as the eighteenth century

TABLE 3-1

LITIGATION RATES (VOLOST COURT CASES PER

1,000 RURAL INHABITANTS, 1891–1915)

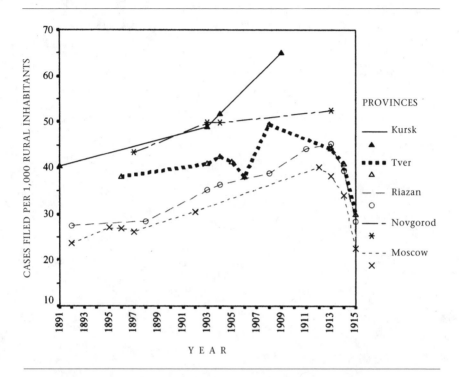

YEAR

Sources: Figures for 1903–1904 are from RGIA, f. 1405, op. 543 (1912), d. 942, ll. 149, 164, 178, 266–71, 369. For Riazan: GARO, f. 695, op. 6 (1895), d. 12; f. 695, op. 10 (1899), d. 5, ll. 180, 203, 226, 237, 263, 278, 286, 301, 313, 344, 352, 367; f. 695, op. 21 (1911), d. 9; RGIA, f. 1291, op. 31 (1909), d. 241, ll. 14–21; (1914), d. 414, ll. 20–21, 24–25, 51–58, 84–91; Frank, *Crime*, 56. Tver: Mikhailovskii, 159–60; GATO, f. 56, op. 1, d. 16882, ll. 181–89, 358–64; RGIA, f. 1291, op. 31 (1909), d. 247, ll. 19–25; (1914), d. 85, ll. 26ob.–32, 50ob.–57, 91ob.–98. Moscow: TsIAM, f. 62, op. 2, d. 317, ll. 1–13; op. 4 (1895), ll. 7–8; op. 1, d. 7191, ll. 255–62; RGIA, f. 1291, op. 31 (1914), d. 416, ll. 19ob.–20, 23–4, 56–9, 87–90. Kursk: RGIA-otchety, "Vsepoddanneishii otchet Kurskogo gubernatora za 1891," vol. 48:20; *Obzor 25-letniia deiatel'nosti krest'ianskikh uchrezhdenii v Kurskoi gubernii* (Kursk, 1912), 41. Vladimir: RGIA-otchety, "Vsepoddanneishii otchet Vladimirskogo gubernatora," vol. 15:9, 15–16, 86; Frierson, "I Must Always Answer to the Law," 328; RGIA, f. 1291, op. 54 (1898), d. 170b, ll. 311–12; op. 31 (1914), d. 225, ll. 15–16, 27–33, 61–67, 99. Novgorod: RGIA, f. 1291, op. 54 (1898), 170b, ll. 86–87; op. 31 (1914), d. 438, 18–19, 24ob.–25. Population data for calculating litigation rates are taken from Adrian Niel Jones, "The Peasants of Late Imperial Russia: Economy and Society in the Era of the Stolypin Land Reform" (Ph.D. diss., Harvard University, 1988), table 2.13; *Svod statisticheskikh materialov kasaiushchikhsia ekonomicheskogo polozheniia sel'skogo naseleniia Evropeiskoi Rossii* (St. Petersburg, 1894), 34–41.

TABLE 3-2

RATES OF LITIGATION IN VOLOST COURTS (SELECTED PROVINCES, 1904)

PROVINCE	Cases filed per 1,000 rural inhabitants	Cases filed per 1,000 rural households
Viatka	28	193
Vologda	33	191
Kaluga	34	227
Novgorod	50	331
Iaroslavl	36	178
Tver	42	258
Moscow	34	231
Riazan	36	240
Tambov	48	329
Penza	39	216
Voronezh	48	339
Orel	54	380
Kursk	52	378
Mogilev	71	638
Kherson	68	522
Chernigov	74	487

Source: RGIA, f. 1405, op. 543, d. 942 (1912), ll. 49, 64, 71, 103, 149, 162, 164, 178, 207, 266, 359, 369, 397, 404, 411.

citing appropriate laws and decrees—villagers had limited opportunity to record their litigiousness. Most crimes and disputes had been arbitrated within the village itself or were dealt with by the seigneur or his bailiff, who retained broad punitive powers.[17] While the Kisilev reforms had given state peasants (approximately 45% of the peasant population) their own volost courts in 1839, the jurisdiction of these was quite narrow, and they functioned primarily as an appeal instance for village courts (sel'skie raspravy) in which the village elder played a central role.[18] After 1861 villagers did not immediately appreciate the utility of the new courts. Turning to the newly sanctioned peasant court to resolve internal disputes no longer had the weight of appealing to higher authorities nor the convenience of addressing the village assembly, volost elder, or council of elders. It naturally took some time for peasants to familiarize themselves with the new courts and appreciate the advantages of using them.

One of these advantages was that disputes were potentially removed from the village political arena and its local networks of power and influence. In spite of frequent assertions by rural observers that bribery was ubiquitous and that custom was manipulated by all-powerful scribes who sold their influence over impressionable peasant judges to the highest bidder, it is difficult to see the volost courts merely as a hegemonic institution controlled by wealthier peasants. As already seen, the alleged power of the scribe was largely mythical. Some of the same correspondents to the Tenishev bureau who cited a host of anachronistic proverbs to illustrate the venality of the courts proceeded to explain that the drinks offered to judges and witnesses—by both sides in a dispute—were compensation rather than bribery, that peasants sought to elect judges known for their honesty, and that the most credible witnesses were known for their sobriety.[19] Such contradictions were overlooked by commentators of the Tenishev materials, while sordid tales of drunken judges and egregious examples of corruption and influence peddling were prominently published in journals and the provincial press and resurfaced in official investigations of the state of rural institutions. The fact is that the volost court, where never more than one judge came from the same village as the litigants, could dilute the strength of village networks of influence, factionalism, and rivalry, ensuring that sometimes the weaker party would win.

This probably explains why women were assiduous users of the court—in some instances responsible for over a third of all complaints filed.[20] And these women sometimes won even on issues that commentators claimed the courts were most reluctant and unable to adjudicate. For instance, the judges in Sinkovo volost (Moscow province) awarded support—in effect sanctioning separation—to mistreated wives five times in 1913: two young wives without children were allowed to reclaim their dowries, two wives with children were awarded a modest monthly stipend of three rubles, and one woman who had gone deaf from her husband's beatings was awarded a cottage, a barn, and part of the household grain.[21] In the 1880s the mother of the future peasant activist Ivan Stoliarov became a convert of the court after winning a case against the village elder who had denied her a favorable spot at the local market. Even though that faith would turn out to be misplaced, as the household later lost a crucial land case involving the same abusive elder, the lesson was that sometimes the weaker party could win.[22] In understanding court usage, the fact that weaker parties were at times able to redress imbalances of power is as significant as the statistical reality that the wealthier and well-connected parties were more likely to be able to use the courts to their advantage.

After 1861 villagers also had more opportunities to learn about legislation that concerned them. As more peasants served as judges, a growing pool of local inhabitants gained familiarity with the rudiments of rural laws and regulations, especially after the introduction of three-year terms in 1889. Not only did male literacy rates (defined narrowly as ability to read) increase from an estimated 10 to 15 percent in the 1860s to over 50 percent on the eve of the revolution, but the complex pre-Emancipation regulations that had restricted the publication and dissemination of laws to those who needed to know them (usually the officials responsible for their application) were decisively abandoned.[23] One avowed goal of the reformers was to teach peasants about the law. The General Statute was distributed to each volost, and new laws were published in the official provincial press *(Gubernskie vedomosti)*. These laws were also supposed to be posted in volost administration buildings. Private presses published hundreds of cheap guides to rural laws and administrative procedures, and by the 1900s most popular rural periodicals ran legal advice columns.[24]

Although most peasants hardly had the time, the literacy, or the inclination to consult these publications, there were people in the village who did—the loudly decried "underground advocates." In a context where trained and accredited lawyers remained in the cities, and where the zemstvos were forbidden to hire lawyers to provide free legal consultations, villagers sought help in formulating their petitions from any literate neighbor (such as a volost scribe, schoolteacher, or retired officer) who had a reputation for dealing successfully with authorities.[25] The press almost unanimously blamed these self-appointed amateur jurists for fanning the flames of village discord, labeling them a curse and a "poison." Publicists portrayed them as descending upon hapless villages like locusts, seeking out their clients by exploiting ignorance and frustration, and writing groundless complaints in exchange for a few kopecks or a bottle of vodka.[26] Yet, peasant petitions reveal that rural inhabitants were in fact getting decent legal advice. Petitions show a high level of familiarity with new legislation and with procedural regulations. If "underground advocates" sometimes interpreted laws rather loosely to the advantage of their client, their opportunism was arguably not unlike that of any good, modern North American lawyer. The patently absurd petition that so roused the lyrical indignation of publicists by rambling on for pages in a single sentence, or by making shotgun reference to a wide array of irrelevant Senate rulings or articles from the General Statute, was the exception.

Another factor contributing to growing court use was the reduced availability of other options. Most contemporary observers assumed that informal means of resolving disputes were eclipsed as rising migration, higher literacy rates, and the infiltration of urban culture into the countryside weakened the authority of household heads and village elders, thereby undermining the ability of the community to conduct its internal business on its own. Equally important was the fact that after 1889, elders were vulnerable to complaints to land captains that they had misused their powers, and thus were less likely to feel comfortable playing a judicial role. As already noted, elders were reluctant even to use those legal powers granted them to fine or arrest fellow villagers for petty misdemeanors. Village assemblies did continue to fulfill a judicial role, if only because legislation placed certain legal questions—such as banishment, use of allotment land, family divisions—within their jurisdiction. But land captains were on the lookout for resolutions that overstepped these bounds, and assemblies themselves were more likely to recuse themselves from examining disputes.[27] A major thrust of the 1889 reforms had been to instill respect for law, authority, and moral order, and authorities viewed extrajudicial dispute resolution, which could not easily be controlled and verified, with considerable mistrust. The effectiveness of government controls certainly should not be exaggerated, however. While numerous Tenishev correspondents found no informal courts in the 1890s, just as many reported that elders and assemblies continued to serve as mediators. The land captain Aleksandr Novikov, for instance, reported that Tambov villagers in the 1890s continued to elect unofficial arbiters whose decisions were never appealed.[28] Nevertheless, the choice to address the courts was not always a reflection of preference but included an element of compulsion, as extra-judicial dispute resolution was not always a viable option.

The willingness of villagers to take their disputes to the new courts ostensibly signaled that state authorities had succeeded in their goal of penetrating the countryside, and that villages embraced—willingly or not—officially sanctioned legal institutions. But the simple fact that peasants went to court does not reveal whether villagers were satisfied, whether they perceived decisions as being fair and consistent, or whether the courts ultimately fulfilled their primary function of resolving disputes. Nor does it reveal much about the nature of that court experience, or about litigants' motives and expectations. Finally, statistics by themselves say little about how village attitudes toward justice intersected with state priorities While each of these issues will be examined in the rest of this chapter, it is with the third that the account will begin, since it is by examining procedure—or more broadly legal styles—that one can begin to evaluate the meaning of court use for rural inhabitants.

GOVERNMENT REGULATIONS AND PEASANT USE OF THE COURTS

The 1889 Temporary Regulations for Volost Courts, inspired as they were by hostility toward "artificial" rules and animated by the conviction that legal procedures and formal law were obstacles to fairness and "internal justice," accorded the rural tribunals considerable flexibility in the conduct of local justice. Not only were judges permitted to follow custom in regulating inheritance but they were enjoined to rule "according to conscience" and to try to bring about peaceful settlements in civil cases. In the interests of ensuring accessibility, no fees were to be levied either in the volost or on appeal. Formalities were to be kept to a minimum. Ceremonial procedures that were common in the general courts—such as requiring the audience to stand when the verdict was announced—could not be imposed. Written evidence was not automatically to be given greater weight than witnesses' oral statements. Litigants could not be compelled to file written complaints, and they had to appear personally at their hearing if they lived within fifteen kilometers of the court (as most did unless they were away for work). In a frequently cited circular from 1891, the MVD reminded rural authorities that none of the regulations from the Code of Civil Procedure written for the general courts could be applied either in the volost or in appeal instances, as any detailed instructions "would undermine the patriarchal character of the institution."[29] Everything was done to ensure that the courts remained accessible, free of formal requirements, and close to the population.

On the other hand, the 1889 legislation betrayed a degree of mistrust of rural justice left to its own devices. The entire point of the reforms was to remove the courts from the alleged influence of *miroedy*, corrupt scribes, fancy-talkers (*govorilshiki*), vodka-inclined judges, and other perverters of justice. The laconic eighteen articles of 1861 were replaced by a more detailed document of forty-two articles, which had in turn expanded to eighty-two articles by 1903. Peasants no longer had the right to elect up to twelve judges who could rotate office during their three-year term (a practice followed in 42 percent of the courts studied by the 1872 Liuboshchinskii Commission). Instead, three judges had to sit for the full three-year term so as to give them time to acquire knowledge and experience. Gone was the confidence that virtually any peasant would know the local norms of custom and be a good judge simply by virtue of being a peasant. The land captain had supervisory powers over the courts: he chose judges from among eight candidates elected by the volost assembly; he had the right to fine them or recommend their removal; and he was responsible for reviewing the merit of appeals to be forwarded to the district congress. Inspectors also sought to supervise judges by routinely quizzing them on points of law to ascertain their knowledge of legislation. In order to combat corruption and graft, salary levels were set by the district congresses (even though judges were still paid with volost funds). Stricter rules of record keeping were instituted to ensure transparency and guard against manipulation by the rich and clever: all peaceful settlements were to be entered in the register of decisions. While peasants remained free to take disputes to a mediator of their choosing, mediated decisions also had to be registered in the volost office, whereupon they became binding and could not be appealed.[30] In spite of St. Petersburg's continuous talk of the benefits of simple and informal justice, increasingly detailed rules of procedure, jurisdiction, and bookkeeping sought to limit the discretionary powers of the judges and potentially reduced the independence of the reformed courts.

Much of the government's legislation on the volost courts was based on the premise that the substance of "customary law" could be retained if only the obstacles to peasants' traditional sense of fairness were removed. In practice, however, this left few concrete guidelines and much discretion for inspectors from the Ministry of Internal Affairs and the provincial boards to judge whether fairness was in fact prevailing. The evils of partiality, corruption, and drink rarely showed themselves openly, so supervising officials were always alert for indirect signs of their presence. In the process, officials came to condemn many of the practices inherent in local courts of custom that had been mandated to encourage reconciliation and rule "according to conscience." Peaceful settlements, instead of being interpreted as a sign of successful mediation, could be read as a reflection of judges too intimidated to render judgments. Inconsistency, inevitable in a court that ruled situationally, became interpreted as partiality. Inspectors were bound to find the courts wanting, and their reports repeatedly identified disjunctions between peasant practice and official expectations. For officials who worked with the courts, evidence that the informality of village judicial practices continued to infiltrate the rural tribunals was a matter of grave concern.

One consistent official complaint related to the failure of the peasant judges to distinguish properly between criminal and civil cases. It was not unusual for victims of a crime to ask for—and to be awarded—civil compensation. While such practices were permissible for petty crimes, both the Temporary Regulations and the Regulations on Punishments Imposed by the Justices of the Peace (which continued to regulate much of the volost court's criminal jurisdiction) listed a broad range of misdemeanors that had to be punished regardless of the wishes of the accuser. The 1889 legislation might have required the court to encourage reconciliation (*primirenie*) between litigants in civil matters, but the volost court was also to serve government policy: reconciliation could not be allowed for crimes that upset the social order, such as theft, fraud, libel, threats, insulting peasant officials, and disturbing the peace.[31]

The courts nevertheless regularly allowed peasants to reconcile or receive compensation, even for serious criminal matters. Observers since the 1860s noted that, with the exception of actions or behavior that threatened the economic well-being of the community (such as horse theft), most criminal cases were regarded as disputes between individuals, and plaintiffs retained control over prosecution. As one respondent to the 1872 Liuboshchinskii Commission explained, "Anyone can withdraw a complaint, as if it had never been filed."[32] There is little evidence that attitudes had changed by the turn of the century. Some plaintiffs did comply with official procedure so far as to arrive in court to announce that a complaint had been filed "by mistake," or that they had to drop the case because of "lack of witnesses"; but otherwise the inspectors' exhortations had little effect. In 1908 inspectors from Tambov were still complaining of the "complete confused understanding between civil and criminal cases, and [the failure to] distinguish between private and public accusations."[33] Peasants continued to withdraw complaints as they saw fit.

The MVD was deeply concerned about peasants' apparent indifference to crime. It quickly introduced safeguards designed to ensure that the crimes it cared about were prosecuted. In 1891 the ministry instructed land captains to suspend decisions even without appeal in a broad range of circumstances: if a case was outside the court's jurisdiction, if reconciliation had erroneously been allowed in a criminal case, if they considered the decision unjust (nepravosudnyi), or if the courts had permitted civil compensation in criminal cases. The first section of these instructions was to be incorporated into the land captain legislation in 1896. In 1894 the ministry told governors that if judges did not find enough grounds to sentence an accused, the police could present the dossier to the land captain for further action.[34] In spite of such measures, authorities remained largely absent from the volost court. The police, overworked and understaffed even after the significant expansions in its forces in 1878 and 1903, and after several years of campaigns against rural "hooliganism," initiated but a small proportion of accusations: 9 percent in Izhevskoe (Riazan province) in 1910, 9 percent in Ignat'evo in 1908, and 12 percent in Sinkovo (Moscow) in 1913 and 1915, for example.[35] The overwhelming majority of criminal cases were initiated by the victim. Given the absence of any public prosecutor even in cases initiated by a police report, and given that all cases were heard by the same judges under a uniform procedure, there was little to encourage judges to distinguish between private complaints and misdemeanors that threatened public order, or to apply punishments in spite of the wishes of the accuser.[36] Litigants retained considerable leeway to define their disputes as they wished.

Another common and related error noted by inspectors was the propensity of peasant judges to drop cases because the accuser did not appear in court. In Ignat'evo volost (Moscow) between 1900 and 1915, nearly half of all cases were dropped for absence every year, with the peak in 1908 even reaching over 60 percent. In Arkhangel'skoe volost (Tambov) 93 of 149 (62%) criminal complaints, and 422 of 802 (58%) civil suits were dropped in 1908, and that pattern was remarked upon in almost every inspection report.[37] In addition to being troubled by the fact that crimes were being ignored, most officials interpreted high absenteeism as evidence that peasants lacked respect for the institution and were filing frivolous or ill-founded suits.[38] Yet, many of the cases dropped for absence of litigants were hardly frivolous. They ran the gamut of villagers' concerns, from the most petty claim of fifty kopecks to land disputes with life or death consequences for the economy of a household. It is difficult to know for certain what happened to cases that were never heard in court.

Most likely, the vast majority were reconciled before they went to trial. Peaceful settlements were a common outcome of volost court cases: in Moscow in 1895, as well as in Riazan in 1892 and 1899, close to 40 percent of all complaints ended in a peaceful settlement.[39] Unfortunately, after 1900 provincial authorities stopped collecting data on the outcome of volost court cases, but individual court registers extending to 1915 from Tver, Tambov, Moscow, and Riazan all indicate that between one-third and one-half of all complaints never required a decision by the judges.[40]

Ministerial inspectors tended to interpret absenteeism by plaintiffs as a manifestation of peasants' excessive recourse to reconciliation. They feared that judges, vulnerable both to vengeful acts by their neighbors and to punishment by the land captain if they made an error, were reluctant to impose sentences. Unfortunately, the brief entries in the court records rarely indicate the motives behind settlements and do not reveal pressures that might have been brought to bear on judges. But the dogged persistence with which judges continued to contravene administrative regulations does not suggest timidity before the land captain. Although fear of revenge may have played a role in particular cases, the pressures on judges were more subtle. As temporary electees, not only did judges live in the community, but they might in the future find themselves in the role of litigant before one of the very peasants they were judging. It was important under such circumstances to avoid exacerbating the tensions behind a dispute, and to try to bring peace between the litigants. Observers frequently repeated that peasant judges sought to rule "so that no one [would] be offended" *(chtoby nikomu ne bylo obidno)*.[41] While this tendency should not be exaggerated—courts did fine, punish, or rule for one side in at least half of the cases that reached them—there certainly was little reason for judges to inflame quarrels when a modicum of local peace had been established.

It remains to be explained why peasants filed complaints in such large numbers if much of the time they did not even appear to pursue them. One common motive was no doubt strategic: a court filing could induce a rival to negotiate. Even a verdict did not necessarily signal the end of a dispute but could serve as a point of departure for negotiation. This is revealed most clearly in disputes in which reconciliation was announced after the judges had rendered a decision and the plaintiff had ostensibly already received what he wanted. Much of the countryside's judicial business continued to be conducted outside the courts, if in conjunction with it.[42] Extra-judicial modes of dispute resolution adapted to the expansion of the formal justice but did not disappear.

The registers of Sinkovo volost (Dmitrov district, Moscow) are unusual in providing details that uncover the range of motivations behind peaceful settlements. In 1913 the court registered fifteen post-verdict reconciliations out of a total of 156 decisions. Twelve involved criminal complaints (a third of all criminal decisions rendered), and six of these involved crimes for which out-of-court settlement was prohibited: theft, fraud, libel, and public scandal accompanied by assault.[43] In four of the cases, women who had complained of violent mistreatment by their husbands announced reconciliation after the court had ordered the incarceration of their husbands for up to fifteen days. Presumably, they felt it would not do them much good in the long run to have their husbands stew in jail for one or two weeks, and they had little alternative but to forgive them for fear of the consequences. As many observers of rural justice noted, volost courts were ill equipped to deal with cases of domestic dispute, and judges knew it. Requests for separation were outside the courts' jurisdiction, and judges could go to great lengths to encourage reconciliation.[44]

In other cases, especially in accusations of slander or insult, it appears that the plaintiff was seeking public vindication, and there was little point in carrying out the sentence once this had been achieved. One Natal'ia Ul'ianova, for instance, accused her mother-in-law of slander, as the latter had spread the rumor that her daughter-in-law had syphilis. When Ul'ianova produced a medical certificate testifying to her good health and the judges ordered that her mother-in-law be imprisoned for seven days, Ul'ianova dropped her case. It is possible that the subsequent reconciliation even strengthened her moral position, as it demonstrated that her motives were neither vengeful nor pecuniary.[45]

Peasants were especially likely to pursue out-of-court settlements in cases of theft or destruction of property, preferring compensation or restitution over the arrest of the guilty party. One Sivkov, for instance, filed a complaint with the police reporting the theft of some boards worth five rubles. When the court ordered the incarceration of the defendant for three days, Sivkov declared he was dissatisfied with the decision and later announced reconciliation, presumably in exchange for some kind of compensation or restitution.[46] Observers had long noted this preference for restitution over punishment in cases of minor theft. Even in cases such as insult or beatings, which did not involve material loss, villagers frequently requested compensation. This may explain the actions of Fedor Malkov, who reconciled with his neighbor after the latter was sentenced to fifteen days in jail for having beaten him during a holiday gathering.[47]

In some cases there were other motives beyond desire for monetary gain, for plaintiffs also reconciled even after they had been awarded compensation. Pelagia Lavrova, for example, asked for, and was granted, six rubles from a peasant who had taken hay from her land, but she then requested that the verdict be suspended because she had settled.[48] One can only guess as to the motives of the successful plaintiff in such cases. Perhaps the main purpose of Lavrova's suit had been to prove ownership of the land from which the hay was taken, and there was no reason to exacerbate relations with her neighbor once this had been established.

But there may also have been a more subtle dynamic at work in favor of peaceful settlements, a sense that good people should try to settle their disputes. A number of nineteenth-century ethnographers noted that peasants who repeatedly addressed the courts were thought ill of by their neighbors. In one report to the Tenishev bureau of a court session in Penza, the judges shamed the plaintiff into settling: "Have you thought what people will say about you—a brigand, they'll say—always hanging around the courts."[49] When questioned directly about peasant attitudes toward court use, many Tenishev respondents asserted that villagers disliked chicanery, even though in response to other questions they reported that peasants were litigious. The potential contradiction can be explained if one considers the court session as but one episode in a process of disputation. Going to court was not enough to mark someone as litigious; insisting on rights to the detriment of settlement could be. Regardless of the motives for reconciliation, the ability and willingness to settle ensured that litigants retained some control over the judicial process.

For the MVD's inspectors, another, even more troubling, manifestation of the volost courts' informality was the tendency of judges to rule "according to the person" *(po cheloveku)*. Not only was the character of the litigants an important factor in evaluating conflicting claims, but the reputation of witnesses was also taken into account when weighing testimony. The practice was particularly difficult for inspectors to combat, for the simple reason that it was not, strictly speaking, illegal. Judges were instructed to rule "according to conscience," and the MVD even reminded rural officials in 1891 that since the purpose of the volost court was to be close to the population and since the Temporary Regulations had not specified formal rules of evidence, a judge could use his personal knowledge in arriving at a decision.[50] As long as judges remained within the limits of their jurisdiction and followed the broad guidelines regulating punishment, they were free to consider reputation in weighing the credibility of complainants and witnesses.

The reputation of the parties and their witnesses could at times become the only factor enabling judges to distinguish between rival claims. The court records from Sinkovo volost again are unusual in providing occasional indications of the judges' reasoning. Thus, in one accusation of insult, the judges decided to dismiss one witness's testimony because he was "only giving himself airs of authority," whereas "the exemplary conduct of the village elder (the defendant)" was well known.[51] Judges occasionally went further, acknowledging the veracity of a complaint but nevertheless acquitting the defendant. When Mariia Budnova, exasperated that her husband was "drinking off the household property" and frustrated that her complaints to the local authorities had gone unheard, broke the windows of the local tavern, the court ruled that her actions were justified. In another case, Aleksandra Andrianova was found guilty of slander for having publicly accused a neighbor of stealing firewood, although she had no proof for the claim. Apparently, she was not alone in her suspicions, for the judges accorded her "extenuating circumstances" and gave her only a reprimand. This was an extraordinarily mild sentence for a libel case, insufficient to restore the plaintiff's good name, and it is no surprise that it was appealed. Other cases only hint at the reputation of the litigants. In some accusations of insult, a defendant who explained that he had been provoked was acquitted, while in other similar disputes, both litigants were fined or jailed. For some defendants, drunkenness was accepted as a mitigating circumstance, whereas for others it aggravated their guilt. Some defendants having beaten up a fellow villager were jailed for one day because they expressed "sincere repentance," while others, who were publicly forgiven by their accusers, were jailed for seven days.[52]

For provincial and MVD inspectors of all political stripes, such irregularities smacked at best of favoritism, at worst of bribery and corruption. Few practices so clearly underlined the fundamental shortcomings of rural administration, as they flew in the face of efforts both to instill in peasants a respect for the law, and to protect rural inhabitants from the cabals of village leadership. Since inspectors were unable to dictate judges' rulings, they resorted to a stricter interpretation of rules of jurisdiction, procedure, and bookkeeping. In addition to verifying that rules for reconciliation were followed, the inspectors chided judges for awarding compensation for crimes and giving jail sentences in civil disputes. They criticized the failure to postpone cases when witnesses did not show up, especially when such absences led to acquittals for lack of evidence. They found fault with volost elders for not exercising their right to fine peasants who neglected to appear when called as witnesses. Inspectors also noted those instances in which they believed a punishment was too lenient (a fine of fifty kopecks for insulting a watchman) or too strict (thirty days in jail for insult).[53] And they fulminated helplessly against scribes, who rarely wrote down the motives behind court decisions, or wrote down motives that were "stupid." In the words of one inspector, a simple declaration of the "inner conviction of the court" did not constitute proof that a defendant was guilty or that a plaintiff was lying.[54] But short of complaining, there was little inspectors could do to remedy the situation.

The reasoning for most decisions could not be easily summarized and was often based on little more than the "inner conviction" of the judges. Whereas by the turn of the century, written documentation had become a virtual requirement for the recovery of debts, the resolution of most other disputes depended on the testimony of witnesses—in other words, on what neighbors had seen and heard. And given the extraordinary transparency of village life, neighbors had always seen or heard something, even in the most private domestic disputes. How many times a wife had been seen bruised, whether a peasant was hard-working and kept his household in order *(khoziaistvennyi)*, even rumors about the type of life a son led while he was off working in Moscow—all these were considerations that went into determination of a verdict. One case from Sinkovo, in which a wife accused her husband of withholding her food, was decided against her on the evidence of witnesses who said she had spoken crudely to her husband and had once been seen to address him with a rude gesture. Another woman was able to obtain a five-ruble monthly allowance from the father of her illegitimate child on the strength of testimony by villagers who had seen them together on numerous occasions. Semen Ezhov was unable to obtain the exclusion *(vydel)* of his son Afanasii from his household, because witnesses claimed that the arguments between father and son were not that frequent, and in any case the mother-in-law's unjustified attacks against Afanasii's young wife were to blame. Ezhov was instructed to make peace with his son.[55] In each of these cases, public opinion played a vital role in determining the verdict. As numerous respondents to the Tenishev bureau explained, crime was not considered as a fact separate from the life of the accused. Nor for that matter were civil disputes. Witnesses described events that were quite peripheral to the immediate circumstances of a case, and their testimony served to establish the veracity of a complaint. Reputation was evidence.

The prevalence of absenteeism, reconciliation, and a style of reasoning that broadened the focus of a hearing beyond the immediate circumstances of a dispute suggests that the reformed courts were fully integrated into the fabric of village political life. Villagers used the courts more frequently, but there is little indication that formal litigation reduced the prevalence of informal dispute resolution. The courts did not serve as a final recourse that reflected the failure of earlier levels of mediation. Instead, many peasants took their problems to the judges in the early stages of a dispute, expecting the ultimate solution to be reached in an out-of-court settlement. This strategy carried relatively little risk, for the volost courts were cheap, accessible, local, and familiar; and it was unlikely that the plaintiff would lose control over the case and suffer unexpected consequences, for he or she could always withdraw a complaint.

While the government had hoped to institutionalize the application of norms of custom in civil cases and to instill a respect for order and impartiality in criminal cases, the rural courts succeeded instead in institutionalizing informal judicial procedures. But this is only part of the story. For after all, if the volost courts were simply doing the same thing that village elders had done before, then why would peasants have gone before the judges in such large numbers?

Types of Cases before the Volost Courts

In order to understand what volost courts could accomplish that informal dispute resolution methods alone could not, it is necessary to identify the types of cases that increased most rapidly. Peasants addressed the courts for a wide variety of reasons, and with a variety of audiences in mind. Much of the time the courts served as yet another arena for the conduct of village politics and family squabbles. But court practice also responded to economic and social changes taking place in peasant society, as well as to changes in state legislation. The tensions engendered by the Stolypin agrarian reforms were especially important in reinforcing the need for written agreements and for more formal settlements that would be recognized by higher authorities. Ultimately, the volost courts retained greater autonomy in dealing with criminal accusations than they did in addressing civil disputes.

While the statistics collected by the provincial boards over the years are incomparable and make a detailed analysis of shifting trends over time impossible, the data do show that civil cases increased more rapidly than criminal cases, at least for the period after 1889 when statistical reporting—incomplete and inconsistent as it was—became part of administrative practice.[56] In Riazan, between 1892 and 1913, the number of criminal complaints increased by 114 percent, while the number of civil suits filed in volost courts grew by 156 percent. An even greater discrepancy occurred in Tver, where, between 1896 and 1913, the average annual increase for criminal complaints was only 1.3 percent, but for civil suits 3.2 percent. Comparable growth patterns occurred in Novgorod, Kursk, and Moscow provinces (see tables 3-3 and 3-4).[57]

The relative stability in the per capita rate of criminal complaints belies official and public assumptions that declining morals and the dissipation of patriarchal authority were leading to an alarming rise of petty crime in the countryside.[58] A breakdown of the statistics, however, reveals a dramatic increase in specific categories of complaints. A survey compiled by the Ministry of Internal Affairs in 1912 showed that cases falling under the rubrics of disturbance of the peace (public drunkenness, spreading false rumors, public fighting, illegal sale of alcohol), disruption of public order (insulting judges or elders, ignoring the instructions of a village official), and personal insult (verbal insult and "insult by deed," such as tearing clothes, pulling beards, hitting) had each increased by more than a third during a five-year period in Riazan. A similar precipitous rise was recorded in Penza, Tula, Chernigov, and to a lesser extent in Tver and Tambov.[59] The first two rubrics of the MVD survey, relating to public order, reflected official priorities and the concerns of a society that was panicking over rural "hooliganism." As Stephen Frank has convincingly argued, the reported increases likely resulted from more assiduous policing and especially from changes in the way crimes were categorized. One thrust of inspection reports was, after all, to get scribes to record disputes under the proper criminal article of the Regulation on Punishments, allowing for readjustments among categories that did not necessarily reflect real changes in behavior.

Such recategorization is unlikely in the case of insults, however, as these were difficult to confuse with anything else. In addition, cases involving insult were initiated not by the authorities, but by peasants them-

TABLE 3-3

LITIGATION RATES (NUMBER OF CRIMINAL CASES PER

1,000 RURAL INHABITANTS, 1891–1915)

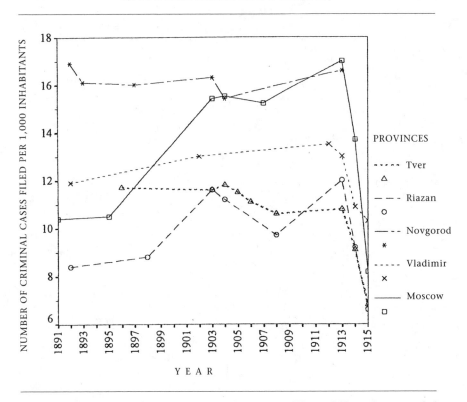

Sources: See table 3-1. In addition, Putilov, "Zametki o vremennykh pravilakh o volostnom sude," *ZhIuO*, no.7 (1895), 60.

selves. Registers from individual courts also point to the rising frequency with which peasants dragged each other to court to defend their good name. In Ignat'evo volost for instance, forty of ninety-two criminal complaints (43%) involved verbal or physical insult in 1891. Records from 1895, 1900, 1908, and 1911 register a steady increase in both numbers and proportions of accusations of insult, until by 1914 they accounted for 179 of 192 complaints, or 93 percent of all criminal cases.[60] Ignat'evo's astonishingly high rate was not unique: between 65 and 95 percent of Iagunino's criminal caseload between 1895 and 1911 was taken up with insults, while the range in Khotinsk volost (Tver province) in 1901 to 1904 was 88 to 93 percent. Insults were the largest category of criminal cases throughout European Russia. In both Tver and Riazan provinces in 1908, 57 percent of all volost court criminal

TABLE 3-4

LITIGATION RATES (NUMBER OF CIVIL CASES PER

1,000 RURAL INHABITANTS, 1891–1915)

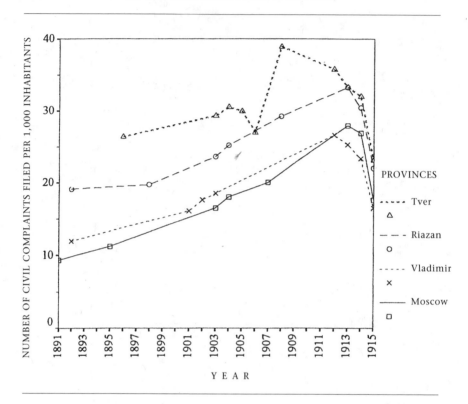

PROVINCES

..... Tver
△

— — Riazan
○

..... Vladimir
×

——— Moscow
□

Sources: See table 3-1. In addition, Putilov, "Zametki o vremennykh pravilakh o volostnom sude," *ZhIuO*, no.7 (1895), 60.

cases were classified as personal insult. The same pattern can be found in 1904 in Tula (61%) and in 1913 in the courts of Tambov (60%), Moscow (56%), Vladimir (41%), and Novgorod (40%).[61]

Villagers were quick to seek vindication for a wide range of real or perceived slights and threats. Peasants demanded redress not only for insults of the crudest sort (many of these implying sexual misconduct), but also for being called a thief, a witch, or even an "unkempt devil." Mothers filed complaints against disrespectful sons. Some villagers merely objected to being called a "good-for-nothing" during a drunken brawl. Judges themselves sued for being accused of bribery during a court hearing or of having measured out a field like a "village wench" *(baba derevenskaia)*.[62] The seemingly petty nature of many of these complaints did not mean that peasants viewed them as frivolous. A number of observers speculated that the complaints expressed the former serfs' developing sense of self-worth—

perhaps, although such intangibles are notoriously difficult, if not impossible, to document. What is clear is that villagers could go to great lengths to defend their reputations, as did one Ivan Biriukov, who twice appealed his own victorious defense of his wife and daughter's sexual reputation because, in his view, such a grave insult should not be punished with ten days in jail, "but much more." Similar determination can be found in depositions arguing the relative gravity of being called a "bitch" as opposed to a "thief," or a "whore" as opposed to an "arsonist."[63] Reputation mattered and attacks against it demanded public vindication.

Disputes over insults most clearly show how the volost courts were woven into the fabric of village politics. Anthropologists have tended to see gossip and reputation as a form of community regulation, in which verbal pressure—including derogatory nicknames, harmful epithets, cursing, and rumor—could be applied to regulate behavior, enforce conformity, and wield influence. Community reputations were fragile, fluctuating, and contested, however. Insults, harmful gossip, and slander were not so much a reflection of community consensus as an expression of the continual power struggle for social capital in a process that Jeffrey Burds has aptly called the "politics of reputation."[64] Complaints alleging insulting words or harmful rumors could involve contests over status and access to resources, and not infrequently they concealed a broader dispute that may or may not have reached the courts. It was therefore not unusual to find the same peasants appearing in a series of cases over the course of several years: suits could lead to countersuits on seemingly unrelated issues, and rivals could file mutual accusations of theft, trespass, illegal cutting of wood, or defamation. Complaints about insult were but one episode in prolonged disputes. A woman in Stepanovo volost (Tver), for instance, first filed a complaint against her brother for insulting her at the village assembly. This suit was soon followed by another claiming that her brother had refused to relinquish her share of the land inherited from their mother. According to the complainant, their mother had obtained the assembly's approval to transfer the household land to her son only temporarily, with the stipulation that the daughter could later request her share.[65] Under the circumstances, the seemingly minor—and private—conflict over an insult was in fact a crucial step in an acrimonious battle for the main witness in a land dispute, the village assembly.

The judges understood very well the stakes involved. While they limited their investigations of the numerous drunken quarrels that reached the court to determining who had started the fight, in cases of insults that had been proffered soberly and especially publicly, they often looked into the underlying causes. When the defendant argued that his action had been justified, the focus of a hearing could stray far afield from the original complaint. An accusation of slander could lead to the plaintiff's imprisonment for theft, or to his having to pay the defendant for hay taken from a field—outcomes loudly decried by provincial and ministerial inspectors for going beyond the bounds of the original complaint.[66]

Verbal insults could be dealt with quite severely. A. Kh. Gol'msten, who examined the 1865–1885 court registers from Kemets volost (Novgorod province), concluded that peasants treated verbal insults more severely than "insults by deed." He noted that peasants felt a particularly offensive insult could not be "washed away with rubles" and in such cases requested punishment "according to the law" rather than compensation. Sixty percent of verbal insults thus led to a criminal punishment (jail or fine), as against only 40 percent of physical insults.[67] Inspectors after the turn of the century also noted the severity of punishments for defamation. One inspector in Tambov, for instance, deplored the fact that the Gagarin volost court punished insults with fifteen days of arrest but gave only seven days for theft.[68] Likewise, in Sinkovo volost in 1913 and 1915, the average jail sentence for verbal insult was seven days, but only three days for theft.

What the prevalence of insult cases suggests is that peasants used the volost courts as a public forum, bringing into the written record behaviors that previously had been hidden. Accusations of insult were important within a larger complex of rivalries. They were a form of public posturing, establishing the righteousness of an individual's position, and defending reputation in a context where the opinion of neighbors mattered to one's ability to trade, marry, sell, speak with authority in the assembly, or successfully prosecute a court case. Insult, even when it occurred within the private confines of the family, was a public matter. By removing contests over honor from the arena of local networks and rivalries, the volost courts may have provided a new forum for the defense and constitution of reputation, but the targeted audience remained the village.[69] Use of the volost courts did not necessarily reflect a change in the values of litigants nor did it change the stakes of local battles, merely the means by which they were fought.

The rise in the incidence of civil disputes, on the other hand, was more closely related to economic and social transformations, as well as to legislative changes. Among civil cases, two broad categories of disputes stand out: land disputes and "miscellaneous claims" (all claims up to a value of 300 rubles except those relating to immovable property). "Miscellaneous claims" *(po vsiakogo roda sporam i iskam)*, by far the larger group, was an umbrella term for a great variety of cases: torts, breaches of contract, debt claims, and small property claims. There was also great diversity in the case profiles of different volosts, as these were linked to the economic activity of an area. In Sinkovo volost, for instance, in spite of a high level of seasonal out-migration, agriculture remained the central focus of the local economy—and of local quarrels. Most of its civil claims were disputes over ownership of hay, potatoes, or firewood. The Ignat'evo volost court, by contrast, dealt overwhelmingly with cases of unpaid goods taken from local stores or trading stalls, and, to a lesser degree, with disputes over unpaid salaries. This volost was well known for its rural industries, and agriculture played a subsidiary role. Local shopkeepers were regular clients of the court, arriving three or four times a year to collect a series of outstanding debts. Here, written documentation played a much greater role, and deliberation and judgments were largely routine: if the claimant had a receipt, he won; if not, he lost. By 1908 such cases comprised the bulk of the civil caseload in Ignat'evo volost.

Many contemporary analysts interpreted the rise of small claims to be the result of the monetization of the economy. They assumed that transformations of the rural economy had rendered community norms obsolete, thus feeding litigiousness and court use.[70] What these analyses overlooked, however, was that if monetary claims were increasing in absolute terms, they were declining in relative terms. If the increase in small claims appears so spectacular, it is only because they were so numerous. Although "miscellaneous claims" were responsible for approximately half of the total absolute increase in the civil caseload between 1903 and 1913, the per capita growth rate in Riazan and Moscow hovered at around 2 percent per year, and in Tver it declined by 0.5 percent. Even while the volost courts were adapting to the changes sweeping through certain regions, "miscellaneous claims" as a proportion of the total civil caseload declined; for instance, from 89 to 76 percent in Vladimir, and from 83 to 72 percent in Riazan (see table 3-5). Other types of cases were increasing much more quickly.

After the turn of the century it was the category of land disputes that grew most rapidly. As the second largest category of civil cases, land disputes accounted for anywhere between 5 percent (Vladimir 1901) and 17 percent (Riazan 1913) of the civil caseload; they were followed by inheritance and household partitions (from 4.7% to 13.4% of cases). Land and inheritance disputes grew by as much as 30 percent a year in some provinces during the second half of the decade. The most obvious contributor to the courts' business after 1906 was the Stolypin agrarian reforms. Contemporaries assumed that the reforms greatly exacerbated tensions within the village, and the press printed daily accounts of villages divided into antagonistic camps, battling through the volost courts over the location of boundaries and fences, or access to pastures and meadows.

The impression was so prevalent that in 1911 the Ministry of Internal Affairs issued a circular to provincial governors asking them to substantiate the press portrait of pervasive chaos and conflict, and to report on the number of volost court cases directly related to the November 9 legislation. The MVD query was inconclusive. Most governors reported no "significant" conflicts due to the agrarian reforms, or only a handful of incidents. Their responses give the impression of great calm reigning in the countryside, although one suspects provincial officials of being somewhat disingenuous in their efforts to portray their provinces in the best possible light. Only three governors bothered to place their data into statistical context, giving some indication of how land reforms could affect the work of the courts and belying their colleagues' sanguine assessments. The governor of Simbirsk stated that the number of cases related to the 9 November

TABLE 3-5

LAND CASES AS PROPORTION OF CIVIL CASELOAD

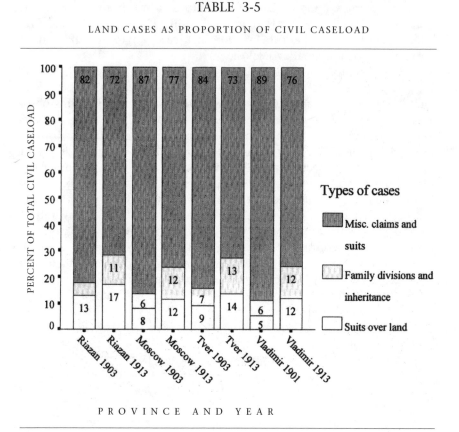

PROVINCE AND YEAR

legislation had risen from 6 percent of the civil caseload in 1908 to 9 percent in 1910, accounting for slightly less than half of the total increase in civil disputes. The reports from Penza and St. Petersburg both showed a significant rise in a wide range of disputes: disputes between households over allotment land, battles over the rights of renters to continue using land, and disagreements over who in the household was to be considered its head. Penza registered a doubling of land cases, raising them from 19.8 percent of the civil caseload in 1908 to 26 percent in 1910. St. Petersburg traced volost court decisions back to 1906, and found that land cases had risen from 9.2 percent to 19.3 percent of all civil cases.[71]

Unfortunately, more precise statistical correlation of the agrarian reforms with court activity is impossible. Volost level data on granting of titles (ukreplenie) and consolidation of land are largely absent from the archives. But, the findings of the Penza and St. Petersburg governors are hardly surprising. The 1906 legislation allowing a head of household to request title to his or her share of communal land greatly raised the stakes of land disputes. Under the former legislation, in repartitional communes any loss of land could conceivably be reversed at a later date. The process of titling land under the new legislation could permanently fix past losses, concessions, and even injustices. Given the earlier propensity of households to engage in private land exchanges without written documentation, it suddenly became vitally important to fix in writing who precisely held user rights only temporarily, who precisely was using whose land, and who in fact was the head of household with the right to request title and ultimately to sell off the family farm.

The Penza and St. Petersburg governors were quite right to cast their nets widely in search of the repercussions of agrarian reform. Acrimonious land disputes could be accompanied by much posturing and bluster as well as diversionary tactics—not to mention heightened sensibilities—giving rise to court cases that on the surface had nothing to do with titling or consolidation. S. T. Semenov, in his three-year battle for land title and consolidation in his native commune in Moscow province, described a long series of legal obstacles put up by the opposition to thwart his projects. In the first case, the village elder and his acolytes persuaded an absentee to file a complaint alleging that Semenov was using a share of his land temporarily abandoned to the commune when he had gone to work in Moscow. A second case was threatened when an exasperated land settlement agent, after a particularly stormy assembly, rhetorically asked the opponents of Semenov's consolidation: "Does everyone have to follow the *mir* like sheep?" "He called us sheep!" protested Semenov's enemies, threatening to file a complaint for insult. Another tactic consisted of denying that Semenov had a voice in the assembly, as his elderly father should in fact be head of household.[72] Were a historian to come across these cases in the archives, only one would give any indication of being related to land reform.

The trends reported by the St. Petersburg and Penza governors were evident in other provinces as well. In Riazan, Tver, and Moscow, land and inheritance cases increased much more rapidly than other types of suits, accounting for nearly half of the overall increase in the civil caseload registered in the Stolypin period.[73] It is possible, as the St. Petersburg governor's report proposed, that the increase in land cases reflected changes in jurisdiction introduced by the 5 October 1905 decree, which lifted the requirement that households obtain permission from the assembly for a household division. This is unlikely, however. Cases of disputed partitions *(razdely)* had already been within the jurisdiction of the court before 1905, and the requirement of assembly approval had rarely been respected anyway. And household partitions were only one of the categories of land cases that increased during the Stolypin agrarian reforms.

The raised stakes are reflected in the sharp increase of non-adversarial cases of inheritance and pre-mortem household partition. In Sinkovo volost in 1913, 51 cases concerned inheritance or *razdel:* 32 of these were simply requests for confirmation of arrangements made out of court, in some instances several years, even decades, earlier. Nothing in the law required such a confirmation; nevertheless the Sinkovo peasants successfully used the volost courts to notarize domestic arrangements.[74] Sinkovo was unusual in its high rate of registered divisions, but even volosts with small numbers of registered land disputes saw an upturn in inheritance and partition cases at some point in the Stolypin period. The Iagunino volost judges saw an average of only 3.8 cases of inheritance or partition a year between 1901 and 1905. Then these cases gradually became more common: from 8 in 1907, they grew to 16 in 1908, finally reaching 40 cases (out of a total of 141) in 1916.[75] The new land legislation greatly spurred the need for formal settlements that would be recognized both inside and outside the village.

Registered inheritance arrangements were worded specifically to avoid future conflicts. Agreements on household divisions typically included conditions stipulating how sons were to support their aging parents. When one of the parents retained part of the land, the court verdict specified that children would request no further share of the property in the future. In some divisions, a separating son agreed that upon his death, his property and share of communal land would revert to his brothers and nephews. The inheritance disputes that reached the courts stood as testimony to the dangers of not leaving a paper trail to family arrangements: estranged sons claimed not to be separated and requested part of their deceased father's property; widows found themselves dispossessed by their in-laws; or brothers found it impossible to reclaim a sibling's land that had escheated to the commune.[76]

This need for formal recognition meant that the ability of litigants to adapt the volost courts to the needs of local politics, which was so apparent in criminal accusations, was restricted in land and inheritance disputes. The fact that family and property disputes were also those most likely to be brought before the instances of appeal and cassation (land captains, district congresses, provincial boards, Governing Senate) potentially restricted the autonomy of local practices even further. The appeal process meant that local courts had to adjust their rulings according to criteria defined from above. Before considering the issue of land disputes further, therefore, it is necessary to examine some of the external administrative constraints on rural legal practices that existed even before 1906.

DEFINING THE BOUNDARIES OF LAW AND CUSTOM

The volost courts did not function as autarkic institutions. The 1889 regulations for the reformed volost courts greatly expanded opportunities for appeal, thereby ensuring that a significant proportion of disputes went beyond the village and that state officials became arbiters of rural disputes. Appeals were first heard by the land captain, who ruled on all civil disputes valued at less than thirty rubles, and on all criminal cases that carried a fine of no more than five rubles or a jail sentence of no more than three days. Any such case in which the captain found a breach of procedure was forwarded to the district congress. All other appeals were forwarded with the land captain's recommendation to the district congress, which usually then ruled on substance, although it could also return a case for reexamination by a different volost court. The district congresses thus heard approximately two-thirds of all appeals. Gareth Popkins has estimated that during the reformed volost courts' first decade, between 10 and 20 percent of all rural households had dealings with a district congress. This conservative estimate should no doubt be revised upward, especially for later years: the district congresses of Riazan province in 1908 alone reviewed over 12,000 cases, involving an estimated 5–7 percent of the province's peasant households. This proportion reached roughly 9 percent by 1913, while the proportion ranged between 6 and 7 percent in Vladimir, Novgorod, Moscow, and Tver. Given these numbers, it would be surprising if fewer than half of a province's households had dealings with the appeal bodies in the decade before the 1917 revolution.[77]

The assiduity with which villagers appealed is all the more significant as appeals had a relatively good chance of success. A 1900 MVD study covering sixteen districts in eight provinces found that over half of the decisions reaching twelve district congresses were overturned, a number consistent with other reports spanning the entire period from 1890 to 1915.[78] For the peasantry, the district congresses were not an abstract and distant authority. Their decisions had a very real and direct impact on village life, often at crucial moments in the life of peasant households. The appeal process meant that state officials potentially gained an extraordinary opportunity to guide the work of the volost courts, to mold peasant understandings of property relations, and to influence how and why peasants used the volost courts. What use was made of this opportunity is the question to be addressed in the remainder of this chapter.

The new rules of appeal in many ways merely sanctioned and regularized practices that had flourished before 1889 in spite of official restrictions that only allowed requests for cassation on procedural grounds. By the 1870s two converging pressures had contributed to turning the congresses of peace arbitrators (to 1874) and the district boards (1874–1889) into full appeal instances. On the one hand, the 1872 Liuboshchinskii Commission had found that the lack of recourse against an unjust decision was one of the peasants' most frequent grievances against the volost courts. Peasants (or at least their advocates) quickly became adept at translating substance into procedure, filing complaints against bribery, improper questioning of witnesses, or incomplete examination of documents. It is rather ironic that the emancipators' concern for the sanctity of "custom" probably did more to encourage the flourishing of illegal advocates than any other single measure, as the necessity of filing a request for cassation as opposed to an appeal on substance required considerable lawyerly skill. At least one observer attributed outsiders' impressions that courts were ruled by bribes and alcohol to the frequency with which such factors were mentioned on paper rather than to reality, as appellants needed to hunt for grounds to file an appeal for cassation. Members of the cassation boards were only too ready to read into the resulting accusations of corruption, bribery, and drunkenness demonstrative proof that justice did not exist in the countryside, and that peasants had to be defended from the arbitrariness of the volost courts. Accordingly, officials overturned cases for reasons that went far beyond the narrow bounds of cassation as defined in legislation: because a punishment was "too strict," because a household had to be responsible for its members' debts, or because the rights of orphans could not be neglected in cases of inheritance. Not only did such decisions limit the autonomy of the volost courts but in practice they amounted to decisions on substance.[79]

Although evidence is scant, peasants appear to have increasingly availed themselves of the right to request that decisions be overturned. In his study of Kemets volost (Novgorod), Gol'msten noted that very few peasants appealed in the first decade after Emancipation even though nearly a third of the litigants declared that they were dissatisfied with their verdict. The appeal rate increased rapidly after that, for it stood at 17 percent for the entire period between 1865 and 1885. Dashkevich, in a study of several Kiev volosts, found appeal rates to have gone from 5 percent to 20 percent of all verdicts over the same period.[80] Peasants, who had already managed to appeal volost court decisions before 1889, made frequent use of their new right once restrictions were removed. In the province of Kursk, 15 percent of all volost court cases were contested in 1891, and in Novgorod the figure was 10 percent in 1897. In Vladimir in 1893 the appeal rate stood at 10 percent, and it rose to 15 percent in 1902.[81] These figures, included in governors' annual reports, are somewhat misleading, however, for they counted appeals as a proportion of all complaints filed in court. Yet disputes that were reconciled, as well as the numerous disputes that were dropped because the sides never appeared in court, were not even subject to appeal. It was in the governors' interest to report low appeal rates, as these were interpreted to reflect peasant satisfaction with the reformed courts. If reconciliations are excluded (over a quarter of all complaints filed), the rate of appeal in Tver in 1896 rises from 8.5 percent to approximately 12 percent. In Moscow province in 1891, peasants appealed 13 percent of all criminal verdicts as well as 21 percent of civil decisions, while Riazan litigants appealed roughly a quarter of actual verdicts in 1892.[82]

It is impossible to know for certain whether there was any significant change in appeal patterns over the next two decades, as provincial authorities ceased reporting on case outcomes. Registers from individual volosts suggest instead that appeal rates fluctuated widely from year to year. For instance, in Ignat'evo volost between 17 and 35 percent of verdicts were appealed between 1891 and 1908. The range in the Iagunino court was from 10 to 40 percent, and in Timonovo between 9 and 23 percent. In some years, fully half of all civil decisions were challenged.[83] In Riazan, the volost of Izhevskoe saw much smaller fluctuations (21–26%) from 1900 to 1913.[84] Such variations can be attributed in part to changes in personnel and to the fact that some judges were less skilled at rendering acceptable judgments. The judges of Ignat'evo in 1906—a peak year for appeals of criminal cases—followed the uncharacteristic practice of fining both sides in insult cases. If they hoped thereby to motivate the litigants to reconcile, they failed utterly, and the majority of these sentences were contested. Some land captains, afraid of encouraging litigiousness, tried to forbid courts from announcing the rules and time limits for appeals at the end of hearings. Others attended court sessions and guided the work of the judges; in such cases, dissatisfied litigants were less likely to see the use of filing an appeal that would only have to cross the desk of these same land captains. A number of district congresses allowed only appeals of decisions that went against the defendant. Others gained a reputation for regularly reducing volost court sentences.[85] Each of these measures had an appreciable, if temporary and local, influence on appeal rates.

In spite of fluctuations, the ranking of appeal rates for different types of cases remained remarkably constant from year to year and from volost to volost. The most frequently appealed disputes were those with the potential to create a long-term precedent. The 1900 MVD study of court practice in sixteen districts shows that verdicts in inheritance and land disputes were twice as likely to be appealed as "miscellaneous suits."[86] More detailed data for two Moscow volosts show a similar pattern a decade later (see tables 3-6 and 3-7). Among civil cases, disputes over land, rights of passage, inheritance, and household divisions were those most often taken to higher authorities, while domestic disputes and "miscellaneous suits" were infrequently contested. Of the criminal cases, neither verbal nor physical insults were likely to be appealed, while complaints that peasants called "libel" (kleveta—a peasant who was called a thief could complain either of insult or libel) almost always went beyond the volost court. Complaints that involved plowing over a boundary or taking produce from someone else's land tended to be filed under samoupravstvo (taking the law into one's own hands) and were more likely to be appealed than complaints of theft. The absolute value of a dispute was not the determining factor: a boundary dispute involving fifty kopecks' worth of fodder was as likely to be appealed as a household division. In cases central to the allocation of resources between and within households, villagers did not hesitate to draw higher authorities into their local battles.

TABLE 3-6

APPEALS OF VOLOST COURT VERDICTS (SINKOVO VOLOST,

MOSCOW PROVINCE, 1913 AND 1915)

CIVIL	no. of verdicts	verdicts appealed	appeal rate	CRIMINAL	no. of verdicts	verdicts appealed	appeal rate
right of passage	3	3	100%	libel	3	2	67%
land disputes	12	10	83%	samou-pravstvo	10	4	40%
inheritance: adversarial	32	18	56%	assault	14	2	14%
property disputes	17	5	30%	insult	18	0	0
request for financial support	11	2	18%	disorderly conduct	6	0	0
domestic disputes	13	2	15%	theft	7	0	0
claims (iski)	40	4	10%	threats	0	0	-
inheritance: non-adversarial	69	0	0	misc.**	7	0	0
misc.*	12	1	8%				
Total	209	53	25%		65	8	12%

Source: TsIAM, f.1981, op.1, dd.2, 3.
*Contracts with priimaki, breaches of contract, building regulations.
**Carelessness with fire, fraud, blocking passages, keeping dangerous domestic animals, non-fulfillment of duties by a peasant official.

It is also clear that larger numbers of appeals were reaching the higher instances. As the Senate and the MVD clarified regulations, land captains lost much of their discretionary powers to limit the number of cases reaching the district congresses. The growth in the caseload of the appeal instances far surpassed the increased volume of cases reaching the volost

TABLE 3-7

APPEALS OF VOLOST COURT VERDICTS (IGNAT'EVO VOLOST,

MOSCOW PROVINCE, 1908)

CIVIL	complaints filed	no. of verdicts	verdicts appealed	appeal rate	CRIMINAL	complaints filed	no. of verdicts	verdicts appealed	appeal rate
right of passage	6	3	2	67%	libel	3	3	3	100%
land disputes	36	25	8	40%	samou-pravstvo	16	3	3	100%
inheritance	29	13	7	54%	assault	41	11	2	18%
property	16	6	3	50%	insult	63	19	5	26%
financial support	9	7	4	57%	disorderly conduct	13	9	2	22%
domestic disputes	6	5	1	20%	theft	9	6	0	0
claims (iski)	255	151	22	15%	threats	9	2	1	50%
misc.*	5	2	0	0	misc.**	5	4	0	0
Total	362	212	47	22%	**Total**	159	57	16	28%

Source: TsIAM, f.1112, op.1, d.19.
*Contracts with priimaki, breaches of contract, building regulations.
**Carelessness with fire, fraud, blocking passages, keeping dangerous domestic animals, non-fulfillment of duties by a peasant official.

courts (see table 3-8). But it was the civil caseload that was entirely responsible for this growth: by 1913 verdicts on criminal cases were, if anything, less frequently contested than two decades earlier. The growth in numbers of civil disputes reaching the district congresses was two to three times the growth of volost court cases. And a significant proportion of these cases dealt with land, inheritance, and family divisions. In Riazan in 1903 these categories together constituted 38 percent of the civil caseload of the district congresses; by 1908 the proportion was 44 percent (as opposed to 16% and 28% of the volost caseload for the same years). This meant that by 1908, 28 percent of all volost court verdicts dealing with land

and inheritance were being rejudged at the appeal level, while the proportion for all other civil cases was less than 12 percent. Levels in other provinces were similar: the district congresses of Tver, Vladimir, Moscow, Novgorod, and Vladimir each reviewed approximately a quarter of the volost courts' land and inheritance cases. It was in the area of property relations that appeal instances had the greatest opportunity to affect the behavior of the lower courts.

But it was also precisely in this area that the greatest confusion reigned. The new right to appeal a volost court decision on substantive grounds rapidly accentuated problems that had already surfaced in pre-1889 cassation practices. The jurist A. A. Leont'ev, in a study published in 1895, most forcefully exposed some of the dilemmas caused by the appealability of "custom." According to Leont'ev, no codifiable norms of customary law existed in Russia. While in one village, allotment land left vacant by an extinct household went to the closest living relative, in the neighboring village it could only escheat to the commune for general redistribution. If an absentee brother returned to the village after a long absence and demanded a share of the patrimonial allotment, the court might in one instance rule in his favor, but in an analogous case two weeks later rule in favor of the brother who had remained in the village. In each case, argued Leont'ev, the court was ruling according to considerations that could not be codified or even noted in the brief records that all volost courts were obligated to keep. Worse still—for the jurist in search of norms—the decisions of peasant judges were by their very nature ad hoc and could not create precedent. What unified the practice of all villages, argued Leont'ev, was a "legal vision" *(pravovoi vzgliad)* that took into account the character and reputation of the individuals involved, their economic solidity or seriousness *(khoziaistvennost')*, and their past contribution to the upkeep of a household.[87] Such inconsistency, lack of norms, and absence of a system of creating precedent began to matter once peasants regularly used the higher legal and administrative institutions.

On what basis could a district congress possibly review the decisions of the peasant judges? How was custom to be recognized so as to provide reliable criteria for reviewing appeals? In rare cases, land captains and district congresses studied local practices and encouraged village assemblies to pass resolutions fixing their legal customs. The land captain Polivanov, for instance, noticed that in his district all appeals of court decisions regarding trampling of fields *(potrava)* were overturned by the district congress, which insisted that volost courts could not fine the owner of a field as being responsible for maintaining fences in good repair. Only after Polivanov urged assemblies to draw up written regulations governing such disputes did the district congress begin upholding local court verdicts.[88] This was a relatively straightforward situation, however, hardly applicable to the complex circumstances that typically surrounded disputes over inheritance or household divisions. Cases in which the decision of a peasant judge turned on considerations of reputation, character, or past behavior

TABLE 3-8

GROWTH OF VOLOST COURT CASELOAD

AND OF APPEALS SUBMITTED TO DISTRICT CONGRESSES

	rural population increase	increase in volost court caseload		increase of volost court appeals heard in district congresses	
		CIVIL	CRIMINAL	CIVIL	CRIMINAL
Riazan 1892–1913	33%	160%	113%	480%	111%
Moscow 1895–1913	37%	226%	117%	627%	70%
Tver 1896–1913	30%	76%	28%	205%	60%
Vladimir 1892–1913	43%	210%	n.d.	481%	n.d.
Vladimir 1902–1913		74%	20%	99%	16%

Sources: See Table 3-1. Additional district congress data come from RGIA f. 1291, op. 31 (1914), d. 225, ll. 15–18 (Vladimir); d. 414, ll. 20–21, 24–25 (Riazan); d. 416, ll. 4ob.–5ob. (Moscow); d. 85, 9ob.–12; Mikhailovskii, 161 (Tver).

were difficult to argue on appeal. A defendant could always point to ostensibly analogous cases in the past that had been decided differently, giving rise to conflicting testimony and complaints that a "custom" had been invented or dictated by the volost scribe.

The Kharkhov district congress went further than most in seeking a solution by launching a district-wide investigation of local customs in 1890, the results of which were published as supplements to the provincial calendar from 1893 to 1896. The congress maintained that if custom was to have the validity of juridical norm, then it had to be known to the judges and should not have to be proven by the litigants as if it was a mere fact in the case.[89] But the Kharkhov solution, elegant in its apparent simplicity, glossed over difficulties that jurists and ethnographers had already confronted for two decades. Critics pointed to the dangers of drawing principles from two or three random examples, thereby neglecting local variations and then imposing principles that were in fact foreign to a given locality. More serious objections pointed to the difficulty of distinguishing between normative customs and mere social practice.[90] If the criterion for identifying a custom was that it had been followed for some length of time, then how could the judge distinguish between habit and custom? If villagers had the habit of sealing an agreement with a round of drinks, should the practice really be raised to the level of legal norm and accepted as evidence in court on a par with written documentation? If peasant judges recognized the right of husbands to beat their wives, should this be recognized as permissible under customary law? As one critic quipped, why not then accept theft as customary law on the basis of its ubiquity in rural society? The dilemma could not be resolved by rejecting customs considered immoral or illegal, for custom was inherently outside the written law.[91]

The MVD was fatalistic about such dilemmas. Minister D. S. Sipiagin, who in 1901 rejected the governor's proposal to extend the Kharkhov project to the rest of the empire, explained: "At present, as long as customary law exists only in the consciousness of the people, gaining knowledge of it is in practice, if not impossible, then in any case extremely difficult."[92] The MVD's resistance to codification must be understood within the context of the long-standing rivalry between administration and the judiciary. Codification would put a premium on experts in laws (leading to pettifoggery and formalism) as opposed to experts in people, on lawyers and judges as opposed to land captains with their alleged intimate knowledge of local conditions and the special character of rural life. Even allowing appeal instances to build up and rule from a body of precedents would constrain administrative discretion. The point of allowing appeals had been to redress abuses, not to "peasantize" higher courts. In short, either codification or rule by precedents would undermine the ideal of flexible paternal authority that was at the core of the 1889 reforms.[93]

In view of the ambiguous status of custom, the rulings of the Governing Senate were crucial for providing guidance to local officials. The Senate defined custom to consist of nonwritten juridical rules recognized as obligatory by inhabitants of a given locality who consistently submitted to them. On the question of the "local" character of custom, the highest court of cassation tended to ignore variations within provinces, accepting for instance in one ruling the MVD's assertion that "in the province of Nizhegorod" there was no custom allowing widows without male children to retain communal land.[94] In this case, the Senate chose simplicity rather than exactitude. On some issues the Senate went even further, in effect creating norms extending to all peasants of European Russia. An 1885 ruling, for example, established that communes could not remove allotment land from women heads of household except temporarily and in case of arrears, as was already the case for men. Applying the principle that the peasant household was a labor unit, the Senate specified in 1885 and 1897 that allotment land and related movable property could not be willed. Under the same principle, the head of household could not unilaterally dispose of property needed for farming, and household members' personal debts could not be covered by household property.[95] Each of these rulings was binding for the lower courts and effectively defined "custom" regardless of previous local practices. Senate rulings fell far short of full de facto codification, however. On most issues, the substance and applicability of custom still had to be determined locally on a case by case basis.

The second practical problem for appeal instances consisted of determining under what circumstances custom could be applied. The General Statute was notoriously imprecise on this issue. According to article 13, "in regulating inheritance of peasant property, the court is permitted to follow local custom." Yet there existed no consensus among jurists about the meaning of this "permission." Did it mean that peasants could choose to apply either custom or the general civil code? Or did it mean that the peasantry as a whole had the right to be subject to different norms from those prevailing in the rest of society, but that these norms were obligatorily applied to the peasantry as a whole? The latter interpretation was the most accepted among legal scholars and students of the peasant courts, if not necessarily among the administrators responsible for reviewing peasant appeals. Leont'ev, for instance, argued that it would be absurd to think that peasants could pick and choose among laws when they arrived in court. This would deny custom the status of legal norm regulating social relations both in and out of court. In any case, he added, the 12 June 1889 law on the reformed volost courts unambiguously stated: "In suits and quarrels among peasants, especially in cases concerning household partition or peasant inheritance, the court is to be guided *(rukovodit'sia)* by local custom."[96] The proponents of the mandatory nature of custom frequently cited an 1878 Senate ruling specifying that "the application of local custom, in those situations allowed by the law, is obligatory for the justices of the peace . . . . Article 13 of the General Statute cannot be understood to mean that local peasant custom regarding inheritance is applicable only upon agreement of the litigants."[97] The Senate thus agreed that the applicability of custom could not be left to the discretion of litigants; otherwise, litigants would refer simply to the law that best suited their interests.

A number of legal scholars vehemently dissented, however, arguing that the applicability of custom was in fact extremely limited. After all, the General Statute defined former serfs as "free rural inhabitants" to whom extended "all general civil laws regarding family rights and obligations" (article 21). Freed serfs could not be excluded from general civil laws, they argued, especially since the customs of an enserfed population could hardly serve as the basis of legal relations among members of a free population. Instead, the application of custom had been granted as an exception, to be applied (as stated in article 107 of the 1861 General Statute) only in the absence of an agreement registered in the volost office. In addition, the Senate had repeatedly decreed that peasants were "permitted," not "obligated," to regulate inheritance according to custom: "Local customs are not the only and unconditional norms governing transfer of property between peasants. . . . [T]he application of custom to decide legal disputes . . . is possible only on condition that the sides refer to local custom."[98] Even the 1878 decision that had confirmed the obligatory nature of custom specified that justices were first obliged to verify that any invoked custom indeed existed. Proponents of the narrow application of custom took these rulings to mean that custom could never be applied unless it was explicitly invoked by the litigants and then certified as valid. Without such a restriction, critics of custom feared, jurists and administrators might reify what peasants did into "customary law," and then the obligation of the volost courts to rule according to "conscience" would be tantamount to allowing arbitrary rule.[99]

These were powerful arguments, closer to the land captains' conception of their tutelary role and to the reform-minded bureaucrats' vision of the pedagogical value of law and administration. How, they might ask, could local officials possibly protect the weak and defend the helpless if the decisions of the peasant courts were to be declared "custom" and were therefore to be upheld? To idealize custom would ensure that the knowledge necessary to adjudicate would remain in the hands of the local community, or—more likely—of local strongmen. Rural officials' growing distrust of custom was reflected in the 1902 provincial and district committees' responses to Sergei Witte's Special Conference on the Needs of Agriculture. The majority of the committees explained that there was no "customary law," or that it had long ago disappeared. Instead, "each *baba* has her own custom," and the courts were governed by "arbitrariness" *(proizvol)*, "discretion" *(usmotrenie)*, and "corruption" *(zloupotreblenie)*. Peasants instead aspired to live according to the civil code, critics argued in an opinion often echoed in the legal journals. Some of the local committees added that Senate practice was artificially freezing peasant custom, at a time when peasant society itself was rapidly evolving and adapting to increasing contacts with urban Russia.[100]

Support for custom had further eroded by 1912 when the MVD conducted a survey among provincial officials with a view to preparing a new rural inheritance code (which was never completed). Thirty-nine of the forty-five provincial committees concluded that succession among peasants should follow a revised civil code. Even the Riazan committee, which sided with the minority advocating a continued role for custom, did not necessarily reflect the opinion of the provincial officials closest to the daily practice of rural justice. While a member of the provincial board maintained that "custom" was alive and well and responded beautifully to the demands of peasant life, all seven land captains who filed responses emphasized the difficulty of identifying custom, the unreliability of processes for certifying its existence (with individuals or assemblies who were often interested parties), its imprecision, its apparent malleability, and the absurdity of applying custom to titled communal land, a form of land-ownership that had virtually not existed but six years earlier.[101]

Given the obstacles of identifying and defining "custom," many district congresses preferred to avoid the problem altogether by applying the general civil code. While Senate rulings that required litigants to invoke custom had been written for the higher courts, district congresses sometimes extended the requirement to the volost court.[102] This eased the burden of administrators and meant that the written code was to be applied by default, while the right to be judged according to custom required that its existence first be proven. The presence of a legal professional in the district congresses—the district member of the circuit court—probably encouraged this tendency. The circuit court official, the member most likely to prepare cases for hearing, could most be expected to be sympathetic to references to written law, generally assumed in judicial circles to represent the final stage in the evolution toward civilization and social maturity.[103] He also had a propensity to carry into the district congresses habits gained from his work in the circuit court, where the laws and procedures of the written code applied.

Needless to say, the requirement that custom be invoked could cause considerable confusion and dismay among peasant litigants, especially when district congresses ruled according to the civil code simply because neither side had mentioned custom. As one bewildered woman complained in precisely such a situation: "The volost court knows local custom perfectly well. If it did not refer to it, then that is *its* oversight."[104] The requirement that appellants provide proof of custom (through witness testimony, certification by elected peasant officials, or assembly resolution) could create additional difficulties. Assemblies rarely issued certifications, perhaps simply because villagers feared creating binding precedent from the particular circumstances of one dispute. In addition, not all appellants were equally able to defend custom-based arguments. Village assemblies and elders were not always disinterested parties, and certification could be bound up with contests for power. For instance, in 1913, Evdokiia Strenina was unable to prevent the belated claim to half of her father's household plot *(usad'ba)* by her sister, who had long left the village. She explained to the Moscow provincial board that according to custom she was her father's only heir, since she had always remained and taken care of him. However, she added: "If you ask for a proof of this custom, I would be unable to show it, as the commune itself was involved in a court case with me over this land, and the assembly would not give me a resolution."[105] As the Kharkhov district congress had feared, custom was being contested on a par with factual evidence.

But district congresses did not consistently favor the civil code. Within Riazan province in 1910–1911, the Skopin district congress was ruling on inheritance disputes only according to custom (regardless of whether litigants had invoked it); the Spassk congress varied its rules from session to session depending on the officials present; and the Riazan provincial board required proof of custom.[106] Even the presence of the district member of the circuit court did not guarantee a uniform approach to custom. Opinion among judicial personnel was as divided as opinion among scholars who wrote in legal journals. And the judicial sessions of the district congress were as burdened with work as the administrative sessions, precluding careful consideration of the complexities of each case. Judicial practices of the appeal instances remained, above all, highly inconsistent.

In short, by the turn of the century, there were at least three different bases for legal practice in the Russian countryside: peasant practice, "custom" as codified by the Senate and interpreted by the district congresses, and general statutory law. In practice, the tensions emerging from the coexistence of divergent legal practices resolved themselves in ways that depended on the type and nature of a dispute, the local balance of power governing control of witnesses, and the personal preferences of the officials reviewing the appeals. The result was that by the end of the nineteenth century Russia was close to what anthropologist Clifford Geertz has termed "legal eclecticism," in which the lack of consensus as to the bases on which decisions were rendered left "the subjects of these complexities [without] much hope of comprehending it at all, save opportunistically."[107]

THE APPEAL PROCESS

With all the practical difficulties of identifying custom and determining the circumstances under which it could be applied, district congresses' rulings were notoriously unpredictable. Contemporary observers were keenly aware of the potential problems that this inconsistency could cause, although they disagreed on what it meant for peasant attitudes toward law. Reformers tended to assume that peasants aspired to live according to the general civil code, and that they were frustrated by appellate courts' insistence on applying ill-defined customs no longer appropriate to modern village life. Other commentators claimed the contrary: peasants were bedeviled by the imposition of foreign legal concepts that upset traditional notions of fairness. Yet another view was that litigants came to refer to "the law" or to "custom" exclusively according to their interests. In fact, one can see all three of these dynamics at work, but with such irregularity that it is difficult to speak of a dual or "bifurcated" legal system. District congresses sometimes ruled according to a principle of "custom" that neither side had mentioned. Other rulings ignored references to custom and applied the civil code. It was especially common for the higher instances to rule according to procedural regulations that bore no relation to the arguments advanced by the litigants. And there certainly is plenty of evidence of opportunistic reference to law and custom. But if the legal system made strategic behavior possible, it also prevented peasants and their advocates from learning which strategies carried the best chance of success, decreasing the likelihood that any single verdict would be final.

The consequences of confusion over law and custom were greatest in cases of inheritance. Observers of the peasant courts noted that, in adjudicating inheritance and household division *(razdel)*, judges and assemblies generally considered the litigants' relative labor contribution to a household. They deduced that one fundamental principle lay behind the apparent discrepancy in local practices: in the phrase consecrated by Senate rulings, the peasant household was an "economic-labor unit." Thus, according to peasant and Senate practice, adopted sons had equal claims with birth sons during a household division. Sons who agreed to take in or support elderly parents had the right to a greater share. Sons who had left for work in the cities and did not send earnings home could be excluded from a division. A daughter who took her labor into another household when she married was likewise excluded. If she brought her husband into her natal household, however, the in-marrying son-in-law *(ziat'-vlazen, priimak)* received the rights of a birth son, while losing his rights to the land of his paternal household.[108] The Senate consistently upheld these practices by extending the definition of the peasant household as a labor unit *(trudovoi soiuz)* within which property was held in common.

Such considerations would not enter into the decisions of the district congresses if these were guided by the civil code, which privileged relations of consanguinity. The tendency to apply the civil code was noted by numerous commentators as early as the mid-1870s: a district board might, for instance, overturn a case in which a brother or sister had been denied part of the household property as a result of having married out, on the basis that they had been denied their inheritance; or the pre-mortem separation of a son *(vydel)* could be overturned because he had not received an equal share of the property. The rights of adopted sons and in-marrying sons-in-law *(priimaki)* were particularly precarious in the higher instances. Neither the adoption of an adult man (undertaken by childless couples concerned about support in their old age), nor the inheritance rights of a woman when she married a *priimak,* nor the loss of inheritance rights of a son who married into another household was recognized by the civil code. Even when arrangements regarding *priimaki* were formalized in a written contract, they might be overturned for failing to meet the formal requirements of an official will.[109]

The contradictions between custom and law were variously resolved. Cassation and appeal practice was, above all, inconsistent. While statutory law was frequently applied to peasant practice, on other occasions custom might be enforced when peasants chose the general civil code. In some courts, for instance, informal wills were taken into account when the allotment of a deceased head of household was being partitioned.[110] Yet, the practice of willing communal land was theoretically contrary to the principle that the household was a labor unit in which the head was merely the manager of the common property. On this basis, peasant wills could be overturned by a district congress intent on upholding "customary law." Or, alternatively, if the volost court overturned a testament disinheriting one of the deceased's sons, the district court might rule that the testament was formally correct and should be upheld.

A few examples drawn from the Spassk district congress (Riazan) illustrate the difficulty that appellants faced in attempting to predict how higher authorities would resolve conflicts between law and custom. In

1910, for instance, a peasant returning to his native village tried to reclaim use of his uncle's allotment land. The villager who was using the disputed land presented a document testifying that the uncle had sold him the land, and the volost court ruled for the defendant. But the returning peasant filed an appeal claiming, plausibly, that the document was forged. The district congress ruled that the issue of the authenticity of the document was irrelevant, as allotment land was in any case the property of the commune and could "not be acquired by inheritance according to the law."[111] A few months later, two daughters who were using their deceased father's allotment according to his informal will were threatened by the claim that the land had escheated to the commune. The volost court had sided with the commune's argument that according to custom, married daughters lost the right to the parental household's share of communal land. The daughters protested that "government law does not recognize land to be escheated if there are heirs," and the district congress upheld their claim.[112] Did the difference in the rulings of these two cases arise from the fact that one involved collateral kin, while the other related to the rights of direct descendants? Or that one involved a returning peasant and the other involved village residents? The Spassk congress mentioned neither. Nor did it explain why it deemed irrelevant the properly certified reference to custom in the second case. The only general principle mentioned in the rulings related to the inheritance of communal land. So, could the use of a household's share of communal land be passed on according to an informal will? For villagers and their advocates, the answer seemed to depend entirely on the mood or the makeup of the congress on a given day. It is not surprising that litigants would conclude, as one peasant told land captain Ianovich, that "each [court] has its own law."[113]

The growing partiality of the appeal instances for the civil code had grave implications for the situation of women, and widows in particular. Village practices governing land distribution in the post-Emancipation period were subject to wide regional variations, yet the common practice had been to allow a widow to retain her husband's allotment after his death, and this right was virtually universal if she had male children. Rodney Bohac has shown that while the inheritance rights of women under serfdom were limited, widows could serve as guardians of property, protecting the patrimony of their children against the claims of distant relatives.[114] The Geographic Society and Free Economic Society surveys of the late 1870s found that this custodial role remained important in the post-Emancipation period. In most areas a widow could retain her allotment when she brought a new husband into her household. Even if a widow was unable to maintain the household and lost her allotment through failure to pay taxes and redemption payments, her sons, and in some places married daughters, retained the right to reclaim land upon reaching majority. These rights could be precarious. In villages where even unmarried daughters usually retained the land of their deceased fathers, women's holdings were ultimately subject to the discretionary approval of the assembly.[115] Generally, however, communes preferred to avoid impoverishing a household to the extent that it would have to depend on neighbors for handouts, and they rarely removed the land of a woman head of household.

The civil code, in contrast, guaranteed wives one-seventh of their deceased husbands' real property and one-eighth of his movable property. Daughters had the right to a fourteenth part of their father's real property and one-eighth of the movables. Ostensibly, as Rose Glickman has argued, the civil code could represent an improvement for peasant women, because it reduced their precarious dependence on the goodwill of the assembly.[116] It certainly did represent an improvement for most daughters, who customarily received only a small dowry when they married, for childless widows with no custodial role, or for widows who lived in complex households. The latter, even if they had sons, frequently found their husbands' brothers reluctant to recognize the rights of their vulnerable nephews. However, the civil code also guaranteed that widows could receive *only* a one-seventh share, thereby undermining one niche in which women could potentially achieve a measure of status and independence within peasant society. While justices of the peace and later district congresses had often favored the civil code in the countryside in order to defend the position of peasant women, the same provisions could be turned against women by their in-laws. It was not uncommon, especially after the 1906 land reform decree, even for a son who had left to work in the city to contest his mother's right to remain head of the household. The application of the civil code allowed absentee sons to gain control over the bulk of the household's land. If successful, they could then request a land title in order to sell the land. The stakes were enormous, and it is hardly surprising that non-adversarial cases on inheritance and household partition filled the volost courts after the turn of the century as households sought to secure their domestic arrangements.

It is also no coincidence that fourteen of the eighteen court cases registering inheritance arrangements in Sinkovo volost in 1913 were filed by individuals whose rights, under the civil code, could easily be contested. Twelve of the cases confirmed a woman as heir: the wife, daughter, or daughter-in-law of the deceased. Four further specified that use of communal arable land was to pass to the woman. The cases of confirmation of inheritance by males also represented potentially precarious situations: three widows requested inheritance of their husbands' property for their minor sons, and one adopted son presented the agreement he had made with his adoptive parents. Only two adult birth sons bothered to register their inheritance with the court.[117] At first glance, the rulings of the Sinkovo judges would suggest that the court was successfully defending custom by formalizing precarious claims.[118] Yet, some of the claims were precarious within either system (notably inheritance by a daughter-in-law). Conflicting invocations of law and custom should not be read merely as conflicts between tradition and change, as many contemporary observers were wont to do. The important thing was to defend inheritance arrangements against potential challenges according either to custom or to law. It is even possible that in the interstices between law and custom, some peasants were able to use the volost courts to obtain greater flexibility to dispose of their property. But nothing guaranteed that the district congresses would respect the volost courts' certification of what was, in effect, an informal will.

The high stakes involved in land disputes guaranteed that uncertainty as to the bases on which decisions governing inheritance were to be made extended into the village. Peasant petitioners could appeal alternatively to "custom" or to "the law" *(zakon)* according to their interests. For instance, in the Moscow village of Iagunino in 1905, Mikhail Kondratev requested that he be recognized as heir to his uncle's property, adding that his childless aunt, according to law, should receive only one-seventh of immovable and one-fourth of movable property.[119] In another 1915 inheritance case, the widow Tatiana Morozova requested to be confirmed, along with her stepson, as heir to her "legal share" of her husband's property. The volost court confirmed the inheritance, specifying that stepson and widow each had the right to one-half share. The stepson appealed the decision, shrewdly taking note of the expression used by Morozova in her petition: "She herself said 'legal share,' and that means according to the law, and she must get 1/7."[120] Simple opportunism was an important part of peasant strategies of argumentation.

Use of courts and appeals cannot be understood only in terms of opportunism, however. Litigants also spoke of moral obligations, fairness, and relations of enmity. At times, they mentioned neither law nor custom and were surprised to find the district congress ruling against them for this oversight.

How did peasant appellants argue their cases? It is here that the authorship of petitions becomes of interest. Peasants—even when literate—rarely made an appeal without the aid of an advocate. At first sight, most peasant petitions appear oddly schizophrenic. On the one hand, they describe the substance of the dispute, outline sometimes irrelevant background circumstances of their case, try to elicit sympathy by exposing difficult personal circumstances, and refer to moral obligations and the ill will of enemies. On the other hand, the petitions invariably conclude with legal terminology and a dry enumeration of articles of law codes or procedural regulations. In fact, most peasant petitions had three authors: the petitioner, the scribe, and the state. D. Ilimskii, a jurist who wrote about his experience as an informal advocate during two years of exile in Irkutsk, explained that his clients demanded petitions that were long on details and circumstances. When he tried to explain that such details were superfluous and that judges would deem them irrelevant, the client threatened to go to a more verbose scribe who "for just a half-bottle will fill you up whole pages."[121] Any advocate with good business sense and judicial knowledge wrote out his clients' objections—sometimes verbatim, judging from a writing style close to direct speech—and added relevant legal arguments with proper reference to articles of law, procedural regulations, and Senate decisions. In any case, the point here is not to look for that ever so elusive authentic peasant voice. The advocate worked to translate his client's case into terms that conformed to the dictates of the authorities.

The problem was that no one seemed to be certain what those dictates were. The third author, the state, was no longer providing a clear script.[122] Peasant "custom" was alternately idealized and ignored. The civil code sometimes trumped "custom" and sometimes was deemed inappropriate to the special conditions of rural life. Peasants were invited to petition the land captain and district congresses for protection, and to appeal to the courts (who happened to be the same land captains and district congresses) to defend their legal claims. There existed no standard structure for appeals that would govern the dialogue between petitioners and authorities. That peasant petitions typically included three or four conflicting arguments in support of an appeal was not a reflection of the ignorance and opportunism of advocates, as contemporary critics usually assumed. It was a rational strategy made necessary by the impossibility of knowing what a particular congress on any particular day might choose to focus on.

What was the clever appellant to do if he wanted to put forth a strategic argument that had a chance of gaining the sympathy of the appeal court? A popular solution was the "shotgun" approach, such as that taken in 1910 by an absentee peasant-worker protesting the volost court's approval of a household division with his elderly widowed mother. The court had granted an ailing widow a third of the household property on the grounds that her son had failed for years to send any money home to aid her. The wayward son gathered an impressive array of incompatible arguments in his appeal. According to custom, if a parent could no longer support herself, she should go live with her children. In any case, according to civil law a widow should get only a one-seventh share, not a third. In addition, his mother had not followed proper procedure—if she was unhappy that he did not send money, then she should have filed a civil suit about that. He indignantly added a moral argument: a mother should "not try to take away from her own son, a family man, his last home, and destroy his peasant household." And finally, he argued that the volost court's decision should be overturned on procedural grounds, as the communal assembly had sent a representative to court to testify in favor of his mother's request and had thus overstepped its jurisdiction. The district congress was typically laconic, ruling on grounds that had not even been mentioned by the appellant: since the mother was incapable of running the household and conducting agriculture without outside help, she did not even have the right to request a household division.[123] None of the arguments raised in the appeal, in the mother's counter-appeal, in the volost court verdict, or in the assembly's testimony were addressed in the ruling.

It was quite common for district congresses to bypass the arguments presented in petitions. Congresses, which had to hear as many as 30 or 40 cases per session, seemed especially keen to grasp at procedural flaws as a means to facilitate their work. They relied on the testimony of witnesses handpicked by the litigants. They also depended on the litigants to know the custom according to which they were supposed to rule. Yet, suspicious of manipulation and abuse of power by village strongmen, they distrusted appellants who could put forward properly certified evidence of custom. It was easier not to engage in the contest of who had the right to determine what custom was. Attention to formal and procedural requirements at least gave district congresses control over the proceedings and provided them with some firm basis on which to rule.

Even when rulings were consistent and correct, they rarely addressed the many motives and issues of fairness raised by the sides. The arguments presented in cases of disputed family divisions were usually quite extensive, involving as they did moral obligations and contests over authority. One 1910 case from Zaraisk district illustrates particularly well the extent to which the disjunction between arguments and decisions could leave underlying tensions unaddressed. In this protracted dispute over a household division, Grigorii Gudkov claimed that his share of property in the separation from his mother and brothers was unequal and unfair, since he had received an inferior portion of the family holdings (a calf instead of a cow, the old cottage instead of the new, a new plot to settle on rather than the old homestead, for example). In addition, he claimed that his mother had sold off some of the household property prior to the division merely to deprive him. When the district congress ruled simply that he had not appealed the listing of the household property within designated time limits, and that any complaint against illegal dispersal of household property would have to be filed in a separate civil suit, Gudkov was outraged. In an appeal to the provincial board (on substance in spite of the fact that the board could only rule on procedure), he protested that "the congress should divide property, not give one side all the property, and the other side the right to sue." But his mother, who had ostensibly won, was equally outraged. She reminded the provincial board that her son's behavior was

> neither legal nor moral . . . He considers himself the head of household so wants to take the lion's share of the property. . . . [He] wants to proceed in the way he finds fair, and this is what he considers fair: that his mother and brothers are thrown off into another place and he stays where it is convenient for him. If truly this is according not only to the law, but also to the moral point of view, to not recognize one's mother as parent *(roditelia)* and not recognize her as head of household *(khoziaika v dome)*, then all that is left is to be surprised at the modern cleverness of a son against his mother.[124]

The congress's procedural ruling had sidestepped all the substantive issues that it had the right (and from the petitioners' point of view the obligation) to consider: evidence relating to the "fair" division of property, obligations between sons and mothers, and the issue of headship and authority. While one litigant might withdraw from such a case puzzled by the "modern cleverness" of a son manipulating law to the detriment of his moral obligations, the other might wonder about the ponderous inefficiency of those same laws. And neither side would receive much satisfaction from the verdict of the provincial board, which could not rule on substance. Although boards did have the right to send back a case for a new hearing when the district congress had not examined the facts, they did so only in the presence of other procedural errors, and then only if the appellant had explicitly raised the objection. In this dispute, the Riazan board merely—and rather typically—confirmed the lower court's decision. Although the quarrel was decided, none of the underlying issues had been arbitrated.

Arguments exposing relations of enmity got particularly short shrift from the appeal instances. Petitioners frequently invoked the ill will and power of enemies to explain why an appeal had not been filed within the prescribed time limits (fifteen to thirty days), why a case previously decided should be reopened, or why a grievance more than ten years old (the civil statute of limitations) merited a hearing on substance. Sally Falk-Moore's observations on conflicting notions of "judicial time" in the British colonial courts of Africa are relevant here: local disputes were "defined in terms of ebb and flow of micropolitics [so that] what might be impossible at one time, becomes possible with an emigration, death, change of alignments." The result, according to Falk-Moore, was a society "constantly seething with latent claims" as villagers made "strategic use of time for the purposes of litigation."[125] Similarly, Russian peasant villagers might seek to reopen a case after a long period because a shift in the local balance of power and influence produced willing witnesses or different testimony from new village elders. Dar'ia Egoreva, for instance, filed a request to reexamine a land case decided four years earlier, because she now had witness testimony to support her claim. One Biriukov in 1910 sued for the return of some land removed by the commune seven years earlier, explaining that he had not appealed earlier for fear of revenge. A peasant worker who had returned to his native village and been unable to obtain land requested that his case be reopened: while the previous ruling had been based on the evidence of custom presented by the commune's representative, he now had an assembly resolution to support his claim. In this case, the provincial board ruled simply that new evidence was not allowed in cassation, a ruling that was rather typical as administrative instances either ignored references to ill will, revenge, and misuse of power, or deemed them to be irrelevant.[126] In spite of the official mantra about the importance of being "close to the population," the appeal boards were constrained in myriad ways—by lack of training, by overwork, and by procedural rules—from considering the local power relations that were at the center of many appellants' appeals to justice.

If one of the mandates of the administrative courts was to teach peasants respect for the judicial process, congresses were ill-equipped to fulfill that mandate: turnover in personnel, overwork, and decisions made without reference to earlier cases precluded continuity and consistency. Usage could not turn into custom, and decisions could not create precedents. The congresses did not have the necessary local knowledge to rule situationally in accordance with the ideals of paternal justice, but neither did they have the judicial tools for rule according to law. Under the circumstances, it was difficult—if not impossible—for the volost courts or for peasant appellants and their advocates to know how to adjust their practice and arguments to satisfy the higher court. The inconsistency among rulings (even within a single district) made it impossible for petitioners to learn what the law might be, and it prevented them from rendering the complexities of their cases into universally understood arguments that could be adjudicated.[127] This made it less likely that verdicts could finalize disputes. The number of written exchanges between rural inhabitants and authorities did indeed increase, but to the detriment of communication, as there were no mutually understood rules governing the terms of the dialogue. The 1912 reforms of the volost courts, which retained the right to rule according to custom and the same appeal instance guided by identical procedural rules and Senate decisions as before, could do little to resolve this fundamental problem.[128]

◆ ◆ ◆

It would be an error to project the chaotic situation reigning in the sphere of inheritance rights to volost court practices as a whole. Peasants made a differentiated usage of the courts, distinguishing among the audiences to whom their suits were directed. Some suits were turned inward toward the village, while others required decisions that would be recognized both inside and outside the community. The Russian volost court retained many of the characteristics of what legal historians and anthropologists have called "community justice."[129] Especially in criminal matters, peasants retained considerable control over prosecution. The courts were largely impervious to the notion that crimes constituted a public offense and should thus be punished regardless of the will of the victim. Likewise, the courts failed to distinguish strictly between crimes and civil claims (and between punishment and compensation); they made widespread use of reconciliation; and punishments were made to "fit the criminal rather than the crime." In addition, peasants frequently used the courts creatively in their day-to-day battles, filing complaints to scare off rivals, to force negotiation, to shame family members into different behavior, to defend honor and reputation—in other words, to achieve goals that had little to do with the substance of law. These features would suggest that judges in their rulings sought to reestablish local peace in such a way as to avoid the interference of outside authorities. Certainly, land captains' supervision of the courts was no more effective than their control of other spheres of peasant administration. Inspections remained sporadic and superficial, transcripts of proceedings were often too succinct for even the most knowledgeable inspectors, and no one verified whether verdicts were implemented. Peasants were largely left to appropriate the volost courts to their needs.

This is only half of the story, however. The courts stood at the threshold between official and peasant Russia and were not unaffected by outside pressures and influence. Behavioral issues, embedded in a village framework of dispute settlement, could respond to the logic of village politics in ways that disputes over land could not. The possibility of appeal increasingly implicated villagers in the broader administrative system, its concerns, and its procedures. But if peasants' willingness to implicate higher authorities in local affairs provided the state with an extraordinary opportunity to gain greater control over the countryside, then that opportunity was squandered. Where the autonomy of the court was most constrained—in the realm of property relations—there was little in the practice of the appeal instances to encourage the development of specific notions of defendable rights. And after making appeals to outside officials to intercede, villagers were more often than not bound to be disappointed. In case after case, the final rulings had little to do with the original complaint and did not take into account circumstances that peasants considered to be central to the dispute: issues of morality, authority, or relations of enmity. Administrators and peasants were often speaking different languages, such that in the end, decisions were rendered, but disputes could continue to simmer only to resurface when the situation allowed.

Under the circumstances, it is unlikely that the peasant courts served as "a school in modern institution building," as some scholars have argued.[130] It is true that on one level, the volost courts were immensely successful, if only because of the sheer number of cases presented to them. To the extent that local disputes were taken to an officially sanctioned institution, peasant use of volost courts could be interpreted as part of a process of monopolization of judicial power by the state and might even be said to reflect recognition of that monopoly. But to the extent that a minimum requirement of rule of law is that it "provides reasonable predictability for the legal security of one's actions," then the Russian rural judicial system fell far short.[131] This failure did not bode well for Prime Minister Stolypin's modernizing projects. By default, volost courts and the related rural administrative appeal bodies were assigned the task of resolving disputes arising from the agrarian reforms. Both were poorly suited to serve as an instrument for transmitting the new legislation and resolving the conflicts that would arise from it.

THE VILLAGE ASSEMBLY AND CONTESTED COLLECTIVISM

♦ ♦ ♦

The disappointment that many officials expressed about the volost court paled in comparison with the almost universal censure directed at the village assembly *(skhod).* The *skhod* had once elicited the greatest hopes for rural society. In the first decades after Emancipation, populists and Slavophiles still tended to see in the village assembly a potential expression of peasant direct democracy, egalitarianism, and solidarity. For government officials, the patriarchal authority embodied in the assembly of heads of household was a convenient administrative unit and a guarantor of order and social stability. Yet, the actual conduct of this pivotal village institution betrayed the hopes placed in it, and after 1861 it was increasingly decried as "one of the evils" of village life representing the rule of the loudest, the wealthiest, and the most corrupt villagers.

Certainly, the disorder that generally characterized the *skhod* hardly corresponded to an administrator's concept of good government. A description of an assembly in Arkhangel'sk province in the mid-1890s gives a rather typical picture of the chaotic boisterousness with which village affairs were conducted.

> In larger communes the gathered crowd of 150–300 people does not even fit into the meeting house, but spills out into the entryway and into the streets, yelling, arguing . . . culminating sometimes in fights. But in any case, no one even knows what is being discussed in the *izba,* what opinions are being expressed, which of these are reasonable, etc. Then, getting bored waiting for the end of the assembly, which drags on sometimes long past midnight, some doze off and fall asleep right there on the ground, others scatter into

the neighboring houses. At last, the resolution is passed, usually under the influence of a few people . . . and the signing begins. Those who are illiterate and half asleep, having not heard or discussed anything, entrust the signing to a literate [peasant] and hurry home . . . for tomorrow the lost time has to be made up. Literates, if they find out what the affair is all about, also sign without objection, for if it was decided, then there is nothing to be done, it would only make enemies.[1]

The themes raised here resurfaced in virtually all discussions of the peasant assembly: the absence of calm, reasoned discussion, the role of influential people, unanimity enforced to the detriment of illiterates. The behavior of such "wild, screaming hordes," in the words of one particularly censorious land captain, seemed proof that peasants were incapable of abstract thought. They did not decide questions according to general principles and for the general good, but only according to particular circumstances and in their own personal interests. Bureaucratic reformers as well as conservative supporters of land captain paternalism agreed that the assembly was not, by its very nature, capable of making wise and measured decisions in its collective interest.[2]

The prevailing despair over the state of village assemblies stemmed not only from the fact that they failed to live up to ideological visions of good government but also from a generalized ethnographic misconception. Sketches "from the village" were typically juxtaposed against an ideal type purported to have existed in the past. In the 1860s, ethnographers discussed the reduced role and authority of elders, "no longer" repositories of custom and local wisdom in a world increasingly in economic and cultural contact with the outside. In the wake of Emancipation, ethnographer Petr Efimenko observed that the traditional elders were shouted down with cries of "it was that way in your time, but not now."[3] Through the 1880s and 1890s, observers pointed to increasing household divisions that brought younger heads of household into the assembly, exacerbating generational conflicts and reducing the moral authority of the *mir*. If unanimous decisions could still be found, they no longer signaled the strength of a unified peasant worldview, but bribery, vodka, and manipulation. Local officials asserted that by the turn of the century, villagers had lost respect for *skhod* decisions. The Stolypin agrarian reforms were likewise said to have undermined village solidarity, and the "current" practice of voting at the assembly was a departure from the "previous" custom of arriving at unanimous decisions.[4] The work of Soviet ethnographers of the 1920s echoed that of their predecessors, but with judgment reversed: the "new" practices of voting and the influence of women and youth were salutary indicators of the influence of Soviet culture.[5]

The famous tradition of unanimous decision making was thus repeatedly declared moribund from the 1860s to the 1920s. Yet it is doubtful whether it ever existed. Historian N. M. Druzhinin summarizes a list of laments from the 1840s about the prevalence of disorder, corruption, elections governed by alcohol, pro forma resolutions, and rule by clever strongmen that differ not one bit from laments of sixty or seventy years later.[6] There obviously is something wrong with the repeated discovery of the same "new" developments decade after decade over the course of seventy years—and their attribution successively to emancipation, migration, rising literacy, land reform, or revolution. The historian who takes such statements of transformation in peasant behavior at face value runs the risk of falsely reifying tradition and misrepresenting the nature of change in peasant society.[7]

That nineteenth- and early twentieth-century Russian ethnographers, publicists, and government officials, steeped as they were in progressive visions of history and societal transformation, should so starkly juxtapose tradition and change is no surprise. These writers were primarily interested in understanding the place of the commune in the transition from tradition to modernity. Debate centered on identifying the primary function of the commune and was informed by the assumption that it was in a stage of transition from one form to another. Analysts focused their efforts on determining whether the assembly was an expression of village solidarity, an instrument of domination by the strong, or simply a mechanism of rule by the state. These questions were good ones, and they remain valid today. The various functions ascribed to the *skhod,* however, cannot be approached as alternatives. The assembly was each of these things, sometimes simultaneously and sometimes in alternation under varying circumstances. It is one purpose of this chapter to explore the nature and dynamics of these varying circumstances. Increasing state presence in the village, demographic pressures, limited availability of land, rising migration, each could potentially reduce the power of the assembly. Only by examining the interaction of these various pressures can one begin to understand the conditional nature of village solidarity and to identify some of the fault lines that threatened that solidarity.

But first and foremost, the assembly was an arena in which village conflicts were negotiated and resolved. This was where the shifting boundaries of what the community was—and was not—were established and contested. This was where peasants argued about taxes, access to commons, use of resources, welfare obligations, and especially about land tenure and property. Increasingly, internal village arguments were conducted in relation to the legal and fiscal framework established by the state. But state officials, obsessed by the fact that they were unable to control the outcome of village conflicts, tended to misread the assembly. Everywhere they looked, they thought they saw the manipulations of the *miroed,* failing to recognize the extent to which government-sponsored concepts of "property" and "right to land" had penetrated the village.

THE *SKHOD* AND THE LAND CAPTAIN—
THE CASE OF BELOOMUT

In spite of the apparent detail with which the 1861 statutes regulated the assembly, much in the legislation was in fact vague. The precise limits of the *skhod*'s jurisdiction—who was to be considered a head of household, how often or on what basis redistributions were to be carried out, under what circumstances a resolution could be appealed, what in fact constituted the proper fulfillment of the village's obligations—all this would be worked out through administrative practice in subsequent decades. Senate rulings and MVD instructions, along with interventions by peace arbiters, land captains, police, and zemstvo officials all aimed at limiting local autonomy and turning village institutions into better executors of state policies. How successful were they in this task? Or, to rephrase the question from the perspective of the commune, to what extent was the assembly—what it did and how it went about doing it—shaped by government intervention and legislation?

The resolutions *(prigovory)* of Verkhne-Beloomut in northern Riazan (Zaraisk district) illustrate some of the effects of the government's efforts to better define and circumscribe the village assembly's activities. Beloomut was not a typical, and even less a "traditional," village. With its 460 peasant households and a resident population of approximately 2,800 by 1884, it had been deeply affected by processes of industrialization due to its proximity to the factories of Moscow province, to the Moscow-Kazan railway line, and to an important port on the Oka river. The village did not have any arable land, and households lived from a combination of dairy farming, cottage industry (tailoring), and outwork. By the turn of the century, half of the village's households had abandoned agriculture altogether and rented out their entire land allotment. These combined activities brought a relative degree of prosperity, as testified by the village's two churches, two schools, and a municipal library. There were also several hundred outsiders living in the village, mostly peasants from neighboring villages who had come to work in the tailoring industry.[8] The commune was also exceptional in that its peasants were "free agriculturalists" *(svobodnye khlebopashtsy)*, former serfs liberated in the 1840s by the famous radical Nicholas Ogarev. After the village's land debt had been fully paid off in 1878, households had become "full proprietors" under hereditary household tenure, bound neither by the regulations on collective responsibility for redemption payments nor by restrictions on disposal of allotment land.[9] Beloomut's very exceptionalism makes it an interesting case, for it illustrates the extent of the assembly's role even in communes with hereditary land tenure and highlights the effects of a combination of administrative, demographic, and economic pressures that all villages bore to varying degrees.

According to the local press, the town's administration was rife with corruption and its agriculture was a model of inefficiency. As in many larger villages of Russia's central provinces by the turn of the century, Beloomut had its own village correspondent. This amateur journalist, "Makar" (as he signed his columns) was only one of a growing number of peasant correspondents regularly publishing sketches from their native villages in Riazan's two daily newspapers, *Riazan Life* and *Riazan News*. Generally literate, young, with some experience of city life, they were representatives of the "new people," as volost elder Sergei Matveev called them. Matveev characterized them as sober, honest, but hard *(zheskie),* stingy and joyless. Deeply involved in communal affairs, they were at the forefront of any movement that would bring "progress" to the village: cooperatives, temperance movements, reading circles, agronomy societies.[10] Reports "from the village" were central to the press's educational mission and its determination to demonstrate the evils of blind adherence to tradition and the benefits of progress, sobriety, and education. Generally relegated to the back page rubric "Miscellanea" under such titles as "Savage custom" *(Dikii obychai),* "Benighted village" *(Temnoe derevnia),* or "In the dark" *(Vo t'me),* these articles betrayed a generalizing predilection for the sensational and the appalling.[11] While the village correspondents' brief accounts reveal much of the writers' bitter disapproval of rural life, they are less useful in gauging subtle changes in communal practices.

Makar, like his colleagues, sang the praises of science, bemoaned the frightful state of the "dark village," called for the need to bring "light" and "civilization" to the superstitious peasant. Beloomut needed a theater to "show how other people live, how people should live." It needed a second library to reduce the number of hours villagers spent in the tavern. Makar's columns regularly outlined the shortcomings of Beloomut's communal agricultural activities: the fields regularly flooded because drainage ditches were not cleaned out, the communal forest was becoming "a desert" for lack of replanting, the "communal bulls are so weak, the wind could blow them over." His conclusion, invariably, was that peasants must now walk "the new path lit by science." And when the elder who had overseen all these alleged horrors was reelected, Makar noted that on the evening preceding the *skhod,* the taverns were full: "And this is in Beloomut! Again vodka! Again bribes! And this is in 1913! Shame! Shame for people, for their dignity, for everything, shame!"[12] Makar and his colleagues contributed in no small measure to the impression that discipline and order in the commune had declined.

Village resolutions paint a substantially different picture of increasing regulation and defense of communal resources. In the 1880s only a small proportion of assembly resolutions dealt with agricultural tasks. Beloomut's system of landholding, referred to in zemstvo publications by the rather awkward term of "communal-parceled" *(obshchino-uchastkovoe),* did not correspond to any form of property and land usage outlined in existing legislation. Households owned user-rights to a fixed number of shares of hayfields whose location was determined each year by drawing lots. Households in arrears for communal taxes lost their user-rights for the year—their shares rented out through auction. Once haying had been completed, the fields reverted to undivided communal use and were used for grazing cattle. Pasturing was reserved for households who owned a share of meadow and was regulated by stints (set at seven head of livestock "but not for commercial purposes"). Pastures and woods were likewise undivided in common use. In the early 1880s the assembly's role in regulating agriculture was alluded to in resolutions setting the time for beginning haying, hiring cowherders, electing peasants responsible for setting boundary markers, and forbidding fieldwork on Sundays and church holidays (a restriction—illegal after 1904—that would disappear from later registers). The assembly began recording annual distributions only in the 1890s, after the arrival of the land captain who was charged with reviewing them.[13]

The assembly vigorously defended communal resources from outside encroachment. The expulsion of six families of gypsies in 1883 (and especially their horses) was a relatively straightforward matter. More troublesome was the land commune's relation to the one hundred or more non-peasant agricultural households and the increasing number of newcomers who worked in the tailoring industry. The conflict with outsiders began in the 1880s. No legislation restricted the right of free agriculturalists to sell their land. As a result, 156 of the village's 1,820 shares of hayfields had ended up in the hands of outsiders, primarily merchants and villagers from neighboring Lower-Beloomut. In 1880 several of these owners sued the village for access to communal woods and pastures in equivalent proportion to their holding of hayfields. Beloomut defended itself energetically, appealing its case to the palace of justice *(Sudebnaia palata)* after an initial loss in the lower courts. The commune argued that its forest and pastures could hardly be equated with its hayfields, as the former were held in common and undivided, while the latter were held individually and redivided annually. The court agreed with this argument, thus sanctioning the commune's definition of differences in forms of land possession. While the hayfields and household plots were personal inheritable property and therefore could be sold, the woods and pasture were common and therefore unalienable. Outsiders might be able to buy rights of land use, but they could not thereby buy into communal membership and concomitant access to commons.[14]

The commune did not rely exclusively on its court victory to restrict outsiders' access to its resources. The assembly established restrictions on disposal of wood cut from the commune's forest. Villagers had to request permission to cut trees for construction or heating, and the assembly specified how many trees each petitioner could use. An 1883 resolution added that buildings built with "our communal wood" could be sold only to a member of the commune, and only with permission from the assembly.

By 1907 the assembly further restricted access in response to the increase in the artisan population, revoking resolutions from 1894 and 1895 that had allowed resident outsiders to buy the right to cut specified quantities of firewood.[15] Contrary to Makar's assertions, the assembly was taking measures to prevent overuse of communal resources.

Between the 1880s and the 1910s, the assembly of Beloomut underwent significant changes: more peasants participated, meetings became less frequent, resolutions became ever more detailed and respectful of the General Statute's formal requirements. In the 1880s the village assembly had generally gathered every two weeks, and in the busy spring season as often as three times in one week. Contrary to later practice, resolutions indicated neither the number of households in the commune nor the number of peasants attending. In 1883 the number of peasants signing resolutions (either themselves or through proxies) ranged between 79 and 130 (17% and 28% of householders), a proportion far below the legal requirement of 50 percent. Yet there is no indication that the district board overturned any of the resolutions on grounds of insufficient participation. District authorities in Zaraisk, as elsewhere in the 1880s, were lax in enforcing formal regulations.

With the arrival of the first land captain, resolutions began indicating, as required in the General Statute, the number of eligible householders. In 1890 this number totaled only 236 "present households"; contrary to repeated Senate rulings, Beloomut was not counting absentee households. Only in the mid-1890s did the assembly comply with all the formal requirements regarding participation: the official number of eligible households more than doubled to include absentees, and participation rates reached the required 50 percent. It is impossible to know for certain whether this was a real or a "paper" increase in participation. The Beloomut correspondent to the Tenishev bureau reported that it was not uncommon for village officials to make the rounds of homes in the days following a village meeting to collect the requisite number of signatures. Nevertheless, it is likely that at least some of the registered increase in participation was real. Given that meetings were less frequent (less than once a month), it had become less burdensome to attend. And the presence of a particularly active land captain between 1894 and 1910 made it ever more delicate to manipulate signatures too openly, a maneuver also complicated by rising literacy: the proportion of signatories able to affix their own names rose from an average of 45 percent in 1883 to 68 percent in 1909.[16]

The presence of the land captain, and a growing awareness of the legal value of a duly signed village resolution in case of conflict, gave rise to longer resolutions: rental agreements, hiring contracts, obligations of elected officials, and annual accounts were all recorded in ever increasing detail. The 1883 agreement to hire herdsmen, for instance, specified only the amount to be paid for each head of livestock. The 1909 *prigovor* added that the herdsmen were to be "of sober lifestyle" and that they were accountable for any losses of cattle or damage to crops. The contract further established fines for taking in livestock not belonging to a villager, specified how the cattle were to be disposed in pasture, how they were to cross bridges, and when the cowherd had to hire a helper.[17] It may seem surprising that even self-evident tasks should be spelled out in such detail, but precise codification of assembly decisions made it easier to enforce regulations and contracts before the increasingly busy volost courts and appeal instances.

Most striking, however, was the increase in responsibilities falling to the commune and a concomitant proliferation of elected petty officials. In the 1880s, in addition to those hired voluntarily for communal tasks (field elders to supervise redistributions, watchmen for the hayfields, herdsmen and their assistants, and an envoy to represent the commune in court cases), the village had to elect and pay for a much larger number of peasants responsible for fulfilling its obligations to the state: the elder, his assistant, volost court judges, police deputies (desiatskie), the tax collector, a church caretaker and his assistant, and four peasants to verify the tax roles. In 1883 the district board's permanent member compelled the community to hire four forest wardens. By the turn of the century, after one unscrupulous tax collector had embezzled an astonishing 5,000 rubles, came the periodic verification of the elder's accounts; the assembly annually elected three peasants for ten rubles each. The land captain enforced zemstvo fire-prevention measures, requiring the commune to hire two chimney sweeps every year and to establish a rotation of watchmen.[18] It is no wonder that villagers eyed the arrival of outside officials with some trepidation. The Tenishev bureau correspondent explained that relations with the land captain were especially tense, as every time he appeared, the commune incurred another expense.

The proliferation of village offices, the growing expenses linked to the multiplication of state-imposed obligations, and increasingly standardized record keeping suggest that Beloomut showed little ability to defend local autonomy, and that the government had successfully transformed village institutions into tools of enforcement of its priorities. The resolutions remained prescriptive documents, however. Given the difficulties that land captains had in finding out what truly was happening in the village, communal respect for formal requirements could even serve to shield, to obfuscate, and thus to protect local autonomy. A number of correspondents to the Tenishev bureau remarked that although villagers would appear to listen eagerly to the captain's advice, they would then fulfill his orders slowly and only after repeated reminders.[19] Feigned compliance coupled with foot dragging are well-known classic weapons in the repertoire of peasant passive resistance.

But rarely could assemblies simply say one thing and then do another, especially on the crucial question of local taxes (mirskie sbory). The ambiguous results of communal resistance to the imposition of ever more obligatory communal expenses are especially evident in the confrontations between assemblies and authorities over communal welfare *(prizrenie)*. Critics of the commune had long pointed to its minimal welfare contributions as testimony to the *mir's* failure to guarantee subsistence for its members. Already in the 1880s, a few particularly enterprising district boards had made a concerted, and allegedly successful, effort to encourage assemblies to institute local levies for the construction and support of orphanages and shelters for the ill and destitute. Such campaigns only intensified with the arrival of the land captains. In Beloomut, land captain Melgunov worked for over two years to formalize the village's legal obligation to provide support to any member incapable of work and without relatives in the village as stipulated in article 179 of the General Statute. Beginning in 1885, he repeatedly harangued volost and village assemblies—sometimes even brandishing threats of arrest—to establish a special welfare fund. He finally succeeded in 1897, getting the assembly to approve a ten-kopeck levy on each share of land. The proposal had again met with virtual unanimous opposition and Melgunov had to gather the assembly three times before villagers, faced with the prospect of being called to repeated and time-consuming meetings, reluctantly succumbed.[20]

The land captain's victory did not fundamentally transform the way the village dealt with its indigent members, however. By 1908 the commune had accumulated a fund of 10,000 rubles of capital earmarked for welfare, but with over 13,000 rubles of annual expenses, it distributed only 539 rubles to the poor and elderly.[21] The village had lost—householders paid the extra tax—but so had the land captain, as the funds were not spent as intended. Beloomut tried instead to ensure that none of its members would become a burden on the commune. When a villager needed to sell his house, he or she had to get permission from the assembly. Most sellers were single or widowed women, and if the assembly found that they had no other means of support, it forbade the sale on the grounds that the house had been built with communal wood. A resolution of 1885 stipulated that a woman with no other property or means of support could sell only on condition that the buyer took upon himself the payment of "all possible dues . . . and would support her in old age and infirmity from his own resources." The assembly still enforced this provision twenty-five years later.[22] Since collective responsibility for taxes did not apply in Beloomut (due again to the commune's particular legal standing), communal interference in a household's right to dispose of its property did not arise from the fear that the entire village might be liable for the arrears of its improvident members. Rather, restrictions on disposal of property were motivated by fear of mendicity.

Confrontations such as those described above were repeated in numerous other assemblies, and the result was often the reinforcement of rules aimed at circumventing the application of article 179. Village societies rarely designated individuals as responding to the criteria for support outlined in the General Statute. The volost assemblies of Simbirsk, Saratov, and Smolensk provinces, ordered by their governors in 1888 to compile lists of individuals unable to work, without means, and without relatives, found but 17,300 for a population of 4,500,000. Of these, only 733 received some type of formal aid from their communities.[23] Assemblies of St. Petersburg province in the 1890s limited requests for aid by allowing land transfers only on condition that the recipient support the previous holder. When land captains ordered a commune to provide support to one of its members, assemblies responded that the petitioner had a cousin, stepson, or other distant relative who should take him in. There remained no trace of the orphanages and welfare funds established with much fanfare throughout the province a decade earlier.[24]

Less than 1 percent of communal expenses in European Russia went toward welfare in 1894, and this level remained unchanged in 1905. In Tver in 1896, welfare expenditures were virtually the same as the cost of renewing imperial portraits in volost buildings and holding memorials for the deceased Alexander III.[25] As late as 1914, a small zemstvo survey in Moscow province found that 19 percent of 137 communes gave some sort of aid to orphans, while 22 percent supported the elderly and infirm. Nearly half of these communes, however, had merely passed a resolution rotating the obligation to feed and shelter the petitioner. This was but a formalization of the widely reported and long-standing practice whereby the needy made the rounds of more fortunate households to ask for food (or "making the round of the mir"—*idti po miru*).[26] In spite of land captains' successes in getting assemblies to pass resolutions defining welfare provisions, communes preferred to restrict rights of land use and disposal to limit the burdens of welfare obligations. Meanwhile, the law on communal charity had become a source of constant, if low-level, conflict between captains and assemblies.

The fact that peasants were exclusively responsible for village and volost administrative expenses was also a source of tension. Peasants were particularly resentful of zemstvo taxes in kind, such as road corvée or fire fighting. Unlike zemstvo monetary taxes, these taxes were not levied on the entire tax-paying population of the province but were distributed among a district's communes. In the 1890s communes and volosts throughout Russia increasingly tried to extend taxation to those who were exempt by assessing nonpeasant residents and owners of nonallotment land. These individuals would sometimes acquiesce, haggling only over the amount levied, but more often they were ready to appeal their cases, all the way to the Senate if need be.[27] The problem became more acute where there were more outsiders. At the same 1907 Beloomut assembly that rescinded the right of nonmembers to cut wood for heat, some villagers proposed to tax households that took in outside lodgers a rather astronomical twenty-five rubles per year.[28] In 1911 several villages in Moscow province passed resolutions refusing to clean village roads that served through-traffic. Since so few villagers had horses, the resolutions explained, the filth *(griaz)* obviously came primarily from passers-by. One village elder emphatically added that the commune refused to clean the road and ditches "forever," since they were not used exclusively by peasants.[29] One 497-household commune in Sapozhok district engaged in a five-year legal and administrative battle attempting to assess 80 nonpeasant residents for their share of fire-fighting expenses. One can also find attempts to place a head tax on absentees still registered in the volost, but who held no land.[30] The association of local levies (both in money and in kind) with possession of communal land was so entrenched that after 1906 some peasants who had taken out title requested that their land henceforth be exempt from local assessments. Their appeals were unsuccessful, though not before exacerbating tensions in the village.[31] Such requests also initially confounded administrators, as they pointed to the difficulties of untangling the overlapping administrative functions of the village society from the land management functions of the commune.

Village efforts to limit local taxes were ultimately unsuccessful, and expenses grew dramatically after the 1880s. Measuring the evolution of Beloomut's expenses is unfortunately not possible, for early accounts are all too sketchy. Data from the Central Statistical Committee, however, show that combined volost and communal expenditures in forty-six provinces of European Russia, which stood at 32 million rubles in 1881, reached 42 million rubles in 1891 (an increase of 25% per *desiatina* of allotment land). Expenditures rose more rapidly after the arrival of land captains, reaching 57 million in 1894. The total for fifty provinces was 61 million rubles in 1894, and 73 million by 1905. According to Nikolai Brzheskii, head of the Department of Direct Taxation in the late 1890s, the average cost of local taxes for one desiatina of land was 50 percent greater in the second half of the 1890s than in the first half of the decade.[32]

It is possible that the data artificially inflated the rate of increase. There is evidence that some communes increasingly allowed payments for the hiring of replacements in lieu of labor obligations. Since reported figures did not include service levies, an unknown proportion of the increase reflects a shift in how obligations were met. In addition, communal expenses were not covered exclusively by tax levies, but also from leasing of communal property (such as rights to operate mills, brick factories, river crossings, etc.), so that an increase in expenditures did not necessarily translate into an increase in the tax burden. In 1891 such income covered approximately one-quarter of communal and volost spending. There is nevertheless some justification for equating communal and volost expenditures with taxes, for the income from communal resources was largely tied to mandatory expenses and unavailable for other purposes. Incomplete as they are, the data on communal expenses do demonstrate that the costs for peasant self-government were a considerable burden on peasant households. The 45 million rubles spent in 1891 were slightly higher than the empire's redemption payments assessed for that year. According to zemstvo budget studies, in the early 1880s communal and volost taxes accounted for nearly one-fifth of peasant tax obligations, and this share continued to grow into the 1890s.[33] Volost and communal taxes (86% higher than zemstvo taxes in 1881) had grown ten years later to twice the level of zemstvo taxes. In Riazan province, this sum represented 25 percent of a peasant's entire tax obligations, in Tver 37 percent.[34]

Absence of empire-wide data makes it difficult to trace trends after 1905. Communes did get significant relief as zemstvos and the central government took a more active role in funding medical care and education (these had accounted for 11 percent of reported expenditures in 1905). Beyond that, it was difficult for communes to reduce their expenses, even when these were voluntary. An MVD circular of 1889, reconfirmed in a 1904 Senate decision, specified that once an assembly "voluntarily and consciously" took on an expense, it could not then go back on that decision: voluntary assessments were in essence turned into mandatory taxes.[35] The apparent dramatic decreases reported in some provinces are attributable in large part to accounting changes: statisticians began separating out fees for communal agricultural tasks (such as renting land, hiring of herdsmen and field watchmen, which accounted for 15% of outlays in 1905) from administrative expenses, and these were no longer included in reported totals.[36] On balance, communal and volost taxes did probably decline. Data from Tver province, for instance, suggests that the burden of communal taxes dropped from approximately 3.4 to 2.5 rubles per household between 1896 and 1908 but still accounted for approximately one-quarter of all direct taxes.[37] Communal and volost taxes remained a significant proportion of a peasant household's tax bill and a significant source of resentment.

The resolutions of Verkhne-Beloomut illustrate three processes observable throughout Russia's central provinces. The first is that the 1861 legislation, by imposing a single institutional framework, contributed to a homogenization of *skhod* activities. The assembly's role as tax collector, as manager of land use, as legal entity before the courts, all muted the distinctive legal status of the village. While zemstvo statisticians, agronomists, and land reformers sharply distinguished between hereditary *(podvornye)* and repartitional *(peredelnye)* communes, the differences between these two legally distinct forms of land possession were less than the similarities. At one end of the spectrum, the ideal-type redistributional commune had only household plots in personal property, while arable land was under communal ownership and household user-rights were allotted temporarily through periodic land repartitions. At the other end, land in the hereditary commune was the personal property *(lichnoe sobstvennost')* of each household and could not be redistributed or removed for arrears under the provisions for collective responsibility. Most communes did not fit into these neat legal categories but combined a varying mix of communal and hereditary elements. And in both, the assembly played a crucial role in regulating agricultural tasks peculiar to open-field farming, in determining the share of each in the use of common land, in defending communal resources from overuse. Community cooperation was enforced through a great deal of compulsion, bolstered by fines and an army of guards and watchmen. There was much in village collectivism that was coercive.[38]

The second general characteristic of communal activity is that the realities of local administration played havoc with the distinction the 1861 Emancipation Statute had tried to make between the land-management functions of the land commune and the administrative functions of the village society. Assemblies discussed the village society's administrative affairs at the same meetings as those of the land society, with exactly the same peasants attending. The system of taxation that associated the obligations of estate-specific taxes with holding of allotment land favored a merging of the two, as did the regulations on communal welfare.

Finally, the assembly's recorded actions were strongly marked by government intervention. Contrary to the hopes expressed by historical anthropologist M. M. Gromyko, assembly resolutions are not the place to look for the expression of peasant ideals.[39] They were resolutely part of what James Scott has called the "public transcript," at the center of the administrative dialogue between land captains and assemblies.[40] The strength of community and welfare functions did not stand in opposition to state intervention but was forged in adaptation to it. As the government sought to broaden village societies' responsibilities, all the while maintaining limits on their ability to extend taxation to individuals who were not members of the land commune, village reaction was to define more carefully who could have access to communal resources and under what conditions. Unwelcome measures passed under duress promoted adjustments that divided as much as they united. The assembly sought to draw more firmly the boundaries between outsiders and insiders in ways that strengthened the core while excluding others. The boundaries of community, far from being stable products of a united worldview grounded in tradition, fluctuated in reaction to perceived destabilizing threats.

MIROEDY, UNANIMITY, AND THE THEATER OF VILLAGE POLITICS

For the officials who observed the stubborn ability of assemblies to subvert the intent of government regulations, there was one dominant explanation: the *kulak-miroed* used his money, literacy, and cunning to control the assembly. It was the *kulak-miroed* who plied the assembly with vodka; it was he who ensured that acolytes were elected as village officials; it was he who rented communal land for a song, thus preventing the community from accumulating capital that could be put to productive use. The rich peasant was a formidable opponent because he transformed his economic power into political power, and vice versa. He was allegedly able, for instance, to keep his compatriots in poverty by preventing the village elder from forwarding requests for loans from the commune's granary, thus ensuring a local market for his own surplus grain. Poor peasants purportedly voted with the local bosses out of fear that opposition could provoke vengeful measures to collect arrears. It was the ability of these few powerful individuals to bend the assembly to their own short-term interests that explained the "herd principle" *(stadnost')* of communal decisions and that frustrating, united front with which villagers seemed to oppose any new, useful, or progressive measure.[41] In short, the *miroed* provided a coherent and all-encompassing explanation for the difficulties encountered by officials in penetrating the village. Ultimately, however, the very convenience of the explanation was an obstacle to overcoming those difficulties.

The synonymy of *miroed* and *kulak*—with both connoting exploitation arising from the concentration of wealth, power, and local knowledge in the hands of a single person—emerged as an uncontested way of understanding the countryside only toward the end of the nineteenth century. While officials and writers of the 1870s and 1880s already saw the *"kulak-miroed"* as a parasitic exploiter, they identified the threat to peasant well-being as coming from outside the peasant community, from the non-peasant traders and loan sharks. And this usage coexisted with another quite different one. The authoritative prerevolutionary dictionary of Russian language (compiled in the 1850s and 1860s) gave several definitions for *miroed,* none of which had much to do with wealth. The word's first meaning identified a peasant who loafed about and lived off others; he was an idler, a sponger, a parasite. *Miroed* could also refer to any peasant official, or to those who served as solicitors for communal affairs. In this capacity, the *miroed* lived off the *mir,* fleecing peasants through clever trickery or by constantly instigating lawsuits.[42] It was this emphasis on involvement in communal affairs that was privileged by a local correspondent for the Geographic Society in the 1880s: *miroed* referred to whoever

> spoke a lot, confidently, continuously, with cries, but at the same time enjoys the trust [of the *skhod*] that defers to him. This talker-*miroed [govorun-miroed]* is always at the fore upon the arrival of any kind of official, and also is entrusted to petition about communal affairs when necessary.[43]

Neither were kulaks necessarily associated with wealth: the kulak was a trader, a middleman, "especially in the grain trade, at bazaars and docks; not wealthy himself, he lives off deception, overcharging, and false measures."[44] The occasional identification of a protagonist in village disputes as a "poor kulak" *(nebogatyi kulak)* is thus not the oxymoron it first appears to be.

The activities of one of these "commune-eaters" were well described by Nikolai Astyrev in the 1880s. A native of St. Petersburg in need of work, Astyrev had decided to put his literacy to use in the provinces and found employment as volost clerk in Voronezh. In his account of his years of rural service, he described one Parfen who was at the center of all village business. This peasant, whose counterpart could be found in any large village, "is a mental force. It is absolutely not required that he be wealthy, but it is necessary that he have the opportunity to 'feed' off the *mir*, that he receive some material advantages for his handling of communal affairs."[45] Parfen was indispensable to the community by virtue of the fact that most villagers did not know exactly where each allotment was located or its quality, who was about to give up an allotment, how much the communal herdsman had been paid so far that year, and so on. It was he who found out when an assembly could be gathered by consulting with the most important villagers, and he who bargained and arranged rental of communal land before auctions. In short, he was consistently involved in the assembly and kept track of all business and expenses, in the process skimming a sum for himself in compensation for his efforts. As M. M. Gromyko has argued, it was the *miroed*'s influence that was emphasized rather than wealth, and this influence could not be pegged to a specific social group or interest. The ambivalence of villagers' relation to the *miroed* was captured by the sentence offered as an example of usage in the Dal' dictionary: "He is a *miroed* . . . but without him we could not get by *(a bez nego ne prozhivesh)*!"[46]

By the turn of the century, this meaning of the word *miroed* had been largely forgotten in writings about the countryside, and the term was conflated with *kulak* primarily to refer to wealthy peasants. Whereas Astyrev's Parfen wielded power through the control of information and had a recognized function in the community, the *kulak-miroed* used that control for economic exploitation. In this second incarnation, if he was legally a peasant, culturally he was a suspect peasant. Successful penetration of the village depended on separating him out from the "genuine" agricultural peasantry. Characteristically, a 1906 MVD brochure distributed before elections to the second Duma called on peasants not to elect villagers who were cut off from village life: the wealth of such *miroedy* was foreign, other *(chuzhaia)*, coming as it did from trade and usury.[47] The political leanings of the rural activist mattered little: both conservative land captains and progressive cooperative agents or schoolteachers identified the *kulak-miroed* as the enemy of literacy (which he monopolized), sobriety (which deprived him of his most useful tool, vodka), and more generally of morality and fiscal responsibility. Analysts from across the political spectrum saw him as the primary obstacle to outside influence, resisting anyone who might threaten his control, authority, and vested interests.[48]

Also caught in the trend toward semantic simplification was the rich, regionally varied vocabulary referring to active participants of the peasant assembly. Ethnographers from the 1870s through the 1890s had identified a cast of characters within the melee of the *skhod,* each with his (and more rarely her) appointed role and position. There were the "pretty-talkers" *(krasnobai),* the "sharp-ones" *(rezaki),* the "bellowers" *(gorlany),* or the "chatterers" *(govoruny).* Some were known for their seriousness and ability to sway a crowd. Others were reputed as effective compromisers. And central to any assembly were the "yellers" *(krikuny).* Reputed for their glib eloquence and their willingness to outyell, outargue, and outswear their opponents, these village orators typically argued through the use of jokes and incisive witticisms, building on their opponent's character, exposing personal weaknesses, and playing with popular sayings, all to the particular delight of their audience. Anyone who had a stake in the outcome of the assembly sought their assistance.[49] And *krikuny* did not shy away from practicing their skills with visiting officials; the assembly could rely on them to voice objections to land captain demands. As Nikolai Brzheskii explained, summarizing the views of local committees for the Special Conference on the Study of the Needs of Agriculture, "they simply say aloud what the others are thinking."[50] Most land captains were less generous, grouping *krikuny* with all sorts of rural troublemakers, dismissing them as hooligans for hire.

What most observers failed to see was the theater of the *skhod.* The volost elder Sergei Matveev is one of the few informants to take his readers behind the scenes. In his volost assembly, two irreconcilable minority factions stood at the sides of the elder's table, the better to harangue the middle. On the right stood the traditionalists (three "black hundreds," one "poor kulak," and two women), railing against youth who wore city jackets and peasants who shaved like squires. To the left stood the "new people," a group that had emerged after 1906 and were partisans of change. In the middle stood the vast majority, and on the front bench the respected patriarchs, the first to arrive at any meeting, well-off heads of large families, and partisans of compromise solutions. When the elder proposed a question for consideration, the *krikuny* from the flanks were the first to step in with strong positions that would stir up passions and provoke much yelling, insults, and lengthy side-arguments. The leader of the "new people" would follow the proceedings and dispose his troops as needed: for violent attacks he would turn to one acolyte and whisper, "Tear him apart, Ivan!" For strong provocative positions, he turned to another of his allies, and when the assembly had argued itself out, he sent in yet a third, known for calming things down with compromise solutions that would please the middle. Meanwhile, the land captain, "who knew the peasant world through the old literature," aroused considerable puzzlement among the participants when he spoke "as if the *miroed* existed and controlled the assembly."[51] Matveev's account suggests that the dynamics of the assembly are probably better understood within the framework of factionalism. The point here, though, is that there was more order to the assembly than would appear at first sight, but for those who did not know the actors involved, that order was unintelligible. The observer saw only a frightening, "screaming horde," "wild crowd," or "undisciplined mass." Whether *krikun, miroed,* or *gorlan,* all these terms evoked, in the words of one writer, the "fearful" state of the "benighted village" where a few village exploiters controlled the *mir* with the aid of rabble-rousing troublemakers.[52]

If there was more order, there was also less unanimity than was immediately apparent. For most writers, chaos was the expression of the *miroed*'s influence, and the "herd principle" *(stadnost')* was the result. Yet there is no need to resort to machinations to explain the vast majority of unanimous decisions. Most questions considered by the assembly were routine administrative matters, with resolutions repeated verbatim year after year. These were the types of issues least likely to bring high participation, for which elders had to make the rounds of households to collect the requisite number of signatures and for which there was little cause for dissension. The formulaic declarations that typically opened a written resolution also accentuated the impression of consensus: "We, the peasant-proprietors of the village of X, having discussed without compulsion among ourselves, have unanimously agreed . . . ." Yet the phrase often meant no more than unanimity of the majority. It was not uncommon for opponents of a resolution simply not to sign, thereby falsely maintaining the appearance of unanimity. For instance, in the village of Iumasheva in 1882, when twenty-one *skhod* participants refused to sign a resolution on land redistribution, the remaining sixty-three "unanimously agreed" to proceed. Even more revealing are resolutions opening with the standard declaration of unanimity, yet concluding with two columns of signatures indicating those "for" and "against."[53]

One should not exclude the possibility that the formulaic declarations reflected an ideal or at least a preference for unanimous decisions. After all, peasants frequently told investigators that this was what they strove to achieve. The middle groups of solid patriarchs in Matveev's account preferred conciliatory solutions. Similar statements appear in numerous sources: a good resolution is one "that would offend no one" *(chtoby nekomu bylo obidno),* "that is good for everyone," that is "without offence."[54] On the rare occasion when an assembly deprived a member of his right to participate, it was because "he tries to do everything against the *skhod,*" "he persistently opposes *skhod* resolutions," or because he "is a person with his own morals *(samonravnyi),* who by his actions and pride always speaks aggressively *(nemiroliubno)."*[55] It is within this context that one can understand how informants' statements that "the assembly almost always comes to a unanimous decision" could be followed by lengthy descriptions of voting procedures.[56] Unity could remain the ideal, even if it rarely was to be found in reality.

Land captains were correct to doubt that expressions of unanimity necessarily reflected consensus. It is another thing, however, to assume that a village elite systematically imposed fictitious concord through intimidation and bribery. Instead, a unanimous decision can be seen as a snapshot of the balance of power at a given time. As historical anthropologist Sally Falk-Moore has argued for African villages under British colonial rule, "what appears to be equilibrium from the outside is often a temporary moment of agreement in which a dominant segment of the group has prevailed and everyone recognizes that predominance and acquiesces in all public behavior."[57] As a result, shifting circumstances that changed the perceived cost or benefit of a certain decision could lead to dramatic shifts of village opinion. In Sergei Semenov's bitter battles for land reorganization in his native commune of Moscow province, only minorities came out strongly for or against consolidation. The majority kept quiet, assessed the relative strengths of each side, filed applications for consolidation when they feared the commune would lose its best lands, and withdrew them when it seemed that consolidators would not receive sufficient land. This waffling majority voted in the same indecisive way, resulting in a succession of contradictory resolutions, one to proceed with a redistribution that would widen strips, one stipulating that all households would take out title (thus blocking redistribution), and one (passed unanimously and immediately appealed) resolving that all households would consolidate.[58] Such apparent wild fluctuations in the assembly's actions make little sense without consideration of peasants' changing expectations of what they perceived to be possible.

The difficult process of building majorities was at its most fragile, and its most acrimonious, when it came to deciding whether to proceed with a general land repartition *(peredel)*. The decision to redistribute allotment land was almost always a long and arduous process. One Shustikov, an educated member of a Vologda commune, described the process in his native village in the late 1880s. Talk of redistribution had been going on for a long time, and by the time the assembly addressed the question, arguments were heated and tempers flared. Proponents of redistribution objected to the fact that some households had engaged in private exchanges of plots, so they were using more land than in 1858 even though they still paid taxes and redemption according to the 1858 criteria. One peasant emphasized the unfairness that his fields were located far from the village and of poor quality: "We both pay for two shares, but you get five times more grain," he pointed out to one of the opponents of redistribution. Another wanted to get back land exchanged twenty years earlier against a small loan. Others mentioned that their sons would bring in wives so the household would have more mouths to feed, while others with many daughters would not need so much land when the girls married out. The opponents were just as adamant: they had held land for thirty years, paid redemption over that period so that only ten years of dues remained, and fertilized and improved their strips through hard work while others went off for easy earnings. Finally, when the assembly was argued out, in a lull in the discussion, a leading opponent of redistribution conceded that he would not go against the *mir*. As one Riazan peasant explained in the same period, "the minority realizes there is nothing to be done and join the rest."[59] But arguments did not end there, continuing over the division of each field, as case-by-case adjustments were made to the criteria of distribution. Although the commune had decided to divide according to the number of "eaters," those getting the best fields could be persuaded to receive a bit less: a family with only daughters could get an extra allotment in anticipation of an in-marrying son-in-law *(priimak)*; a family with a son who had long left the village would not get a share for him.[60] These types of case-by-case adjustments could serve to reconcile the losing side.

Astyrev went further in describing the internal village politics behind a *peredel* in a large commune of 510 households in Voronezh. There, the arguments were much the same as in Vologda, but discussions lasted through numerous assemblies for almost two years. Households that stood to gain or lose significant amounts of land were both in the minority, but some *"miroedy"* (according to Astyrev) who would lose communal land that they were renting for a good price joined forces with the opponents. These renters even tried to bribe the scribe to "read the law" in such a way as to block the redistribution. In exchange, they promised to switch sides within a year, when their leases were up. Even though Astyrev did not play along, the renters did indeed eventually switch sides, by which time the neutral party was resigned to repartition. Approximately forty households stood to lose quite a bit of land, but knowing that the balance of power had shifted, they felt it was useless to continue opposition and they did not even come to the assembly. The result of two years of acrimonious arguments was a unanimous resolution.[61] The village "strongmen" had been able to delay, but not to prevent redistribution, and in the end the unanimous resolution was not the one they had wanted.

The two land redistributions described above both occurred before the arrival of land captains, "before authorities were always about," as Shustikov put it. Given the arduous process of arriving at the decision to redistribute and of choosing the criteria, the presence of a land captain with his own ideas about what was just could be extremely disruptive. Whereas a minority opposing a redistribution of land might have reluctantly submitted to the inevitable, the arrival of a land captain who personally questioned each householder could reopen old arguments and resentments, not to mention new hopes that other means could be found to block redistribution. Land captains discovered upon investigation that in spite of a unanimous resolution, some peasants stated that they were opposed (as indeed they had been). This only reinforced officials' convictions that the assembly worked according to the "herd principle." The land captain Ianovich noticed that after a resolution passed with ten peasants opposed, on the day of verification there would be forty. Typically, he concluded that "vodka talks."[62] The passage of a new law on redistributions in 1893 also was disruptive as it insisted on distribution according to equal criteria for all households. If a land captain cleaved too closely to the letter of the regulations, the types of case-by-case adjustments that greased the wheels of reconciliation became impossible.[63]

One paradox is that in spite of all the concern and talk of the *miroed,* the closer one comes to the village, the less one hears about him. When the Geographic Society in the 1880s asked local correspondents about their village strongmen, the response was almost invariably "we have no *miroedy.*" Local respondents to a Tver provincial zemstvo survey from the 1890s aiming to establish a list of village kulaks identified but six peasants in the province.[64] Villagers simply did not recognize their wealthier neighbors as alien or sinister. When the Tenishev survey asked whether rich peasants commanded respect within the village, the answer was invariably yes. Peasants were said to admire the ability to buy and sell at the right time, while external signs of wealth—especially good clothes, good horses, or good harnesses—were all a source of pride. One correspondent explained that peasants went to their wealthier neighbors for advice, bowed before them and used patronymics, asked them for loans, but "these relations do not exceed the normal peasant bounds." Another specified that there were dozens of wealthy peasant traders in his district for whom agriculture was a secondary occupation, but that they were respected "since kulaks are the exception."[65]

Given the predilection of land captains to seek out the exploiter, one might expect villagers, applying strategies of manipulation of dominant discourse found in so many historical contexts, at least to frame issues of contention in terms of wealth when they appealed cases to higher authorities. Yet, in the hundreds of court cases and administrative appeals examined for this study, only a handful of petitioners referred to their enemies as either kulaks or *miroedy,* and only a few more mentioned wealth and influence. The exceptions tend to prove the rule, for they can almost always be attributed either to individuals who had embraced the challenge of introducing science and rationality into village life (Matveev's "new people") or to extreme situations in which membership in the community was at stake.

Among the most virulent denunciators of kulaks were the village correspondents. Their contributions to the press were particularly important in reinforcing dominant conceptions of village life, for they had the credibility of reporting "from the inside" as enlightened peasants. To the extent that the language of *kulachestvo* and *miroedstvo* (kulakdom) entered the village, it was probably in large part through such representatives of the "new people." Yanni Kotsonis has argued that organizers of credit cooperatives, who worked to exclude "nonproductive" kulaks from the new organizations that granted low-interest loans, also "gave villagers reason to care how they were labeled."[66] But those who cared the most about the label were precisely the new-type village activists: virtually any issue of a provincial daily newspaper in the 1910s included a contribution by a village correspondent on the cooperatives' and the schoolteachers' battles for progress against the "spider's web" of the *miroedy*.

In the cauldron of village politics, "kulak" and *"miroed"* became little more than epithets. Sergei Semenov characterized his enemies, opponents of land reorganization, as typical *miroedy*: they were the old manipulative village bosses, tradition-bound, uneducated, superstitious adherents to the notion that productivity depended only on the will of God. Meanwhile, his enemies fueled their anger by going to a tavern in the neighboring village that subscribed to the conservative newspaper *Russkoe slovo* (The Russian Word), and there they could read vituperative attacks on predatory kulaks who took advantage of the land reform laws to destroy the peasant community.[67] "Kulak" and *"miroed"* had little sociological meaning, existing in the eye of the beholder and used as an insult to denigrate an enemy with whom reconciliation had become impossible.

Appeals against banishment were another of the few occasions when villagers mentioned wealth to outside authorities. With a two-thirds vote, the assembly could hand over to the state authorities for exile to Siberia any of its members deemed to exhibit "devious and harmful conduct" posing a threat to the well-being of the community.[68] The long and tearful petitions protesting banishment decisions almost invariably spoke of the long-standing enmity of influential neighbors. Out of malice *(po zlobu)* these enemies had seized the opportunity of an unfounded suspicion or fabricated accusation to settle old scores and manipulate the assembly into opting for exile. Petitioners hoped to raise doubts as to the credibility of the commune's judgment by insisting that spiteful enemies were hand in glove with the village leadership and were able to use their wealth to bribe the assembly. The father of one exile wrote that "our *miroedy* and the volost and village leadership found some kind of hooliganism. The *miroedy*, who hang out every day at the volost are very harmful people for the village. They call for exile and the entire commune lines up behind them."[69] Another petitioner lamented that wealthy neighbors, who had long coveted his four shares of allotment land, used their "strong voice in the *skhod*" to pressure villagers to sign the banishment resolution.[70]

Such appeals would be expected to gain a sympathetic hearing from land captains, ever on the lookout for the machinations of the *kulak-miroed*, especially since Senate rulings specifically instructed the captain to investigate allegations of partiality and of manipulation by influential members of the assembly. Officials were rarely receptive to these pleas, however, almost invariably upholding the commune's decision. The fact is that exiles were not credible peasants, a point belabored in the banishment resolutions. Banishment was almost exclusively reserved for peasants who had by their overall improper behavior placed themselves morally beyond the pale of the village community. Resolutions not only listed the specific offenses imputed to a peasant but also gave a characterization of his general dissolute way of life. The same elements reappear in almost every case, in a litany of references to drunkenness and rowdiness and to a marginal economic existence. "They do not have a sober way of life, they constantly get drunk, and do not work," stated one resolution. The "depraved" targets of another petition "[support] themselves as they can on the backs of the other householders of the commune." They always drink and commit outrages, said another, their "economic way of life . . . is completely different from the peasant's."[71] Banishment was a measure of last resort for communes, applied almost exclusively to marginalized individuals, vagrants, migrants, drunkards, suspected arsonists, and thieves who could not be dealt with through regular village pressures and institutions. Reference to the influence of *miroedy* was likewise a defense of last resort, invoked by those who stood outside the village networks of alliances and rivalries.

In more ordinary disputes—complaints against land redistributions, against removal of allotment land, against volost court decisions—the land captain bent on combating *kulak-miroed* influence had to ascribe guilt with precious little help from peasants. Failure of the concept of *miroedstvo* to guide practical actions did not discredit it. On the contrary, the apparent absence of the kulak was interpreted only as further evidence of the extent of his power and cunning. Nothing else seemed to make sense of unanimous votes passed in the face of opposition, of consecutive votes that could adopt opposing positions, or of the resurgence of bitter debate after consensus had ostensibly been reached. What most officials failed to understand was the extent to which their own presence was disruptive, contributing to bring out into the open behaviors that few administrators in the past had even had occasion to observe. These widely deplored behaviors were possible not because a handful of strongmen kept the village closed to outsiders, but because of the ways local quarrels intersected with legal and administrative pressures coming from without.

PARTICIPATION AND THE RIGHT TO LAND

Belying the dominant image of growing peasant apathy toward the assembly was the frequency and passion with which villagers fought over the right to participate. Historians have long noted that participation in the village assembly broadened in the decades following Emancipation. Household partitions brought younger heads of household into the assembly, growing migration facilitated the participation of women representing their absent husbands, and bureaucratic insistence on quorums accentuated these developments. It is misleading, however, to characterize the process as one of democratization. Demographic, generational, social, and bureaucratic developments often collided, and increased participation by one group could occur to the detriment of another. The question of who had a voice in the assembly could be quite a contentious issue: recognition as head of household determined who had the right to make decisions regarding household property, who had a right to a share of communal property, and who was liable to which taxes. The thorny issue of participation shines a spotlight on underlying village cleavages, and these cleavages fell primarily along generational and gender lines.

Rural observers in the 1880s and 1890s were convinced that peasants cared little for the assembly, viewing it as an obligation rather than a right. If two-thirds attendance was required, the responsible official had to make the rounds of the village two or three times to "drive" *(sgoniat')* recalcitrants to the meeting. Land captains and provincial authorities were deeply concerned about chronic absenteeism. Low rates of participation, compounded by unanimous decisions, raised suspicions of influence peddling. In the 1910s—after twenty years of land captain exhortations and controls—provincial inspectors opened their reports with descriptions of the village assembly house deploring the fact that the structures were too small to accommodate even a small proportion of the village heads of household. Inspectors were ever on the lookout for evidence that the village leadership had resorted to signing for absentees, which was especially easy to do where illiteracy rates were high.[72] Even if no obvious illegalities could be found in the registered resolutions, inspectors were quite right to be suspicious: in some rosters of resolutions, signatures of illiterate peasants were listed in the same order year after year. Other resolutions included no signatures at all, and it was quite possible that they had been written up "just for form, and not at the *skhod.*"[73] Everywhere inspectors looked, they seemed to find confirmation that the majority of peasants were excluded, demoralized, or indifferent about communal affairs.

Much of the apparent indifference toward village affairs has a very simple explanation: the vast majority of questions decided at the assembly were routine. Most of the resolutions passed in Beloomut, for instance, were repeated verbatim from previous years. Such matters as renewing the employment of the village herder or naming a legal guardian simply did not require the active participation of most villagers. When the assembly had to address issues that would significantly change this routine, when it sought to levy new taxes, and especially when it envisaged conducting a general repartition, peasants became passionately involved. And when denied the right to participate, they did not hesitate to complain to the land captain. S. Dediulin, who served in the 1890s, noted that the great majority of complaints in his precinct centered on questions of participation.[74] In Riazan and Moscow provinces, hardly an appeal to the land captains did not include charges of writing in absentees, of recording illiterate peasants against their will, of including individuals who were not legitimate heads of household, and of collecting signatures by going house to house without having convened the assembly. The combination of apparent apathy toward the village assembly, reluctant and forced attendance, along with impassioned defense of the right to participate when it was threatened was not unique to Russian peasants, but can be found in contexts as diverse as eighteenth-century France and twentieth-century Spain.[75] Peasants did care about the right to participate in the *skhod*.

In spite of the continued inability of authorities to ensure proper attendance for every meeting, their interventions nonetheless did change patterns of participation. When a villager felt unfairly excluded, there was an official to call upon who was likely to be sympathetic. Unable to suppress the village strongmen, land captains hoped at least to dilute their influence by insisting on participation by the largest proportion of heads of household possible. The difficulty was that local officials had little to guide them in determining who in fact had the right to vote. The 1861 legislation had been particularly laconic on this question, only setting a quorum of half of all heads of household for most resolutions and specifying that two-thirds of eligible households had to agree on important questions such as land repartitioning, banishment, or the levying of voluntary communal taxes. The legislation did not specify who was to be included in the count of eligible householders. Should this count include only members who held arable land, or also those who held nothing but a household plot *(usadba)*? Should households that no longer conducted agriculture, such as migrants, be included in the total? Could households that had divided illegally, without official assembly approval, each send a representative?

In the absence of legislative guidance, post-Emancipation communes determined eligibility on their own, and practices varied widely from village to village. In some areas, landless peasants were allowed to participate, while in others they could only discuss non-land questions or were excluded altogether. Likewise, there was no general rule governing the participation of women. While some communes excluded all women, others allowed widows to attend when the issues discussed concerned them directly. Still other communes included the wives of absentees and recognized widows as heads of household with full rights. When the Voronezh provincial board set out to study local practices in the early 1880s, it found variation not only between villages but also from one meeting to the next, as participation depended on the issue under consideration.[76] Without some elaboration of regulations and a degree of standardization, authorities had no basis to evaluate whether the composition of assemblies was valid.

Provincial authorities quickly called upon the Senate to clarify rights of participation, which the highest court systematically broadened. One of the first issues brought before the Senate centered on absentees. The 1861 legislation did not specify whether the commune was obligated to count them in the total for purposes of determining legal quorums or majorities. Assemblies in areas of high out-migration found that even if quorums could be reached, then gaining a majority on divisive issues became virtually impossible, so they resorted to counting only "present households." As one commune explained, including absentees in the count of "householders with a voice in the *skhod*" would be the same as counting their voices against a resolution. "We consider that we have as much right to count them among those who agree," it added.[77] But excluding absentees could have particularly grave consequences in cases of land redistribution, as migrants could find their landholdings reduced in their absence. In 1881, the Senate specified that majorities had to be counted as a proportion of all households in the commune, and not just those present at the assembly. In 1884 and 1889, the Senate further ruled that even if a member of a commune did not conduct agriculture and had neither allotment land nor a household plot, he could not be denied a voice in the assembly. The insistence that absentees be counted pressured village societies—if sometimes reluctantly—to include the wives of absentees, without whom legal *skhody* could not be assembled in areas of high migration. Other rulings inexorably tended toward wider participation: households that had divided without the approval of the assembly had to be recognized, as well as households headed by women.[78] These rulings greatly simplified the task of provincial authorities, who could increasingly rely on household lists to determine whether quorums had been respected. They also tended to fix participation, reducing variations by issue, and further facilitated the conflation of the administrative and land societies.

Demographic pressures also forced changes in the composition of the assembly. While there has been some controversy over the precise extent to which household partitions increased in the wake of Emancipation, there is little doubt that the number of households rose faster than the population in much of European Russia. The number of households in forty-nine provinces grew by 42 percent between 1877 and 1905, and by another 25 percent between 1905 and 1915. As a result, the average household size had declined from 8.4 in the 1850s to 6.1 by 1900.[79] In 1889, 70 percent of Riazan's households only had between one and two workers (men between the ages of 18 and 60 or women between 18 and 55). In other words, most households included no more than one conjugal unit, as adult married sons were setting up their own households.[80] The increase in the number of household partitions thus brought younger heads of household into the assembly, peasants who earlier would have been represented by the family patriarch *(bol'shak)*.

Population pressures did not, however, broaden participation in a linear and uncontested manner. The link between high out-migration and female participation in village affairs was hardly automatic. In some areas of high migration, one finds a large number of women signing resolutions, while in adjoining volosts, one finds none at all. In some villages of northern Riazan, for instance, as many as one-fifth of the signatures on resolutions in the Stolypin period are female names. In such villages, one finds a pattern close to that outlined by Barbara Engel for the province of Kostroma, where women were not only active in the assembly but occasionally filled village offices.[81] In contrast, in nearby Beloomut, where already in 1889 over 60 percent of the male adult population engaged in seasonal work outside the village, there were no female names among the signatures in the resolutions. On the rare occasion that the Beloomut assembly counted women's voices, male proxies were signing the resolution.[82]

What could account for such wide variation of practices governing female attendance? First, much depended on the attitudes of the local authorities. Some officials felt that the presence of women in the assembly was beneficial, leading to less squandering of resources on drink. On the other hand, the Voronezh provincial board in 1883 concluded that if the General Statute had meant to admit women into the assembly, then it would not have used exclusively the masculine form of "householder" (domokhoziain). Thirty years later, a Kursk official railed against the evils of baby-skhody: while the presence of the occasional widowed head of household was consonant with peasant tradition, he argued, the systematic replacement of absent worker-husbands by their wives "radically changes the entire social-administrative structure of the village commune. . . . Neither the village elder nor the deputies (desiatkie) can manage with this undisciplined, wailing, screeching crowd of female citizens."[83] Such hostility toward female participation was probably widespread. Even the government's 1907 project to reform village and volost administration had proposed to exclude women from the new assemblies. As late as 1915 the MVD received requests from land captains to suspend assemblies until the end of the war because of the absence of too many male heads of household.[84] An active land captain could compel assemblies to include women throughout his precinct (the price of not following instructions being the difficulty of achieving quorums and voided resolutions), while an official convinced that female participation reduced the likelihood of reasoned discussion could simply turn a blind eye to local exclusions.

Another reason for regional variations in female participation rates is that the issue was closely tied in with conflicts over establishing criteria for land repartition. In most redistributional communes, land had been allocated according to the number of males present in each household at the time of the 1858 census (referred to as revision souls). In the decades following Emancipation, population pressures and the increasing number of household divisions resulted in increasing anomalies in landholding within communes. Formerly large households that had lost members since the last repartition nevertheless still held a large number of allotment shares. On the other hand, households that had grown had to content themselves with the share allocated sometimes decades earlier. Newly formed households were especially handicapped: they had little choice but to share with siblings the arable allotment land they inherited and to crowd onto their parents' farmstead (usad'ba). As a result, new or growing households clamored for a shift from old "revision souls," to new "present souls" (nalichnye dushi).

The shift toward including households created after Emancipation rarely occurred without conflict. Peasants who stood to lose land understandably resisted transfers to "present souls." Since redistributions had to be approved by two-thirds of the assembly, a determined minority could block changes for years or even sometimes decades. Observers reported that general repartitions almost disappeared in the central black earth provinces in the 1870s, only to pick up again in the 1880s.[85] According to one compilation of zemstvo surveys conducted in 6,830 communes of Saratov, Moscow, and Vladimir provinces, there was a marked evolution in redistribution practices between 1880 and 1902. In that period, the proportion of communes that had not conducted a redistribution since Emancipation declined from 65 to 12 percent. By 1902, 59 percent had distributed according to the number of males, 8 percent according to the number of workers, and 19 percent according to the number of "eaters."[86]

The new households were successful not only because their growing numbers gave them the necessary votes to force redistribution, but also because of a growing assertiveness in defending the legitimacy of their claims. As members of the younger generation were increasingly likely to have spent some time working outside the village, they were also more likely to be financially independent, more confident, and more vocal. Many press and ethnographic observations remarked on the desire for independence exhibited by younger peasants. The younger electors of the volost of Znamenskoe (Riazan) in 1907 felt that "new times and new songs" required a change in the elder who had served over thirty years by ensuring the election of his relatives to the volost assembly.[87] Universal military service, introduced in 1874, also played a role. Contrary to the pre-1874 system of military draft that ensured that few draftees serving out their fifteen- or twenty-five-year term returned to the village, the new system brought conscripts back after six years. By the mid-1880s, there were enough of these former soldiers to make a difference in debates on *peredely*. One commune in 1886, for instance, gave as its reason for redistributing land the fact that "many young people have even done military service and set up families that they do not have the land to feed."[88] In one particularly acrimonious dispute from Tambov, where proponents of redistribution fell one vote short of the necessary two-thirds, petitioners complained that their adversaries wanted "to wipe us from the face of the earth, and leave us to the mercy of fate." This was all the more intolerable since a number of the petitioners had fought in the Russo-Japanese War. "Of these present souls are many who served defending the Russian land (*zemlia i otechestvo*) . . . but to their sorrow, they did not even have land back in Russia for which they were laying down their lives."[89] The notion that military service should be rewarded with land, an idea voiced with increasing insistence by soldiers during World War I, had its roots in arguments over repartition since the 1880s.[90]

Generational pressures that favored the autonomy of younger heads of household could come into conflict with pressures bringing women into the assembly. If younger peasants were ready to challenge their fathers' authority and control of resources, they would be even readier to do so when households were headed by women. One particularly acrimonious case from St. Petersburg district—which dragged on from appeal to appeal for eleven years—deserves to be discussed at some length as it reveals the stakes behind tensions that existed in numerous villages in more muted form. In 1898 thirteen peasants from the village of Volynkino passed a resolution distributing income received from the leasing of communal land among the communes' twenty-two households in proportion to the number of people in each household ("present souls"). The resolution was appealed by twelve villagers who claimed that it was invalid, since the assembly had excluded women householders. The case then went through a series of appeals and counter-appeals, resolutions and counter-resolutions in an astonishing display of the ponderous inefficiency of the system of administrative appeal. The case became so confusing that the Senate had to hear it five times, the last hearing made necessary by the fact that the Senate itself had issued conflicting rulings on this one dispute, and that a resolution overturned in 1906 had already been implemented (with the Senate's accord) four years earlier.

Ostensibly, the contested issue was whether the village had a custom allowing women heads of household to participate in the assembly. One faction claimed that women had been allowed in the 1880s and 1890s only when questions directly concerning them were discussed, and presented resolutions covering a ten-year period showing that women were signatories in only 22 of 262 resolutions. The other faction claimed that the partial participation of women did constitute sufficient custom to warrant their inclusion in the future. The local land captain agreed with this latter interpretation, and in February 1900 he called a full assembly (with female householders attending), which passed a resolution stipulating that henceforth its proper composition would be twenty-three householders. The members of the original, restricted assembly howled in protest at the land captain's interference, and at the apparent malleability of custom. The land captain, they objected in an appeal to the Senate, had arbitrarily suspended the village elder, who refused to call an enlarged *skhod,* and directed the volost elder, who was himself a member of the commune and an interested party, to head the meeting. The Senate, "which is the guardian of the stability of law and of the purity of the sources of customary law," could not possibly sanction such an interpretation, they added. By the time the case again reached the Senate in 1906, there were not only conflicting interpretations of past custom, but there now existed a "currently established custom" dating from 1900.[91]

What makes this case unusual is that women headed fifteen of Volynkino's households. Ten of these fifteen households had no men whatsoever, and the other five had a male member of the household represent them at the assembly. Of the seven heads of household signing each protest (which constituted a majority of the restricted *skhod*), only one was an uncontested head of household in both the enlarged and the restricted assembly. The others appear to have been junior members of a household headed by a woman, or else landless peasants (holding only a household plot, which in most of St. Petersburg district where this case took place would not have given them a voice in the assembly). The real issue of contention had in fact little to do with the role of women in communal affairs but had to do with land use. The famous resolution of 1898, which had initiated the long dispute by restricting the assembly to males, had allotted land according to the number of members in each household (distribution by "present souls"). This was a break with the previous practice of counting a household's right to its share of communal resources according to the number of revision souls (i.e., according to the number of males at the time of the 1858 census). In the words of the supporters of the new criteria, distribution according to present souls would "eliminate the unfair accumulation of several shares in a few hands to the detriment of large families and the indigent peasants of Volynkino."[92] As the population of the village had almost doubled since Emancipation, some families had grown considerably, yet received no more land. Meanwhile, other families—such as that of the volost elder and some of the households headed by widows—had retained a hold on a disproportionate share in the communal wealth. The power of the female heads of household was in direct conflict with younger peasants who clamored for readjustments in the relative weight of households. The only way to break that power was to restrict the right of women to participate in the assembly.

Five Senate resolutions failed to resolve the case. In 1915, the 1906 Senate decision recognizing the original resolution that had excluded women and thereby divided land by present souls remained in force, although it had never been implemented. The entire debate resurfaced in 1915 when two women requested title and consolidation of their share of land, this time according to present souls. The commune filed an appeal, countering that the 1898 resolution remained unimplemented, and that therefore the petitioners had the right only to "revision souls." The dispute landed this time in the Ministry of Agriculture. It sidestepped the issues under contention, ruling that since the landholders did not themselves farm their land but rented it out for the cultivation of vegetables for the neighboring St. Petersburg market, land reorganization in this case would only disrupt production and thus bring no overall benefit "in these trying times."[93] Chances are the dispute would outlive the regime.

The example from Volynkino was obviously highly unusual, given the inexplicably high proportion of widows in the community, but this exaggerated feature serves to highlight processes that were at work in many of the villages of European Russia. Redistributions according to "new" (usually male) souls could lead to the exclusion of women and frequently gave rise to complaints by widows who found themselves with little or no allotment land. In 1882 four opponents of a *peredel* in the village of Iumasheva

(Riazhsk district, Riazan) protested that "in many households the men have died and only women are left, and this family paying redemption 20 years will have to give up its allotment land to someone who has not paid." In another case the same year, three widows likewise referred to years of redemption payments to claim that the commune had "violated [their] rights of peaceful possession *(vladenie)* granted to us by Merciful Manifesto."[94] The forty-six opponents of redistribution in Bakhmacheev (Riazan district) placed great emphasis on the five widows among them who had lost all their land because of "this scrap of paper called a resolution": the assembly had unfairly excluded the women, they argued, and the fact that the district board accepted this was "illegal." The result, concluded the petitioners, was that "land that should by right and fairness belong to us is divided between others to whom it does not belong."[95]

The pressures toward "democratization," abetted by a combination of population growth, household divisions, and a rise in seasonal or year-round migration did not necessarily benefit women, nor did they necessarily benefit young men. Whether they did one or the other depended on the specific circumstances of each village—the demographic balance, the ebb and flow of the balance of power between factions, and the attitude of the local land captain. More generally, the will of assemblies cannot be deduced in advance from a priori assumptions about peasant culture. Instead, it was highly volatile, responding to economic, social, and administrative fluctuations that could be eminently local.

GENERAL LAND REPARTITIONS

Thus far village disputes have been discussed primarily in terms of strategy. They cannot be reduced *only* to strategy, however. Arguments over land took place within an increasingly well-defined framework that shaped conceptions of what constituted the legitimate right to hold land. One striking feature of each of the appeals cited in the previous section is that the petitioners were hardly begging for charity or protection. They were asserting rights, in these cases rights that derived from redemption payments and from their status as householders. These rights could be rallied in support of communal tenure, or in support of individual household tenure, but both sides agreed on the terms of the arguments. Both the opponents and proponents of redistribution spoke of "property." But what did peasants mean when they spoke of property? How were rights of land tenure in redistributional communes conceptualized, and how did this fit with legislation and shifts in state policy?

The 1880s and early 1890s were a crucial moment in constituting or consolidating post-Emancipation attitudes toward land tenure. It was in this period that the pressures for redistribution forced many communes to confront the meaning of tenure and property. Two decades beyond Emancipation, men born after the 1858 revision were entering adulthood and starting families, and an increasing proportion of these young fathers had served in the army or worked outside the village. At the same time, peasant-workers struggling from industrial compression were pulled back to the village, demanding land they had earlier been only too happy to give up to the commune. Compounding the pressures for redistribution was the reduction in the financial burden of holding allotment land. After 1881 the government reduced redemption payments for former serfs by 20–30 percent (depending on the province), and it phased out the poll tax between 1883 and 1887. Meanwhile, former state peasants—who had traditionally repartitioned after a new "revision"—gave up their wait for a census that did not come when they were included in the redemption process in 1886.[96] By the end of the decade a wave of repartitions swept through regions where they had virtually disappeared since Emancipation.

The impact of the tax reforms varied according to region. In villages with poor land (primarily in the northern non–black earth regions), where taxes could not be covered by the income from allotment land, redistributions had been frequent (sometimes annual) in an effort to spread the burden of payments. Once tax obligations were more in line with what the land could produce, the assembly no longer had to compel households to take on land they did not want, and resistance to redistributions grew while the period between them lengthened. In regions where land had already been profitable and where redistributions had been rare, the pressures for *peredely* increased.[97] In both cases, communes confronted a change in the status quo that led to protracted and acrimonious battles between the proponents and opponents of redistribution.

The arguments advanced in the debates reported by Shustikov and Astyrev were repeated in village after village and were closely linked to the process of redemption. The opponents of redistribution cited improvements that they had made to their strips, the hard labor that they had expended, but especially the burden of the redemption payments that they had borne. Numerous nineteenth-century students of the land commune concluded that redemption payments encouraged proprietary sentiments, because peasants could not reconcile themselves to the fact that they could pay for their land for years only to lose it. The legal scholar O. Khauke argued further that although redemption dues were levied on an entire commune, the fixed repayment period of forty-nine years (forty-four for state peasants) meant that only the first generations after Emancipation bore the brunt of payments. As a result, a growing proportion of peasants believed that the household was in effect buying the land for its descendants, paying off the land for itself rather than for the commune.[98]

Khauke's assessment is borne out by an examination of peasant appeals to administrative authorities against repartitions. Villagers protesting the loss of land invariably justified their request in terms of redemption payments. A villager working in Moscow disputed the reduction of his holdings in 1885 by half a share on the grounds that he had paid for twenty-four years without arrears, so this land had become his property *(sobstvennost')*. "Have the commune return the land for which I paid heavy taxes," requested one Riazan petitioner in 1890. "According to what law did the elder allow a resolution [to be passed] about another's property," asked another. Some petitioners went so far as to demand (unsuccessfully) reimbursement of payments on land lost in a *peredel*.[99]

The reasoning linking redemption to individual property rights was not entirely without legal logic. Article 166 of the Redemption Statute specified that allotments acquired not by the commune, but by individual householders were the personal property of each household. Proponents of hereditary household property overlooked the fact that the legislation was referring to the type of document signed with former owners (agreements signed between landlords and a village society automatically placing the village in communal tenure) and not to the reality of who was actually making the payments. The language of property suffused the Emancipation legislation: former serfs and state peasants acquired the status of "peasant proprietors" *(krest'iane-sobstvenniki)*, an appellation regularly used in the opening sentence of village resolutions. The entire redemption process was for the "acquisition of property." The legislation also specified that an allotment once redeemed became the personal property *(lichnaia sobstvennost')* of the household.[100] For many peasants it seemed only fair that land could become property even before completion of the redemption process. As one uncharacteristically ironical petitioner put it: "I have fertilized and paid redemption for 20 years. . . . It would have been even better had I paid 48 years, and during the last 49th year the land had been removed to give to another [who had not had] the labor of redemption but redeemed it."[101]

The arguments of the proponents of redistribution are more difficult to pin down as assemblies seldom recorded their reasons for conducting *peredely*, at least not until 1906 when authorities' greater hostility toward redistributing forced villagers to defend more vigorously their right to do so. A few resolutions cited the need to reduce fragmentation and inter-stripping or the need to cut out additional household plots from arable fields. Some added that repartition was necessary to reduce the number of disputes and court cases. More often, they mentioned the need to balance landholding with household size: land was to be removed from households that had lost members "to those with greater need," to "those families who have more 'eaters,'" or to "those who need to obtain a means to earn a living."[102] These types of arguments were familiar to—and frequently mentioned by—contemporary students of the commune. Conspicuously absent was any mention that "land is God's," a phrase frequently attributed to peasants by nineteenth-century ethnographers. Either that argument was reserved for battles against private, noble landowners, or its prevalence has been assumed, projected onto the peasantry as a whole from the pronouncements of a few, such as the 1905 Peasant Union or peasant deputies in the State Duma.[103]

An influential study published in 1906 by Karl Kachorovskii identified two opposing principles at work in conflicts over redistribution, the "right to labor" and the "right of labor." While Kachorovskii saw the first as the cornerstone of communal principles—asserting that each household had a right to have access to land to survive—the second reflected nascent conceptions of private property. There are some problems with such a stark opposition and the implication that one set of claims derived from communal culture while the other reflected private interest. The first is that arguments implying the rights of "invested labor" should not be equated with arguments for unencumbered rights of property. In much of early modern Europe, these had stood in opposition, the rights of "invested labor" invoked to resist the revocation of usage rights.[104] What was at stake in Russian village contests over repartition were claim rights and usage rights, and no one was arguing for the detachment of rights from usage.

A second problem with Kachorovskii's conclusion is that the proponents of redistribution also spoke of property but insisted that land was the property of the commune. Since each member household shared in the obligations of communal membership (and these could not be renounced), then each should have "fair" access to communal property. One Spassk commune, for instance, explained in the preamble of its resolution dividing land by "present souls" that since Emancipation some families had gained additional members while others had shrunk. As a result, those with the most land use it "absolutely unfairly . . . because allotment land belongs to the entire commune with equal rights *(v ravnom prave)* for each person, and some households with few revision souls but the exact same rights to communal land do not have enough grain."[105] There was also ample support in the law for this interpretation: article 160 of the Redemption Statute stated clearly that as long as a village society was redeeming land, allotments remained the common property of all householders whose assembly had the right to apportion use among its members. Senate rulings throughout the 1880s and 1890s consistently reaffirmed that members held only user-rights to communal property.[106]

The third shortcoming inherent in reading pleas for repartition as a reflection of collectivist values and the rebuttals of opponents as individualism is that the two sides had in common the tendency to link the rights of tenure with the burdens of obligation. The position of a specific householder was determined in the nexus of local rights and obligations that could change over the life of the household. Once a battle against redistribution had been lost, the link between individual redemption payment and individual land possession was broken, but not the link between redemption and possession. A household that had lost land after arguing against *peredel* on the grounds that land was the property of the household was likely to feel that it could—indeed should—regain allotments if household composition again changed, in other words argue for *peredel*. Preferences for individual household as opposed to communal property cannot be deduced from a priori assumptions about peasant mentalities. The position of any individual household for or against repartition could shift depending on the history of each commune, determined in relation to the redemption process.

A redistribution in effect set up certain expectations for the future and increased the likelihood of subsequent redistributions. This becomes apparent in the resolutions of a few particularly prudent communes that spelled out those expectations. The village of Degtianoe (Riazan), for instance, after dividing according to the number of workers in 1888, set out conditions that henceforth would govern tenure. The resolution limited rights of disposal, specifying that householders could rent out or exchange their land only temporarily. If any household ceased paying redemption payments, then the commune would take over and rent out its land. At any time during the period of redemption or after, abandoned land escheated to the commune; any widow without male children could retain the household's allotment until the girls were married, after which it would escheat to the commune. Finally, after the end of redemption (expected in 1907), the signatories agreed that land would continue to be distributed according to workers, and that no one would be allowed to sell or mortgage; allotment land was to remain in "common use" (in fact in individual use, but as property in common available for redistribution).[107] Participation in redemption gave claim rights to shares, strengthening the notion that allotment land was the property of the commune, not only temporarily until the end of the redemption process, but for good.

It is in this context that one can make sense of the fact that householders could vote for a redistribution even though they would lose land. A study of thirty-one communes in Saratov in the 1880s found that slightly less than half of member households (enough to block any redistribution) lost 10 percent or more of their land during redistribution. Why would a household vote for redistribution if it was losing land? First, a household's economic interest cannot always be measured purely in terms of area. Redistributions could be an opportunity to get better land or better situated land, to reduce parcelization and thus the number of strips held by each household, to increase the size of household garden plots. Second, it is important to keep in mind that landholding was expressed in terms of shares. A household retaining the same number of shares would lose a small amount of land since the overall number of shares had increased with the rise in population.[108] But that loss was minor compared with the promise that the household might gain shares in the future when the need arose. In other words, the loss of land could be accepted as the price of insurance, an insurance that remained valid as long as allotment land remained the property of the commune.

While observers were fond of noting that peasants were confused by the terminology of property, that confusion was inevitable given the ambiguities of the Emancipation legislation itself. A degree of implied property rights had been endowed simultaneously in the land commune and in the household: in the commune as long as allotment land was being redeemed, and in the household once it was redeemed. The fact that the two could conflict became ever more evident in the late 1880s with the escalation of quarrels over redistribution, and as a small but growing number of peasants retired their redemption debt and took out title to their share of communal land according to article 165 of the Redemption Statute. The government had two options to clarify existing legislation. The first would have been to reaffirm the evolutionary provisions of the Emancipation statutes by strengthening the clauses linking redemption to household property. The clause that most pointed in this direction was article 36 of the General Statute. It provided that "each member of a village society can demand that, from the land fund acquired as society property *(obshchestvennaia sobstvennost')*, a parcel be separated as private property in proportion to the share of his participation in the acquisition of said land."[109] This was the article that most closely echoed peasant claims that redemption payments legitimized household—and not communal—tenure.

The second option, which was the one the government chose, was to strengthen communal property rights and limit the rights of individual households to claim their share of communal land as personal property. With its 14 December 1893 law for the "prevention of alienability of peasant allotment land," the government suspended the right of a household to pay off its share of redemption to separate from the commune without the latter's approval (part 2 of article 165). According to the majority opinion of the State Council, peasants had shown insufficient maturity to use this right responsibly. Instead of being used to consolidate strips and improve agriculture, article 165 was allegedly leading to land sales, speculation, and landlessness. It threatened to undermine what the State Council saw as the primary function of allotment land to serve as a special land fund "for the preservation of the peasant way of life *[byt]* and for the proper fulfillment of obligations to the state." Further, the State Council reasoned that since the commune had the right as proprietor to apportion land among members and to regulate its use during the redemption process, then that right was all the more unassailable once land was redeemed. Finally, the State Council deemed that unless the assembly could veto withdrawals, the danger existed (after redistribution) that a householder could redeem land for which neither he nor his ascendants had paid.[110] Over the next two decades, administrative and judicial rulings consistently reinforced the prerogatives of communes to restrict the rights of its members to use and dispose of its holdings in ways that could threaten communal property.

The renewed emphasis on allotment land as a special fund for the preservation of peasant existence had wide repercussions. It was at the center of key Senate rulings on a broad range of issues. It was the main reason given for an 1891 ruling confirming the right of village societies to restrict land uses by individual households that might exhaust the soil. An 1897 ruling limiting the testamentary right of heads of household explained that "peasant property owners *(sobstvenniki)* are possessors *(vladeltsy)* not on the basis of the right of ownership of property as defined in [the civil codes], which gives the owner full control over the property. [Rather they are owners] on a completely unique basis born of a general aim of state policy to protect where possible the way of life of the tilling estate."[111] The Senate gave similar reasons for rulings confirming that even in communes under hereditary tenure, the head of household could not dispossess those whose labor had contributed to redeeming household land. The household head was merely the manager and not the owner of household property. Household property could not be seized to cover the personal debts of its head, nor could the head sell movable property necessary for agriculture without agreement of members of the household.[112] The government's determination to protect allotment land also affected *peredely,* adding force to peasant arguments for redistribution. These were increasingly read by land captains and district congresses not only as reflecting basic peasant notions of "fairness," but as consonant with the intent of the emancipators.

◆ ◆ ◆

Proprietorial sentiments fostered by the burden and the fixed term of redemption payments could reinforce attachment to communal tenure as they could reinforce attachment to individual tenure. Whether they did one or the other depended in large part on shifting local circumstances. Village factionalism rarely emerged from dogmatic positions based on alternative values, class interests, or ideological visions. Opposing sides in fights over land largely agreed on the terms of the debate, and these terms had been established by the modalities of Emancipation and redemption. It is impossible to say that the *mir* "enclosed peasants in a separate world, with its own moral codes and legal customs, in hostile opposition to the state."[113] Villagers did not hesitate to draw in outside authorities to intervene in internal disputes, especially on that most crucial of issues—who in the commune had the right to hold, claim, and till communal land.

Even if land captains were rarely able to obtain the results that they wanted, their very presence encouraged appellants to frame issues in terms that could be adjudicated. Disputes over repartition shaped arguments over entitlement and fostered debate over the link between property and redemption payments that echoed those taking place in Russia's foremost legal journals. During the 1890s, the government channeled its administrative, legal, and rhetorical energies into bolstering communal property, protecting claim rights, and preserving allotment land as a protected reserve that would keep at bay peasant landlessness and impoverishment. Land captains tried to limit communal tendencies to exclude or marginalize members whom villagers perceived to be a potential drain on resources. The state's priorities fit well with arguments presented in support of the commune's right to redistribute, of the rights of peasant-workers to return to the village, and of the right of widows to retain their allotments. The Stolypin agrarian reforms, which brought into the countryside officials determined to inculcate peasants with proprietorial sentiments they allegedly lacked, would not so much assault peasant conceptions of land tenure, but challenge conceptions of property as they had been built up and reinforced by the Emancipation legislation and by the special measures of the 1890s. Ironically, reformers underestimated the task of transformation partly because they underestimated the extent to which authorities had succeeded over the previous two decades in strengthening the idea that communal holdings were indeed property.

THE CHALLENGES
OF PROPERTY
REFORM,
1906–1916

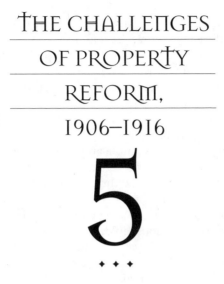

In early 1917 a dedicated but discouraged supporter of the Stolypin agrarian reforms, land captain Polivanov, ventured that "had our legislators thought clearly about who was going to implement the laws, they would have been much more careful."[1] In fact, the architects of the reform—including Prime Minister Petr Stolypin—had given the issue considerable thought. The 9 November 1906 decree, which allowed peasants to claim their share of communal land as personal property and enclose it in a single parcel, was to have been accompanied by a broad range of administrative reforms constituting a significant departure from the principle of indirect rule through corporate bodies. But the failure of these proposed changes to garner sufficient support in the Duma, the State Council, and even among Stolypin's ministerial colleagues, meant that property reform had to be implemented within the legal and administrative framework established in the 1890s. The volost courts retained their jurisdiction over the new peasant proprietors, even on issues such as inheritance and land use, but with little more to guide them than the General Statute's ambiguous permission to rule according to custom. The assembly voted on individual petitions for title as well as for consolidation, and the village society remained the local administrative unit for both titled and communal households. Land captains heard appeals when assemblies refused to grant title, and they were charged with investigations when conflicts over land reorganization arose. District congresses and provincial boards, guided by experience and the body of Senate cassation rulings built up over the previous half-century, still heard appeals against decisions by all lower authorities. Volost scribes remained a primary conduit for information between the village and state authorities, while village and volost elders received and forwarded petitions for title and consolidation.

The tasks that local administrative bodies had to face after 1906 were immense. Caseloads and backlogs grew at all levels of the administrative ladder, as peasants deluged the authorities with petitions and complaints. The simple act of obtaining a land title *(ukreplenie)* could be extraordinarily divisive even if the petitioner never undertook the second stage of consolidation but kept his scattered strips within the commune's open-field system. The new land legislation greatly heightened tensions that had already existed in the village prior to 1906 by raising the stakes in local disputes and introducing further complications in an already tangled legal situation. Since householders who obtained title gained considerable autonomy from the village assembly, the logic of the rights of land usage and tenure within the commune was fundamentally transformed. No longer could the assembly, during a general land redistribution, alter the quantity of land held by the household. No longer would the land of a departing household automatically escheat to the commune, as titled land could now be sold to outsiders. No longer could conditional allotments of land be enforced, as temporary holders could conceivably make that allotment permanent by requesting a land title. There was nothing surprising here, for the 9 November decree was intended to undermine the administrative and fiscal means through which the commune had previously controlled its members' lands. But the new legislation also had a whole series of collateral consequences—secondary or tertiary repercussions that were not at the center of the reform's goals but which played no small part in increasing peasant diffidence. Issues that had already been contentious in the 1890s, such as defining the commune's relationship to resident outsiders, allocating communal taxes and exemptions, enforcing the provisions of communal welfare, and determining household headship were all reopened in relation to the new proprietors.

It is over these issues that most of the disputes of the Stolypin period were fought. While the agrarian reforms have often been analyzed in terms of the confrontation between the principles of communal landholding and those of private property, these lines were often blurred in the myriad day-to-day conflicts that emerged after 1906. This is not to say that communal opposition did not exist. After all, 70 percent of individual petitions for title were rejected by assemblies and had to be forwarded to land captains and district congresses for administrative ruling.[2] Peasants did occasionally burn down the cottage of a consolidated homesteader, and they did sometimes attack surveyors. But in spite of Soviet historians' best efforts to track peasant resistance to the agrarian reforms, they found relatively few violent confrontations with authorities. The fact is that the vast majority of villages remained outwardly peaceful.[3] The most widespread, if not the most dramatic, conflicts occurred not with police or surveyors over consolidation, but in the volost courts and before the land captains over titling and its repercussions. In the central provinces especially, where only a small minority of households consolidated, the place to look for the repercussions of reform and for the peasant voice is neither in the few complaints filed with or against the local land settlement committees, nor in the rather sparse police archives, but in the thousands of peasant petitions, assembly resolutions, and letters of complaint filed with volost courts, land captains, and district congresses.[4]

The new property laws posed a number of related challenges both for villagers and for authorities. The first was that the government's rhetorical emphasis on property rights overlay existing understandings of property and possession that had emerged in the post-Emancipation decades. When the 9 November legislation was being drafted, its authors had briefly considered granting property rights along the lines earlier outlined in article 36 of the 1861 General Statute. Had this option been adopted, each household would have received the right to demand title to a share equal to its participation in the redemption process. In response to the practical difficulties of following this route—many villages had not kept adequate records—the commission determined instead that households could title land received after the most recent repartition that was in their "actual use."[5] This seemingly minor decision complicated the task of implementation, as local administrators were asked to grant property rights on the basis of usage claims. Meanwhile, most peasants framed their claims in terms of property rights that derived from redemption payments. These were property rights conceived in local terms and argued in relation to the specific history of each household and commune. But authorities paid little attention to these considerations: increasingly, the arguments advanced by petitioners and the motives outlined in administrative rulings had little relation to each other. The often haphazard and sometimes crude ways in which authorities untangled references to claim rights, "property" rights, "fairness," law, and "custom" opened the door ever wider to strategic uses of law and procedure, decreasing the likelihood that rulings could finalize disputes.

A second challenge for both communes and administrators was that the new laws again raised the question of the relation between the land and the administrative communes (zemel'noe and sel'skoe obshchestva). Developments over the previous half-century had favored a merging of the two; the rights to claim possession of land in one derived from the obligations borne in the other. The new legislation, while seeking to uncouple land from administrative functions, did so imperfectly. Most notably, the village society lost control over how householders could use or dispose of land; the result was that, although the village society was still responsible for local welfare, it could no longer control the flow of requests for support. This incongruity quickly became a leitmotif of petitions against titling. The fear that "masses" of impoverished compatriots would now overwhelm the village society with requests for support distilled many of the anxieties that the new property laws awakened—fears of landlessness, of impoverishment, of insecurity, of losses never to be recouped, and of neighbors who would be better able to take advantage of the new laws. Complaints about abusive welfare claims took on a symbolic and rhetorical importance that authorities were loath to recognize, even as the issue became a stand-in for much that peasants deemed to be unfair about the reforms.

Finally, the property reforms challenged existing definitions of communal membership. There was hardly a village that was not confronted with the issue of land tenure by individual households who filed—or who could potentially file—for title. Even a cursory look at the list of cases heard by land captains and provincial boards reveals sharp divisions within villages when it came to deciding who had a legitimate claim to hold (let alone request title to) a share of communal land. Administrative authorities after 1906 were showered with appeals from peasants who had been refused an allotment by their commune, or whose allotment had been taken from them. More broadly at issue was the definition of what it took to be a member of the commune with full claim rights to allotment land. The reforms greatly weakened the means by which communes could deal with unusual circumstances, namely the claims of marginal members whose rights to land had been fragile and conditional. The legislation provided minimal guidance for dealing with the resulting problems, and as had earlier been the case, solutions had to be improvised, tested, and adjusted through countless ministerial explanations, Senate rulings, and gubernatorial circulars. The resulting inconsistencies and shifts in policies on ostensibly peripheral issues created a host of new grievances but did not establish a legal, normative, or institutional framework to address them.

Tenure Changes and the Commune

In early 1914 a group of villagers petitioned Nicholas II to complain about the losses they were allegedly suffering at the hands of a small group wishing to separate from the commune: "We live far from towns, railroads, factories; we survive only from agriculture, but we managed to build a church. . . . All was well and we were happy. Then in November 1912 everything fell apart. Seven malefactors showed up—artisans and city-folk—and asked to separate [their land] with the goal of putting it on the market."[6] The image of pre-reform idyll, that "all was peaceful before," was a stock phrase in petitions after 1906. Obviously, this was a rhetorical device; neighborly bickering, insulting, and suing had long been very much part of village life. What peasants were expressing was a perception that their intensity was now greater. The rules governing land disputes had dramatically changed: the stakes were much higher, the risks associated with losing were acute, and the mechanisms of conciliation were weakened.

Although changes in property laws were secondary to the government's goal of improving agricultural efficiency through land reorganization, they are central to understanding villagers' reactions to the agrarian reforms as a whole. Titling by individual households was the 1906 legislation's most widely used provision.[7] Villagers' attitudes to the titling of land must be understood in light of the evolution of redistributional practices over the previous decades. Any head of household registered in the commune had retained a right to claim land according to the number of "souls" in the household. The entire system had rested on the confidence that any land lost could be recouped if the household again grew—that land would be taken from the dead to give to the living, as peasants frequently expressed it. The transfer of land from communal to "personal" property threatened this fundamental logic in a variety of ways, according to the motives of those requesting title. As had been the case prior to 1906, it was not the tensions between rich and poor that were the greatest, but tensions between young and old, male and female heads of household, and residents and returning migrant workers (otkhodniki).

The group most often mentioned by critics of the land reform as disruptive to village peace were the mnogodushniki. These households—those that had lost members since the last general repartition and therefore held more "souls" of land than would be warranted under a new redistribution—were among the first to petition for land titles to protect their holdings, an action that aroused the hostility of communes for the entire process of reform.[8] According to a famous 1910 survey conducted by the Free Economic Society (FES) in 183 communes of the Central Agricultural Region, 28 percent of the households titling land by 1911 succeeded in appropriating more land than their family size would have warranted under the repartitional system.[9] These households were not necessarily those with the most land. Even in the first year of the reforms, the average holdings of households receiving title were smaller than those remaining within the commune, and the gap only widened in subsequent years.[10] In Riazan, for instance, in 60 percent of the villages where titles were granted within the first four months of the reforms, the new proprietors held more land than they would have received had their commune redistributed according to male souls. Nevertheless, titled households held an average of 6.5 desiatina of arable land, while those that remained within the commune retained 10.8. By 1916 the figures for the entire province stood at an estimated 3.5 and 5 desiatina, respectively.[11] Soviet historian S. M. Dubrovskii estimated that by 1916 approximately 22 percent of the empire's households titled 14 percent of communal land.[12] Those who titled, including the mnogodushniki, were frequently small and precarious households.

Many of the households that stood to lose the most during a general repartition were headed by unmarried women and widows without male children who had managed to hold onto one share of their father's or husband's allotment; these women risked losing all their household's land if the commune redistributed according to male souls. A request for legal title was a means of protecting holdings. The commune's opposition to these women's claims is easy to understand. Personal property was subtracted from the commune's land fund, reducing the amount of land remaining for redistribution. Even the withdrawal of the small widow's allotment from future redistributions threatened the integrity of the communal land fund just as surely as did a withdrawal by the largest households. Such withdrawals did not have to happen very frequently to feed the perception that communal land was being unfairly lost.[13]

More common than the *mnogodushniki* were households requesting titles in order to sell all or part of their allotment. In European Russia, this group represented approximately a third of all households separating from the commune, in Riazan between 35 and 45 percent.[14] Data collected by the Land Section of the Ministry of Internal Affairs for 1914 indicated that many sellers were simply liquidating their farm because of economic difficulties. Others sold out in order to migrate, or to transfer land to a family member. Only a minority sold land in order to "improve agriculture" (for instance, in order to buy land elsewhere). The largest category of sellers was absentees: these constituted nearly 40 percent of the Riazan households selling land in 1914.[15] In Tula between 1910 and 1912, slightly over a quarter of all land titles were issued to absentees, and nearly one-half of these subsequently sold their holdings. In contrast, only 4 percent of resident proprietors sold land. In eight central provinces, 37 percent of those selling in the first half of 1914 no longer farmed. In Novgorod, 25 percent of sales were undertaken by absentees, in Simbirsk, 52 percent.[16]

While any sale could potentially be a source of resentment, as the commune or one of its members found itself in effect buying back "its own" land, the claims of absentees created the most problems. As one zemstvo correspondent from Vladimir objected: "These are people who personally do not need the land."[17] The return of migrant workers to their villages had been a source of conflict ever since peasants had begun leaving for lengthy periods to work in cities. In many cases, a departing peasant had rented his allotment to a fellow villager, often for a nominal fee; the latter would understandably be loath to give it up. Requests to reclaim land that had been left to the disposition of the commune could also have far-reaching consequences. Resident households that had been granted use of an absentee's allotment might—should they lose this land—have to be accommodated elsewhere. The claims of absentees, therefore, could on occasion feed renewed talk of repartition. The new threat that returnees could now not only reclaim land but also sell it only exacerbated these tensions.

Publicists reported that the 9 November decree precipitated a virtual flood of requests for land titles by absentees. Factory workers and migrants to Siberia, who had been all but forgotten in their native villages, having left ten, twenty, or even thirty years earlier, suddenly remembered land once held by them or by their fathers. "Absentees now try with all their strength to get back land in order to sell," wrote one FES respondent from Tula. "They expend time and their last means on all these useless attempts, providing income for unscrupulous illegal advocates."[18] It was no coincidence that well over a quarter of the letters requesting legal advice from the semi-official newspaper Sel'skii vestnik inquired whether allotment land given up to the commune could be titled and sold.[19]

The sale of allotment land created additional resentments when the purchaser was an outsider to the village. Although allotment land still could not be sold to a non-peasant and no individual could buy more than six shares, the legislation implied that the purchaser was also buying the right to use a share of common resources (pasture land, woods, and so on).[20] The commune thus lost some of its discretionary power to accept or refuse new members, a power that had been doggedly defended even in communes under hereditary household tenure, as in the case of Verkhne-Beloomut.

Hostility toward sales is well illustrated by events in the large commune of Izhevskoe (Riazan, Spassk district). By 1913 an increasing number of lots had fallen into the hands of outsiders. Although land held by outsiders amounted only to 200 of 5,200 shares, rumors began to circulate that a redistribution would soon reclaim land from purchasers.[21] Izhevskoe was under hereditary household tenure, so any redistribution that changed the quantity of land held by each household would have been illegal. Contrary to the assumption that the new laws permitting title changes barely affected villages already under hereditary household tenure (or even for that matter redistributional communes that had never repartitioned), they in fact undermined the means that had allowed communes to find a modus vivendi with non-native owners. The result, rather ironically, given the legislation's goal of strengthening hereditary tenure, was at times a resurgence of debate over the advantages of communal principles.

It is very difficult to know how often outsiders effectively bought into communes, as the MVD began collecting detailed data on transactions in allotment land only in 1914. That year, approximately a quarter of purchasers in the Riazan districts of Spassk and Riazhsk were from outside the village.[22] But even resident purchasers were not necessarily insiders to the commune. Historian M. S. Simonova found that in Voronezh 37 percent of allotment land sold was bought by landless peasants. Some of these landless villagers undoubtedly already held a household plot and were therefore administratively part of the community. But in most communes, possession of a household plot did not in itself give access to the commons. As one Riazan resolution explained: the commune "never received any dues from them and does not have anything in common with them."[23] In addition, a number of the landless purchasers were undeniably complete outsiders, tavern-keepers, petty merchants, or shopkeepers registered in the volost, who were not even members of the village society. Although correspondents to the FES indicated that some communes sought to restrict sales to outsiders or to buy up land, communes were in fact rarely able to come up with the money necessary to buy the land of departing villagers.[24] Ultimately, villagers' ability to prevent the influx of outsiders was severely restricted.

The sale of allotment land also potentially intensified discord within households. The enormous powers of the household head had hitherto, except under exceptional circumstances, not included the power to disinherit his children. According to a Nizhnii-Novgorod report, in 1910 nearly 10 percent of all administrative cases resulting from the land reforms consisted of disputes among family members over the title of head of household, who under the new regulations would have the sole power to request title and dispose of household property. A household head could brandish the threat of titling to maintain control over disgruntled sons, threatening to transfer the property to another relative of his choice. In fact, 9.7 percent of the sales completed in Riazan in 1914 were undertaken precisely in order to transfer property to relatives.[25] Wives or children on occasion sought to block a title by having themselves named as tutors of the household property on the grounds that the head of household was a squanderer (rastochitel'). The rather cumbersome procedure in place until 1911, requiring a preliminary investigation by the governor's office, which then transferred the request for review by the assembly, was by all accounts increasingly undertaken after 1906. Absentee sons complained that their father's intentions to sell deprived them of the land for which they had paid by sending home earnings. Disgruntled wives also sometimes requested trusteeship over their allegedly drunken or wayward husbands. The authorities repeatedly had to remind petitioners that the desire to sell allotment land was not in itself a proof of squandering, although it is doubtful that this was of any comfort to the petitioners. As one frustrated wife exclaimed: "If one agrees [with that view], then trusteeship can only be established over people who already have nothing."[26]

Junior family members intent on preventing titling and sale sometimes found support in the village assembly. Villagers worried about finding themselves responsible for an impoverished compatriot (or his children) who had so improvidently sold off his last means of livelihood. Izhevskoe villagers claimed to be distressed at the increasingly frequent reappearance of children of landless migrants who got "used to the easy-going (veselaia) life" and drank up the proceeds from a land sale. The assembly even passed an illegal resolution forbidding households to dispose of their last piece of land. Respondents to the FES study explained that they feared the rise of village mendicity, and that the sellers would drink up their money and become a burden on the commune.[27] Even after jurisdiction for trusteeship had been transferred to the volost courts in 1911, the assembly could be a decisive witness testifying for the side deemed least likely to sell.

Communal opposition to land sales fed into long-standing concerns about the moral qualities and seriousness of peasant-workers. A word pop-

ularly used to designate a migrant worker chasing after higher wages—
letun (flier)—could have ambivalent connotations, suggesting not only the
freedoms associated with city life but also the dangers of instability and
rootlessness. As a peasant from the southern district of Ranenburg explained: "The new law is bad for many peasants. Since they have received
the right to sell their land, the head of household as well as all his descendants end up as poor landless peasants *(bobyly bezzemel'nye)*, incapable of
any other profession besides agriculture."[28] Correspondents from Vladimir
province expressed similar misgivings: "The young generation will be
landless," they said. "Where are [the sellers] going to settle their sons?"[29]
Such apprehensions occasionally found a sympathetic hearing with
provincial officials. A Riazan report to the MVD on hooliganism claimed
that the land reforms contributed to disorder in the countryside by allowing peasants to sell their land and drink up the proceeds, thus allowing
parents to disinherit their children.[30] The image of an uprooted, landless,
and denatured peasantry threatening the social and moral order, which
had been an important part of the ideology of the land captain reforms,
remained a powerful one.

Peasants' fears that they would be overwhelmed by mendicants exacerbated long-standing conflicts with authorities over communal welfare. By
reducing the powers of the commune to control the economic actions of
its members, the 1906 law threatened to further undermine local control
over welfare expenditures. The village of Ulitino (Moscow), for instance,
protested one widow's request for land title on the grounds that "she
[would] sell it and then request aid for the sick and elderly."[31] Bitter battles erupted in assemblies over what to do with indigent landless peasants.
Some communes felt that whoever bought their land should be responsible for putting them up, while some recommended rotating the obligation. Most, however, felt that a seller's own irresponsibility excluded him
from the village and from the right to demand support. As one commune complained: "We weren't asked [our opinion] when this new law
was set up."[32] The commune of Baichits (Riazan, Mikhailov district) vo-
ciferously refused to provide aid to a returning widow on the grounds
that the rising number of landless peasants rendered the old law on
communal welfare obsolete. In a petition to the provincial board, the
commune conceded that while this law might have made sense under
the regime of collective responsibility for taxes (abolished in 1903), this
was no longer the case after 1906:

> Many peasants have sold all their property and are registered in the com-
> mune only as numbers *(dlia scheta)*; now all these people reappear . . . and
> demand lodging and support. Should it really be expected that the commune
> give all these people support? No, such a situation can't be, and such a law
> can't exist. How could it be that government authorities, making a law allow-
> ing peasants to sell everything and thereby allowing them to be destitute, did
> not determine [that the volost or the district] should give them support?[33]

Yet, such a law did exist. A special meeting of Moscow land captains, called in 1910 by the governor to clarify and ensure the uniform application of the 9 November decree, identified the law on communal welfare as one of the main factors slowing the reforms and recommended its abrogation.[34] It was not repealed, however, and the MVD had to continually remind rural officials that the reform legislation did not in any way free communes from the obligation of providing support to their indigent members, whether or not the latter had received title. This policy only aggravated the sentiment of many longtime residents that the new laws were not only disruptive but unfair.

The 9 November decree also heightened the insecurity already felt by many migrant workers. Not all returnees were opportunistically trying to cash in on the new property laws: many continued to view their ties to their village as security in case of unemployment or illness. While all government observers and zemstvo statisticians concurred that the net flow of migration was into the cities, there was nonetheless a circular flow bringing some workers back to the village, especially in periods of economic downturn. In six Saratov volosts, 31 percent of peasant workers who had been absent in 1884 had returned by 1899. Likewise, in Viaz'ma district in Smolensk, 29.3 percent of the 1884 absentees were back in their villages in 1900.[35] Statements from peasant correspondents collected by the Moscow zemstvo in 1910 even suggested that while the number of peasants leaving for factory work in the city in search of "the easy life" was increasing, so was the return flow. As one villager summarized the situation: "Although peasants leave for outside work, they do not abandon their land, in spite of everything, considering it the provider (kormilitsei). . . . Many peasants throw aside their land and run off to the city, but after living there a little while, they don't make it, and they run back to the village. . . . Recently even more of these peasants have begun running back to the village." The result upon return was a "veritable scandal" over land.[36] One peasant correspondent from Simbirsk described the additional vulnerability felt by migrant workers with the introduction of the new laws:

> The goal of my attempt [to request title] was primarily to find out the mood of the commune and thus to let them know of my rights in case they all decided to take out titles. Now one has to fear that the entire commune will up and claim all the land as personal property, if not today, then tomorrow. After that, from where would I be able to receive land? These days the position of the worker is so unstable, that you don't know today what will be tomorrow. Just one denunciation or suspicion—and beat it! In the commune there already won't be any land, or you don't know whether there will be or not.[37]

Thus, not all absentees were motivated by a desire to liquidate their holdings. Some were moved, on the contrary, by the apprehension that their native land commune would melt away while they were not watching.

Numerous analysts—including some reform officials—observed that fear was a major factor driving the progress of titling. As the first households claimed title, they initiated a domino effect; overall communal holdings diminished, and the burden of accommodating returnees increased for those remaining in the commune. The incentive, therefore, was for villagers to file for title before too many absentees returned, and for absentees to claim land before there was none left. The commune thus found itself caught up in a headlong "race for land" as each sought to protect its continued access to land. The neo-populist publicist A. V. Peshekhonov even predicted that the process spelled the end of communal landholding, as ever-widening circles of peasants were drawn to claim their land as personal property in order to protect it.[38]

Peshekhonov's rather logical scenario for the demise of the redistributional land commune did not play itself out, however. The government's shift in emphasis after 1910 away from individual land titles toward whole village consolidation slowed the flow of defensive titling that had marked the first years of the reform. By then, many of the households most threatened by the loss of land had already requested title. As some reform officials also remarked, peasants in communes falling under article 1 of the 1910 law (which automatically converted to hereditary household tenure communes that had not repartitioned since Emancipation) came to realize that even without titles, their holdings could no longer be reduced.[39] In addition, again contrary to Peshekhonov's predictions, short-term, or seasonal, migration had little impact on the progress of titling. In Riazan, for instance, the proportion of households separating from the commune was lowest in the districts with the highest overall levels of seasonal migration.[40] In spite of strong out-migration in the northernmost districts of Spassk and Kasimov, few households had abandoned agriculture completely. One FES respondent from Kasimov suggested that it was precisely the near universality of seasonal male migration that made titling unnecessary and consolidation impossible. How, he asked, could a *baba* alone be expected to take care of a separate farmstead?[41] Households engaged in seasonal migration could have a more defensive attitude toward communal tenure, a factor inhibiting the process of titling.

But the "race for land" did take over in certain localities. It was reported from regions of Moscow and Vladimir provinces where long-term migration was prevalent.[42] It was not so much the rate of out-migration that was important, but the degree to which these migrants had abandoned their ties to agriculture. In regions where long-term migration was prevalent, returnees could play a significant role in initiating a cascade of defensive titling, but this was a local phenomenon, statistically diluted in province and district level data. It would be only at the most local level that one could measure the effect of long-term migration on titling. Such data exist for one Riazan volost (Koz'modem'ianskoe, Riazhsk district) (see table 5-1). The volost was relatively homogeneous among its nineteen villages

TABLE 5-1

LONG-TERM MIGRATION AND LAND TITLES IN

KOZ'MODEM'IANSKOE VOLOST, RIAZAN PROVINCE (19 VILLAGES)

Proportion of households renting out entire allotment (1887)	Tax per *desiatina* (1887)	Land per worker (in *desiatiny*) (1887)	Households receiving title (1915)
low (mean = 8.4%) 6 villages	3.7	4.7	26%
mid (mean = 18.4%) 7 villages	3.9	3.5	32.5%
high (mean = 29.7%) 6 villages	3.7	3.8	48.2%

Source: GARO, f. 70, op. 15 (1916), d. 5.

in respect to tax levels, size of landholdings, and quality of land. The key variable affecting titling levels was long-term migration (as measured by the proportion of households that had been renting out their entire allotments in the late 1880s).[43] It is here, at the village level, that one can find the "race for land" so well described by many observers yet diluted in provincial level data.

The tensions examined thus far have been analyzed in terms of conflicting interests, and there was nothing particularly new either about the interests or the conflicts. Distrust of the intentions of returning workers, of the elderly and of widows, and of outsiders had all been integral to village politics for decades. What made these conflicts more acrimonious was the fact that losses could now be permanent. As long as land had remained the property of the commune, losing claims could remain alive, if in abeyance. A death, a departure, a shift in the balance of power, and especially a partial or general distribution, could reverse previous losses. By proposing to settle outstanding disputes once and for all, the new land legislation tended to bring these seething claims to the surface. The stakes were higher, exacerbating any number of anxieties: that fathers could dispossess their sons, that masses of landless compatriots would demand aid from the village society, that clever city folk would make abusive claims on communal resources, that land would go to outsiders. If prereform village relations were portrayed in peasant petitions as peaceful and happy, it was not because peasants had forgotten former disputes; it was because post-reform disputes were more acrimonious. And it was also because former mechanisms for resolving conflicting claims were largely incapacitated by the new laws, an issue to be examined in the rest of this chapter.

COMMUNAL LAND REDISTRIBUTIONS AFTER 1906

In villages where individual title claims were perceived as threats to communal property and finances, assemblies had other ways of protecting themselves against the 9 November legislation besides defensive titling. One means, in theory, was through a general redistribution of land according to "present souls," whereby allotments of formerly large households, of widows, and of absentees could be removed to reduce incentives to apply for title. Numerous commentators noted that a wave of defensive redistributions swept the central provinces in 1907–1908, and most historians agree that these became an important tool in the commune's arsenal of defense against the reforms.[44] What is striking about this "redistributional fever," however, is that it in fact translated into many attempts, but few successes. One effect of the new legislation was to bring redistributions to a virtual halt. But while some reform officials were quick to celebrate the apparent ease and speed with which *peredely* declined and even some analysts hostile to the reforms declared the commune "moribund," the growing difficulty of conducting redistributions did not necessarily signal the end of the desire to do so. The obstacles to repartition could violate the notion—earlier reinforced by the government itself—that land was the property of the commune available to those who had carried the burden of redemption and local dues, and who needed it to live. The decline of repartitions did not mark the end of disputes, but disputes now had to be addressed by other means.

The extent to which communes could (or would wish to) proceed with general land repartitions would depend in part on the extent to which they had conducted *peredely* prior to 1906. While the 1905 land survey indicated that 95 percent of land communes in twenty-nine Russian provinces of European Russia were still legally classified under communal tenure, not all of these had in fact availed themselves of the right to readjust holdings. Communes in which households still held land according to "revision souls" found themselves de facto under hereditary tenure. According to the MVD, these constituted a majority. The ministry in 1910 had asked provincial boards to compile data in view of applying article 1 of the 14 June 1910 law, which provided for the automatic conversion from communal to hereditary household tenure when a commune had not undertaken a general redistribution since lands were allotted at Emancipation.

The new legal status of these communes meant that they could no longer legally repartition. Article 1 simplified the task of issuing titles, through a simple process of certification. It also meant that, should just one household receive title, then all households in the commune would be reclassified under personal ownership, and only half of all households (rather than three-quarters for villages still under communal tenure) could force village-wide consolidation. The MVD's figures reported that 58 percent of communes in forty provinces of European Russia had not undertaken a general repartition since Emancipation. (These encompassed only about a third of all households, however, given that larger communes were most likely to repartition.) Some historians have concluded from this that even prior to 1906, peasants had been rejecting the repartitional commune and thereby preparing the path for individual tenure and the Stolypin reforms.[45]

The MVD's 1910 data are problematic, however. They contradict almost every other major study on the question. The ministry's own earlier data, published in 1905, indicated that nearly three-quarters of land communes in twenty-eight central provinces had conducted *peredely* in the previous twenty-five years.[46] These figures are quite close to those reported by Karl Kachorovskii on the basis of zemstvo surveys of some 74,000 communes. Kachorovskii calculated that 71 percent of communes (encompassing 80% of surveyed households) had conducted general or partial redistributions. While, according to the MVD's 1910 survey, 77.3 percent of Tver's communes fell under article 1, zemstvo studies from the 1890s found that only 41 percent still held land according to revision souls.[47] And, in the 1880s, even before a well-documented wave of repartitions swept the province's southern black earth districts, the Riazan zemstvo had identified as many repartitional communes as the provincial board would report after 1910.

A closer look at the Riazan data can help identify some of the reasons for the discrepancies between the MVD and the zemstvo data and allow a rough estimate of their relative accuracy. One glaring disparity is that many more communes in the northern districts of Egorevsk, Kasimov, and Spassk were classified as redistributional in the 1880s than in the Stolypin period (see table 5-2, columns 1 and 3). Government and zemstvo statisticians were not always counting the same thing. Zemstvo data included communes practicing distributions by "revision souls," whereby the land of extinct households could be reallotted to newly formed households; the location or disposition of allotments was changed, but not the overall number of shares held—and paid for—by each household. The problem is that it is impossible to know the precise number of this type of "qualitative" (as opposed to "quantitative") repartition. Zemstvo reports combined them with redistributions by "miscellaneous other criteria" (notably the household's economic strength). Together, this broad category accounted for a third of the province's *peredely,* and almost all were concentrated precisely in the three northern districts. This was a region of poor land and high out-migration, where it was common to distribute according to ability to pay, which did change the number of shares held by each household (and therefore uncoupled redemption payments from individual holdings). The zemstvo data thus overstated the prevalence of quantitative redistributions in the province's northern districts, but not by enough to account for the incongruence with the MVD's 1910 data.

Neither of the two compilations, on the other hand, included partial redistributions *(skidki-nakidki, svalki-navalki)* in their totals. The choice to include *skidki-nakidki* in data measuring the prevalence of redistributional activity would not be unwarranted, for the adjustment of holdings among individual households could postpone the need for general redistributions and often reflected similar attitudes toward communal holdings. The commune of Orekhovo, for example, explained that *skidki-nakidki* had been conducted annually "from time immemorial according to the needs of peasant families [depending on] which families need to obtain means to live, on whether land taxes are a burden, etc."[48] If zemstvo figures are readjusted to include partial redistributions but to exclude three-quarters of the category *"peredely* by revision souls and miscellaneous criteria"—a very rough but cautious estimate—then 33 percent of the province's communes were redistributional, close to the MVD's finding of 35 percent two decades later (see table 5-2, column 2). Yet, as of the 1880s, redistributions had barely begun in the province's southern districts. The MVD's assertion that two-thirds of Riazan's communes had not undertaken a general repartition since land had been allotted after Emancipation was thus highly dubious. In fact, over three-quarters of households of Riazan province lived in communes in which there had been at least one redistribution since Emancipation.

One reason for the MVD's inflated results was that the forms provided in 1910 to volost clerks and land captains for reporting communal activities gave the strictest possible definition of redistribution, excluding both qualitative and partial redistributions. In addition, some local officials interpreted the phrase "since land was allotted" to mean "in twenty-four years," an error widespread enough that it has been repeated by otherwise meticulous historians.[49] The land captains' method of compiling data was ill-designed for accurate reporting of an activity that frequently left no written record. Upon receiving orders to report on redistributions, many volost clerks merely consulted the notoriously incomplete registers of village resolutions. Some communes had undertaken illegal—consequently unrecorded—redistributions before 1906 precisely so as to avoid administrative interference. The law of 8 June 1893 stipulated that repartitions should not occur at less than twelve-year intervals and forbade partial redistributions altogether. The ease with which these restrictions had been simply ignored is evident from data collected in Vladimir indicating that 38 percent of the province's communes conducted illegal adjustments. In Saratov, 30 percent of communes conducted partial distributions in the

TABLE 5-2

PERCENTAGES OF COMMUNES CONDUCTING REDISTRIBUTIONS

SINCE EMANCIPATION (RIAZAN PROVINCE)

District (north to south)	1880s (zemstvo studies)	1880s adjusted	1911 (MVD data)	1911: percent of households in repartitional communes (MVD)
Egorevsk	72	49	51	67
Kasimov	61	57	40	56
Spassk	42	41	31	65
Riazan	5	n.d.	32	53
Zaraisk	11	14	6	4
Pronsk	14	19	19	59
Skopin	n.d.	n.d.	38	94
Mikhailov	42	46	70	91
Sapozhok	28	33	30	60
Riazhsk	16	21	19	37
Dankov	9	15	37	49
Ranenburg	4	12	61	83
Province	33	33	35	65

Sources: Italics indicate incomplete data: For 1911, 15% of communes are missing for Skopin, 8% for Ranenburg. For the 1880s: 48% of Riazan district communes were unstudied, 15% in Pronsk, 12% in Sapozhok. Figures for 1911 are compiled from GARO, f. 695, op. 21 (1911), d. 12, ll. 123–25; f. 695, op. 23 (1913), d. 13, l. 1; RGIA, f. 1291, op. 121 (1916), d. 4. Zemstvo data for 1880s are from Selivanov, 89–90, 120; Riazanskoe gubernskoe zemstvo, *Sbornik statisticheskikh svedenii*, vol.1, *Riazanskii uezd*, 22–23.

1890s, and 16 percent did the same in the next decade. Overworked land captains tended to turn a blind eye to partial redistributions. In Vladimir, interventions aimed at enforcing the 1893 law affected fewer than 5 percent of all communes.[50] In short, a considerable proportion of the communes' repartitional activities occurred without official sanction and without leaving a paper trail.

It was also not uncommon for communes to conduct illegal general repartitions. In the Moscow volost of Iagunino (Zvenigorod district), for instance, only three of the twenty-nine villages conducting *peredely* prior to 1906 did so with the sanction of a recorded and confirmed village resolution. In Vladimir, repartitions overturned by land captains were carried out nonetheless.[51] The situation was much the same in Riazan. The commune of Semkina (Riazan district) had gone so far as to pass a fictitious resolution in 1870 transferring to hereditary household tenure in order to avoid the application of the law on collective responsibility for taxes. Meanwhile, the village had conducted three unsanctioned and unrecorded general redistributions. Such situations would only be discovered by the authorities after the 9 November legislation drove communes to try to secure repartitions in writing so as to avoid claims according to former, now fictitious, holdings. More irregularities emerged in the wake of the 1910 law, when one household applied for a certification of personal ownership and thereby initiated the process of officially introducing hereditary household tenure for the entire commune. It should be noted that the Riazan district zemstvo published a detailed description of Semkina and its fictitious resolution in 1882, along with descriptions of several other analogous villages.[52] The zemstvo methods of investigation, which consisted of sending out investigators to gather assemblies and question villagers, were more apt to give an accurate picture of communal redistributional practices than the provincial board's reliance on volost records.

What is clear is that manifestations of communal landholding went far beyond what a strict count of recorded general repartitions would indicate. The MVD figures were intended to provide the basis for the broadest possible application of the 14 June 1910 law, but they reflected much wishful thinking. Within months of publication of the law, even the MVD recognized the futility of taking a purely legalistic approach to determining a commune's status. The minister instructed provincial officials not to include under article 1 communes that had conducted illegal or unrecorded repartitions, "the goal of the law not being the forceful destruction of the commune, but only the strengthening of hereditary tenure where it has appeared." By 1911 the MVD was even more cautious, recommending that provincial authorities further exempt communes that had undertaken qualitative *peredely,* since such distributions also often served to equalize holdings among households.[53]

The MVD's willingness to recognize the validity of unrecorded repartitions solved only one problem, however. According to Sergei Matveev, the 1906 decree had brought immediate confusion and tension to his Samara volost, as actual holdings rarely coincided with what was recorded on paper. In spite of the restrictions on partial redistributions imposed by the 1893 law, some communes had continued to adjust holdings annually. In addition, again contrary to legislation, land had rarely been distributed according to clearly defined norms but instead had balanced the work capacity of the household with its consumer needs. As a result, the most recent *peredely,* conducted prior to the introduction of the new laws, had been rejected by the district congress. But by the time the redistributions were invalidated, they had already been carried out and the overturned resolutions simply forgotten. When a few enterprising peasants then applied for title, the fact that actual holdings were not legally recognized suddenly became vitally important. Some of the households that had lost land went to court to try to regain it, while those who feared losing land rushed to title it. Assemblies gathered to conduct new redistributions in an effort to prevent titling on holdings that existed only on paper. As always, such efforts quickly led to lengthy arguments, and as usual, the first meetings drifted into the streets until the quorum was lost. But by then, each party knew where he stood, and at the end of the meeting, those who had the most to lose came back in and presented requests for title. Even if this group was small, its action ended all discussion, as the very purpose of redistribution had by then been defeated. And there the matter ended in village after village.[54]

Matveev's account fits poorly with the assumption that villagers were able to use the redistribution mechanism to defend against the new laws. P. N. Zyrianov, the historian who has studied the issue most closely, argues that a wave of repartitions followed the announcement of the 9 November decree, as communes hurried to remove allotments from households that held more than their share. Zyrianov's analysis suggests a vitality of communal land practices that survived the disruptions of the reforms. The problem is that he gives little sense of how post-1906 repartitional activity compared to what had been happening before. It is possible to do this, however, for the one complete data set he presents, that of Bogorodsk district in Moscow province. This was the most actively redistributional district of the province, and according to the provincial board, only 65 of the district's 412 communes potentially fell under article 1 of the 14 June 1910 law. At the pre-reform rate, one could expect as many as 230 (56%) of the district's communes to undertake a redistribution over the course of the eight peacetime years following the 9 November decree. Yet Zyrianov found that 110 communes (26.7%) passed redistribution resolutions between 1907 and 1914, and that half of these were overturned by the authorities.[55] That is, only a quarter of the communes that could be expected to redistribute at the pre-reform rate in fact successfully did so after 1906. The contrast is even more striking if one compares the seven resolutions per year approved between 1907 and 1914 with the fifty-three general repartitions of arable land conducted annually between 1858 and 1878.[56] Far from a flurry of redistributional activity, one sees a dramatic drop.

Riazan province also saw a decline in general redistributions after 1906. In 1908, 106 assembly resolutions falling under the 8 June 1893 law were presented to the district congresses that were supposed to review all *peredely*. Even assuming that all of these concerned general redistributions (which they did not, as some related to the removal of allotments from individual households), this is fewer than one could expect in a pre-reform year. Communes in Riazan at the turn of the century redistributed land on average every 13.6 years. Assuming that just 35 percent of the province's communes were redistributional (which was the provincial board's low estimate), then one could expect as many as 142 redistributions annually. In Ranenburg district alone, there had been 27 redistributions a year between 1900 and 1902.[57] Yet, by 1913, only 35 redistribution resolutions were presented to the authorities province-wide, 45 in 1914, and a mere 18 in 1915—and of these a third were overturned by the authorities.[58] It is possible that communes continued to practice illegal redistributions, but this was much less likely to happen than before 1906, for unless a resolution was duly reviewed and approved, any household that lost land could request title according to the last registered record of the village's landholding arrangement. The records from Moscow and Riazan suggest, in accordance to Matveev's testimony, that if redistributions were much discussed, they stalled in many communes during the period of the agrarian reforms.

Further local studies will be necessary to learn whether these conclusions can be extended to European Russia as a whole. The trend is hardly surprising, however, for the option of requesting a title for allotment land changed the politics of general redistributions. Opponents to a *peredel* now had an important new weapon to avoid losing land, as a request for land title could be filed any time up to the day the vote passed in the assembly. They also had greater incentive, because any losses could now prove to be permanent. Since land redistributions were never snap decisions but gave rise to debate, negotiation, and posturing that could sometimes last for years, opponents had plenty of time to request titles.[59]

Communes wishing to repartition also faced administrative obstacles, in spite of instructions from the center to let communes die a natural death. When some governors exhorted land captains to keep track of rumors of land redistributions in their districts so that they could identify possible malcontents who could be persuaded to request land titles, the MVD frowned on the practice. The ministry in 1909 instructed that "instead of facilitating the transition from communal to individual tenure, [repartition] can, on the contrary, encourage the further retention of communal forms of landholding." Inspectors reprimanded land captains in Ekaterinoslavl, Voronezh, and Saratov for their tolerant attitudes toward *peredely*.[60] It is hardly surprising, therefore, that provincial boards frequently overturned resolutions. In Riazan, 60 percent of general repartitions, from a random sample of eighty-seven for the period from 1907 to 1914, were overturned. In 1914 over half of the resolutions presented for confirmation in thirty-five provinces were annulled.[61]

But did the wane of repartitions mean that the commune was moribund? If what is being measured is the ability of the government to change the way peasants acted, then the answer is probably yes. Whether peasants were applying for title in order to embrace reform or to defend against it, in the long run the result in both cases was to upset customary practices and to facilitate sales and land reorganization. But if one is gauging peasant attitudes, especially in the short term, then the answer is not so straightforward.

The end of redistributions could be resented as highly unfair. The cancellation of redemption dues after January 1907 had further strengthened the notion that land was due in return for past payments.[62] When a village had conducted land redistributions after Emancipation, redemption payments were grounds for rejecting a transfer to hereditary household tenure. If one household had lost some of its land because of a temporary reduction of its size, or the temporary departure of a member, it then could no longer expect an adjustment when the family grew again. "That means," explained a correspondent to the newspaper *Sel'skii vestnik*, "that he paid off the land for someone else, while he himself must sit impoverished without land."[63] The village of Semkina, for example, appealed the district authorities' refusal to confirm its redistribution in 1907, asking:

> How could we now possibly go to household tenure, when we have paid off the land all together *(smesheno vsem obshestvom)*? And to whom can we give the right amount of land? If we give Ivanov's household 7 *desiatina*, as is indicated in the 1870 resolution, Ivanov died 20 years ago. The land was then paid for by Stepanov, and after Stepanov for 10 years the Razanovs paid, and so on. And the same goes for the entire commune.[64]

The end of repartitions broke the logic underpinning the system of communal property, whereby loss of land could be accepted as the price of insurance. The question "To whom can we give the right amount of land?" was one that the new laws resolved, but in all too crude a fashion. The legislative "right amount" was whatever a household was using at the moment. This could be quite different from the "fair amount," a concept that was eminently local and depended on the specific histories of each commune and each household.

Given the enormous stakes involved, local fights over repartition reached a level of complexity and acrimony rarely seen in the 1880s and 1890s. The seventy-two opponents of a *peredel* in a commune of Ranenburg district asserted bluntly that "with the decree of 9 November 1906 all land became property, and property is sacred *(sobstvennost' Sviata)* and unalienable."[65] The opponents of a 1908 repartition in Dmitriveka (Egorevsk) protested that repartition was entirely unfair: "We had more land when dues were high. . . . It is impossible to equate us with those peasants who are receiving land only now and who participated in redemption either indirectly or in insignificant amount." They added ominously that should this "illegal resolution be implemented, there could be disorders in [their] commune."[66] In another village, the supporters of repartition blamed their opponents for the local disarray: "Everything is all in a mess, there are arguments, even fights and then court cases and arrests."[67] Whereas the commune of Gavrilovskoe (Spassk district) had repartitioned without complaints in 1896 and the resolution had been confirmed within a month, the 1908 repartition immediately gave rise to no fewer than four appeals requiring five hearings at the district congress. These cases took a year and a half to work their way through the administrative system, and further appeals were filed as late as 1913 and 1915.[68] Finality in the outcomes of disputes was rare; some losing parties continued to appeal even years after repartitions had been confirmed or rejected.

Any solution was likely to leave simmering resentments. If a commune repartitioned without protests and individuals subsequently applied for title on their new holdings, then complaints that "land was taken from those who paid to give to those who did not" could appear on the land captain's desk. If a commune that had not partitioned since Emancipation succeeded in doing so despite all the odds between 1907 and 1909, the opponents were likely to revive their efforts to return to "revision souls" after the 1910 law suggested that had they only held out a few more years, their commune could never have repartitioned. Households that had taken out titles merely to protect their holdings tearfully begged authorities to allow them back into the commune when they found themselves forced onto consolidated plots (a right that communes received with the 1910 law). Majorities that had failed in their bid to repartition did not give up but repeatedly submitted bitter appeals to local authorities.[69] In short, there was hardly a solution that was not liable to create a constituency of discontent.

What is remarkable, given the extent of administrative and tactical obstacles, is that any repartition proposals at all managed to gather the necessary two-thirds majority. Those that did tended to bristle with restrictive clauses designed to ensure that conditional allotments could not be transformed into personal property. One Moscow commune, for example, specified that no absentee could receive land unless he either had a building in the village or filled one of the village society's obligatory offices. Any person from outside the commune who was taken into a home—such as an in-marrying son-in-law—could never receive land (only rent it), a stipulation that ensured that an outsider would not receive an allotment upon the death of the head of household into which he was taken.[70] Other communes added a number of other restrictions: that the commune reserved the right to adjust holdings every three (or six) years; that when an allotment was abandoned it was being forsaken "forever"; or that no household could request a land title until the next redistribution.[71] As the consequences increased of allotting land to marginal members—to a precarious household or to someone who was not firmly implanted in the village—communes became stricter in their allotment of land. But all these clauses and restrictions were illegal, and district congresses refused to confirm resolutions that contained them.

Even more remarkable is that it is still possible in this period to find *peredely* in which more than half of all households lost land.[72] The fact that this could still happen suggests that one cannot understand the social and cultural impact of the new property laws in terms of strategic behavior alone. The idea that communal land was the property of all households was strong enough that, in some rare cases, villagers were able to overcome fears of individual strategic maneuvering that the new legislation had exacerbated. In most villages, however, this did not happen. The new property laws opened the door to individual attempts to take advantage of new opportunities. The 1906 and 1910 laws had disabled one of the primary mechanisms by which local rivalries could be managed; they had torn down the framework within which peasants could argue over land. The attendant rivalries, tensions, and distrust made it virtually impossible for the village to mount a united opposition to the reforms. Peasants had to find other means to settle their differences, and these means required intervention from outside authorities.

ARGUING CLAIM RIGHTS AND PROPERTY RIGHTS
BEFORE THE AUTHORITIES

In 1915 a widow from Moscow's Bogorodsk district complained to the district congress that her village society was refusing to return to her one share of allotment land that it had removed ten years earlier. In 1905, with her husband recently deceased and two sons serving in the Russo-Japanese War, she had requested to be temporarily relieved of one share of land for which she was no longer able to pay taxes. The village society did not contest the facts of the case: it agreed that "according to custom" the allotment should have been restituted upon the sons' return from military service. The problem, it claimed, was that for some time there had been no free land in the village; the Krutovs would have to wait either for an allotment to free up or for a general repartition. Under the new laws, both scenarios were highly unlikely, which explains Krutova's rather desperate pleas. Could it really be, she asked, that "the village society, in the guise of doing me a favor, in fact took away my land forever?" The district congress's answer to that question was yes: Krutova herself had agreed to the removal, the assembly had properly voted and signed the resolution, and the widow had passed the ten-year statute of limitations for appealing it. Krutova raged at the formalism of the decision:

> It is possible according to the articles of law to turn down my complaint; it is something else altogether if this affair is examined according to substance. In 1905, two sons were off at war with Japan. These sons are now again off at war. . . . When my sons returned, the society refused to return land for which we had paid for 42 years, saying that I myself had agreed to the removal. Is it really possible that I would have preferred to gift land to the commune and deprive my own children of a piece of bread, all while they, sparing neither health nor life, fulfill their sacred duty toward faith, the Tsar, and the fatherland?[73]

Krutova conceded that the ruling was formally correct, but not that it was just. Rarely did petitioners so explicitly express disillusionment about the law. What this case had in common with thousands of others, however, was threefold: the persistence of the petitioner, the expressed fear that losses would be "forever," and the disjunction between the arguments advanced on appeal and the grounds of the administrative ruling. Krutova's predicament was an indirect result of the property reforms, and her case was typical of the types of conflict that existing laws, procedures, and regulations were ill-suited to address.

The decline of repartitions did not end the practice of removing allotments from some households *(otobranie zemli)*, or of refusing to allocate land to others *(nenadelenie zemli)*. Slighted villagers had little choice but to solicit intervention from the authorities. The Nizhnii-Novgorod governor, for example, reported that by 1910, cases of land alienation constituted nearly 20 percent of the district congress caseload relating to the 9 November decree. Penza authorities calculated similar proportions, adding that the caseload had doubled between 1908 and 1910. Cases of unfair land transfers were the most common complaints against communes to be heard by the district congresses of Riazan's southern black earth district of Riazhsk and of the northern district of Spassk.[74] Prominent among these were appeals by absentees, not only city dwellers who had left decades earlier but also soldiers, members of households that remained in the village, and workers who wished to return.

Disputes between communes and absentees were difficult for authorities to deal with. Gaps in the legislation easily allowed alternative interpretations as to who retained rights to communal land. The 9 November decree itself specified only that the head of each household with a holding in the commune had the right to title his or her share of allotment land. But who among the absentees in fact still had a holding? The issue had to be resolved through Senate rulings, MVD circulars, and administrative practice—and these were frequently in conflict.

The Senate continued to defend the right of peasant workers to return to their commune of origin, ruling repeatedly that resolutions on land redistribution had to list absentees, with the amount of land to which they were entitled, according to the same criteria used for resident villagers. Upon their return, the commune was then obliged to provide these absentees with their share of land. Senate rulings created a dilemma for the MVD: allowing the right of return might strengthen claim rights—in other words, communal principles. It might also encourage profiteering by workers with no real interest in the land. Yet disallowing absentee claims could worsen landlessness and impoverishment. The ministry quickly issued official clarifications to provide some protection against abuse by returnees. It specified that land could be claimed as personal property only if it was in the "actual use" *(fakticheskoe pol'zovanie)* of the petitioner, and only if the petitioner could claim residency *(osedlost')* in the village.[75] A peasant-worker who wanted to receive title for his share of communal land had to go through two stages: first, prove that he had land in "actual use" in the village (or, if that failed, show that he was to be allotted land); then, request a land title.

There was also the problem of what to do with returnees when all or most households had transferred to hereditary household tenure. The MVD's solution was simple: if claims on titled land were allowed, then proprietors would still be bound by outstanding communal obligations. Accordingly, the ministry in 1907 instructed local authorities that in such cases absentees lost all their rights: if there was no commune, there could be no claims on it. A few months later, in an attempt to cover situations in which only some households had titled, the ministry advised that when a commune had no free communal allotments, then it should provide monetary compensation. Yet, the MVD did nothing to publicize its opinion. As late as 1912, when the Ufa provincial board requested guidance on the issue, the ministry responded only that difficulties of implementation should be referred to the volost courts.[76]

The reason for the MVD's discretion was simply that its instructions violated Senate rulings. The Senate ruled repeatedly that the 1906 and 1910 laws did not change or overturn rules set out in the General Statute regarding the mutual obligations between a village society and its members who had rights to use communal allotment land. Titled—even consolidated—households owed land to returning members. The MVD quite rightly pointed to the incongruity of village societies inheriting claims from dissolved land communes. As historian George Yaney has aptly noted, the "law did not evolve to the point where it guaranteed new property rights against traditional claims."[77] The ministry continued to file objections when pertinent cases came before the Senate, arguing that communal claim rights could exist only under communal tenure.[78] By 1917, however, the issue had still not been settled.

Given the conflicting messages coming out of St. Petersburg, the resolution of disputes was left to the discretion of local officials. But the rulings of these officials were highly inconsistent. In 1910, for example, the Riazan provincial board's permanent member instructed land captains that absent members had lost their right to request allotment and could only sue for compensation through the courts, but the same year, a conference of land captains in Moscow province concluded that if absentees had transferred use of their allotment through rent "or under other conditions," they could still claim "actual use."[79] Some district congresses and provincial boards gave up altogether any attempt to apply general principles, ruling on a case-by-case basis according to principles known only to themselves. Even the Riazan provincial board did not cleave to its own instructions. In March 1910, for instance, the board logically rejected the claims of a returnee on the grounds that since the petitioner did not conduct agriculture, he could not demand an allotment. The board took no notice of the absentee's argument that such a requirement was impossible: "I cannot conduct agriculture without land, so now [I face] the menace of remaining landless forever." But in July of the same year, the board accepted this last argument: an absentee could not be denied land on the grounds that he did not live in the village, as he could hardly do so without land.[80] The board at other times tried to guess intentions, rejecting petitioners who seemed to be claiming land "for the purposes of exploitation, and not for farming."[81] There were similar inconsistencies on the issue of what to do when the entire commune had titled. In late 1915 the board turned down a claim on the grounds that the commune had transferred to hereditary household tenure. Yet, in an analogous 1916 case, the board ruled that the transfer of a commune to hereditary tenure did not have any bearing on the case.[82]

With the stakes so high, such inconsistencies only intensified petitioners' strategic efforts to rally all possible legal, moral, and procedural arguments. They also decreased the likelihood that verdicts would resolve conflicts. It was not unknown for a single dispute over land alienation to rise up the ladder of appeal to arrive before the Senate three or even four times.[83] The increase in judicial appeal rates discussed in chapter three, as well as the rise in administrative caseloads, reflected a declining willingness on the part of appellants to accept authorities' rulings as final.

In the battles between returnees and communes, the latter had the distinct advantage. The gaps in the legislation allowed communes to define residency and actual use so as to undermine the claims of absentees. The first response by a commune faced with a request for land by an absentee was simply to deny that the latter had any land. Inquiries sent from Moscow and St. Petersburg to the Iagunino volost authorities (Moscow), asking who at that time was using "my land," invariably elicited curt replies to the effect that there was no land in the village, and "no one in the village remember[ed] if there ever was."[84] Volost authorities seemed to have great difficulty producing copies of past village resolutions and tax receipts. Even if the returnee had a written rental agreement, it could take considerable determination and a willingness to appeal all the way to the provincial board—even to the Senate—to overturn a village assembly's refusal to return an allotment.[85]

If the petitioner persisted in spite of the difficulties of obtaining necessary documentation, the assembly could pass a resolution declaring that there was no free land left in the village for the moment. Although communes were theoretically obliged to set aside shares for returnees, the amount of land reserved was always grossly inadequate, sufficient only for a handful of returns. If the lack of free allotments was substantiated, the land commune was freed from the obligation to allocate land until the next general repartition. Here, then, was yet another reason not to repartition. One St. Petersburg resident who had successfully sued his native Novgorod commune for land complained:

The proposal to wait for *peredel* is the same as refusing land, since repartition can be put off precisely in order . . . not to allot me any land, and I will completely be denied the possibility of ever receiving land in actual use. . . . The decision [of the district congress granting me land] is not difficult to implement: since there is a court decision, the role of the executive authorities is to get the commune somehow or other to return my land. . . . The proposal to receive money is patently unfair. . . . How can they offer me money, when I was granted land that I intend neither to sell nor dispose of?[86]

Even absentees who obtained administrative rulings technically in their favor could thus lose on substance.

Many of the conflicts between communes and returnees revolved around the question of who could claim the "actual use" of land that had been left in the care of a relative, or rented out to a fellow villager. While the MVD recognized that renting out allotment land constituted legitimate "actual use," rentals were often difficult to document, as city workers typically preferred to lease their land for long periods, receiving all the money up front without any written agreement. Young workers from the village of Pokrovskoe in southern Riazan, for instance, transferred the right to use their allotments for six to twelve years before going off to work in the Donets coal mines. In exchange, they received ten to fifteen rubles a year, and the renter agreed to pay all taxes and fees, and to fulfill natural obligations.[87] In instances where the renter was loath to give up the land he had held for so long, much depended on the testimony of most likely sympathetic villagers, and on the discretion, political preferences, and idiosyncratic interpretations of the land captain.

While communes were generally successful in excluding absentees who did not actually take steps to return to their village, they had a harder time when a claimant did go through the motions of resettling. According to Senate rulings, the commune was not obligated to allocate land to absentees "until their return and their acquisition of a farm." But, as many petitioners pointed out, the requirement that absentees return and resume agriculture before receiving allotment land was an almost insurmountable obstacle. How could they move to the village without at least assurances that they would receive allotment land? Yet, for the village, a petitioner's mere declaration of intent to return and take up agriculture was often met with skepticism. "He only wants land in order to sell" was a common phrase in communal refusals to allot land. The assembly of Aleksandrovka (Riazan, Sapozhok district) explained its refusal to grant twelve shares of land to a peasant who had left with his family for Siberia in spite of the fact that he had bought a house in the village: "Undertaking peasant agriculture consists of more than the simple purchase of a building. . . . Kuleshov is not capable, and in fact he does not want to sit tightly on his native land."[88] The commune's understanding of residency, based on close family ties, bearing the burden of communal obligations, and the conduct of agriculture, overrode the paper ties of rental agreements, passport registration, and tax receipts.

A dispute from Nikol'skaia Sloboda (Pronsk district), which dragged through all appeal instances for three years, deserves to be discussed at some length, for it illustrates many of the difficulties that daunted both peasants and officials. In 1913 one Petr Lavrenov complained to his land captain that, although he had purchased a household plot in his native village in order to return and take up agriculture, the commune had refused to give him his rightful share of allotment land. The commune responded that it did not have any land left. Upon investigation, the land captain discovered that the commune had conducted an illegal *peredel* in 1911 and redistributed all absentee land among remaining residents, and that most of these households had subsequently hurried to take out titles to their new holdings. The authorities faced an unpleasant choice: either they sanctioned an illegal repartition or they violated property rights.

The land captain and district congress each ruled that Lavrenov had met all conditions for a return to his village: if the requirement that a petitioner conduct agriculture was defined too strictly, absentees would never be able to return. In any case, it would be wrong to deny the petitioner land that had been removed on the basis of an illegal redistribution. On appeal, the commune countered that Lavrenov was not a resident, as he lived in the city of Pronsk (one kilometer from Nikol'skaia); nor could he conduct agriculture, since he was a blacksmith. The provincial board finally ruled in its favor, betraying a continued mistrust of the new commercialization of allotment land. Lavrenov had first to return to live in the village; the mere stated intention of conducting agriculture did not suffice, for "intentions cannot be verified and can easily be changed." The board added—in an interpretation of law permitted only by the Senate—that the law's emphasis on residency "clearly demonstrate[d] the law's intent to present land only to those who work it themselves while living in their village."[89] The highest instance of appeal of Riazan province had sided with the villagers' understanding of what it meant to be a peasant with claim rights to communal land, and this interpretation favored exclusion.

Peasants were obviously well aware of the ambiguities of legislation and the inconsistencies with which appeal instances ruled and rallied all the appropriate legal arguments available to them. But that does not mean that petitioners' behavior can be understood only in terms of opportunism. Their strategies took form within a legal, economic, and cultural framework grounded in lived local experience and past exposure to law, courts, and officials.[90] At the core of arguments over land were redemption payments. Thus, one Riazan commune howled in protest when the Ranenburg district congress allowed one Orekhov, a returnee, to claim land: "The commune has bought off this land, has carried the burden of all natural and monetary taxes; Orekhov has contributed neither payments nor taxes, and presented his request for land when it was already all paid for by the commune."[91] The very reasoning put forth by the State Council in 1893 to restrict rights of disposal on redeemed allotments—that peasants would redeem land for which neither they nor their forebears had paid—was precisely the argument most often invoked after 1906 to counter the claims of absentees.

Absentees, who were ostensibly making traditional claims of right to land (or "right to labor" according to Kachorovskii's formulation), also spoke of redemption. They argued that since land was paid off, it was now property—*sobstvennost'*. Considerations of usage and residency could not vitiate this basic fact. A peasant from southern Riazan who appealed his assembly's rejection of his title application, explained that "although I do not live in my native village and do not farm there, and the commune used my land until 9 November 1906, since the end of redemption payments the land has become the property of each member of the commune, and since it is property, then it is unconditional and each can use it as he wishes."[92] Peasants who were refused their initial petition for land and were turned down in their appeals to the land captain could go to considerable lengths to stake their claim. A peasant whose land had reverted to the commune after he had resettled in Siberia, for instance, complained that since he had paid off the redemption payment in its entirety, his commune of origin now was using his land "as if it was a renter."[93] Another sued his natal commune for thirty-one years of back-rent on the four shares of land his fellow villagers had used in his absence.[94]

At first sight, many such petitions smack of crass opportunism. Could the redemption payments of two or three decades earlier really affect the attitudes toward land of the sons and the grandsons of those who had paid? Again and again, peasants insisted that was the case. Even before 1906, claims could lie dormant for years and memories of losses and resentments be passed from generation to generation, only to resurface in court or administrative appeals years later. In addition, until the mid-1880s, conflicts had been more likely to arise when a peasant-worker tried to free himself of his rural ties, and from the obligation to pay taxes and redemption payments on land that he no longer farmed himself. This was especially true in areas where redemption payments had surpassed what the land could earn. Historian Boris Tikhonov found that, in Moscow province, communes bent on collecting back payments frequently refused to renew passports to absentees who were in arrears, leading to panicked appeals to provincial authorities by urban dwellers who stressed that they had long ago lost their "settled" status *(osedlost')* in the village.[95] It is no surprise, then, that a peasant-worker who had his passport revoked for missing a payment after years of timely dues would later find this once unwelcome burden to be a perfectly valid basis for claiming the right to a share of communal land. As one worker instructed the district board reviewing his case in 1914: "Young people do not know

TABLE 5-3

TAX LEVELS AND LAND TITLING IN 1880s (31 VOLOSTS, RIAZAN PROVINCE)

taxes per *desiantina* (1887)	Size of landholding (*desiantina* per worker 1880s)	Proportion of household renting out land (1887)	Rent cost / tax ratio (1887)	Proportion of households receiving title (1912)
low (mean = 2.4 rubles) N=10	5.1	12.3%	3	13.4
mid (mean = 2.9 rubles) N=11	4	8%	3.1	17.9
high (mean = 3.7 rubles) N=10	3.3	19.7%	2.3	25.8
correlation with titling = .690	-.533	.708	-.052	

Sources: The rent/tax ratio measures the cost of renting one *desiatina* of land in relation to the tax burden. This is a very rough index of how profitable allotment land was. In all cases here, a departing peasant could expect to rent his allotment for more than the taxes and payments due on it. The 1880s data is for the second half of the decade, after redemption dues were lowered. They are drawn from the "Volostnaia tablitsa" section of the following volumes: Riazanskoe gubernskoe zemstvo, *Sbornik statisticheskikh svedenii po Riazanskoi gubernii*, v.6, *Pronskii uezd* (Riazan 1886); vol. 8, pt. 1, *Spasskii uezd* (Riazan, 1887); vol. 9, pt. 1 *Sapozhkovskii uezd* (Riazan, 1888); and vol. 10, *Riazhskii uezd* (Riazan, 1888); RGIA, f. 1291, op. 31 (1912), dd. 46, 514; GARO, f. 70, op. 15 (1915), d. 5; f. 81, op. 23 (1915), sv. 26, d. 84.

that I answered for all dues and taxes when land was a burden, when peasant holdings took everything down to the last kopeck. About that, you will have to question the older villagers."[96]

And peasants not only spoke about redemption payments; they also acted on them. Data from thirty-one volosts of Riazan province suggest that householders whose taxes had been high in the 1880s were precisely those most likely to take out title (see table 5-3). It did not matter whether the land was good or not. Volosts in which the holdings in the 1880s had been the smallest and the taxes had been the highest were precisely those in which peasants were most likely by 1912 to take out title. Obviously, this single statistical sample is too small to be conclusive in itself. But it conforms to what petitioners kept repeating—that the right to claim or keep land derived from past redemption payments.

The conflicting references to "actual use" and "property" cannot be read as necessarily reflecting conflicting attitudes about the commune. On the one hand, villagers defended communal land by resisting the ability of title holders to dispose of allotment land, but they did so by restricting claim rights and membership. On the other hand, attempts to maintain continued access to allotment land, which had been a cornerstone of the communal system, were usually framed in the language of property rights. Such ambiguities did not simplify the task of the appeal instances charged with untangling conflicting claims. More often than not, local officials simply ignored references to "property" and redemption and focused instead on "actual use," a tendency that did not address petitioners' underlying arguments and concerns. The inconsistencies with which appeal authorities ruled did little to alleviate fears, and perhaps even less to finalize disputes.

Both the fears and the resentments of absentees probably took on greater acuity with World War I. The notion that land was due as a reward for military service, present in petitions since the 1880s, overlay and reinforced older arguments for entitlement. The appeal of one native of Spassk district was quite typical in the way it juxtaposed moral and legal grounds to justify the right to an allotment. The petitioner complained that he had paid off his share of communal land, returned regularly to the village, sent home earnings, and taken care of his father. Still the commune would not return his land. "How could I possibly be left landless? Now I am serving in the Franco-Russian factory; I am serving government defense while many members of our village society are not serving the fatherland in any way, instead occupying my native land that my uncle and father farmed."[97] Such righteous indignation brought together elements that could be identified as "traditional" (right to land) and elements that were decidedly "modern" (rights attendant to service to the fatherland). The local and the national were linked very concretely through the village plot of land.

Property and "Custom" in Inheritance Strategies

Absentees were not the only nominal members of the commune to be challenged in their right to keep or claim allotment land. Among the files that piled up on the desks of the land captains and provincial boards after 1906 were a high proportion of appeals by widows, single women, sons-in-law, and adopted children. Before 1906, levels of communal land rights could vary according to gender, age, residence, and even capacity to work. The property label threatened to erase such distinctions. Women, in-marrying husbands, and sons adopted into households with no male heirs had long faced obstacles in establishing their rights as full heads of household. While traditionally recognized as legitimate, their claims were nonetheless considered to be necessary but often temporary aberra-tions from normal rules of succession. For these groups, right to land had been conditional, and the new legislation raised the stakes of land disputes by threatening to make temporary and conditional arrange-ments permanent and unconditional. Communes responded by trying to draw the line more firmly between insiders and outsiders, effectively disenfranchising targeted groups of villagers by blocking their access to allotment land. Such efforts to exclude marginal members, conjugated with continued uncertainty over the boundaries, definitions, and appli-cability of law and custom, introduced even greater confusion in inheri-tance disputes. A growing minority of villagers found that the new prop-erty laws heightened their insecurity.

The role of widows as guardians of household land had been well at-tested in the nineteenth century and, given their high number in the Russian countryside, was especially significant. In Iaroslavl province, for instance, 11.5 percent of women between the ages of thirty and fifty were widowed, and in Riazan province, the 1897 census found one widow for every 4.5 married women. In some villages in the early twen-tieth century, as many as 30 percent of households were headed by women.[98] The problems that women's holdings might pose under the new laws were threefold. First, relatives could no longer be assured that the principle of guardianship would be respected, as titled land could be disposed of without their consent or the commune's approval. For the same reasons, communes potentially lost control over conditional wid-ows' allotments. Finally, communes bristled at the prospect that a woman might sell the land that had been granted to prevent her impov-erishment and then officially request communal charity on the grounds that she was landless. As one commune expressed the fear, there could now be "masses" of requests for charity "since female householders [would] quite freely transfer their allotment to relatives or sell it for money, and then demand support from the commune."[99] While it is un-clear whether "masses" of women did in fact flood communes with re-quests for aid, it is known that some women did succeed in selling their allotments: 15 percent of the land sales of Riazan's Spassk and Riazhsk districts conducted in 1914 were effected by women.[100]

The perception that women were more likely to title and sell drove a number of communes to place special restrictions on women's allotments: they could be held only for the widow's lifetime, only until the next repartition, only as rent (albeit free), or only if she did not marry outside the village.[101] In 1909 the commune of Borok (Riazan, Spassk district) even tried to return to a distribution system based on male souls after having distributed according to "eaters" in early 1906. The assembly justified transferring to hereditary tenure on the basis of the number of males present in each household: "The last redistribution criteria is inapplicable under local conditions, as girls, having received an equal share of land, get married when they come of age. There have been instances in our village of brides taking land to a household that is a complete stranger to the commune."[102] Clearly, women had married outside the village before. Until 1906, however, they had been unable to keep their land when they did so.

Such blanket restrictions on women's allotments rarely survived scrutiny by higher authorities. Both the MVD and the Senate, in an effort to prevent excessive landlessness, continued until 1917 to defend the rights of female heads of household to an allotment. The rulings of the Senate specified that not only did a widow retain her right to her husband's allotment after his death, but in the event of her remarriage, the commune was obliged to grant her new husband a share of land. The fact that the new husband was not registered in the village was not grounds for removing the widow's allotment.[103] The MVD consistently issued instructions to inform provincial officials of these rulings.

In spite of these instructions, however, women were subject to the same pressures that pushed out absentees. If a peasant who had continued paying all taxes and dues in his absence was unlikely to get any land back, his widow had an even slimmer chance. Even if a widow lived within the village, assemblies would not accept her mere declaration of intent to want to continue farming the land herself but measured her sincerity, her capabilities, and the likelihood that she might become a burden on the village. In one case from Moscow province, the commune held that a widow's project to build a house was a sham. Instead, they believed that one of the villagers had agreed to pretend to begin construction for her in exchange for the right to buy the land after appropriation was approved: "Ivanova herself is not in any position to build any kind of house, nor is she capable of conducting agriculture."[104] As another commune explained in its justification for removing an allotment from an 83-year-old widow, it would be entirely unfair to expect the commune to provide both land and aid to cultivate it.[105] Any hint that a woman was too old, too weak, or lacked the necessary hands in her household raised suspicions that she might sell out.

While the motives for denying women allotment land were similar to those leading to the exclusion of absentees, the dynamics and terms of the disputes were quite different. After all, a resident widow usually had "actual use" of contested land. The point of contention, therefore, shifted from the issue of defining residency (osedlost') to that of determining whether a woman was in fact an independent head of household. While absentees were challenged by the entire commune, women were generally in conflict with family members as well. The reasons are easy to understand. The 9 November decree gave a head of household hitherto un-heard-of powers: only he (or she) could title and then sell allotment land, and do so in spite of the objections of other members of the household. An absent husband could thus conceivably dispossess his wife, or a mother could deprive an absentee son of land he had paid for by sending his earnings home.

Virtually the only way to block titling by a male head of household was to request trusteeship over him for drunkenness or squandering. It was much easier to block a woman, especially after the 14 June 1910 law fur-ther undermined the strength of women's claims to head households. While all titled land automatically became the personal property of the head of household, article 48 of the legislation specified that allotments held by a household consisting of a woman and her children or other di-rect relatives could only be titled as the common property of all its mem-bers. One practical effect of the provision was to make it simpler to block requests for titles filed by women. It was quite common for a widow's rela-tives to try to obstruct her claim to title by arguing that the household's land should be registered as common property. The Senate noted local au-thorities' tendency to mistakenly extend article 48 to cover indirect rela-tives.[106] In one case from Riazhsk district, for instance, a man was able to block his sister-in-law's petition for land title, even though he had sepa-rated from his brother twenty-five years earlier. The widow was able to produce a copy of the volost court decision to prove the separation, but to no avail. It appears that the division had never been noted in the house-hold register *(posemienaia spiska)*. On that basis, both the provincial board and the Senate overturned the land appropriation—and this in spite of the fact that the brother-in-law withdrew his complaint.[107]

The provision for "common property" further strengthened the assem-bly's role in resolving disputes over headship. Since the great majority of family divisions had occurred without written documentation, assemblies were called upon to provide testimony about past household arrange-ments. Relatives were in some cases able to merge previously separated households after a male head of household died, forestalling any inde-pendent action by his widow. Widows were especially vulnerable to the claims of male in-laws, who were better placed to curry the favor of the as-sembly, especially when the latter played on fears that land could go to an outsider. One man in Moscow province, for instance, was able to persuade the assembly to pass a resolution transferring the household headship from his mother-in-law to himself, a move the matriarch promptly protested. In its defense, the commune explained that Agrafena Kolpet-skaia had herself turned down the headship, and that in any case she was not "capable" *(sposobna)*. The son-in-law had put the household back on its feet, and "now if she takes it back she will again destroy it, since she in-tends to claim it as property and to sell everything." Uncharacteristically, the provincial board in this case turned down the son-in-law's request for headship, surmising that the village resolution had been passed behind Kolpetskaia's back.[108] This was an unusual ruling; appeal and cassation instances usually accepted the assembly's word as to whether or not a household partition had taken place, this in accordance with Senate instructions. If boards too easily doubted assemblies' declarations, the Senate opined, virtually any ruling could be overturned on the grounds that it had not been examined on substance.[109]

While confusion over the rights of female householders should in theory have been limited to requests for land title, in practice it also extended to the allocation and removal of communal allotments, as well as to inheritance disputes. The new law not only enhanced the ability of male relatives to make claims against women but made assemblies leery of leaving temporary usage of allotment land to a widow. In the village of Zhernavki (Skopin district), a 1908 general repartition according to "present males" was appealed by three widows without male children and six absentees. The absentees won their appeals; the provincial board found that since each had close relatives in the village, it would be improper to deprive them of an allotment as if they did not have residency. The widows, on the other hand, did not have so much luck, as the land captain found that each had a relative who had received an allotment. The previously independent widows were thereby reincorporated into extended households (headed by a brother-in-law, a grandson, and a nephew), that could easily refuse them support (as the widows argued at the hearing).[110]

It is perhaps because of their vulnerability that female petitioners did not rely on the arguments of inheritance and redemption payments alone. In contrast to the petitions filed by male returnees, the pleas of women present classic examples of what Kachorovskii defined as the "right to labor," or the right of each to receive land necessary for survival. As the widow Ermolaeva protested in response to the commune's removal of her allotment: "I live alone and I cannot live without land and without an income."[111] Women's appeals commonly took the form of tearful entreaty. "I am with five minor children and do not know where to put down my head," pleaded a widow who wanted to return to her husband's village after his death deprived her of any income.[112] Another "poor widow with children and without a piece of bread" complained that the commune had refused to name a guardian for her two daughters, choosing instead to redistribute her husband's allotment to her brother-in-law and thereby leaving the daughters "to the mercy of fate . . . with nowhere to put down their heads."[113] Such appeals for merciful protection, however, were no more likely to be noted by administrative appeal instances than arguments based on "property" and redemption payments.

Women did not always find much support among higher authorities, who could be ignorant of or indifferent to Senate rulings. Given the extraordinary confusion reigning at all levels of rural administration, which was only exacerbated by the new legislation, patently incorrect rulings were not uncommon and hardly surprising. Neither the 1906 decree nor the 1910 law gave any indications of how the new property laws might affect the regulation of inheritance. However, recognizing titled land as the personal property of the head of household (when the latter was not a woman), rather than as the common property of the household was a significant departure from the understanding of family property that had hitherto regulated inheritance. As a result, the land reform legislation reinforced the tendency on the part of officials to apply the civil code to land in personal ownership.

The MVD encouraged the shift to the civil code in a December 1906 circular: henceforth, conflicts over allotment land claimed as personal property were to be ruled according to custom only when the litigants could demonstrate the existence of custom. Likewise, the general assembly of the Senate ruled in 1910 that, in the absence of demonstrated local custom, inheritance of land in personal ownership should only take into account relations of kinship and not labor participation.[114] Yet, the second department of the Senate consistently ruled that, since land registered as personal property retained its designation as allotment land, permission to rule according to custom remained valid. And since the allotment was the holding of the "working family union," inheritance was to be determined by the relative economic participation of each of the parties in the household.[115] The prominent legal scholar A. E. Vorms concluded in 1912 that disputes over both communal land and land claimed in personal property were to continue to be regulated by custom. Nevertheless, he found that local authorities had a growing predilection for applying the civil code.[116]

The reigning legislative confusion left much discretionary leeway for local authorities and only accentuated the inconsistencies evident in appellate and cassation rulings of district congresses and provincial boards. At times, a district congress might deem that a titled allotment should by definition be more secure and on that basis uphold a female petitioner's right to keep her holdings. In other cases, authorities could rule that since the disputed land was personal property, then no existing customs applied to it, and the widow should receive the share specified in the civil code.[117]

The application of the general civil code also limited the alternative inheritance strategies available to a precarious household to ensure its survival. Throughout the post-Emancipation period, families without male heirs could either adopt a son into the household or bring in a son-in-law. Likewise, a widow could defend her household and allotment against the claims of collateral relatives (such as brothers, uncles, or nephews of her first husband) by remarrying. Men in each of these cases were referred to by the same term, reflecting their similar status—*priimak*.[118] Higher instances ruled on disputes surrounding the rights of *priimaki* with the same inconsistency as in cases involving widows. In one case where the nephew of a widow successfully sued to regain his uncle's allotment, for instance, the provincial board agreed with the decision, ruling that the rights of *priimak* could not be conferred by a widow, and that after 1906, in the absence of direct reference to custom, the civil code had to be applied. The widow therefore only had a right to a one-seventh share of her husband's land. A few weeks later, however, the same provincial board ruled an analogous case in favor of a widow, judging that her second husband was a *priimak,* and therefore should receive land in his wife's village.[119] In another case, which represented an even clearer departure from "custom" as defined by the Senate, one E. Delitskaia lost the two shares she had received from her father in the process of registering her husband from a neighboring volost into her own commune. Delitskaia appealed her case all the way to the provincial board, but the authorities agreed with the commune that, with her marriage, the woman had lost her registration in the village.[120]

While a widow's status as householder and landholder had never been particularly secure, the compound result of the changes introduced with the 1906 legislation further undermined that status. The provisions for "common property," in conjunction with the growing uncertainty over the applicability of law and custom, made it easier for male relatives to make successful claims against widows. The position of independent women heads of household became more precarious and dependent on the will of the assembly.

The war added to that precariousness and dependence, and not only because of the growing proportion of widows and soldiers' wives in the village. Even households holding titled land could find it difficult to defend their holdings in the absence of the male head. The MVD insisted that since the household head of titled land was its sole proprietor, wives could not take measures that would affect this property. A soldier's wife, therefore, could not act in court without her husband's document of proxy. Yet, as the Riazan provincial board pointed out, the impossibility of obtaining proxies from the growing ranks of prisoners and the missing left women unable to defend themselves in court against encroachments by neighbors or in-laws.[121]

Growing numbers of soldiers' wives *(soldatki)* bypassed the courts to appeal directly to the general staff about land encroachments, repartitions, land alienation, and land reorganization. Military authorities regularly forwarded these complaints to the MVD for investigation, and in March 1916 General A. N. Kuropatkin, commander of the northern front, protested to the minister of internal affairs that land settlement commissions, in their zeal, were undermining morale at the front, as rumors that soldiers might lose their land elicited "bitter feelings . . . from the consciousness of the defenselessness of their family."[122] Some governors likewise noted the rise of tensions and the attendant dangers to army morale, requesting permission from the MVD to suspend *peredely* until the end of the war for fear that soldiers' families would lose land.[123] The MVD made few concessions to the exigencies of war, however. Land reorganization work was suspended in November 1916, but on the other issues the ministry merely exhorted land captains to ever greater vigilance to ensure that soldiers' families were properly defended. Land claims and rights were even more dependent than before 1906 on particular circumstances, on the ability to rally local support, on favorable testimony by the assembly, and on the zeal and personality of the overworked local official receiving complaints.

◆ ◆ ◆

In the majority of disputes over allotment land heard by the appeal instances after 1906, the commune had the advantage. Both proceduralism and the rule of "actual use" favored the status quo, even if the latter had arisen from previous illegal actions. Without official documentation to prove past rental agreements, household divisions, or inheritance arrangements, both absentees and women heads of household found their land claims difficult to uphold. This is not to say that communes were completely successful in halting the process of granting land titles. Obviously, many households did succeed in transferring their allotment land to personal property, and many of these did in the end sell out. Village reactions to the new land legislation were eminently local: in one village, group titling came from a desire to improve agricultural methods; in another, the same action was undertaken to defend against initiatives by a few individuals. In one village, absentees could title and sell without arousing objection; in another the same action would raise a storm of protest. In some cases a widow was supported by the assembly against in-laws or absent sons; in others the contrary was the case. But underlying this local variety was a strengthening of exclusionary tendencies. Overall, individual petitioners lost 103 of the 185 appeals (62%) examined—and that included a final ruling of the provincial board. Absentees won 42 percent of their appeals, while among female petitioners, only 32 percent ultimately received satisfaction. The apprehensions so consistently voiced in petitions were not groundless.

The new laws drove communes to redefine the rules governing access to land, and villagers were able to use the terms of the legislation itself to do so. In spite of the flurry of Senate rulings and MVD instructions, determined communes retained considerable flexibility to remove and reallocate allotments as they saw fit. In practice, the application of the new land laws involved efforts to disinherit many women and peasant-workers whose claims to land had earlier been fully legitimate, but who after 1906 found themselves disadvantaged in the settlement process by their existing marginal status. The reforms thus meant violating not only understandings of "custom" but also understandings of "property"—at least as they were held by those who lost out.

The seemingly minor decision made in 1906 to apply the rule of "actual use" complicated the process of resolving disputes. While a revival of

article 36 of the General Statute would probably not have created less conflict, it would at least have built on a logic that had already taken hold in
the countryside. This was a logic that sometimes favored communal property and sometimes favored individual property, but it was one that peasants consistently appealed to—even as authorities consistently ignored
it—suggesting that they were willing to recognize it as fair. Tying property
rights to past redemption payments would also have provided local authorities with a standard against which to evaluate conflicting claims that would
have freed them from the endless and impossible task of evaluating the particular circumstances and intentions of litigants. As it was, the knowledge
necessary to evaluate disputes remained embedded in the community, and
rulings were unlikely to be perceived as fair or consistent. This made it unlikely that disputes could be finalized, and more likely that claims would remain dormant, ready to be revived when circumstances allowed, undoubtedly contributing a great deal to the turbulence associated with the
resurgence of the commune after the collapse of the tsarist regime.

The paradox is that property reforms, while designed to introduce
greater security in land rights, for a substantial minority of villagers did
just the contrary. The 1906 and 1910 laws opened the door ever wider to
individual strategic use of state rules and institutions. Not only did this
erode the ability of communes to present a united front against the reforms but it nourished fears of permanent loss, alarm that neighbors
might make better use of new opportunities, defensive "races for land,"
and open-ended resolutions. Fear was an important factor driving the
movement to title, especially since access to land remained the only viable
welfare system. World War I only exacerbated these fears. With the mobilization of some 15 million men over the course of the war, what had
been unusual (absent men, widows, women serving as de facto heads of
households) became more and more common. Yet the state offered no
way to unravel such a tangle of exceptional situations. Under the circumstances, it is no surprise that villagers resorted massively to repartitioning
after the collapse of the tsarist regime. Regardless of what peasants might
have thought about the agronomic advantages or disadvantages of repartitioning, it remained the only viable mechanism for untangling the rival
claims that the Stolypin reforms and the war had created.

CONCLUSION

✦ ✦ ✦

On the eve of World War I, the Russian village had lost much of the administrative self-sufficiency it might once have enjoyed. Peasants depended on the rulings of outside officials to pursue their disputes with neighbors, kin, and communes. If the knowledge necessary to adjudicate disputes remained in the local community, the ability to settle did not. The volost court had been gradually dispossessed of its capacity to resolve conflicts over land, while the mechanism of land redistribution—which was also a mechanism for periodically settling accounts—was largely disabled. Meanwhile, the new property laws had raised the stakes of land disputes, providing new incentives and opportunities to defend, revive, or invent outstanding claims. But the government's reluctance to establish a framework within which new types of conflicts could be argued meant that settlements were open-ended. Claims lost on the basis of "custom" could be revived under the aegis of "law" (and vice versa); those lost on procedural grounds could be reopened on substance. Litigants were increasingly able to challenge the very existence and substance of "custom." Cases could rise all the way to the Senate, only to begin anew from the volost court the climb up the ladder of appeal. Disputes had a disconcerting ability to survive verdicts. The lack of finality in the legal and administrative system not only made strategic behavior possible but made it virtually the only viable response to the added insecurity introduced by the new property laws. State officials had penetrated the village. But their presence contributed to many of the problems that they, in theory, ought to have mitigated, notably insecurity of rights, especially rights in land and property.

I am not arguing here that Russia's prewar administrative system was in an untenable crisis and on the brink of collapse. The types of tensions, disjunctions, and inconsistencies that I have described in this book were probably not enough by themselves to bring down the regime. Peasants' primary mode of action after all was still to appeal, petition, and sue. Senate rulings provided the legal system some flexibility even in the face of legislative immobility, and with some continuity behind dramatic legislative about-faces. Village officials may not have had much authority to do the government's bidding, but neither did they have much power to be exceptionally corrupt. The most effective land captains accommodated, even if they were reprimanded for doing so. And when recourse within the legal and administrative system was exhausted, peasants turned to the tsar, his wife, his ministers, or his generals to request merciful extra-institutional intervention.[1]

But neither could the peasants' engagement with state institutions be a source of stability. On the contrary, the weaknesses of Russia's system of rural administration undermined the country's ability to confront the inevitable strains of war. In the same way that peasant reactions to the Stolypin agrarian reforms cannot be analyzed without reference to developments over the previous two decades, so reactions to the war must be understood in relation to changes introduced with the Stolypin reforms. When peasant families were forced to face the mobilization of men, livestock, and money, the countryside was already seething with unsettled claims and unaddressed fears. Likewise, the sullen lack of enthusiasm with which villagers greeted officials' calls to provide ever greater aid to families of mobilized men can be understood only in the context of decades of conflict over communal welfare.[2] The point is not just that World War I destabilized Russian rural society, but that tensions permeating villages prior to 1914 ensured that the disruptions of war would have devastating effects.

Rural administrative institutions were particularly ill-prepared to confront the emergencies of war. Within six months of the start of hostilities, 35 percent of the country's land captains had been mobilized. Because of lack of replacements, the MVD extended the practice of assigning responsibility for a vacant precinct to a neighboring official. By late 1915 well over half of the country's precincts had to share a land captain, and the latter could expect little help from village officials. In some provinces, half of all volost elders were mobilized. Those that remained were solicited to take on ever more numerous tasks: in addition to their regular duties, elders were called upon to aid in the requisition of horses, carts, and harnesses, in the distribution of aid to soldiers' families, and in the settlement of refugees. Even though the number of cases filed in the volost courts fell to nearly half of their prewar level by 1916, appellate and cassation instances were unable to keep up with appeals. Backlogs in district congresses and provincial boards two or three times the prewar level were not unusual.[3] For an administrative system dependant on the initiatives, investigations, and rulings of local officials, the absence of so many individuals was debilitating. The government had even fewer means than before to address complaints, to reassure soldiers that they would not be dispossessed in their absence, or to protect the rights of the growing ranks of soldiers' wives—the *soldatki*—and widows.

In the face of administrative emergencies, the MVD and governors responded with ever more exhortation. The war brought about an almost reflexive revival of the language of paternal duty. When peasants misunderstood a government circular to mean that all land reorganization work was to be suspended, the Tula governor reminded his *zemskie nachal'niki* that as "the authority close to the people," they were to explain the importance of land reorganization on every possible occasion, at assemblies, in their offices, on tours of their precincts. When rumors began to circulate throughout the central provinces that soldiers' families would be exempt from taxes, the Riazan governor prodded land captains to tour their precincts to explain the "real meaning of the advantages granted."[4] The MVD issued circulars in the same vein: in order to ensure that the rights of soldiers were not trampled in their absence, the captains should redouble efforts to personally verify all land transactions and redistributions. If *soldatki* were unable to defend their property in the absence of their husbands, then local authorities were to initiate criminal proceedings against offenders.[5] But if the confident and highly motivated land captains of the 1890s had been unable to keep up with endless requests to "judge, persuade, punish, search, protect," their doubly overworked successors could do little but scratch the surface of the endless urgent tasks they were asked to accomplish.

It is little wonder that villagers would retreat to localist solutions in 1917–1918. The standard textbook story presents the revival of the repartitional commune after the collapse of the tsarist regime as evidence of peasants' attachment to the institution, of their rejection of the Stolypin reforms, and by extension, of the triumph of peasant traditionalism against a reforming state.[6] In evaluating the significance of the continuities and ruptures of the revolutionary and civil war eras, however, it is important to keep in mind that the peasant "commune" and concomitant attitudes toward land and property had been in constant flux over the previous half century, and that they were forged in the process of interaction with state authorities, laws, and regulations. Peasant actions in 1917 likewise cannot be divorced from the broader political context within which they were embedded. With the revolution and the breakdown of state institutions, horizons of political expectations changed dramatically. Under the extraordinary conjunctural conditions of war and disintegration of political authority, communal institutions could be mobilized for social and political change. The "village society," as peasants continued to call it, provided the framework for villagers not only to seize and redistribute lands of private landowners, but also to settle a whole host of accumulated internal conflicts.[7]

The revival of general land repartitions conducted under the authority of the village assembly did not necessarily signal that peasants were acting according to age-old isolationist and parochial impulses. *Peredel* was simply the only mechanism available to confront the consequences of demographic upheaval, to accommodate returning soldiers, to evaluate the claims of workers escaping urban economic crisis, and to deal with the growing ranks of widows. Besides, repartitions were not simply revived according to a well-honed communal ideal. They differed in a number of crucial ways from those of the earlier period. The new rhetorical emphasis on "equalization" had not been a feature of prerevolutionary repartitions, nor had it been an important part of the language of land disputes.[8] As peasants sought to align local conflicts with broader political ideologies, they adapted new vocabulary that in turn would open a new chapter in communal reinvention. Simply too much was changing in these early years of Soviet power to camouflage the shifting dynamics of intersection of the local and the national under the rubric of historical continuity of peasant mentalities.

While this study has paid considerable attention to failings and short-comings of the tsarist government's reform projects, in many ways the state had achieved its goal of reaching into the village. And many of the transformations that it had brought about could be characterized as "modern." The villagers of 1916 were very different from their grandfathers who had been liberated from serfdom. They knew well the path to the courtroom, to the land captain's office, to the district and provincial administrations, and they went there willingly. While villagers effectively "peasantized" the volost court in the course of resolving petty crime, in the realm of civil relations they were forced to adapt to government-sponsored concepts of community, rights, and property. Peasants looked to state-sanctioned institutions and to state officials to resolve internal conflicts, and neither the volost court nor the village assembly acted to minimize outside intervention in order to protect local autonomy. These local bodies were sites of contact and exchange. Even as they did a poor job of transmitting the state's priorities, and regardless of the intent of the individuals who used them, they did frame village disputes. Even on those allegedly most immutable of values—concepts of property and land tenure—peasants tried to argue and act in terms that had been defined in legislation.

Villagers' remarkable propensity to sue and appeal could on the surface be read as a sign of confidence in state institutions. In theory, the very act of appeal—regardless of petitioners' intentions—is an integrative act, giving government authorities final arbitrating power.[9] This, however, neglects the substance of the exchange taking place between rulers and ruled. Russian state policies by the 1890s had fostered the notion that redeemed land was property, had strengthened definitions of community that associated the burdens of obligations with the right to hold land, and had defined the outlines of a "custom" regulating property devolution. Yet when peasants structured their actions and their petitions along these lines, officials were as likely as not to ignore their arguments. The irony is that the more peasants used the institutions and laws available to them, the more they solicited authorities, the greater the obstacles to communication grew. The obstacle was not the inertia of peasant tradition, but the framework of state-peasant dialogue, which no longer worked. Confronted with inconsistent policies, with what appeared to be arbitrary legal responses, villagers' rising expectations of outside intervention were not being met.

The tsarist state was reluctant to accept the consequences of the changes that it had wrought. What advocates of greater state *dirigisme* and those of reinforced paternalism had in common was a fear of accommodations that might lead to "peasantization" of local state institutions. Both rejected solutions that could have structured peasant actions over the long term, such as precedence setting or codification, for fear that this would constrain the instrumental utility of law and administration. There could be, under the circumstances, little "trickle-up process of state-formation."[10] Peasants may have developed more "modern" expectations. The empire's officials, however, were not living in the timescale of modernization theories, but within the much shorter scale of human time. Reformers expressed impatience at what they perceived to be the slow pace of change, but the desire to transform peasants alternated with ambivalence over the wisdom of doing so. When peasants did not behave in accordance to preconceptions, this was read as further evidence that the *miroed* remained the village gatekeeper, that peasants were stubborn, backward, and helpless, and that they were not ready for the responsibilities of citizenship, proprietorship, and civil law. When peasants went to court en masse, they were labeled "litigious"; when they cited official laws and procedures, they were deemed to be manipulated by unscrupulous illegal advocates; when they misused (or manipulated) the myriad laws, procedures, and regulations that sometimes befuddled the most highly educated senator, they were "ignorant."

These attitudes were by no means universal. There were quite talented individuals both in the central bureaucracy and even among land captains whose analyses of peasant society would not surprise a modern anthropologist. Many jurists were well aware of the problematic nature of the very concept of "customary law"; few of them studied peasant society as if it existed in isolation from state and society. But these analyses did not carry the political weight of those that emphasized peasant backwardness. On the eve of World War I, key ministerial posts were back in the hands of individuals with a visceral distrust of establishing a governing framework that would constrain administrative discretion. Reform proposals had been shelved in the name of tending to the rural population's special needs. Resistance in the name of tradition is indeed an important part of Russian history, but it came from the highest levels of the state, not the peasantry.

State resistance to peasant pressures for constructive engagement would survive the Russian Revolution. Soviet authorities inherited conceptions of peasants as backward, ignorant, and bound by the inertia of tradition.[11] Like their tsarist forbears, they tended to misread the opportunities offered by peasant petitions and appeals. In seeking to exploit village cleavages, they tended to pull on the wrong levers. In trying to explain the difficulties they seemed to face in penetrating the village, they blamed the kulak, but with a virulence reinforced by class prejudices. There is indeed striking continuity between the late tsarist and Soviet periods: it is to be found in the governing elite's extraordinary anxiety that the wrong peasants still ruled the countryside.

ПОTES

◆ ◆ ◆

ABBREVIATIONS

The notes use standard abbreviations for Russian archival sources: f. = *fond* (collection); op. = *opis'* (subset or list); d. = *delo* (file); l. = *list* (page). Two subdivisions are specific to the Riazan provincial archives: GO = *grazhdanskii otdel* (civil section); sv. = *sviazka* (bundle)

Archives

GARO	Gosudarstvennyi Arkhiv Riazanskoi Oblasti
GATO	Gosudarstvennyi Arkhiv Tverskoi Oblasti
GATO-Tambov	Gosudarstvennyi Arkhiv Tambovskoi Oblasti
GARF	Gosudarstvennyi Arkhiv Rossiiskoi Federatsii
RGIA	Rossiiskii Gosudarstvennyi Istoricheskii Arkhiv
RGIA-otchety	RGIA, Biblioteka, pervyi otdel, Otchety sostoianii gubernii
TsIAM	Tsentral'nyi Istoricheskii Arkhiv goroda Moskvy

Periodicals and Newspapers

CMRS	*Cahiers du monde russe et soviétique*
IaGV	*Iaroslavskie gubernskie vedomosti*
IuG	*Iuridicheskaia gazeta*
IuO	*Iuridicheskoe obozrenie*
IuV	*Iuridicheskii vestnik*
IuZ	*Iuridicheskie zapiski*
IZ	*Istoricheskie zapiski*
IZO	*Izvestiia zemskogo otdela*
JfGO	*Jahrbücher für Geschichte Osteuropas*
MV	*Moskovskie vedomosti*
OZ	*Otechestvennye zapiski*
PSZ	*Polnoe sobranie zakonov Rossiiskoi imperii*
PV	*Pravitel'stvennyi vestnik*
RB	*Russkoe bogatstvo*
RM	*Russkaia mysl'*

RO   *Russkoe obozrenie*
RR   *Russian Review*
RV   *Riazanskii vestnik*
RZh   *Riazanskaia zhizn'*
SEER   *Slavonic and East European Review*
SG   *Sudebnaia gazeta*
SK   *Severnyi krai*
SM   *Sovremennyi mir*
SR   *Slavic Review*
SV   *Severnyi vestnik*
VE   *Vestnik Evropy*
VP   *Vestnik prava*
VPiN   *Vestnik prava i notariata*
ZhGiUP   *Zhurnal grazhdanskogo i ugolovnogo prava*
ZhIuO   *Zhurnal iuridicheskogo obshchestva pri Imperatorskom Sankt-Peter–burgskom universitete*
ZhMIu   *Zhurnal Ministerstva Iustitsii*

INTRODUCTION

1. V. Anzimirov, "Volostnoi pisar'," *Derevenskaia gazeta*, nos. 26/32 (1910): 2–3.

2. For works outlining the shared assumptions of educated Russians about peasants, see Yanni Kotsonis, *Making Peasants Backward: Agricultural Cooperatives and the Agrarian Question in Russia, 1861–1914* (New York, 1999); Cathy Frierson, *Peasant Icons: Representations of Rural People in Late Nineteenth-Century Russia* (Oxford, 1993).

3. David Moon, "Estimating the Peasant Population of Late Imperial Russia from the 1897 Census: A Research Note," *Europe-Asia Studies* 48, no. 1 (1996): 141–53; V. G. Tiukavkin, *Velikorusskoe krest'ianstvo i stolypinskaia agrarnaia reforma* (Moscow, 2001), 23, 96; Teodor Shanin, *The Roots of Otherness: Russia's Turn of Century*, vol. 1, *Russia as a "Developing Society"* (New Haven, 1985), 133; Vladimir Buldakov, "Soldiers and Changes in the Psychology of the Peasantry and Legal and Political Consciousness in Russia, 1914–1923," *The Soviet and Post-Soviet Review* 17, no. 2–3 (2000): 227.

4. Richard Wortman, *Scenarios of Power: Myth and Ceremony in Russian Monarchy*, vol. 2, *From Alexander II to the Abdication of Nicholas II* (Princeton, 1995).

5. Michael Confino has made this point convincingly in "Present Events and the Representation of the Past," *Cahiers du monde russe* 35, no. 4 (1994): 854.

6. Quotation from David Sabean, *Power in the Blood: Popular Culture and Village Discourse in Early Modern Germany* (Cambridge, 1984), 14. For examination of some of the ways strengthened communal institutions could accompany state centralization in early modern France and Germany, see especially Hilton Root, *Peasants and Kings in Burgundy: Agrarian Foundation of French Absolutism* (Berkeley, 1987); and David Luebke, *His Majesty's Rebels: Communities, Factions, and Rural Revolt in the Black Forest, 1725–1745* (Ithaca, NY, 1997).

7. On "undergovernment" see Frederick Starr, *Decentralization and Self-Government in Russia, 1830–1870* (Princeton, 1972); Neil Weissman, *Reform in Tsarist Russia: The State Bureaucracy and Local Government, 1900–1914* (New Brunswick, NJ, 1981). For discussion of ministerial powers and intra-governmental conflict, see Theodore Taranovski, "Alexander III and His Bureaucracy: The Limitations on Autocratic Power," *Canadian Slavonic Papers* 26, nos. 2–3 (1984): 207–19; Daniel Orlovsky, *The Limits of*

Reform: The Ministry of Internal Affairs in Imperial Russia, 1802–1881 (Cambridge, MA, 1981). On provincial administration: Richard G. Robbins, *The Tsar's Viceroys: Russian Provincial Governors in the Last Years of the Empire* (Ithaca, 1987). On reform, counter-reform, and the bureaucracy in general: P. A. Zaionchkovskii, *Pravitel'stvennyi apparat samoderzhavnoi Rossii* (Moscow, 1979); Francis Wcislo, *Reforming Rural Russia: State, Local Society, and National Politics, 1855–1914* (Princeton, 1990); David Macey, *Government and Peasant in Russia, 1861–1906: The Pre-History of the Stolypin Reforms* (DeKalb, IL, 1987); Thomas Pearson, *Russian Officialdom in Crisis: Autocracy and Local Self-Government, 1861–1900* (Cambridge, 1989); George Yaney, *The Urge to Mobilize: Agrarian Reform in Russia, 1861–1930* (Urbana, IL, 1982).

8. George Yaney, *The Systematization of Russian Government* (Urbana, IL, 1973), 363.

9. Christine Worobec, *Peasant Russia: Family and Community in the Post-Emancipation Period* (Princeton, 1991); Stephen Frank, *Crime, Cultural Conflict, and Justice in Rural Russia, 1856–1914* (Berkeley, 1999); Ben Eklof, *Russian Peasant Schools: Officialdom, Village Culture, and Popular Pedagogy, 1861–1914* (Berkeley, 1986); John Bushnell, "Peasants in Uniform: The Tsarist Army as a Peasant Society," *Journal of Social History* 13, no. 4 (1980): 565–76; Robert Johnson, *Peasant and Proletarian: The Working Class of Moscow in the Late Nineteenth Century* (New Brunswick, NJ, 1979); Joseph Bradley, *Muzhik and Muscovite: Urbanization in Late Imperial Russia* (Berkeley, 1985). For a stimulating discussion of much of the literature on Russian peasant society in relation to the issue of "particularism," see David Moon's "Peasants into Russian Citizens? A Comparative Perspective," *Revolutionary Russia* 9, no. 1 (1996): 43–81.

10. Orlando Figes, *Peasant Russia, Civil War: The Volga Countryside in Revolution, 1917–1921* (Oxford, 1991); John Channon, "The Peasantry in the Revolutions of 1917," in *Revolution in Russia: Reassessments of 1917*, ed. E. R. Frankel, Jonathan Frankel, and Baruch Knei-Paz (Cambridge, 1992); O. G. Bukhovets, *Sotsial'nye konflikty i krest'ianskaia mental'nost' v Rossiiskoi imperii nachala XX veka. Novye materialy, metody, resul'taty* (Moscow, 1996).

11. Moshe Lewin, "The *Obshchina* and the Village," in *Land Commune and Peasant Community in Imperial and Early Soviet Society*, ed. Roger Bartlett (London, 1990), 24. Works that have been particularly attuned to village cleavages include Jeffrey Burds, *Peasant Dreams and Market Politics: Labor Migration and the Russian Village, 1861–1905* (Pittsburgh, 1998); Barbara Engel, *Between the Fields and the City: Women, Work, and Family in Russia, 1861–1914* (Cambridge, 1994).

12. Teodor Shanin, *The Roots of Otherness: Russia's Turn of Century*, vol. 2, *Russia, 1905–07: Revolution as Moment of Truth* (New Haven, 1985). Orlando Figes (departing somewhat from his own earlier work) has gone furthest in interpreting revolution as rooted in a distinctly peasant dream that he characterizes as "instinctive anarchism" in *A People's Tragedy: The Russian Revolution, 1891–1924* (London, 1996), 84–102. The work of historical sociologist James Scott, which has posited an essential continuity between passive and active resistance, has been particularly influential in Russian peasant studies. See *Weapons of the Weak: Everyday Forms of Peasant Resistance* (New Haven, 1985); *Domination and the Arts of Resistance: Hidden Transcripts* (New Haven, 1990).

13. Florencia Mallon, "The Promise and Dilemma of Subaltern Studies," *American Historical Review* 89, no. 5 (1994): 1491–515. For some useful critiques of the limits of the concept of resistance, see Kotsonis, 164–65; Timothy Mitchell, "Everyday Metaphors of Power," *Theory and Society* 19, no. 5 (1990), 545–77; Gilbert Joseph and Daniel Nugent, eds., *Everyday Forms of State Formation: Revolution and the Negotiation of Rule in Modern Mexico* (Durham, NC, 1994); "Special issue: Resistance to Authority in Russia and the Soviet Union," *Kritika* 1, no. 1 (2000).

14. Historians of the pre-Emancipation era also have shown how peasants engaged with authorities in ways that bolstered the institution of serfdom. Stephen Hoch, *Serfdom and Social Control in Russia: Petrovskoe, a Village in Tambov* (Chicago, 1986); Elise Wirtschafter, "Legal Identity and the Possession of Serfs in Imperial Russia," *Journal of*

Modern History, 70, no. 3 (1998): 561–87; Edgar Melton, "Household Economies and Communal Conflicts on a Russian Serf Estate, 1800–1817," *Journal of Social History*, 26, no. 3 (1993), 559–85; David Moon, *The Russian Peasantry, 1600–1930: The World the Peasants Made* (London and New York, 1999).

15. L. I. Zemtsov, ed., *Volostnoi sud v Rossii, 60x-pervoi poloviny 70x godov XIX veka* (Voronezh, 2002), 9; RGIA, f. 1405, op. 543, d. 942, l. 359.

16. This point was eloquently made over thirty years ago by Hamza Alavi, who argued that the focus on peasants in rebellion "does not refer to other contexts and modes of peasant political action" and that "the uneventful normality of peasant social and political life . . . demands no less attention." "Peasant Classes and Primordial Priorities," *Journal of Peasant Studies* 1, no. 1 (1973): 23, 28.

17. The extent to which it is possible to identify an autonomous communal mode of peasant politics at the root of rebellion and resistance has been studied in the context of other European peasantries, most recently and thoroughly in the context of German history. For a particularly useful overview of the debate see R. W. Scribner, "Communalism: Universal Category or Ideological Construct? A Debate in the Historiography of Early-Modern Germany," *Historical Journal* 37, no. 1 (1994), 199–207.

18. Peter Waldron, *Between Two Revolutions: Stolypin and the Politics of Renewal in Russia* (DeKalb, IL, 1998), 92. On the late 1880s as a watershed in economic policy, see Alessandro Stanziani, *L'économie en révolution. Le cas russe, 1870–1930* (Paris, 1998).

19. For works suggesting ways in which tsarist legitimacy depended on distance, transcendence of concrete local conditions, and institutional fluidity, see especially Richard Wortman, *The Development of Russian Legal Consciousness* (Chicago, 1976) and *Scenarios of Power*; Elise Wirtschafter, *Social Identity in Imperial Russia* (DeKalb, IL, 1997).

20. Alfred Rieber, "The Sedimentary Society," *Russian History*, 16, nos. 2–4 (1989): 353–76.

21. V. Efimov, "Volostnoi sud v vidu reformy mestnoi iustitsii," *VE*, no. 8 (1896): 559. *Materialy k zakonu o mestnom sude*, vol. 1 (St. Petersburg, 1912), statistical addendum, 38–71. Total numbers of cases are estimated from the 1,855,000 civil cases in 1903 (40 provinces) and 1,121,191 criminal cases for 43 provinces in 1905 (unlike 1906, not an abnormal year in terms of court use). *IZO*, no. 2 (1905): 58; Frank, *Crime*, 57.

22. The result is that historians have had an understandable—if unfortunate—tendency to believe their sources and read the dynamics of the assembly of their period as something new. More problematic, in my view, is emphasis on the ideal-type *skhod* that leads to a reification of tradition. The "collective ideal" approach to the commune is perhaps most explicitly stated in Orlando Figes, "The Village Commune and Rural Government," in *Critical Companion to the Russian Revolution, 1914–1921*, ed. Edward Action, Vladimir Cherniaev, and William Rosenberg (Bloomington, IN, 1997), 457. The current emergence of interest in mentality among Russian historians also contributes to the reification of tradition. See for instance B. N. Mironov, *Sotsial'naia istoriia Rossii perioda imperii XVIII–nachalo XX v. Genezis lichnosti, demokraticheskoi sem'i, grazhdanskogo obshchestva i pravovogo gosudarstva* (St. Petersburg, 1999), 1:429–84; L. V. Danilova and V. P. Danilov, "Krest'ianskaia mental'nost' i obshchina," in *Mentalitet i agrarnoe razvitie Rossii XIX–XX v.* (Moscow, 1995), 22–39. One of the few attempts to historicize the *skhod* is O. G. Vronskii's *Krest'ianskaia obshchina na rubazhe XIX–XX vv. Struktura upravleniia, pozemel'nye otnosheniia, pravoporiadok* (Moscow, 1999).

23. Sabean, 29.

24. Even Judith Pallot's excellent study has overlooked these materials, the result of which is, in my view, to overestimate the extent and effectiveness of collective resistance. *Land Reform in Russia, 1906–1917: Peasant Responses to Stolypin's Project of Rural Transformation* (Oxford, 1999).

25. David Macey and more recently V. G. Tiukavkin and O. G. Vronskii have argued that the reforms were both realistic and well conceived (although Vronskii with

the important caveat that they arrived too late). In contrast, Judith Pallot and Pavel Zyrianov both maintain that the reforms were flawed from the very start by unrealistic utopian visions. David Macey, "The Peasant Commune and the Stolypin Reforms: Peasant Attitudes, 1906–14," in Bartlett, ed., *Land Commune*, 220–36; O. G. Vronskii, *Gosudarstvennaia vlast' Rossii i krest'ianskaia obshchina v gody "velikikh potriasenii" (1905–1917)* (Tula, 2000); Tiukavkin; P. N. Zyrianov, *Krest'ianskaia obshchina Evropeiskoi Rossii, 1907–1914* (Moscow, 1992).

26. Most recently, Peter M. Jones, *Liberty and Locality in Revolutionary France: Six Villages Compared, 1760–1820* (Cambridge and New York, 2003).

1—Ideologies of Authority and Institutional Settings

1. Anatole Leroy-Beaulieu, *L'Empire des tsars et les Russes* (Paris, 1990), 511, 526.
2. Ibid., 507, 516.
3. Quoted in Heidi Whelan, *Alexander III and the State Council: Bureaucracy and Counterreform in Late Imperial Russia* (New Brunswick, NJ, 1981), 48; Weissman, 27.
4. Derek Sayer, "Everyday Forms of State Formation: Some Dissident Remarks on Hegemony," in Joseph and Nugent, eds., *Everyday Forms of State Formation*, 369–70.
5. There exists a vast literature on the emergence and ethos of bureaucratic reformers ("enlightened bureaucrats") in the nineteenth century. See especially Bruce Lincoln, *In the Vanguard of Reform: Russia's Enlightened Bureaucrats, 1825–1861* (DeKalb, IL, 1982).
6. For discussions of the Editing Commission's deliberations, see L. G. Zakharova, *Samoderzhavie i otmena krepostnogo prava v Rossii, 1856–1861* (Moscow, 1984); Daniel Field, *The End of Serfdom: Nobility and Bureaucracy in Russia, 1855–1861* (Cambridge, MA, 1976); Wcislo, 11–45.
7. "Mestnoe polozhenie o pozemel'nom ustroistve krest'ian, vodvorennykh na pomeshchich'ikh zemliakh v guberniakh velikorossiiskikh, novorossiiskikh i belorusskikh," *PSZ*, 2nd series, vol. 36, no. 36662, 19 February 1861, art. 5.
8. Regulations regarding communal land were included in regionally specific codexes. Only in some regions could communes register as hereditary communes *(podvornoe obshchestvo)* if they already held arable land in inheritable usage (Belorussia notably). And only the communes of New Russia were allowed to chose their status at Emancipation. A commune could vote to change its legal status, but few did so: over 95% of communes of the 29 Great Russian provinces remained classified as redistributional in 1905. "Mestnoe polozhenie," arts. 110–19. Tsentral'nyi statisticheskii komitet, *Statistika zemlevladeniia 1905 g. Svod dannykh po 50 guberniiam Evropeiskoi Rossii* (St. Peterburg, 1907), 80–129.
9. On the *skhod's* jurisdiction: "Obshchee polozhenie o krest'ianakh vyshedshikh iz krepostnoi zavisimosti," *PSZ*, 2nd series, vol. 36, no. 36657, 19 February 1861, art. 51; A. A. Leont'ev, *Krest'ianskoe pravo. Sistematicheskoe izlozhenie osobenostei zakonodatel'stva o krest'ianakh*, 2nd ed. (St. Petersburg, 1914), 71–79.
10. On the modalities of the system of collective responsibility: "Obshchee polozhenie," arts. 187–88; "Polozhenie o vykupe krest'ianami vyshedshimi iz krepostnoi zavisimosti," *PSZ* 36, no. 36659, 19 February 1861, art. 127.
11. "Polozhenie o vykupe," arts. 163, 165–67, 169–70; V. G. Chernukha, *Krest'ianskii vopros v pravitel'stvennoi politike Rossii (60–70 gody XIX v.)* (Leningrad, 1972), 170–96. State peasants remained tenants of state land until 1886 when they were included in the redemption process, with payments spread over 44 years.
12. "Obshchee polozhenie," arts. 64, 78, 81–86.
13. Ibid., arts. 93–110. On custom: arts. 38, 102; on the Rural Code: art. 107. Cathy Frierson, "Rural Justice in Public Opinion: The Volost' Court Debate, 1861–1912," *SEER* 64, no. 4 (1986): 526–29; Peter Czap, "The Influence of Slavophile

Ideology on the Formation of the Volost Court of 1861 and the Practice of Peasant Self-Justice between 1861 and 1889" (Ph.D. diss., Cornell University, 1959), 46–79.

14. Such a code never saw the light of day. When the volost court was reformed in 1889, it was again to follow an outdated code, the Regulations on Punishments, that had been written for the long abolished justices of the peace. As Stephen Frank has aptly pointed out, some ethnographers of the 1870s and 1880s forgot about this legislative oddity, identifying as custom what had in fact been shaped by earlier legislation. *Crime*, 39–42.

15. This formulation is borrowed from Luebke, 2.

16. Wcislo, 31. The most glaring and often cited example of this contradiction was that although the General Statute granted former serfs "rights equal with other free rural inhabitants" (art. 23), peasants remained (until 1904 when corporal punishment was revoked) the only group subject to such punishment. Frank, *Crime*, 226–38.

17. The most precise discussion of the legal issues can be found in O. A. Khauke, *Krest'ianskoe zemel'noe pravo* (Moscow, 1914), 285–97. In English, the best account of the intricacies of peasant landholding in the post-Emancipation era remains Geroid Robinson's, *Rural Russia under the Old Regime* (Berkeley, 1972), 67–70. See also Lewin, "The *Obshchina* and the Village," in Bartlett, ed., *Land Commune*, 20–22; and L. I. Kuchumova, "Sel'skaia pozemel'naia obshchina evropeiskoi Rossii v 60–70e gody XIX v.," *IZ* 106 (1981): 323–35.

18. For examples of such attempts to force the merger of separate land communes: GARO, f. 721, op. 2 (1890), dd. 16b, 16i. Other problems are outlined in N. M. Tsytovich, *Sel'skoe obshchestvo kak organ mestnogo upravleniia* (Kiev, 1911), 31–36.

19. F. L. Barykov, ed., *Sbornik materialov dlia izucheniia sel'skoi pozemel'noi obshchiny* (St. Petersburg, 1880), 193, 238, 257–58; GARF, f. 586, op. 1, d. 120, ll. 49, 69. I am grateful to Stephen Frank for sharing with me materials from the Pleve fond. *Doklady chlenov Riazanskoi gubernskoi zemskoi upravy o revizii volostei uezdov Spasskogo, Sapozhkovskogo, Skopinskogo i Riazhskogo* (Moscow, 1875), 274; Kuchumova, 334–40; Boris Mironov, "The Russian Peasant Commune after the Reforms of the 1860s," *SR* 44, no. 3 (1985): 438–67. Subdivision of village societies was especially pronounced in the 1860s and 1870s. Their number in Vladimir, for instance, grew 60% over this period. *Vladimirskii zemskii sbornik*, no. 9 (1882): 148–49.

20. Only the 1899 law was incorporated into subsequent editions of the General Statute, which otherwise continued to speak exclusively of the *sel'skoe obshchestvo*. Khauke, 285–97.

21. L. Lichkov, "Krugovaia poruka i obshchinnoe zemlevladenie," *RM*, no. 10 (1886): 21–39; Khauke, 279–84.

22. V. Iu. Skalon, *Zemskie vzgliady na reforma mestnogo upravleniia* (Moscow, 1884), 39–41; E. Markov, "Uezdnoe upravlenie," *Russkaia rech'*, no. 9 (1881): 266–315.

23. N. K. Brzheskii, *Natural'nye povinnosti krest'ian i mirskie sbory* (St. Petersburg, 1906), 90–95, 170–72, 211–12; N. M. Astyrev, "Mirskie raskhody," *RM*, no. 12 (1886): 73–100; I. M. Strakhovskii, "Sovremennoe polozhenie i znachenie krest'ianskikh volostei," *VP*, no. 9 (1901): 34; E. Ganeizer, "Mirskie sbory v odnom uezde," *RB*, no. 7 (1896): 145–53.

24. Cited in Pearson, *Russian Officialdom*, 84–85.

25. S. Sashkov, "Russkaia obshchina i ee vragi," *Delo*, no. 1 (1881): 146–48; A. P. "Sovremennye zemtsy i ikh nuzhdy," *OZ*, no. 6 (1881): 70–79.

26. On populist thinking about the *kulak-miroed*, see Frierson, *Peasant Icons*, 139–60.

27. Quoted in Pearson, *Russian Officialdom*, 81. For a good example of one of many "sketches from the countryside" published in the national press about chaos and corruption in the village, see "Ocherki krest'ianskogo samoupravleniia (Iz podmoskovkoi zhizni)," *Russkie vedomosti*, no. 250 (1878): 1–2.

28. Skalon, 87.

29. On the activities and shortcomings of the peace arbiters, see M. M. Kataev, *Mestnye krest'ianskie uchrezhdenii, 1861, 1874, 1889*, 3 vols. (St. Petersburg, 1911–1912), 2:83–85; Chernukha, 26–54, 56, 62; Pearson, *Russian Officialdom*, 28–39.

30. Kataev, 2: 83–104; Skalon, 49–53. The five members of the district bureaus were the zemstvo-elected permanent member, the district police chief, the marshal of nobility, the president of the district zemstvo, and—for review of judicial cases—one honorary justice of the peace. S. A. Korf, *Administrativnaia iustitsiia v Rossii*, 2 vols. (St. Petersburg, 1910), 2:21–22.

31. The provincial board, as an instance of cassation, was hardly designed to address such complaints. It focused on the same procedural questions already examined by the district board, and the motives for its decisions were even more laconic (usually not provided at all). GARO, f. 694, op. 22 (1882), dd. 260, 337, 361–62, 318–19, 349, 372, 497–99, 464–65; op. 29 (1889), dd. 142, 157, 168, 193, 200, 254, 337, 390. See also Leon'tev, *Krest'ianskoe pravo*, 1st ed., 141–44; Kataev, 2:105–9.

32. Tsytovich, 89.

33. Joan Neuberger, "Popular Legal Cultures: The Saint Petersburg *Mirovoi Sud*," in *Russia's Great Reforms, 1855–1881*, ed. Ben Eklof, John Bushnell, and Larissa Zakharova (Bloomington, IN, 1994); B. V. Vilenskii, *Sudebnaia reforma i kontrreforma v Rossii* (Saratov, 1969), 164–67.

34. See, for instance, accounts by former justices: M. N. P., "Sud v derevne (Iz dnevnika byvshego mirovogo sud'i)," *Nabliudatel'*, no. 2 (1882): 95–124; Ia. Ludmer, "Bab'i stony (Iz zametok mirovogo sud'i)," *IuV*, no. 11 (1884): 446–67. On the shortcomings of the justices, see especially Thomas Pearson, "Russian Law and Rural Justice: Activity and Problems of the Russian Justices of the Peace, 1865–1889," *JfGO* 32, no. 1 (1984): 52–71; Jörg Baberowski, *Autokratie und Justiz. Zum Verhältnis von Rechtsstaatlichkeit und Rückständigkeit im ausgehenden Zarenreich, 1864–1914* (Frankfurt am Main, 1996), chap. 4.

35. For further discussion of MVD debates and projects in the 1870s and early 1880s, see N. M. Druzhinin, *Russkaia derevnia na perelome, 1861–1880* (Moscow, 1978), 28–37; Chernukha, 56–65.

36. Wcislo, 71–79; Pearson, *Russian Officialdom*, 119–34. On debates over the role of law in state reform see William Wagner, *Marriage, Property, and Law in Late Imperial Russia* (Oxford, 1994), 1–12.

37. Skalon, 43–44, 77; F. A. Preobrazhenskii, *Voprosy krest'ianskogo samoupravlenii. Sel'skie uchrezhdeniia i dolzhnostnye litsa* (Moscow, 1893), 5–6, 17.

38. A. Pazukhin, *Sovremennoe sostoianie Rossii i soslovnyi vopros* (Moscow, 1886). For discussion of conservative criticism of peasant self-government, see James Mandel, "Paternalistic Authority in the Russian Countryside, 1856–1906" (Ph.D. diss., Columbia University, 1978), 229–99; Frank Wcislo, "The Land Captain Reform of 1889 and the Reassertion of Unrestricted Autocratic Authority," *Russian History* 15, no. 2–4 (1988): 285–326.

39. Macey, *Government and Peasant*, 30. There clearly were more than two positions on the complex question of how Russia should be governed, even within top echelons of the bureaucracy. I have deliberately simplified here divergent views to their simplest common denominators. For more complete and nuanced discussions of autocratic ideals (in addition to works by Wagner, Wcislo, Pearson, and Macey already cited), see Andrew Verner, *The Crisis of Russian Autocracy: Nicholas II and the 1905 Revolution* (Princeton, 1990), chap. 3.

40. The most thorough discussions of the politics behind the Land Captain Statute are in P. A. Zaionchkovskii, *Rossiiskoe samoderzhavie v kontse XIX stoletiia* (Moscow, 1970), chap. 8; Mandel, 125–218; and Whelan, chap. 10.

41. Wortman, *Scenarios of Power*, vol. 2.

42. Korf, 2: 33.

43. *PSZ*, 3rd series, vol. 9, no. 6195, 12 July 1889, 507.

44. "Polozhenie o zemskikh uchastkovikh nachal'nikov," *PSZ*, 3rd series, vol. 9, no. 6196, 12 July 1889, arts. 6–7, 15.

45. Quoted in Wcislo, *Reforming*, 106. Most recent work on Alexander III has convincingly rejected the characterization of the land captain reform as a "noble reaction," seeing it rather as a "statist reaction." See Whelan, 175–85; Thomas Pearson, "Origins of Alexander III's Land Captains: A Reinterpretation," *SR* 40, no. 3 (1981): 384–403, 25; Yaney, *Urge*, 70–80; P. N. Zyrianov, "Sotsial'naia struktura mestnogo upravleniia kapitalisticheskoi Rossii," *IZ* 107 (1982): 262–65. A significant dissenting voice is Seymour Becker's. He rightly insists that even the most reactionary of nobles defined their role as loyal servants of autocracy in terms consonant with the language of the 1889 legislation. What Becker neglects, however, is disagreement over the nature of this service. Seymour Becker, *Nobility and Privilege in Late Imperial Russia* (DeKalb, IL, 1985), 58–62, 221–22.

46. The governor of Tula, for instance, noted in 1892 that local noble leaders were unhappy with the reform, which in their view strengthened bureaucratic power at the expense of local noble influence. RGIA-otchety, "Vsepoddanneishii otchet Tul'skogo gubernatora za 1892," vol. 103:11. For further discussion of noble grumbling, see A. P. Korelin, *Dvorianstvo v poreformennoi Rossii, 1861–1904* (Moscow, 1979), 199–201.

47. For the broadest interpretation of the range of issues falling under article 39, see V. A. Beer, *Kommentarii novykh provintsial'nykh uchrezhdenii 12 iiulia 1889 goda*, 2 vols. (Moscow, 1894–1895), 1:124–31.

48. "Polozhenie o zemskikh nachal'nikakh," arts. 48–50; "Pravila o proizvodstve sudebnykh del', podvedomstvennykh zemskim nachal'nikam i gorodskim sud'iam," *PSZ*, 3rd series, vol. 9, no. 6483, 29 December 1889, arts. 20–28, 162–63; Tsytovich, 92–94.

49. Cathy Frierson, "Peasant Family Divisions and the Commune," in Bartlett, ed., *Land Communes*, 303–20.

50. *PSZ*, 3rd series, vol. 13, no. 9754, 8 June 1893, and no. 10151, 14 December 1893; I. L. Goremykin, ed., *Svod uzakonenii i rasporiazhenii pravitel'stva ob ustroistve sel'skogo sostoianiia* (St. Petersburg, 1898), 1:567. For a superb discussion of the evolution of property laws, see Olga Crisp, "Peasant Land Tenure and Civil Rights Implications before 1906," in *Civil Rights in Imperial Russia*, ed. Olga Crisp and Linda Edmondson (Oxford, 1989).

51. A similar dilemma was faced by British officials in late colonial Africa. Sally Falk-Moore, "Treating Law as Knowledge: Telling Colonial Officers What to Say to Africans about Running 'Their Own' Native Courts," *Law and Society Review* 26, no. 1 (1992): 11–45.

52. GARO, f. 695, op. 1 (1890), d. 7, ll. 12–20.

53. Ibid., f. 58, op. 9 (1891), sv. 1, d. 1, ll. 43–44. For some virulent expressions of such dismay, see A. N. Naumov, *Iz utselevshikh vospominanii, 1868–1917*, 2 vols. (New York, 1954–1955), 1:195; "Zapiska Krapivenskogo uezdnogo predvoditelia dvorianstva," *Grazhdanin*, no. 83 (1892): 1.

54. Alexander III even continued to appoint individuals who held reformist ideas he abhorred to high posts because they had become indispensable for the proper functioning of the bureaucracy. Whelan; Taranovski, "Alexander III and His Bureaucracy," 207–19.

55. Wagner. Peter Liessem has argued that the Senate's use of judicial precedent institutionalized jurisprudence even in the sphere of administrative justice. *Verwaltungsgerichtsbarkeit im späten Zarenreich. Der Dirigierende Senat und seine Entscheidungen zur russischen Selbstverwaltung, 1864–1917* (Frankfurt am Main, 1996).

56. *PSZ*, 2nd series, vol. 39, no. 41475, 20 November 1864, art. 5. On the function and organization of the Senate, see *Istoriia pravitel'stvuiushchego senata za dvesti let', 1711–1911*, 5 vols. (St. Petersburg, 1911), 4:11–57.

57. Korf, 2:29–33.

58. "Polozhenie o zemskikh nachal'nikakh," arts. 126–29; "Pravila o proizvodstve sudebnykh del'," preamble: part 3-1. Many key Senate rulings and MVD circulars on cassation procedures are reprinted in Goremykin, 1:769–77.

59. E. Przhevalinskii, "Novye otsy-Senatory," *IuG*, no. 87 (1895): 2; "O gubernskikh prisutstviakh kak kassatsionnykh instantsiiakh," *SG*, no. 7 (1892): 1. The problems related to the lack of uniformity in the cassation rulings of provincial boards were regularly discussed in legal journals. See for instance, "Iz deiatel'nosti gubernskikh prisutstvii," *IuV*, no. 3 (1891): 410–24; D. L. "Neskol'ko slov o gubernskikh po sudebnykh delam prisutstviiakh," *ZhGiUP*, no. 12, part 2 (1893): 55–67; B. Filatov, "Iz deiatel'nosti gubernskikh prisutstvii," *ZhIuO*, no. 10 (1894): 95–108; V., "Dvoinaia Kassatsiia," *IuV*, no. 2 (1892): 279–84.

60. I. Danilov, *Sbornik reshenii Pravitel'stvuiushchego Senata po krest'ianskim delam, 1890–1898* (St. Petersburg, 1898), 191–92; Kataev, 2:107–8; Leon'tev, *Krest'ianskoe pravo*, 1st ed., 153–54.

61. George Yaney has argued that the requirement of unanimous decisions in effect gave ministers veto power over Senate decisions. In fact, the changes in voting regulations of 1869 required a majority of three-quarters for all cases initiated either by individual complaint or by presentation by lower instances. The new voting rules covered the majority of cases dealing with peasant administration. *Istoriia senata*, 4:252, 444–46; Yaney, *Systematization*, 259–60.

62. *Istoriia senata*, 4: 263–6, 280; "Iuridicheskoe obozrenie," *VP*, no. 1 (1899): 214–23. The text of the 1896 ruling can be found in I. Danilov, 419–24.

63. The text of the first (1894) decision can be found in I. Danilov, 284. The second is in Pavel Briunelli, *Krest'ianskii advokat. Nastol'naia spravochnaia kniga* (St. Petersburg, 1912), 569. For the third, see Zmirlov, "Khronika," *ZhMIu*, no. 3 (1902): 194–95. See also *Istoriia senata*, 4:266–67.

64. Such critiques were especially common in the reactionary *Grazhdanin*, published by Prince V. P. Meshcherskii, who had been instrumental in the passage of the land captain legislation, and in *Moskovskie vedomosti*.

65. GARO, f. 58, op. 9 (1891), sv. 1, d. 1, ll. 4, 23–25, 28, 32, 36–38, 106, 130.

66. Ibid., ll. 31, 39–40.

67. GARO, f. 5, op. 5 (1890), d. 1803, ll. 1–6ob. Richard Robbins discusses the role of land captains in famine relief and describes similar barrages of "governor to land captain" circulars in other provinces. He has concluded that, on balance, most governors and MVD officials judged the land captains to have been "extremely useful" in combating the famine. Given that this assessment is based in large part on annual reports, it no doubt requires qualification. *Famine in Russia, 1891–1892: The Imperial Government Responds to a Crisis* (New York, 1975), 130–8, 149–55.

68. Robbins, *Tsar's Viceroys*, 189–92; Yaney, *Urge*, 297–301.

69. RGIA-otchety, "Otchet Tul'skogo gubernatora za 1896," vol. 103: 7; I. A. Vorontsov, "Tul'skie zemskie nachal'niki," *MV*, no. 47 (1901): 2.

70. Weissman, 28.

71. See especially A. A. Rittikh, *Zavisimost' krest'ian ot obshchini i mira* (St. Petersburg, 1903) and *Krestianskoe zemlepol'zovanie* (St. Petersburg, 1903), 3–24. Several historians have convincingly challenged the view that communal agriculture was necessarily agronomically regressive. See especially Pallot, *Land Reform*, chap. 3; Roger Bidelux, "Agricultural Advance under the Russian Village Commune System," in Bartlett, ed., *Land Commune*, 196–218; Esther Kingston-Mann, "Peasant Communes and Economic Innovation: A Preliminary Inquiry," in *Peasant Economy, Culture, and Politics of European Russia, 1800–1921*, ed. Esther Kingston-Mann and Timothy Mixter (Princeton, 1991), 23–51. Even David Kerans, who has recently argued that peasant agricultural techniques were indeed ineffective and irrational, does not attribute inefficiency to the commune (*Mind and Labor on the Farm in Black-Earth Russia, 1861–1914* [Budapest and New York, 2001]). For a meticulous study of the economic rationality of "traditional" modes of agriculture, see Jean Meuvret, *Le problème des subsistences à l'époque de Louis XIV*, 3 vols. (Paris, 1977–1988), especially vol. 2, which deals with common rights. For a more recent study, which suggests fascinating parallels for Russian agricultural history, see Philip Hoffman, *Growth in a Traditional Society: The French Countryside, 1450–1815* (Princeton, 1996).

72. I. I. Vorontsov-Dashkov, *K proektu pravil o zemel'nykh peredelakh Ministerstva vnutrennikh del* (St. Petersburg, 1892), 5–6, 13–14.

73. A. M. Anfimov, *Ekonomicheskoe polozhenie i klassovaia bor'ba krest'ian Evropeiskoi Rossii, 1881–1904* (Moscow, 1984),101–3; Ministerstvo finansov, Departament okladnykh sborov, *Sushchestvuiushchii poriadok vzimaniia okladnykh sborov s krest'ian*, 2 vols. (St. Petersburg, 1894–1895). This survey, as well as the far-reaching ramifications of the passport system, have been superbly analyzed in Burds, 51–88. See also M. S. Simonova, "Otmena krugovoi poruki," *IZ* 83 (1969): 170–75.

74. N. Brzheskii, *Nedoimochnost' i krugovaia poruka sel'skikh obshchestv* (St. Petersburg, 1897), 408–10; A. S. Ermolov, *Neurozhai i narodnoe bedstvie* (St. Petersburg, 1892); Simonova, "Otmena," 174.

75. Material from the local committees most critical of the commune were compiled in A. A. Rittikh, *Krest'ianskii pravoporiadok* (St. Petersburg, 1904). For discussion of Witte's Special Conference as well as the MVD's parallel Editing Commission for the Review of the Legal Condition of the Peasantry and their role in preparing the terrain for the Stolypin reforms, see Macey, *Government and Peasant;* and M. S. Simonova, *Krizis agrarnoi politiki nakanune pervoi Rossiiskoi revoliutsii* (Moscow, 1987), 155–91.

76. V. N. Snezhkov, *Posobie dlia volostnykh sudov preobrazovannykh po zakonu 12-go iulia 1889 g.* (Moscow, 1912), 291–96; I. S. Uryson, "Zakon 5-go okt. 1906 goda," *Krest'ianskoe delo*, no. 18 (1910): 3–4; "Po povodu Ukaza 5 okt. 1906," *IuG*, (1906) no. 68: 1986–89; no. 70: 2051–53.

77. M. Mys', "Krest'ianskaia konstitutsiia," *VP*, no. 4 (1906): 126–78. The decree also revoked the governors' right to select peasant deputies to zemstvo assemblies from among lists of electors chosen at volost assemblies, thus restoring direct peasant elections.

78. This is the argument advanced by George Yaney in *Urge*, chap. 4.

79. "Ob ustroistve ispytanii," *IZO*, no. 2 (1908): 94–96; RGIA, f. 1291, op. 31 (1911), d. 432, ll. 8–11. Quotation is from f. 1291, op. 30 (1903), d. 49, l. 55a.

80. *IZO*, no. 8 (1905): 323.

81. N. T. Volkov, ed., *Nakaz zemskim nachal'nikam po administrativnym delam* (Moscow, 1907), 8. George Yaney has argued that the MVD gradually ceased to see land captains as rural "knights" and more as mere bureaucratic executors. In fact, few in the ministry saw these two functions as contradictory, either in 1889 or after 1905.

82. Ibid., 13–14. For sample inspection programs, see *IZO* (1912): no. 1, 21–27; no. 4, 145–50.

83. In his 23 January 1906 memo, Witte proposed that land captains be subordinated to the governors. Bulygin's successor, P. N. Durnovo, successfully fought off Witte's proposal, reminding the tsar that the local nobility, which had always expressed sincere devotion to the throne, would interpret such a measure as a sign of distrust and an unmerited insult. RGIA, f. 1291, op. 30 (1906), d. 71, ll. 2, 12–13ob.

84. GARO, f. 695, op. 1 (1890), d. 6, n.p.

85. *PSZ*, 3rd series, vol. 26, no. 28528 (1906), 970–74; and vol. 30, no. 33743, 1910, 746–53. The law of 29 May 1911 ("O zemleustroistve"), regulated land reorganization: *PSZ*, 3rd series, vol. 31 no. 35370 (1911), 453–71.

86. "Neotchuzhdaemost' krest'ianskikh nadelov," *Pravo*, no. 5 (1908): 280–87; *IZO*, no. 9 (1912): 402–3; Yaney, *Urge*, 263–64.

87. Quoted in Geoffrey Hosking, *The Russian Constitutional Experiment: Government and Duma, 1907–1914* (Cambridge, 1973), 150.

88. Quoted in A. Posnikov, "Zakon 14-go iiunia," *VE*, no. 9 (1910): 237.

89. See especially Waldron, 60–92; Tiukavkin, 161–69. On property reform, see Kotsonis, 57–67. The debate over goals is in my view somewhat futile when its purpose is to establish a measure against which the agrarian reform's success can be assessed. It is logical that those who have focused on the meticulous studies and projects penned prior to 1906 (such as David Macey) would stress agronomic aims, while historians who study the immediate political context of 1906 would emphasize politi-

cal motives. In addition, there existed a variety of reform visions within the bureaucracy: idealization for the enclosed homestead and unabashed hostility to the commune characterized A. A. Kofod (chief inspector of the land settlement administration); concern for agricultural improvement even within the confines of the commune was the primary concern of A. A. Rittikh (head of land reform administration); while the Octobrists and rightist majority in the Duma wished to destroy peasants' "blind faith in expanse [of land] *(prostranstvo)*" and to inculcate them with respect for property. Judith Pallot has been most attuned to the variety of reform visions coexisting in the bureaucracy *(Land Reform*, chap. 2). See chap. 1 of the same book for a good historiographical overview. Also V. S. Konovalov, *Krest'ianstvo i reformy. Rossiiskaia derevnia v nachale XX veka. Analiticheskii obzor* (Moscow, 2000).

90. For the text of these proposals, with explanatory notes: "Proekt o polozheniia o posel'kovom upravlenii," *IZO*, no. 3 (1907): 96–115; "Proekt polozheniia o volostnom upravlenii," no. 4 (1907): 143–54; "Proekt o pravitel'stvennykh uchastkovykh kommisarakh," no. 5 (1907): 187 ff. On the court reforms: *Materialy k zakonu*, vol. 1. On the fate of these and other reform proposals, see Hosking, chap. 6; Waldron, 82–90.

91. N. P. Rudin, *Novyi volostnoi sud* (St. Petersburg, 1915), 23, as quoted in Gareth Popkins, "The Russian Peasant Volost Court and Customary Law, 1861–1917" (Ph.D. diss, Oxford University, 1995), 100. On volost court reforms, see especially P. N. Zyrianov, "Tret'ia Duma i vopros o reforme mestnogo suda i volostnogo upravlenia," *Istoriia SSSR*, no. 6 (1969): 45–62. On the revival of attachment to estate institutions in the MVD after 1911, see Wcislo, *Reforming*, 288–304.

92. Robbins, *Tsar's Viceroys*, 90.

93. On the latter point, see Wcislo, *Reforming*, 116–17, 251. On the importance of the position of land captain or permanent member of the provincial board as a stepping stone to higher administrative positions, see Robbins, *Tsar's Viceroys*, 28–38.

2—LAND CAPTAINS, PEASANT OFFICIALS, AND THE EXPERIENCE OF LOCAL AUTHORITY

1. The 1889 reforms were introduced in stages until 1903 throughout 43 provinces.

2. "Vnutrennee obozrennee," *VE*, no. 3 (1890): 377–81; *IaGV* (1891), no. 70: 1–2; no. 75: 2–3; no. 79: 1–2 (thanks to Stephen Frank for this reference); *PV* (1890), no. 208: 1–2; no. 211: 1–2.

3. *IaGV*, no. 51 (1891): 3–6.

4. RGIA-otchety, "Otchet Vladimirskoi gubernii za 1890," vol. 15:8–9; "Otchet Iaroslavskoi gubernii za 1893," vol. 120:5; "Otchet Tverskoi gubernii za 1891," vol. 98:12, and "Otchet za 1893," vol. 98:15–16; GARO, f. 5, op. 5, d. 1803, "Otchet Riazanskogo gubernatora za 1890," and d. 1984, "Otchet za 1893." For more measured positive assessments, see Ia. Litvinov, "Zemskie nachal'niki, ikh administrativnaia i sudebnaia deiatel'nost'," *RO*, no. 11 (1895): 186–200; and A. Bukeevskii, "Vnutrennee obozrenie," *RO*, no. 3 (1896): 501–9.

5. O. Likhtenshtadt, "Zemskii nachal'nik o dukhe i kharaktere svoi dolzhnosti," *SV*, no. 5 (1896): 305–7; "Vnutrennee obozrenie," *VE*, no. 1 (1894): 451–52; *SV*, no. 1, pt. 2 (1891): 51–52; *IuG*, no. 100 (1892): 1. On forms of address see N. Druzhinin, "Vy i ty," *IuV*, no. 1 (1892): 119–25, and *SG*, no. 8 (1892): 6. On the justice's reputation for dispensing "equal respect," see Neuberger, 237.

6. K. Ia. Kozhukhar, "Zemskie nachal'niki," *VP*, no. 5 (1905): 96.

7. A. V. Shapkarin, ed., *Krest'ianskoe dvizhenie v Rossii v 1890–1900 gg. Sbornik dokumentov* (Moscow, 1959), 36–39, 65, 88–92, 103–8; S. T. Semenov, *Dvadtsat' piat' let v derevne*

(Petrograd, 1915), 86–87; *SV*, no. 1, pt. 2 (1891): 50–51 (Novgorod); "Zemskie nachal'niki," *Grazhdanin*, no. 120 (1895): 5; *IaGV*, no. 79 (1891): 1–2; "Tul'skie zemskie nachal'niki," *MV*, no. 41 (1901): 1; "Zemskii nachal'nik," *Grazhdanin*, no. 129 (1895): 5 (Ufa).

8. RGIA-otchety, "Otchet Tul'skoi gubernii za 1892," vol. 103:11.

9. The Protopopov case achieved notoriety, largely due to a widely reported scathing accusatory speech to the Senate by the procurator and celebrated jurist A. F. Koni. The speech can be found in A. F. Koni, *Sobranie sochinenii*, vol.3, *Sudebnye rechi* (Moscow, 1967), 377–94. For a full discussion of this incident and others, see Sylvain Bensidoun, *L'agitation paysanne en Russie de 1881 à 1902* (Paris, 1975), 348–85; Shapkarin, 88–91, 177–97.

10. In addition to the 29 former justices, 10 Riazan land captains were former peace mediators (or candidates), and 8 had been permanent members of district boards. Only 12 had no prior experience in rural administration. GARO, f. 5, op. 5 (1890), d. 1744, l. 5ob. Data from Tula are from Mandel, 285. Data for 10 provinces are compiled from *PV*, nos. 17, 20, 31, 32, 192, 200, 212, 229, 254, 261, 271 (1890). See also David Macey, "The Land Captains: A Note on Their Social Composition, 1889–1913," *Russian History* 16, nos. 2–4 (1989): 327–51. In 1901–1902, the proportion of former officers for 40 provinces remained at its earlier levels, at 42% (Korelin, 202).

11. GARO, f. 694, op. 27 (1887), d. 6, and f. 695, op. 6 (1895), d. 12.

12. GARF, f. 586, op. 1, d. 123, l. 2.

13. RGIA-otchety, "Otchet Vladimirskoi gubernii za 1890," vol. 15:11–13; *Vladimirskii zemskii sbornik*, no. 9 (1882): 160–71.

14. Kozhukhar, no. 8: 82–89, 58; "Gubernatorskaia reviziia," *IuG*, no. 19 (1892): 2; no. 35 (1893): 3; "Vnutrennee obozrenie," *VE*, no. 1 (1894): 450–51.

15. TsIAM, f. 62, op. 4, d. 27; "Deiatel'nost' zemskikh nachal'nikov Orlovskoi gubernii za 1892," *IuG*, no. 7 (1894): 3.

16. GARO, f. 695, op. 11 (1900), d. 17.

17. "Vnutrennee obozrenie," *VE*, no. 1 (1894): 450.

18. I. M. Strakhovskii, "Krest'ianskii vopros," in *Nuzhdy derevni po rabotam komitetov o nuzhdakh sel'sko-khoziaistvennykh promyshlennosti* (St. Petersburg, 1904), 1:122.

19. V. V. Tenishev, *Administrativnoe polozhenie russkogo krest'ianina* (St. Petersburg, 1908), 63.

20. S. T. Semenov, 86–95, 186–8. For Semenov's biography, see Orlando Figes's lively account in *A People's Tragedy*, 183–84, 232–39, 361–63, 786–89.

21. Naumov, 187–89, 193, 199, 217–19.

22. N. M. Astyrev, *V volostnykh pisariakh*, 1st ed. (Moscow, 1886), 34. See also letters from land captains to the newspaper *Grazhdanin*: "Zemskii nachal'nik," no. 120 (1895): 5; "Khronika praktiki zemskogo nachal'nika," no. 353 (1894): 5.

23. S. Matveev, "V volostnykh starshinakh," *RB*, no. 2 (1912): 79–82.

24. A. I. Novikov, *Zapiski zemskogo nachal'nika* (St. Petersburg, 1899), 37–39, 93–94, 99–102, 204–5. On Novikov, see Samuel Ramer, "Democracy versus the Rule of a Civic Elite: Aleksandr Ivanovich Novikov and the Fate of Self-Government," *CMRS* 22, no. 2–3 (1981): 167–85.

25. "Pis'mo zemskogo nachal'nika," *Grazhdanin*, no. 120 (1895): 5; no. 339 (1894): 4; V. Ianovich, *Itogi shestiletiia (zametki zemskogo nachal'nika)* (Perm, 1902); GARO, f. 5, op. 5 (1889), d. 1744, ll. 6ob.–7; GARF, f. 586, op. 1, d. 123, ll. 25, 34; d. 120, ll. 6, 17, 50, 82; Matveev, "V volostnykh starshinakh," no. 2: 78–86.

26. "Khronika praktiki zemskikh nachal'nikov," *Grazhdanin*, no. 339 (1894): 4; RGIA-otchety, "Otchet Tul'skoi gubernii za 1892," vol. 103:13; "Zemskie nachal'niki v Tul'skoi gubernii," *Russkie vedomosti*, no. 278 (1900): 2.

27. RGIA-otchety, "Otchet Penzenskoi gubernii za 1894," vol. 64a: 8–9; "Otchet Moskovskoi gubernii za 1908," vol. 55:67–67ob.; GARO, f. 5, op. 2 (1900), d. 2235, l. 7ob. On MVD efforts to increase its budget for land captains, see Macey, "Land Captains," 341–42.

28. Naumov, 234; Ianovich, 118.

29. N. Dunin, "Chem dolzhen byt' deiatel'nost' zemskogo nachal'nika," *IuG,* no. 69 (1892): 2; "Zapiska," *Grazhdanin,* no. 83 (1892): 1.

30. Ianovich, 57–60.

31. *VE,* no. 9 (1891): 283; "Oblastnoi otdel," *SV,* no. 6 (1891): 85; *VE,* no. 10 (1892): 839; *IZO* (1909), no. 1:22 and no. 3:54.

32. Naumov, 222.

33. Gurko, *IZO,* no. 8 (1905): 324–25; Naumov, 224; Ianovich, 106–8; Novikov, 36–38; "Vnutennee obozrenie," *VE,* no. 7–8 (1893): 377.

34. Besides the land captains, who served by rotation, the administrative sessions of the district congresses were attended by the chairman of the zemstvo, the police chief *(ispravnik),* and the tax inspector and were presided over by the marshal of nobility. Judicial sessions replaced tax and police officials with the district member of the circuit court, honorary justices of the peace, and municipal judges (by rotation). "Polozhenie o zemskikh nachal'nikov," arts. 71–73.

35. "Vnutennee obozrenie," *VE,* no. 12 (1891): 801; "Vnutennee obozrenie," *VE,* no. 10 (1892): 837; *IuG,* no. 35 (1893): 3; Ia. Gorodyskii, "Praktika sudebno-administrativnykh uchrezhdenii," *ZhIuO,* no. 6 (1895): 76–77; K. I. Tur, *Golos zhizni o krest'ianskom neustroistve* (St. Petersburg, 1898), 160–66; *IZO,* no. 1 (1909): 24–25; RGIA, f. 1291, op. 124 (1911), d. 54b, l. 130; op. 31 (1908), d. 87, l. 240ob.; op. 31 (1911), d. 147, ll. 4, 96–99, 108; Filatov, 107–8; Vladimir Polivanov, "Zapiski zemskogo nachal'nika," *RM,* no. 3–4 (1917): 119–20.

36. RGIA, f. 1291, op. 31 (1914), d. 250, ll. 56–8 and d. 225, ll. 6–9; TsIAM, f. 62, op. 4 (1914), d. 133, ll. 247–54.

37. GARO, f. 695, op. 11 (1900), d. 17; RGIA, f. 1291, op. 31 (1909), d. 247, ll. 15ob.–16 (1914), d. 85, ll. 15ob.–16, 65.

38. RGIA, f. 1291, op. 31 (1909), d. 241, ll. 27–29, 32ob.–33.

39. Mandel, 268.

40. RGIA, f. 1291, op. 31 (1909), d. 247, ll. 15ob–16 (Tver); *IZO,* no. 2 (1912): 64 (Saratov).

41. RGIA, f. 1291, op. 31 (1912), d. 295, l. 6.

42. From the inspection reports of the Land Section, many of which were published for general guidance in its public monthly journal: *IZO,* no. 5 (1911): 227–30. For a similar reprimand of Kherson provincial officials, see *IZO,* no. 3 (1910): 129–30.

43. Naumov, 187; Ianovich, 32–33, 61; S. A. Mikhailovskii, "Sudebno-administrativnye uchrezhdenii Tverskoi gubernii za piatiletie, 1892–1897 gg.," *Sbornik pravovedeniia i obshchestvennykh znanii* (1898), 8:164; D. Bodisko, "Metamorfozii v polozhenii instituta zemskikh nachal'nikov," *MV,* no. 354 (1899): 2.

44. Macey, "Land Captains," 344–45; Abramovich Liberman, "Sostav institut zemskikh nachal'nikov," *Voprosy istorii,* no. 8 (1976): 201–4.

45. *IZO,* no. 5 (1908): 281; no. 8 (1916): 220; no. 2 (1912): 67. Data on vacancies are from RGIA, f. 1291, op. 31 (1913), d. 526, l. 139ob.

46. RGIA, f. 1291, op. 31 (1913), d. 527, l. 126ob.

47. Polivanov, no. 7–8: 59; S. M. Sidel'nikov, ed., *Agrarnaia reforma Stolypina* (Moscow, 1973), 133–34. On the variety of land captain responses to the land reforms, see Zyrianov, *Krest'ianskaia obshchina,* 93–95; Yaney, *Urge,* 288 ff.; David Macey, "Government Actions and Peasant Reactions during the Stolypin Reforms," in *New Perspectives in Modern Russian History: Selected Papers from the Fourth World Congress for Soviet and East Euruopean Studies,* ed. Robert McKean (New York, 1992), 145–48.

48. *IZO,* no. 10 (1908): 321; RGIA, f. 1291, op. 31 (1908), d. 87, l. 242 (Tambov).

49. Novikov, 26–27, 58.

50. Ianovich, 42–44.

51. Boris Mironov has asserted as much, arguing that by the 1910s the volost elders' high salaries, paid by the state budget (on this he is incorrect), had rendered them immune to village pressures. Mironov, *Sotsial'naia istoriia*, 1:465–66.

52. *Svod zakonov rossiiskoi imperii*, vol. 9, *Osoboe prilozhenie k zakonam o sostoianiakh* (St. Petersburg, 1902), 42.

53. V. Gubanin, "Podsudnost' del ob oskorbleniiakh volostnikh sudov," *ZhMIu*, no. 3 (1903): 223–27; N. N. Bystrov, *Sistematicheskii ukazatel' voprosov razreshennykh opredeleniiami obshchogo sobraniia* (St. Petersburg, 1901), 143; K. G. Abramovich, *Krest'ianskoe pravo po resheniiam Pravitel'stvuiushchego Senata: Alfavitnyi ukazatel'* (St. Petersburg, 1902), 126; I. Danilov, 413.

54. There is little evidence, however, that the circuit courts did in fact impose significantly longer sentences than those imposed for insult by the volost courts. GARO, f. 640, op. 42 (1908), sv. 91, dd. 19–20; op. 44 (1910), sv. 97, d. 10; sv. 98, d. 18; op. 46 (1912), sv. 106, d. 6; op. 51 (1908), sv. 184, d. 1022.

55. RGIA, f. 1291, op. 31 (1908), d. 88, l. 107; A. Tiutriumov, "Kul'turnaia rol' zemskogo nachal'nika," *IuV*, no. 12 (1890): 74–80.

56. V. Kharlanov, "Volostnoe pravlenie," *Derevnia*, no. 2 (1901): 65–66. Similar linkages of physical surroundings with moral improvement were made in debates about the state of rural school buildings. Ben Eklof, "*Kindertempel* or Shack? The School Building in Late Imperial Russia (A Case Study of Backwardness)," *RR* 47, no. 2 (1988): 120–21.

57. RGIA, f. 1291, op. 31 (1908), d. 87, ll. 58, 69, 209 (Tver). On volost court ceremony, see Cathy Frierson, "I Must Always Answer to the Law," *SEER* 75, no. 2 (1997): 313–16.

58. For 1880 figures, see Pearson, *Russian Officialdom*, 87; for Tver: A. Nikolaev, *Sel'skoe samoupravlenie* (St. Petersburg, 1906), 14; and for Riazan: GARO, f. 695, op. 19 (1909), d. 76; op. 22 (1912), d. 15.

59. RGIA, f. 1291, op. 31 (1913), d. 421, l. 182 (Tver); GARO, f. 695, op. 23 (1913), d. 1, ll. 20, 58; *GARF*, f. 586, op. 1, d. 118, l. 17 (Riazan).

60. "Na sel'skom skhode," *RV*, no. 204 (1908): 3; A. A. Charushin, *Sel'skie skhody v bytovom ikh osveshchenii* (Arkhangel'sk, 1911), 11–13; Tenishev, *Administrativnoe polozhenie*, 10.

61. The hope was that village societies could at last build up capital funds to meet their social needs. GARO, f. 695, op. 23 (1913), d. 1, l. 76; "Sel'skie skhody i pianstvo," *Sel'skii vestnik*, no. 48 (1913): 4.

62. Some communes went so far as to allow nondrinking householders to receive their share of compensation in cash, entering the costs in the account books as "expenses relating to the sobriety campaign." Ivan Kupchinov, *Iz dnevnika volostnogo pisaria* (Moscow, 1910), 44; Novikov, 41; Polivanov, no. 9–10: 32–33; Tsytovich, 51. Some volost courts were known to accept as evidence of agreement or contract the fact that vodka had been offered by one of the litigants. P. Skorobogatyi, "Dokaza-tel'stvo v volostnom sude," *IuV*, no. 5 (1883): 143.

63. Although land captains were following the letter of Senate instructions, this did not prevent MVD inspectors from condemning such rulings. GARO, f. 929, op. 11 (1911), sv. 1, d. 3, l. 2; TsIAM, f. 62, op. 1 (1910), d. 4027, ll. 2–3, 6; *IZO*, no. 2 (1909): 55. On drink as a symbol of reconciliation, see Worobec, 229.

64. Gurko, *IZO*, no. 8 (1905): 328.

65. Polivanov, no. 5–6: 70; Kozhukhar, no. 8: 96.

66. For an example of the MVD's reprimand in an analogous case from Pskov, see RGIA, f. 1291, op. 50 (1911), d. 292.

67. Kozhukhar, no. 8: 63; Novikov, 36–37; Naumov, 198–99; N. Druzhinin, "Byvshie svobodnye khlebopashtsy," *Zhizn'*, no. 10 (1898): 206, 214–15; *IZO*, no. 2 (1905): 52.

68. "Temnaia derevnia," *RZh*, no. 21 (1913); Charushin, *Sel'skie skhody*, 6; Novikov, 40; Tenishev, *Administrativnoe polozhenie*, 5.

69. RGIA, f. 1291, op. 31 (1912), d. 182, ll. 60–96; op. 31 (1911), d. 401, ll. 13, 62.

70. Ibid., op. 31 (1908), d. 87, ll. 114-15, 247 (Tambov).

71. Polivanov, no. 5-6: 70-71. See also P. Golike and A. Vil'borg, *O volostnom pisare* (St. Petersburg, 1910), 18-19.

72. Polivanov, no. 5-6: 66; see also Ianovich, 49; and Novikov, 35.

73. Zemstvos recognized the unreliability of volost scribes in the 1880s, at which point they established their own networks of respondents for their famous household surveys. For routine tax, fire insurance, and famine relief matters, however, volost scribes remained the primary source of statistical information. On zemstvo statistics, see Allesandro Stanziani, "Statisticiens, zemstva et Etat dans la Russia des années 1880," *CMRS* 32, no. 4 (1991): 445-68; and David Darrow, "The Politics of Numbers: Statistics and the Search for a Theory of Peasant Economy in Russia" (Ph.D. diss., University of Iowa, 1996), especially 208-17.

74. Compiled from MVD inspection reports: RGIA, f. 1291, op. 31 (1908), d. 87 (Tambov); (1911), d. 147 (Riazan); op. 124 (1912), d. 54b (Riazan); op. 31 (1908), d. 88 (Tver); op. 31 (1913), d. 421 (Tver).

75. RGIA, f. 1291, op. 31 (1908), d. 87, l. 295 (Tambov).

76. For examples of citations, see GARO, f. 695, op. 18-1 (1908), d. 241; f. 714, op. 25 (1914), d. 79.

77. RGIA, f. 1291, op. 54 (1910), d. 40, ll. 1-1ob.; op. 31 (1908), d. 89, ll. 106ob., 103ob. (Tver); d. 88, ll. 21, 24-25, 44-45, 46, 51, 85, 119 (Tver); and d. 87, ll. 183, 269 (Tambov).

78. RGIA, f. 1291, op. 31 (1912), d. 46b, l. 203 (Riazan); GATO, f. 488, op. 1 (1914), d. 4286, ll. 1-23; RGIA, op. 54 (1912), d. 177, ll. 20-21; op. 54 (1910), d. 40; d. 29.

79. A catalogue of the ways a scribe could profit from his position can be found in F. Marychev, "Volostnoi pisar' i volost'," *VE*, no. 5 (1902): 247ff.; also *IuG*, no. 57 (1904), 3; Golike and Vil'borg, *O volostnom pisare*, 15-17. One of the few cases of corruption I was able to find in the archives was indeed extraordinary. A scribe in Poltava province had managed over almost 3 years to make 137 appeals of volost court verdicts disappear by forging papers as if they came from the district congress. His scheme was discovered only when a newly appointed land captain finally investigated why peasants were asking about cases that the district congress had never seen. RGIA, f. 1291, op. 31 (1916), d. 317, ll. 19-25.

80. RGIA, f. 1291, op. 31 (1908), d. 88, l. 14ob.

81. Strakhovskii, "Sovremennoe polozhenie," 24; Golike and Vil'borg, *O volostnom pisare*, 10; Astyrev, *V volostnykh pisariakh*, 1st ed., 30-31.

82. G. Pogorelov, *Chto takoe volostnoi pisar'?* (Moscow, 1907), 21-22.

83. GARO, f. 81, op. 21 (1913), d. 13, and op. 16 (1908), d. 169; f. 695, op. 21 (1911), d. 303; RGIA, f. 1291, op. 31 (1910), d. 101, l. 78.

84. *Sel'skii vestnik*, no. 167 (1913), 3. See also no. 166 (1903); no. 191 (1913): 2; no. 217 (1913): 2-3; Kupchinov, 28-33; P. Stashko, *Po sledam istiny. Razskazy iz zhini pisarei*, 2nd ed. (St. Petersburg, 1913), 108.

85. RGIA, f. 1291, op. 31 (1908), d. 87, l. 176 (Tambov); Astyrev, *V volostnykh pisariakh*, 3rd. ed., 241-45.

86. The survey was completed in mid-July 1914 and thus did not record the significant disruptions caused by mobilization. "Statisticheskie kartoteki volostnykh pisarei," RGIA, f. 1291, op. 54 (1914), dd. 146a, 146b, 154a; "Spiski volostnykh starshin," GARO, f. 695, op. 19 (1909), d. 79.

87. "Sluzhebnoe polozhenie volostnykh pisarei," *IZO*, no. 2 (1915): 67-68.

88. *Kozlovskaia derevnia*, no. 3 (1906): 3.

89. GATO, f. 984, op. 1 (1908), d. 7, l. 4; GARO, f. 695, op. 2 (1891), d. 743b, 48-51 (Maklakov's instructions: n.p.).

90. Any of the works cited in this chapter is a good example of such writing, but the masterpiece of the genre, which was singled out by some governors as pernicious reading to be avoided by the volost clerks of their province, was Petr Stashko's *Po sledam istiny*.

91. By mid-1916 the Land Section course had graduated 268 candidates. The Land Section recognized that this was clearly insufficient to meet the needs of the country's 12,000 volosts. *IZO* (1916), no. 7: 260–61; no. 8: 260; no. 10: 258–59.

92. On pensions, see "Itogi perepisi volostnykh pisarei," *IZO*, no. 10 (1916): 258–59. On wage reform: "Sluzhebnoe polozhenie" (1915), no. 1: 19–22; no. 2: 65–68; no. 3: 103–7; no. 4, 142–46.

93. Novikov, 32–33. Also Strakhovskii, "Sovremennoe polozhenie," 20.

94. RGIA, f. 1291, op. 124 (1912), d. 54b, ll. 138–39.

95. Barykov, 163, 185, 198, 212, 266; GARF, f. 586, op. 1, d. 118, ll. 12 , 27 (Riazan); d. 120, ll. 18, 52 (Smolensk); d. 121, ll. 9–10 (Tver); B. M. Firsov and I. G. Kiseleva, eds., *Byt velikorusskikh krest'ian-zemlepashtsev. Opisanie materialov etnograficheskogo biuro kniazia V. N. Tenisheva* (St. Petersburg, 1993), 53, 90 (Vladimir).

96. See, for instance, RGIA, f. 1291, op. 31 (1908), d. 88, ll. 80, 83ob.–84; op. 31 (1909), d. 159, l. 54ob. (Tver); GARO, f. 714, op. 25 (1914), d. 37; GARF, f. 586, op. 1, d. 111, l. 3 (Moscow); Firsov and Kiseleva, 51 (Vladimir).

97. TsIAM, f. 62, op. 1, d. 6786; GARO, f. 695, op. 22 (1912), d. 15.

98. "Mirskie povinnosti," *Entsiklopedicheskii slovar'*, 38:524–25; Ganeizer, 151; RGIA, f. 1291, op. 31 (1908), d. 87 (Tambov); op. 54 (1912), d. 177, ll. 43–45 (Riazan); TsIAM, f. 62, op. 1, d. 7187 (1908).

99. GARF, f. 586, op. 1, d. 118, l. 8. See also Stashko, 6.

100. Novikov, 29; Rittikh, *Krest'ianskii pravoporiadok*, 148–52; GARO, f. 695, op. 22 (1912), d. 23, ll. 14ob.–15; GARF, f. 586, op. 1, d. 121, ll. 9–10 (Tver); d. 120, ll. 18, 52 (Smolensk); Firsov and Kiseleva, 50, 53.

101. GARO, f. 695, op. 26 (1916), d. 29, ll. 266–67; RGIA, f. 1291, op. 54 (1916), d. 75, ll. 3, 39.

102. RGIA, f. 1344, op. 252 (1911), d. 1162. For other examples see: f. 1344, op. 275 (1913), d. 237; *RV*, no. 130 (1907): 3; GATO, f. 255, op. 1 (1909), d. 520.

103. *RV*, no. 130 (1907): 3.

104. Zyrianov, "Sotsial'naia struktura," 254; GARO, f. 721, op. 1 (1896), d. 36.

105. RGIA, f. 1291, op. 31 (1908), d. 87, l. 245.

106. GATO, f. 255, op. 1 (1909), dd. 520, 521, 528. Tver district in 1893 had been singled out by Ministry of Finance inspectors as benefiting from peasant elders ready to use their powers of arrest. Yet, the number of arrests, although two to three times those of neighboring districts, still amounted to only one for every two elders per year. Ministerstvo finansov, *Sushchestvuiushchii poriadok*, 2:89. For further discussion of village officials' shortcomings in combating tax delinquency, see Burds, 46–48.

107. TsIAM, f. 62, op. 1 (1908), d. 7187, l. 80. This file contains numerous cases of a similar nature. Other—mostly unsuccessful—attempts to lower salaries of volost officials were reported in *RV* (1907), no. 61: 3; no. 84: 3; *RZh*, no. 125 (1913): 4 (Riazan); RGIA, f. 1291, op. 31 (1908), d. 87, ll. 174, 249, 252 (Tambov); f. 1344, op. 200 (1907), d. 723 (Nizhnii-Novgorod); and op. 217 (1909), d. 415, l. 2 (Tambov). According to Nikolai Astyrev, assemblies raised and lowered salaries not only according to likes and dislikes, but because they saw no need for equally expensive clerks and elders: if the elder was deemed untrustworthy, the volost assembly sought to attract a competent scribe and then lowered the pay of the elder accordingly. If the elder was competent, peasants saw little need for a highly paid scribe. Astyrev, "Mirskie raskhody," 89–91.

108. GARO, f. 695, op. 21 (1911), dd. 300–301. For the 1890s, see Novikov, 90. For comments by MVD inspectors on the growing propensity of assemblies to lower salaries: *IZO*, no. 6 (1908): 306.

109. GATO, f. 1012, op. 1 (1910), d. 185, l. 15.

110. Naumov, 189. These dilemmas were not unlike those reported by teachers, who had difficulties collecting regular salaries based on an equal assessment for each household, rather than payments per pupil or per lesson. Eklof, *Peasant Schools*, 233.

111. Kupchinov. Use of the phrase "sinless income" to justify venality was by no means limited to peasant officials, but prevailed also within higher echelons of the bureaucracy. Donald MacKenzie Wallace, *Russia* (London, 1912), 308.

112. GARF, f. 586, op. 1, d. 118, ll. 33, 46; d. 120, ll. 26, 59; Firsov and Kiseleva, 63.

113. Kupchinov, 23-24; Stashko, 37.

114. TsIAM, f. 62, op. 2, d. 317; RGIA-otchety, "Otchet Penzenskoi gubernii za 1898," vol. 64a, addendum, n.p.; RGIA, f. 1291, op. 31 (1909), d. 159, l. 78ob.

115. GARO, f. 695, op. 23 (1913), d. 346.

116. For some such cases, see TsIAM, f. 62, op. 1 (1909), d. 5755; op. 4 (1901), d. 1753; GARO, f. 930, op. 17 (1910), sv. 3, d. 9; f. 929, op. 11 (1911), sv. 1, d. 11; f. 81, op. 23 (1915), sv. 25, d. 32; GATO, f. 255, op. 1 (1912), d. 536; RGIA, f. 1291, op. 54 (1911) d. 125, ll. 40, 52, 83, 99, 112, 136.

117. A. K-ov, "Na rodine. Iz zapisok zemskogo nachal'nika," *Drug provintsii,* no. 7 (1910): 47; "Vnutrennee obozrenie," *VE,* no. 7-8 (1893): 383; "Gubernatorskaia reviziia," *IuG,* no. 19 (1892): 2.

118. Decision of the combined First and Civil Cassation departments, 14 December 1891, no. 1, I. Danilov, 145-46.

119. GARO, f. 695, op. 21 (1911), d. 279; f. 714, op. 25 (1914), sv. 64, d. 30; f. 81, op. 23 (1915), sv. 25, d. 30.

120. TsIAM, f. 696, op. 1 (1912), d. 2343; GARF, f. 586, d. 121, ll. 10-11 (Tver); d. 120, l. 18 (Smolensk).

121. GATO, f. 255, op. 1 (1909), d. 522.

122. GARO, f. 929, op. 11 (1911), sv. 1, dd. 19, 22, 27.

123. RGIA, f. 1291, op. 31 (1911), d. 147, ll. 75-76.

124. GARO, f. 79, op. 24 (1913), d. 12.

125. Ibid., f. 714, op. 25 (1914), sv. 65, d. 92. Also TsIAM, f. 62, op. 4 (1910), dd. 1782, 1744.

126. GARO, f. 930, op. 17 (1910), sv. 3, d. 6; op. 19 (1912), sv. 3, d. 3.

127. TsIAM, f. 62, op. 2, d. 317; "Deiatel'nost' zemskikh nachal'nikov," *IuG,* no. 7 (1894): 3; RGIA-otchety, "Otchet Penzenskoi gubernii za 1898," vol. 64a, addendum, n.p.; RGIA, f. 1291, op. 31 (1909), d. 159, l. 78ob.

128. Inspection reports: RGIA, f. 1291, op. 31 (1908), d. 87, ll. 71-73 (Tambov); op. 31 (1910), d. 101, ll. 88, 103ob. (Riazan); op. 31 (1911), d. 147, l. 89 (Riazan); op. 31 (1915), d. 98, l. 121 (Riazan). Land captain hearings: GARO, f. 79, op. 23 (1912), d. 5; f. 929, op. 11 (1911), sv. 1, dd. 18, 20; f. 930, op. 16 (1909), sv. 2, d. 1; TsIAM, f. 62, op. 1 (1909), d. 5755.

129. Firsov and Kiseleva, 50.

130. The contrast with pre-Emancipation village administration is striking. There, the benefits to peasant officials of enforcing the existing social order were enormous, allowing state and serf owners to rule by co-optation. See especially Melton; Hoch, *Serfdom.*

3—Volost Courts and the Dilemmas of Legal Acculturation

1. On nineteenth-century debates concerning volost courts, see Cathy Frierson, "Rural Justice," 326-45; P. N. Zyrianov, "Obychnoe grazhdanskoe pravo v poreformennoi Rossii," *Ezhegodnik po agrarnoi istorii* (Vologda, 1976), 6:91-101.

2. See for instance, David Moon, *Russian Peasants and Tsarist Legislation on the Eve of Reform: Interaction between Peasants and Officialdom, 1825-1855* (Basingstoke, 1992); Wirtschafter, "Legal Identity," 561-87.

3. For approaches examining resistance to state legal definitions, see Frank, *Crime;* Christine Worobec, "Horse thieves and Peasant Justice in Post-Emancipation Russia," *Journal of Social History* 21, no. 2 (1987): 281-93 and *Peasant Russia;* M. M. Gromyko, *Traditsionnye normy povedeniia i formy obshcheniia russkikh krest'ian XIX v*

(Moscow, 1986); Cathy Frierson, "Crime and Punishment in the Russian Village: Rural Concepts of Criminality at the End of the Nineteenth Century," *SR* 46, no. 1 (1987): 55–69. On the breakdown of community, see Mironov, *Sotsial'naia istoriia*, 2:67–78; Frierson, "I Must Always Answer to the Law." This article also emphasizes acculturation, as does Jane Burbank in *Russian Peasants Go to Court: Legal Culture in the Countryside, 1905–1917* (Bloomington, IN, 2004). On the limits and contradictions of acculturation: see Neuberger. Also Gareth Popkins, one of the few historians to examine civil disputes: "Peasant Experiences of the Late Tsarist State: District Congresses of Land Captains, Provincial Boards, and the Legal Appeals Process, 1891–1917," *SEER* 78, no. 1 (2000): 90–114, and "Russian Peasant Wills in the Decisions of the Ruling Senate, 1861–1906," *Legal History* 68, no. 2 (1999): 1–23, and "Code vs. Custom? Norms and Tactics in Peasant Volost Court Appeals, 1889–1917," *RR* 59, no. 3 (2000): 408–24.

4. T. A. Tarabanova, "Volostnoi sud v Rossii v pervoe poreformennoe desiatiletie" (avtoreferat Kand. diss., MGU, 1993), 22. Similar statements were made to zemstvo officials: *Doklady chlenov*, 63, 124, 132, 309.

5. Aleksandr Engelgardt, *Letters from the Country, 1872–1887*, ed. Cathy Frierson (New York and Oxford, 1993), 44, 82–83, 108; also M. N. P., "Sud v derevne," 96, 107–8.

6. P. Skorobogatyi, "Ustroistvo krest'ianskikh sudov," *IuV*, no. 6 (1880): 321; I. Shrag, "Krest'ianskie sudy Vladimirskoi i Moskovskoi gubernii," *IuV*, no. 3–4 (1877): 37; K. Chepurnyi, "K voprosu o iuridicheskikh obychaiakh. Ustroistvo i sostoianie volostnoi iustitsii v Tambovskoi gubernii," *Kievskie universitetskie izvestiia*, no. 9 (1874): 498–99.

7. *Doklady chlenov*, 464. For examples from other provinces, see P. Dashkevich, "Volostnoi sud i kassatsionnaia instantsiia," *IuV*, no. 12 (1892): 526–27; M. I. Zarudnyi, *Zakony i zhizn'. Itogo izsledovaniia krest'ianskikh sudov* (St. Petersburg, 1874), 172–74.

8. V. V. Tenishev, *Pravosudie v russkom krest'ianskom bytu* (Briansk, 1907), 15; A. A. Charushin, "Volostnye sudy v bytovom ikh osveshchenii," *Izucheniia Russkogo severa*, no. 21 (1912): 986.

9. A. P. Smirnov, "Statistika krest'ianskogo byta vo Vladimirskoi gubernii," *Vladimirskii zemskii sbornik*, no. 9 (1882): 172–88.

10. Astyrev, *V volostnykh pisariakh*, 3rd. ed., 262.

11. RGIA-otchety, "Vsepoddanneishii otchet Vladimirskogo gubernatora," vol. 15:9, 15–16, 86.

12. *Doklady chlenov*, 87, 116, 132, 140, 256, 264, 275, 284, 292, 299, 309, 319, 326, 334, 464; RGIA, f. 1405, op. 543 (1916), d. 943, ll. 235–44, 282–86.

13. In the same period, the annual growth rates in Moscow province were 1.6% and 5.2%, respectively. In Vladimir: 1.7% and 3.4%. Kursk (1891 through 1909): 1.9% and 4.4%. Of six provinces studied—those for which a data series covering at least 15 years could be compiled—only Tver (after 1908) experienced a per capita decline of court use before the war.

14. B. Schnapper, "Pour un géographie des mentalités judiciaires. La litigiosité en France au XIXe," *Annales E.S.C.* 34, no. 2 (1979): 403; F. Van Loon and E. Langerwerf, "Socioeconomic Development and the Evolution of Litigation Rates of Civil Courts in Belgium, 1835–1980," *Law and Society Review* 24, no. 2 (1990): 288–89; Christian Wollschläger, "Civil Litigation and Modernization: The Work of the Municipal Courts of Bremen, Germany, in Five Centuries, 1549–1984," *Law and Society Review* 24, no. 2 (1990): 272.

15. TsIAM, "Kniga reshenii volostnogo suda," f. 1112, op. 1, d. 20; "Statisticheskikh svendenii Ignat'evskoi volosti," f. 705, op. 1, d. 818, l. 173.

16. TsIAM, "Kniga dlia zapisei zhalob," f. 749, op. 1, d. 14; *Nasel'enie mestnosti Moskovskoi gubernii na 1912* (Moscow, 1912), 242–43. For examples of equally high rates in other localities, see Popkins, "Peasant Volost Court," 217–20.

17. D. I. Raskin, "Ispol'zovanie zakonodatel'nykh aktov v krest'ianskikh chelobitnykh serediny XVIII v.," *Istoriia SSSR*, no. 4 (1979): 179–92; L. S. Prokof'eva,

Krest'ianskaia obshchina v Rossii vo vtoroi polovine XVIII-pervoi polovine XIX v. (Leningrad, 1981), 157–63; Hoch, *Serfdom,* chap. 5.

18. N. M. Druzhinin, *Gosudarstvennye krest'iane i reforma P. D. Kiseleva,* 2 vols. (Moscow-Leningrad, 1946, 1958), 1:555–56, 569–70, 575–88.

19. GARF, f. 586, op. 1, d. 120, ll. 14, 36, 40 (Pskov), 63–64, 99, 121 (Smolensk); d. 118, ll. 37, 88 (Riazan); Firsov and Kiseleva, 65; Tenishev, *Pravosudie,* 15–17. Stephen Frank has rightly pointed out the dangers of relying on proverbs and other expressions of received opinion, both of which often emerged in an earlier era. Oddly though, he does rely on proverbs to support his argument that peasants saw the volost court as an instrument of the rich. Frank, *Crime,* 98–99, 229.

20. Figures from 6 courts (2 in Tver, one in Riazan, and 3 in Moscow) for 14 different years ranging from 1895 to 1913 show women filing from a low of 13% to a high of 40% of all complaints. It is impossible to determine without local studies what would account for such variations, and whether women increasingly used the courts. Even on the later question, my data shows conflicting trends. For instance, the proportions in Izhevskoe (Spassk district, Riazan) grew as follows: 1889—19%; 1908—25%; 1913—34%. Meanwhile, the figures for Ignat'evo show precisely the opposite trend: 1895—19%; 1900—17%; 1908—13%. Data compiled from GARO, f. 1257, op. 1 (1889), sv. 8, d. 69; f. 811, op. 1 (1908), sv. 4, d. 19 and (1913) d. 30; TsIAM, f. 1112, op. 1, dd. 2, 4, 19; f. 705, op. 1, d. 19.

21. TsIAM, f. 1891, op. 1, d. 2, decisions 75, 98, 110, 112, 115, 141, 146, 156. Beatrice Farnsworth's study of the Liuboshchinskii Commission's published court transcripts shows (even if based on an unrepresentative statistical sample) that in the 1870s the most powerless of women sometimes did win. "The Litigious Daughter-in-Law: Family Relations in Rural Russia in the Second Half of the Nineteenth Century," *SR* 45, no. 1 (1986): 49–64. The nineteenth-century literature emphasizing the helpless position of women in peasant courts is too extensive to cite here. A good example is Ia. Ludmer's, "Bab'i stony," and "Bab'i dela na mirovom sude," *IuV,* no. 11 (1884): 522ff. For further discussion, see Worobec, *Peasant Russia,* chap. 6; and Engel, *Between the Fields,* 24–32. That court practice could be more favorable to women than enumerations of norms would suggest has been noted in other contexts. See for instance Brett Shadle, "'Changing Traditions to Meet Current Altering Conditions': Customary Law, African Courts and the Rejection of Codification in Kenya, 1930–60," *Journal of African History* 40, no. 3 (1999): 411–31; "Porter plainte: Stratégies villageoises et institutions judiciaires en Ile-de-France (XVIIe–XVIIIe siècles)," *Droits et cultures* 19 (1990): 7–118.

22. Ivan Stoliaroff, *Un village russe. Récit d'un paysan de la région de Voronej, 1880–1906.* Translated by Valérie Stoliaroff and Irène Rovère-Sova (Paris, 1992), 35–36, 68–70.

23. Moon, *Russian Peasants,* 10–13; Boris Mironov, "The Development of Literacy in Russia and the USSR from the Tenth to the Twentieth Centuries," *History of Education Quarterly* 31, no. 1 (1991): 234–43.

24. Although the legal guides had relatively small press runs (2,000 to 3,000 on average), they typically went through numerous editions, and a few were published in editions of 15,000. These numbers are comparable to print runs of cheap editions of popular literature, which according to Jeffrey Brooks, rarely exceeded 10,000 copies. A. F. Povorinskii, *Sistematicheskii ukazatel' russkoi literatury po sudoustroistvu i sudoproizvodstvu grazhdanskomu i ugolovnomu,* 2 vols. (St. Petersburg, 1896, 1905); Jeffrey Brooks, *When Russia Learned to Read: Literacy and Popular Literature, 1861–1917* (Princeton, 1985), 154.

25. William Pomeranz, "Justice from Underground: The History of the Underground Advokatura," *RR* 52, no. 3 (1993): 332–38; Joan Neuberger, "Shysters or Public Servants? Uncertified Lawyers and Legal Aid for the Poor in Late Imperial Russia," *Russian History* 23, no. 1–4 (1996): 295–310.

26. The critique of illegal advocates usually took place within the context of the zemstvo campaign to establish free legal services to the peasantry. See, for instance, N.

Sokolovskii, "Derevenskaia konsul'tatsiia," *RB,* no. 3 (1900): 110–38; V. Ilimskii, "Iuridicheskaia bezpomoshchnost' derevni," *Krest'ianskoe delo,* no. 11 (1910): 209–11.

27. For an example of an assembly redirecting a land dispute to the courts, see GARO, f. 714, GO, op. 2 (1891), d. 21.

28. Novikov, 76–77; Tenishev, *Pravosudie,* 63–67; GARF, f. 586, op. 1, d. 118, ll. 7–8, 34; d. 123, ll. 12–13; d. 120, ll. 11, 33, 60.

29. V. Zhdanov, "O neobkhodimosti dopolneniia st.31 vremmenykh pravil," *ZhGiUP,* no. 4 (1892): 24–25; Goremykin, 1: 193–95; Chlen uezdnogo s"ezda, "Oby-chai ili zakon," *SG,* no. 12 (1892): 2; *PSZ,* 3rd series, vol. 9, 12 July 1889, no. 6196, "Vremennye pravila o volostnom sude," arts. 22, 23, 25, 26; RGIA, f. 1291, op. 54 (1908), d. 32, ll. 1–9; A. Tiutriumov, "Grazhdanskoe sudoproizvodstvo volostnyikh su-dov," *IuV,* no. 5–6 (1892): 185.

30. "Vremennye pravila," arts. 4, 7, 14–21, 30–32. According to the Liu-boshchinskii Commission findings, 41% of peasant judges received no compensation in the 1870s. Tarabanova, "Volostnoi sud," 15.

31. "Vremennye pravila," arts. 25–26, 28, 38; N. S. Tagantsev, *Ustav o nakazani-iakh nalogaemykh mirovymi sudiami* (St. Petersburg, 1913), arts. 19–20, 22.

32. Zarudnyi, 108. For discussions of peasant attitudes toward crime, see espe-cially Frank, *Crime;* Frierson, "Crime and Punishment."

33. RGIA, f. 1291, op. 31 (1908), d. 87, l. 115 (Tambov); and op. 31 (1914), d. 182, l. 142 (Riazan).

34. V. Volzhin, "Revizionnyi poriadok otmeny i izmeneniia reshenii volostnoi iustitsii," *ZhIuO,* no. 4 (1897): 89–91; MVD-Ministry of Justice circular, no. 26 (1891), in Volkov, 182–83.

35. GARO, f. 811, op. 1 (1910), d. 24; TsIAM, f. 1112, op. 1, d. 19; f. 1891, dd. 2, 3. Jane Burbank has found similar proportions for 6 of the 7 Moscow province volosts she has studied. *Russian Peasants Go to Court,* 122. The exception is the completely anomalous Nagatino volost. Located on the edge of the rapidly expanding city of Moscow, this volost was more urban than rural. It is unfortunate that Burbank chose to aggregate Nagatino data (apparently one-quarter of her cases) with those of other courts in her statistical sample, as the profile of activity of this volost court differed from rural courts in almost every way. The result is a very odd "average" court. On po-lice and hooliganism see Frank, *Crime,* 30–36, 279–89; Neil Weissman, "Regular Police in Tsarist Russia, 1900–1914," *RR* 44, no. 1 (1985): 45–68.

36. M. V. Dukhovskoi, *Imushchestvennye prostupki po resheniiam volostnykh sudov* (Moscow, 1891), 53–57.

37. RGIA, f. 1291, op. 31 (1908), d. 87, ll. 176, 21, 73, 113ob.–114, 247ob., 251ob, 269; op. 31 (1912), d. 182, ll. 42, 244–8; op. 31 (1911), d. 147, ll. 39–39ob., 44–44ob.; GATO, f. 424, op. 1 (1911), d. 27.

38. RGIA, f. 1291, op. 31 (1908), d. 87, l. 176 (also 20ob., 113ob.–114, 247–48, 251, 268 [Tambov]); op. 31 (1914), d. 182, ll. 244–48; op. 31 (1911), d. 147, l. 39ob.; op. 31 (1910), d. 101, ll. 81, 212 (Riazan).

39. TsIAM, f. 62, op. 4 (1895), d. 27, ll. 7–17; GARO, f. 695, op. 11 (1900), d. 1.

40. GARO, f. 695, op. 6 (1895), d. 12; op. 10 (1899), d. 5; op. 11 (1900), d. 1; GATO, f. 424, op. 1 (1911), d. 9; TsIAM, f. 749, op. 1 (1909), d. 14; RGIA, f. 1291, op. 31 (1908), d. 87, ll. 71, 268, 290ob., 176ob.

41. I. G. Orshanskii, *Izsledovaniia po russkomu pravu obychnomu i brachnomu* (St. Petersburg, 1879), 150; *SG,* no. 1 (1891): 8; GARF, f. 586, op. 1, d. 123, l. 40.

42. Numerous observers commented on the use of judicial complaints and ap-peals as a scare tactic, Dmitrii Ilimskii even comparing them to theatrical props *(buto-forskie tiazhby).* "Bor'ba za pravo (vpechatleniia derevenskogo advokata)," *RB,* no. 4 (1912): 157–58; "K voprosu o sudebnom deiatel'nosti gubernskikh prisutstviiakh," *IuG,* no. 28 (1900): 1–2; *IuG,* no. 17 (1893): 2; *Russkie vedomosti,* no. 120 (1891): 1.

43. TsIAM, f. 1891, op. 1, d. 2.

44. Astyrev, *V volostnykh pisariakh*, 3rd ed., 270–71; I. M. Krasnoperov, "Krest'ianskie zhenshchiny pred volostnym sudom," *Sbornik pravovedeniia i obshchestvennykh znanii* (1893), 1:268–89.

45. TsIAM, f. 1891, op. 1, d. 2, decision 119.

46. Ibid., decision 48.

47. Ibid., decision 60; V. V. Tenishev, "Obshchiia nachala ugolovnogo prava v ponimanii russkogo krest'ianina," *ZhMIu*, no. 7 (1908): 154–56.

48. TsIAM, f. 1891, op. 1, d. 2, decisions 100, 121, 54.

49. Charushin, "Volostnye sudy," 990.

50. The MVD circular had been prompted by some provincial boards that had instructed courts to give greater weight to written documentation than to witness testimony. The MVD responded that since documents were too easily falsified, and that since witnesses and judges often knew when they were, "inner conviction" was the best guarantee of correct rulings. Goremykin, 1:194. On the importance of the reputation of witnesses: GARF, f. 586, op. 1, d. 120, ll. 9–10, 13–14, 29–30, 40, 63; d. 118, l. 19; Firsov and Kiseleva, 66–67.

51. TsIAM, f. 1891, op. 1, d. 2, decision 76.

52. Ibid., decisions 109, 128, 59, 122; d. 3 (1915), decision 135.

53. The maximum jail sentence of 15 days could be doubled for aggravating circumstances. RGIA, f. 1291, op. 31 (1909), d. 149, l. 228; op. 31 (1908), d. 87, ll. 19, 176, 268ob., 290ob., 296ob. (Tambov); op. 31 (1914), d. 182, ll. 244–48, 250ob. (Riazan); op. 31 (1911), d. 147, ll. 39ob., 44ob.; op. 31 (1912), d. 54b, l. 214 (Riazan).

54. GARO, f. 695, op. 23 (1913), d. 1, l. 60; GATO, f. 1012, op. 1 (1910), dd. 185, 188.

55. TsIAM, f. 1891, op. 1, d. 3, decisions 52, 123, 36, 43.

56. Until 1901, provinces reported case outcomes (number reconciled, acquitted, fined, etc.) but shifted to reporting categories of complaints thereafter.

57. In Novgorod the rates of growth averaged 1.6% and 3% respectively, while Kursk, in the brief period between 1903 and 1909, registered an annual decline of criminal cases of 1.2% but an annual growth in civil cases of 9%. Even in Moscow province, the only province where I have found a consistent and significant increase in the per capita rate of criminal cases, the 4% annual increase registered between 1891 and 1907 paled in comparison to the nearly 7% annual rise in the civil caseload.

58. Stephen Frank has shown that much of the increase in crime rates that so worried educated Russians was partly a statistical mirage. See especially his discussion of the effect of state priorities on crime statistics: Frank, *Crime*, chap. 2; cf. Mironov, *Sotsial'naia istoriia*, 2:78–97. On urban attitudes toward rural crime and hooliganism, see especially Stephen Frank, "Confronting the Domestic Other: Rural Popular Culture and Its Enemies in Fin-de Siècle Russia," in *Cultures in Flux: Lower-Class Values, Practices, and Resistance in Late Imperial Russia,* ed. Stephen Frank and Mark Steinberg (Princeton, 1994), 74–107.

59. Smolensk, Saratov, St. Petersburg, and Iaroslavl reported no significant changes. RGIA, f. 1291, op. 54 (1912), d. 174, ll. 84, 99–103, 111–19, 196–97, 207–8, 210–11.

60. The proportion of insults to the total criminal caseload was 62% in 1895, 68% in 1908, and 72% in 1911. TsIAM, f. 62, op. 2 (1891), d. 304; f. 705, op. 1 (1914), d. 781, ll. 92–95 (1895), d. 98; f. 1112, op. 1 (1908), d. 19; f. 705, op. 1 (1911), d. 716.

61. RGIA-otchety, "Obzor Tul'skogo gubernatora," vol. 103:31; RGIA, f. 1291, op. 54 (1901), d. 99, ll. 94ob.–95 (Tver); op. 31 (1909), d. 241, ll. 14–15 (Riazan), and d. 247, l. 21 (Tver); op. 54 (1901), d. 99, ll. 27ob.–28 (Tver); op. 31 (1914), d. 438, ll. 18–19 (Novgorod); GATO-Tambov, f. 233, op. 1, d. 8.

62. GATO, f. 709, op. 1 (1914), dd. 2, 33, 36; f. 589, op. 1 (1912), d. 1555; f. 728, op. 1 (1913), dd. 10, 19.

63. TsIAM, f. 62, op. 1 (1908), d. 5644; f. 1938, op. 1 (1916), d. 17, l. 80.

64. Burds, 208–18. In contrast, M. M. Gromyko tends to see reputation as a rather static instrument of social control. "Mesto sel'skoi (territorial'noi, sosedskoi) obshchiny v sotsial'nom mekhanizme formirovaniia, khraneniia i izmeneniia traditsii," *Sovetskaia*

etnografiia, no. 5 (1984): 75–76. This functional interpretation of gossip as reinforcing community values and cohesion is also emphasized in Max Gluckman, "Gossip and Scandal," *Current Anthropology* 5, no. 4 (1963): 307–16. More recently, anthropologists have tended to examine reputation as part of contests over power, a weapon available to the weak as well as the strong, and one limiting the ability of the latter to consolidate their power. See for instance Karen Brison, *Just Talk: Gossip, Meetings, and Power in a Papua New Guinea Village* (Berkeley, 1992); Catherine Ditte and Olivier Jouneaux, in "Porter plainte," 23–48, 101–18.

65. GATO, f. 424, op. 1 (1911), d. 97, decisions 2, 9, 18. Also TsIAM, f. 696, op. 1 (1912), d. 2343; f. 1938, op. 1 (1916), d. 17, l. 95; f. 1891, op. 1, d. 2, decisions 75–76.

66. See for instance, TsIAM, f. 1891, op. 1, d. 2, decision 97, as well as any of the inspection reports cited above.

67. A. Kh. Gol'msten, "Dvadtsatipiatiletnaia praktika Kemetskogo (Valdaiskogo uezda, Novgorodskoi gubernii) volostnogo suda po voprosam grazhdanskogo prava," in *Iuridicheskiia izsledovaniia i stat'i* (St. Petersburg, 1894), 1:77–78.

68. GATO-Tambov, f. 26, op. 4 (1908), d. 210, l. 13.

69. Compare Burbank, *Russian Peasants Go to Court*, 129–44. Robert Shoemaker, in a study of insult and defamation in London in the seventeenth and eighteenth centuries, has suggested that an increase in litigation reflects the first stages of decline of community as individuals become less willing to accept their neighbors' judgment. Statistics alone, however, cannot lead to this conclusion, especially when there is a significant change in access to courts, as was the case in Russia. "The Decline of Public Insult in London, 1600–1800," *Past and Present*, no. 169 (2000): 97–131. For other useful studies of the relation between reputation, courts, and authority see J. A. Sharpe, *Defamation and Sexual Slander in Early Modern England* (Oxford, 1988); Leah Leneman, "Defamation in Scotland, 1750–1800," *Continuity and Change* 15, no. 2 (2000): 209–34.

70. For further discussion of the relation between court use and economic change, see Frierson, "I Must Always Answer to the Law," 329–33.

71. RGIA, f. 1291, op. 120 (1911), d. 17, l. 94, 97–98, 109, 116, 147.

72. S. T. Semenov, 285–93, 299, 306–12.

73. In Riazan, land disputes grew 128% between 1903 and 1908, cases of inheritance and family division 172%, while the volume of all civil cases was up 41%. In Tver, these figures are 89%, 284%, and 48% respectively. Together, these three types of cases went from 15.6% of the total civil caseload to 25% in 1908 in Tver, and in Riazan from 17.5% to 26%. Land cases in Moscow accounted for a lower proportion of all decisions, but also registered an increase from 17.9% of the civil caseload in 1907 to 23.5% in 1913.

74. Officials from Penza and St. Petersburg provinces likewise reported an increase in nonadversarial cases during the Stolypin period. RGIA, f. 1291, op. 120 (1911), d. 17, l. 98; *IZO*, no. 12 (1909): 411. For a meticulous examination of the issue of peasant wills, see Gareth Popkin's "Russian Peasant Wills."

75. TsIAM, f. 749, op. 1, dd. 3, 13, 38.

76. Ibid., f. 1891, op. 1, d. 2, decisions 108, 12, 37, 130, 44, 61.

77. Popkins estimates for the 1890s that in the central provinces 1–2% of rural households annually had business before the district congresses. Gareth Popkins, "Peasant Volost Court," 167. If we assume, somewhat illogically, however, that each appeal involved just one household, the range of 1–2% is valid only for the 1890s. Already by 1903 in Riazan, 3% of Riazan's households were involved with appeals in the district congresses, 4% in 1908, and 6.5% in 1913. Most cases in fact—except for inheritance and family divisions, family disputes, and those criminal cases initiated by police—involved more than one household. My own count, based on volost court records (8 spanning from 1900 to 1916), shows a consistent range of 1.5 to 1.7 households per case. It is the lower figure that I have used to estimate household involvement with the district congresses.

78. RGIA, f. 1291, op. 54 (1901), d. 163, ll. 8–9, 41ob.–42. Other data show the proportion of overturned verdicts as follows: Moscow 1895—46%; Tver 1892—54%; Tver 1896—59%; Riazan 1892—39%; Novgorod 1891–1893 (criminal cases)—41–45%; Riazan 1908–1909 (4 districts)—35%; Usman district, Tambov 1906–1908—54%; Lipets district, Tambov 1906–1907—27%. "Vnutrenee obozrenie," VE, no. 11 (1893): 372; Mikhailovskii, 161; GARO, f. 695, op. 6 (1895), d. 12; Putilov, "Zametki o vremennykh praviklakh o volostnom sude," ZhIuO, no. 7 (1897): 83; RGIA, f. 1291, op. 31 (1909), d. 149, ll. 195, 201, 227, 252; op. 31 (1908), d. 87, l. 90. See also Popkins, "Peasant Experiences," 100.

79. Dashkevich, "Volostnoi sud," 529–30. It is likely that some governors' triumphant declarations after 1889 that drink had disappeared from the courts meant in fact that it had disappeared from peasant petitions, as appellants could now appeal on substance and no longer had to find procedural flaws in the conduct of their case. On pre-1889 cassation practice, see Orshanskii, 16–31; Astyrev, V volostnykh pisariakh, 3rd ed., 242–46; Zarudnyi, 87, 90–92; Shrag, no. 9–10: 90–91.

80. Gol'msten, 50–51; Dashkevich, "Volostnoi sud," 537.

81. RGIA-otchety, "Otchet Kurskoi gubernii za 1891," vol. 48:20; "Otchet Vladimirskoi gubernii," vol. 15:11 (1893), 86 (1902); RGIA, f. 1291, op. 54 (1898), d. 170a, ll. 86–87.

82. Mikhailovskii, 161. Riazan rates are calculated from GARO, f. 695, op. 6 (1895), d. 12; Moscow: TsIAM, f. 62, op. 2, d. 317; op. 4, d. 27, ll. 7–8.

83. The volost complaint registers more accurately reflect real appeal rates than provincial statistical reports, first because they record all appeals rather than just those approved by the land captain, and second because it is possible to factor out cases not subject to appeal. TsIAM, f. 62, op. 2 (1895) d. 27, ll. 16–17; op. 2 (1891), d. 304, l. 49; f. 1112, op. 1, dd. 16, 19; f. 749, op. 1, dd. 1, 2, 4, 7, 8; f. 1641, op. 1, dd. 7, 19.

84. Compiled from GARO, f. 811, op. 1 (1908), d. 19; op. 1 (1913), d. 30; RGIA, f. 1291, op. 31 (1909), d. 159, l. 86.

85. "Vnutrennee obozrenie," VE, no. 12 (1891): 794–95; VE, no. 7–8 (1893): 375; K. Gen, "Iz kassatsionnoi praktiki," SG, no. 19 (1893): 8–9; Mikhailovskii, 157; I. Maslovskii, "Iz praktika novogo suda," IuG, no. 4 (1892): 2–3; A. I. Novikov, "Novyi sud v derevne," RO, no. 6 (1893): 753–56; RGIA, f. 1291, op. 31 (1911) d. 147, l. 97. On local variations of interpretation regarding right of appeal: Efimov, 575–76; Zhdanov, 26–33; Volzhin, 89–104. The MVD itself was sympathetic to arguments that announcing rules on appeal procedures would encourage litigiousness, but it compromised with the Ministry of Justice on the issue and instructed rural authorities to announce time limits and cite relevant articles of rural legislation. RGIA, f. 1291, op. 30 (1891), d. 13, ll. 3–4, 7–8.

86. The 1900 study reported an appeal rate of 28.5% for land disputes and 25% for inheritance cases, but 14.8% for other suits. Among criminal cases, 19% of insult cases, 27% of theft cases, but 43% of samoupravstvo cases were appealed. Unfortunately, a gross error in the report makes it impossible to calculate the appeal rate for libel cases. RGIA, f. 1291, op. 54 (1901), d. 163, ll. 41ob.–42.

87. Leont'ev was one of the most vocal and well-known advocates for the codification of custom. A. A. Leont'ev, Volostnoi sud i iuridichskie obychai krest'ian (St. Petersburg, 1895), 69–74, 79.

88. Polivanov, no. 9–10: 33–35. Orshanskii described a similar case from the 1870s, in which the district board explained that if the court persisted in calling "custom" what was in fact a crime, the judges themselves would be prosecuted. Izsledovaniia po russkomu pravu, 20.

89. I. S. Illarionov, "Razrabotka obychnogo pravo," VP, no. 1 (1899): 78–91.

90. The issues raised by Russian jurists of the 1880s are remarkably similar to those raised by theorists of legal pluralism today. Sally Merry starkly posed the methodological dilemma for legal historians, asking, "Where do we stop speaking of law and find ourselves simply describing social life?" "Legal Pluralism," Law and Society

Review 22, no. 5 (1988): 878. See also Brian Tamanaha, "A Non-Essentialist Version of Legal Pluralism," *Journal of Law and Society* 27, no. 2 (2000): 296–321; Gordon Woodman, "Ideological Combat and Social Observation: Recent Debate about Legal Pluralism," *Journal of Legal Pluralism*, no. 42 (1998): 21–59.

91. S. F. Platonov, "Ob usloviakh primineniia mirskimi sud'iami mestnykh obychaev, pri razreshenii grazhdanskikh del," *ZhGiUP*, no. 4 (1881): 70–85; I. Tabashnikov, "Zhelatel'noe otnoshenie budushego grazhdanskogo ulozheniia k nashemu obychnomu pravu," *ZhGiUP*, no. 3 (1885): 83–90.

92. "Po voprosu o rasprostranenii znanii obychnogo prava," RGIA, f. 1291, op. 54 (1899), d. 245, l. 6.

93. Jane Burbank (*Russian Peasants Go to Court*, 259) is correct to point out that legality can exist without codification. But codification is only one tool for structuring legal actions. Another, perhaps more relevant to state systems giving a scope to "custom," is attention to precedent. For an example of how precedent setting could function effectively within the context of a paternal judicial system, see Alain Cottereau, "Justice et injustice ordinaire sur les lieux de travail d'après les audiences prud'homales (1806–1866)," *Mouvement social*, no. 141 (1987): 25–59.

94. Decision of the second department, no. 7343, 11 December 1891, in I. Danilov, 144.

95. Abramovich, *Krest'ianskoe pravo*, 102; A. Guliaev, "Khronika. Novoe techenie v Senatskoi praktike po krest'ianskim delam," *ZhMIu*, no. 5 (1901): 189–90; Zyrianov, "Obychnoe grazhdanskoe pravo," 98–99.

96. Leont'ev, *Volostnoi sud*, 97–98. The same argument was presented by A. Vorms in "Zakon i obychai v nasledovanii u krest'ian," *IuV*, no. 1 (1913): 100–103.

97. Decision of the civil cassation department, 12 December 1878, no. 225, quoted in Vorms, "Zakon i obychai," 102; Goremykin, 1:60–61.

98. Quotation from the decision of the General Assembly of the 1st, 2nd and Cassation Departments, 26 January 1898, no. 2, cited in Leont'ev, *Krest'ianskoe pravo*, 2nd ed., 336. Also civil cassation department decisions: 1880, no. 174, and 1885, no. 3, in Tiutriumov, *Obshchee polozhenie*, 141–42.

99. N. P. Druzhinin, *Pravo i lichnosti krest'ianina* (Iaroslavl', 1912), 142–83. See also Tabashnikov, 67–107.

100. Rittikh, *Krest'ianskii pravoporiadok*, 18, 20–23, 27–29, 36, 57–60 (for contrary assessments [from 22 of 93 committees] see 62–68).

101. The committees consisted of the governor, vice governor, marshal of nobility, president of the circuit court, president of the provincial zemstvo, and permanent members of the provincial boards. Although only the last were regularly involved in peasant judicial matters, the committees first surveyed land captains and members of district congresses before composing results to be forwarded to the MVD. The results of the MVD survey can be found in RGIA, f. 408, op. 1, d. 421, ll. 73ff. For Riazan, see GARO, f. 695, op. 22 (1912), d. 238, ll. 9, 16, 20, 27, 30, 36, 47, 55.

102. The Senate never explicitly said whether its rulings on certification of custom extended to the volost courts. It repeatedly ruled, however, that none of the procedural regulations applying to the general courts could be imposed on the volost court. This interdiction extended to the appeal instances, for it would be nonsensical to have appeals heard under different rules from those prevailing in the court of first instance. In short, there remained room for interpretation and legitimate disagreement on the issue. A. M. Andrievskii, "V prave-li volostnye sudy rukovodstvovat' pri razreshenii grazhdanskikh del normami X t. svoda zakona," *IuG*, no. 78 (1906): 2311–13; Goremykin, 1:193–94.

103. It is precisely this evolutionary view of law that was emphasized in the 1892 Ministry of Justice official publication designed to serve as an introductory guide to the principles of law for the administrative personnel who in 1889 took on judicial responsibilities without judicial training. A. Pakharnaev, *Rukovodstvo v sudebnom deledlia zemskikh nachal'nikov, gorodskikh sudei, uezdnikh s"ezdov, gubernskikh prisutstvii i chinov politsii* (St. Petersburg, 1892), 5–6.

104. GARO, f. 721, GO, op. 4 (1911), d. 681.

105. TsIAM, f. 62, op. 2 (1916), d. 3185.

106. RGIA, f. 1291, op. 31 (1911), d. 147, l. 4–4ob.

107. Clifford Geertz, "Local Knowledge: Fact and Law in Comparative Perspective," *Local Knowledge: Further Essays in Interpretive Anthropology* (New York, 1983), 222–26.

108. The literature on peasant property devolution practices is extensive. For a good overview, see especially Worobec, *Peasant Russia*, 42–62. The most thorough treatments can be found in V. F. Mukhin, *Obychnyi poriadok nasledovaniia u krest'ian* (St. Petersburg, 1888); Leont'ev, *Krest'ianskoe pravo*, 2nd ed., 323–45; N. Brzheskii, *Ocherki iuridicheskogo byta krest'ian* (St. Petersburg, 1902), 59–81.

109. The problems faced by the *priimaki* were best described by Pavel Dashkevich. Although the Kiev communes under hereditary household tenure that he studied differed significantly from those in central Russia, the tensions between administrative instances there were similar to those prevailing in the central provinces. "Grazhdanskii obychai-priimachestvo u krest'ian Kievskoi gubernii," *IuV*, no. 8 (1887): 538–65, and "Volostnoi sud," 533–51.

110. Even in repartitional communes, households retained considerable leeway to dispose of their allotment land as they wished between repartitions. This was reflected in the fact that, despite the 1886 legislation requiring assembly approval for a household division, most households divided without permission *(samovol'no)*. On the prevalence of "willful" household divisions, see Frierson, "Peasant Family Divisions," in Bartlett, ed., *Land Commune*, 314–15.

111. GARO, f. 721, GO, op. 4 (1909), d. 479.

112. Ibid. (1910), d. 602.

113. Ianovich, 7.

114. Rodney Bohac, "Widows and the Russian Serf Community," in *Russia's Women: Accommodation, Resistance, Transformation,* ed. Barbara Clements, Barbara Engel, and Christine Worobec (Berkeley, 1991), 101.

115. Barykov, 118, 136, 172 (Riazan), 203 (Tula), 252 (Tver). Overviews of ethnographers' findings on the right of widows can be found in Mukhin, 243–75; E. I. Iakushkin, *Obychnoe pravo. Materialy dlia bibliografii obychnogo pravo* (Iaroslavl', 1896), 2:xxiv–xxix.

116. Rose Glickman, "Women and the Peasant Land Commune," in Bartlett, ed., *Land Commune*, 321–38.

117. TsIAM, f. 1891, op. 1, d. 2.

118. This reaction can be found in other contexts. French peasants after the Revolution, for instance, used their testamentary rights to counter new inheritance laws. Norbert Rouland, *Introduction historique au droit* (Paris, 1998), 213.

119. TsIAM, f. 749, op. 1, d. 8, ll. 10ob.–11.

120. Ibid., f. 62, op. 2, d. 3275, l. 4.

121. D. Ilimskii, 151, 155.

122. On the role of the state in structuring petitions see Madhavan Palat, "Regulating Conflict through the Petition," in *Social Identities in Revolutionary Russia,* ed. M. Palat (New York, 2001), 86–112; Golfo Alexopoulos, "The Ritual Lament: A Narrative of Appeal in the 1920s and 1930s," *Russian History* 24, no. 1–2 (1997): 117–29. The similarities between the pre-Emancipation petitions that Palat studies, and the Soviet petitions analyzed by Alexopoulos are striking. In both periods, "tearful descriptions of misery substituted for legal claims" (Palat, 94). The "ritual lament" emphasized the petitioner's powerlessness, challenging the authorities to act and display mercy in ways that enhanced the sovereignty of the state. There is no continuity from the 1840s through the 1930s, however. The "ritual lament" mode of petitioning did not dominate in the late imperial period.

123. GARO, f. 721, GO, op. 4 (1909), d. 528.

124. Ibid., f. 695, GO, op. 21 (1910), d. 225, l. 6.

125. Falk-Moore, 30–31.

126. GATO, f. 589, op. 1 (1912), d. 1426; GARO, f. 695, GO, op. 21 (1910), d. 89; op. 20 (1909), d. 23; f. 721, GO, op. 4 (1890), d. 9. A number of observers noted that peasants showed the greatest reluctance to accept rules on proscription and time limits. Sokolovskii, no. 1: 115; Skorobogatyi, "Dokozatel'stva," no. 5: 144–45; Dashkevich, "Volostnoi sud," 555.

127. Clifford Geertz has called the process of legal argumentation the "skeletonization of fact so as to narrow moral issues to the point where determinate rulings [could] be made to decide them." It was precisely this process that was impeded in the administrative courts of late Imperial Russia. *Local Knowledge*, 170.

128. Some commentators even feared that the 1912 law would exacerbate the problems related to the applicability and force of custom. A. N. Butovskii, "Primenenie obychaia v mestnom sude," *VP*, no. 21 (1914): 645–48; A. Leont'ev, "Volostnoi sud po zakonu o mestnom sude," *Trudy iuridicheskogo obshchestva pri Sankt-Peterburgskom universitete* (St. Petersburg, 1914), 2:183–212.

129. For some useful overviews, see Cynthia Herrup, "Crime, Law, and Society," *Comparative Studies in Society and History* 27, no. 1 (1985): 159–70; Bruce Lenman and Geoffry Parker, "The State, the Community and the Criminal Law in Early Modern Europe," in *Crime and the Law: The Social History of Crime in Western Europe since 1500*, ed. V. A. C. Gatrell, Bruce Lenman, and Geoffry Parker (London, 1980), 11–48; Rouland, especially chap. 1.

130. David Ransel, in *Village Life in Late Tsarist Russia*, by Olga Semyonova Tian-Shanskaia, ed. David Ransel (Bloomington, IN, 1993), 157. Jane Burbank has developed this argument further, positing that peasants' experience with local courts "constituted [a] . . . foundation for a law based society." *Russian Peasants Go to Court*, 2. Equating participation in the courts with integration within the polity, however, is unwarranted without examining processes of disputation at both the local and appeal levels. For a useful theoretical reflection on the processes of judicial modernization (and its limits), see René Levy and Xavier Rousseaux, "Etats, justice pénale et histoire. Bilan et perspectives," *Droit et société*, no. 20/21 (1992): 249–77.

131. Quotation from William Wagner, "Law and the State in Boris Mironov's *Sotsial'naia istoriia Rossii*," *SR* 60, no. 3 (2001): 563. There exists a striking similarity in jurisdiction, function, procedure, and level of usage between the Russian volost courts and the French justice of the peace courts established after the Revolution. Historians generally credit the French justices with facilitating judicial acculturation. The key differences explaining the different outcome are, in my view, threefold: the French courts did not allow adjudication according to custom; they limited the opportunities for public airing of grievances by excluding witnesses from conciliation sessions; and finally they required relatively high property ownership and education standards for the elected lay judges. Anthony Crubaugh, *Balancing the Scales of Justice: Local Courts and Rural Society in Southwest France, 1750–1800* (University Park, PA, 2001); Annie Bleton-Ruget, "L'infrajustice institutionnalisée. Les justices de paix des cantons ruraux du district de Dijon pendant la Révolution," in *L'infrajudiciaire du Moyen Age à l'époque contemporaine*, ed. Benoit Garnot (Paris, 1996), 291–311.

4—The Village Assembly and Contested Collectivism

1. Tsytovich, 50–52.

2. V. A. Beer, "Sud starikov i sel'skii skhod," *VP*, no. 9 (1900): 132–33; Rittikh, *Krest'ianskii pravoporiadok*, 136.

3. P. Efimenko, "Narodnye iuridicheskie obychai Arkhangel'skoi gubernii," *Trudy Arkhangel'skogo-statisticheskogo komiteta za 1867 i 1868* (Arkhangel', 1869), 199.

4. Skalon, 35–36; Charushin, *Sel'skie skhody*, 14; Sokolovskii, no. 1: 41–47; N. K. Brzheskii, "Sel'skie i volostnye skhody," *Vestnik finansov, promyshlennosti i torgovli*, no. 14 (1906): 6; Matveev, "V volostnykh starshinakh," no. 4: 121.

5. M. Ia. Fenomenov, *Staryi i novyi byt* (Moscow, 1925), 28–30; D. J. Male, *Russian Peasant Organization before Collectivization: A Study of Commune and Gathering, 1925–1930* (Cambridge, 1971).

6. Druzhinin, *Gosudarstvennye krest'iane,* 1:346–48. See also Melton; Hoch, *Serfdom.* For discussion of pre-Emancipation *skhody,* see Prokof'eva, 127–38; V. A. Aleksandrov, *Sel'skaia obshchina v Rossii (XVII–nachalo XIX v.)* (Moscow, 1976), 117–80.

7. This is the tendency in Boris Mironov's work on the commune where it is unclear to what extent the changes he discusses in fact reflect changes in the sources rather than changes of behavior. *Sotsial'naia istoriia,* 1:429–79. For a more successful effort at historicizing the commune, see Oleg Vronskii's *Krest'ianskaia obshchina,* although here too there is insufficient examination of the preconceptions embedded in contemporary accounts.

8. *RV,* no. 4 (1907): 3; TsIAM, f. 1943, op. 1 (1910), d. 183, ll. 3–5ob.; V. P. Semenov, *Polnoe geograficheskoe opisanie nashego otechestva,* vol. 2, *Srednerusskaia chernozemnaia oblast'* (St. Petersburg, 1902), 295–96; A. Selivanov, *Svod dannykh ob ekonomicheskom polozhenii krest'ian Riazanskoi gubernii* (Riazan, 1892), 234. Beloomut's cottage industries were tied into distribution networks radiating from Moscow into northern Riazan province and allowed village women to rework semi-finished suits at home. E. A. Oliunina, *Portnovskii promysel v Moskve i derevniakh Moskovskoi i Riazanskoi gubernii. Materialy k istorii domashnei promyshlennosti v Rossii* (Moscow, 1914), especially chap. 3 describing Beloomut.

9. V. I. Semevskii, *Krest'ianskii vopros v Rossii v XVIII i pervoi polovine XIX veka* (St. Petersburg, 1888), 2:227–31. On the 20 February 1803 law on "free agriculturalists," see Moon, *Russian Peasants and Tsarist Legislation,* 62, 92. Verkhne-Beloomut was also highly unusual in that nearly full rosters of resolutions covering over 30 years have been preserved.

10. Matveev, "V volostnykh starshinakh," no. 2: 76, no. 4: 121; "Iz zhizni sovremennogo krest'ianskogo mira," *RB,* no. 10 (1913): 165–66. The favored themes of prerevolutionary village correspondents (namely the celebration of progress and a predilection for sensationalist examples of the harm done by superstition and tradition) are strikingly similar to those favored by the *sel'kory* of the 1920s. On the 1920s, see especially Steven Coe, "Peasants, the State, and the Language of NEP: The Rural Correspondents Movement in the Soviet Union, 1924–1928" (Ph.D. diss., University of Michigan, 1993).

11. *RV,* no. 207 (1907): 3; *RZh,* no. 21 (1913): 3. On the rural press, see James Krukones, *To the People: The Russian Government and the Newspaper Sel'skii Vestnik, 1881–1917* (New York, 1987). On educated Russia's fears of peasant backwardness: Frank, "Confronting the Domestic Other."

12. *RZh,* no. 21 (1913): 3; no. 37: 3; no. 152: 3–4; no. 153: 2–3; no. 155: 3. The village correspondents' columns told a story that could fit within the "tragedy of the commons" paradigm (positing that land that is no one's will be overused by everyone), as famously expounded by Garrett Hardin in "The Tragedy of the Commons," *Science,* no. 162 (1968): 1243–48. For a recent critique, see *The Management of Common Land in North-West Europe, c. 1500–1850,* ed. Marina De Moor et al. (Turnhout, Belgium, 2002), chap. 1.

13. Selivanov, 108–11; GARO, f. 1943, op. 1, d. 91 (1883), ll. 39–40, 57, 59, 64; op. 1, d. 179 (1909), ll. 66–68, 76–78.

14. Selivanov, 110–13. For similar developments in Iaroslavl province see Druzhinin, "Byvshie svobodnye khlebopashtsy," no. 12, 363–82.

15. TsIAM, f. 1943, op. 1, d. 91 (1883), ll. 10–12; d. 179 (1909), ll. 4–6; op. 1, d. 173 (1907), l. 3; *RV,* no. 4 (1907): 3.

16. TsIAM, f. 1943, op. 1, d. 91 (1883); op. 1, d. 121 (1890); d. 141 (1902); d. 173 (1907); d. 195 (1912); GARF, f. 586, op. 1, d. 118, l. 2. In 1912 the commune inexplicably, and sporadically, again began counting "present households."

17. TsIAM, f. 1943, op. 1, d. 91 (1883), l. 25; d. 179 (1909), ll. 53–56.

18. Ibid., d. 91 (1883), ll. 10–12, 21–24; op. 1, d. 179 (1909), ll. 7–9, 18–20, 60–62; GARF, f. 586, op. 1, d. 118, l. 4.

19. GARF, f. 586, op. 1, d. 122, l. 16 (Tula); d. 120, ll. 7–8 (Smolensk).

20. Ibid., d. 118, ll. 4–7; Tenishev, *Administrativnoe polozhenie,* 40.

21. TsIAM, f. 1943, op. 1 (1909), d. 179, ll. 45–49.

22. Ibid., ll. 12–14, 73–75, 104–6. In 1891 the Senate confirmed that the law on communal welfare gave the village society the right to prevent sales by members who would thereby be impoverished. I. Danilov, 138.

23. O. B., "Sel'skoe obshchestvennoe prizrenie," *VE,* no. 6 (1890): 649–50.

24. "Nishchenstva iz pripisanogo krest'ianskogo naseleniia," *Statisticheskii sbornik po S. Peterburgskoi gubernii za 1897,* vol. 5, *Materialy po nekotorym voprosam, kasaiushchimsia krest'ianskikh uchrezhdenii* (St. Petersburg, 1898), 103–5.

25. Data is for 47 provinces of European Russia. Brzheskii, *Natural'nye povinnosti,* 183; Tsytovich, 102–3. For Tver data: *Sel'sko-khoziastvennyi obzor Tverskoi gubernii za 1896 god* (Tver, 1896), 37, 41.

26. Moskovskoe gubernskoe zemstvo, *Siroty, prestarelye i ne trudosposobnye v Moskovskom gubernii* (Moscow, 1915), 13–17, 31; Engelgardt, 28–31; Efimenko, 195; P. S. Tsypkin, "Opeka v krest'ianskom bytu," in Tenishev, *Administrativnoe polozhenie,* 145–48; Barykov, 173.

27. For example: RGIA, f. 1344, op. 207 (1908), d. 173. Brzheskii noted that this tendency was most prominent in areas of high seasonal migration. *Natural'nye povinnosti,* 104–6; Tsytovich, 68–71; Strakhovskii, "Sovremennoe polozhenie," 75.

28. *RV,* no. 4 (1905): 3.

29. TsIAM, f. 62, op. 1, d. 7360, ll. 162–79.

30. GARO, f. 695, op. 23 (1913), d. 131; f. 930, op. 19 (1912), sv. 3, d. 13.

31. RGIA, f. 1291, op. 50 (1911), d. 7, l. 2; f. 1344, op. 275 (1913), d. 244, ll. 4–5; op. 252 (1911), d. 689.

32. One *desiatina* = 1.07 hectares or 2.7 acres. Figures for 1881 and 1892: *Entsiklopedicheskii slovar',* 38:523; 1894: Brzheskii, *Natural'nye povinnosti,* 94, 194, 207; 1905: Tsytovich, 98–106. Unfortunately, a more careful analysis of the evolution in specific categories of expenses is impossible, as categories that were too broad changed between surveys and were insufficiently explained. For critiques of the numerous shortcomings in official data on *mirskie sbory,* see Brzheskii, *Natural'nye povinnosti,* 152–62; Astyrev, "Mirskie raskhody," 73–100.

33. "Mirskie povinnosti," 523–24. On redemption payments: Steven Hoch, "On Good Numbers and Bad: Malthus, Population Trends and Peasant Standard of Living in Late Imperial Russia," *SR* 53, no. 1 (1994): 46–47.

34. Strakhovskii, "Sovremennoe polozhenie," 7–10; Selivanov, 280–88; I. Krasnoperov, *Svodnyi sbornik statisticheskikh svedenii po Tverskoi gubernii* (Tver, 1897), 1:289.

35. Tur, 199–200; Anfimov, *Ekonomicheskoe polozhenie,* 84.

36. On school funding, see Eklof, *Peasant Schools,* 89–92.

37. If one excludes agricultural expenses from both the 1896 and 1908 Tver data, the share of communal and local taxes actually rose from approximately 21% (1896) to 25% of a peasant household's total tax bill. Tverskoe gubernskoe zemstvo, *Sel'sko-khoziaistvennyi sbornik za 1896,* 20, 32–37; *Statisticheskii ezhegodnik Tverskoi gubernii (1909–1910)* (Tver, 1911), 16–19.

38. On the importance of local institutional frameworks to enforce community regulation and management of common land in other contexts, see De Moor; E. P. Thompson, *Customs in Common: Studies in Traditional Popular Culture* (New York, 1991), 107; Ruth Behar, *Santa Maria del Monte: The Presence of the Past in a Spanish Village* (Princeton, 1986), chaps. 10 and 12.

39. Gromyko, "Mesto sel'skoi obshchiny," 70–79.

40. Scott, *Domination and the Arts of Resistance.*

41. See for instance Novikov, *Zapiski,* 40–41; Tenishev, *Administrativnoe polozhenie,* 33; Rittikh, *Krest'ianskii pravoporiadok,* 129, 134–37, 149.

42. Vladimir Dal', *Tolkovyi slovar' zhivogo velikorusskogo iazyka*, 4 vols. (St. Petersburg-Moscow, 1881– ; reprint, Moscow, 1980), 2:331.

43. Quoted in Gromyko, *Traditsionnye normy*, 95.

44. Dal', *Tolkovyi slovar'*, 2:215.

45. Astyrev, *V volostnykh pisariakh*, 1st ed., 118–23. Cathy Frierson's *Peasant Icons* includes an excellent discussion of the emergence of the kulak "peasant type" in Russian populist thought. Frierson's analysis also emphasizes the evolution of the kulak from "village strongman" into a "synonym for exploitation" but does not consider the *miroed* separately, even somewhat inexplicably translating Astyrev's *"miroed"* as "kulak" in citations (141, 150–51). See also Shanin, 1:156–58.

46. Dal', *Tolkovyi slovar'*, 2:183.

47. *RV*, no. 29 (1907): 3.

48. For example: *RV*, no. 46 (1907): 4; *RV*, no. 1 (1909): 3; *RZh* (1913), no. 21: 3; no. 103: 3; no. 243: 3–4.

49. Tenishev, *Administrativnoe polozhenie*, 34–35; Charushin, *Sel'skie skhody*, 9–10; GARF, f. 586. op. 1, d. 120, ll. 5, 70; Gromyko, *Traditsionnye normy*, 95.

50. Brzheskii, "Sel'skie i volostnye skhody," no. 13: 533.

51. Matveev, "V volostnykh starshinakh," no. 4: 120–30; no. 5: 173.

52. *RV*, no. 21 (1913): 3.

53. GARO, f. 694, op. 22 (1882), d. 318, l. 11; f. 717, op. 5 (1894), d. 82; f. 694, op. 26 (1886), d. 148; Brzheskii, "Sel'skie i volostnye skhody," no. 13: 534.

54. Barykov, 163, 185, 371; Tenishev, *Administrativnoe polozhenie*, 28, 33; Matveev, "V volostnykh starshinakh," no. 5: 174.

55. TsIAM, f. 696, op. 1 (1910), d. 1764, l. 2; f. 62, op. 1 (1908), d. 2738, l. 2; GARO, f. 695, op. 19 (1909), d. 302, l. 3.

56. See for instance GARF, f. 586, d. 121, l. 4 (Tver).

57. Falk-Moore, 32–33.

58. S. T. Semenov, 250–77.

59. Barykov, 163.

60. A. A. Shustikov, "Na mirskom peredele zemli," *Severnyi krai* (1899), no. 32: 2; no. 35: 2; no. 36: 2–3.

61. Astyrev, *V volostnykh pisariakh*, 1st ed., 82–86, 107–9.

62. Ianovich, 79; "Vnutrennee obozrenie," *VE*, no. 7–8 (1893): 383; GARF, f. 586, op. 1, d. 121, l. 4 (Tver); GARO, f. 721, op. 1 (1900), d. 57. In contrast, the procedure followed by district boards prior to 1889 had simply been to entrust investigation to the volost elder who recounted votes and rarely reported anything conflicting with a commune's resolution.

63. These types of on the spot adjustments were mentioned by numerous observers: communes rarely adhered to a single criterion in allotting land but might take into account special family circumstances (extra mouths to feed could result in an allotment slightly above norm, men not capable of working could on the contrary lead to reduction, etc.). In regions where high redemption burdens on poor land forced a large proportion of men to work outside the village, the household's overall tax-paying capability became the crucial criteria. See for instance: V. Trirogov, *Obshchina i podat'* (St. Petersburg), 13–27; Tur, 124–26; RGIA, f. 91, op. 2, d. 776, ll. 12–13; M. M. Gromyko, *Mir russkoi derevni* (Moscow, 1991), 167; Burds, 49–64.

64. Barykov, 163, 185, 198, 212, 266. Information on Tver comes from Burds, 249.

65. Firsov and Kiseleva, 89–91.

66. Kotsonis, 153–59. Quotation from page 153.

67. S. T. Semenov, 256–61, 304.

68. Communal banishment was deemed both by peasants and authorities to be an extreme measure to be applied only in last resort. For further discussion, see Frank, *Crime*, 236–41.

69. RGIA, f. 1291, op. 54 (1913), d. 12, l. 20.

70. GARO, f. 695, op. 18-1 (1908), d. 181, l. 28.

71. Ibid., op. 11 (1911), d. 225, l. 16; RGIA, f. 1344, op. 217 (1909), d. 279, l. 6; f. 1291, op. 54 (1913), d. 12.

72. RGIA, f. 1291, op. 31 (1908), d. 87, ll. 115, 177, 252 (Tambov). On the practice of collecting extra signatures after the assembly: Brzheskii, "Sel'skie i volostnye skhody," no. 13: 534–35; Tenishev, *Administrativnoe polozhenie,* 8, 13, 42; Rittikh, *Krest'ianskii pravoporiadok,* 132; GARF, f. 586, op. 1, d. 122, l. 6 (Tula); d. 121, ll. 6, 18 (Tver); d. 120, ll. 15, 76 (Smolensk); Firsov and Kiseleva, 49.

73. Brzheskii, "Sel'skie i volostnye skhody," no. 13: 534; TsIAM, f. 1964, op. 1 (1907–1909), dd. 1–2; RGIA, f. 1291, op. 31 (1909), d. 149, l. 245ob.; GARF, f. 586, d. 121 (Moscow), l. 4; d. 125, l. 33 (Iaroslavl').

74. S. A. Dediulin, *Krest'ianskoe samoupravlenie v sviazi s dvorianskim voprosom. K voprosu o peresmotre zakonopolozhenii o krest'ianakh* (St. Petersburg, 1902), 86.

75. For France, see Root, 71–82; Spain: Behar, 160–74.

76. Firsov and Kiseleva, 45–48; GARF, f. 586, op. 1, d. 121, l. 2 (Moscow); d. 120, l. 76 (Smolensk); Brzheskii, "Sel'skie i volostnye skhody," no. 13: 532, 535, no. 14: 5; B. Kremnev, "Proekt ob uporiadochenii sel'skikh skhodov," *IuV,* no. 5 (1885): 143–46.

77. GARO, f. 694, op. 22 (1882), d. 319, l. 3.

78. Goremykin, 1:69–70; V. Prugavin, "Sel'skaia zemel'naia obshchina v po-volzhskom krae," *IuV,* no. 5 (1885): 95–100.

79. Frierson, "Peasant Family Divisions," in Bartlett, ed., *Land Commune,* 310–11. For a critique of the assumption that there was a shift from complex to simple households following Emancipation, see Worobec, *Peasant Russia,* 76–117. Empire-wide figures are from Dorothy Atkinson, *The End of the Russian Land Commune, 1905–1930* (Stanford, 1985), 81, and "The Statistics on the Russian Land Commune, 1905–1917," *SR* 32, no. 4 (1973): 786; Mironov, *Sotsial'naia istoriia,* 1:221.

80. Selivanov, 56–57, 62–63.

81. TsIAM, f. 1964, op. 1, d. 2; f. 808, op. 1, d. 49; *RV,* no. 84 (1907): 3; Barbara Engel, "The Woman's Side: Male Out-Migration and the Family Economy in Kostroma Province," *SR* 45, no. 2 (1986): 257–71.

82. It is difficult to gauge the extent of women's public presence from signatures alone, however, as they were more likely to be illiterate, and in such cases it was common practice to list them under the name of the male household head. Brzheskii, "Sel'skie i volostnye skhody," no. 14: 6; Selivanov, 245; TsIAM, f. 1943, op. 1, d. 183 (1910), ll. 4–5ob.; d. 174 (1907).

83. On Voronezh: Kremnev, 149, 155; Kursk: RGIA, f. 1291, op. 54 (1912), d. 176, l. 18.

84. RGIA, f. 1291, op. 51 (1915), d. 150, ll. 2–15; op. 54 (1915), d. 26, ll. 2, 9, 12.

85. K. Kachorovskii, *Russkaia obshchina. Vozmozhno li, zhelatel'no li ee sokhranenie i razvitie?* (Moscow, 1906), 278; P. Veniaminov, *Krest'ianskaia obshchina* (St. Petersburg, 1908), 61; V. S. Prugavin, *Russkaia zemel'naia obshchina v trudakh ee mestnykh issledovatelei* (Moscow, 1888), 46–51; Khauke, 91–94.

86. The remaining 2% made partial adjustments to existing holdings (conducted *skidki*). Veniaminov, 119–21. On the evolution of redistribution criteria, see 107–54.

87. *RV,* no. 130 (1907): 3. On the role of migration in accentuating the "generation gap," see Burds, 29–38.

88. GARO, f. 694, op. 26 (1886), d. 128, l. 4–4ob.

89. RGIA, f. 1344, op. 199 (1907), d. 68, l. 2–2ob. On the growing assertiveness of youth, see Burds, 34–38; Zyrianov, *Krest'ianskaia obshchina,* 247–50.

90. On the World War I debate over proper reward of soldiers, see for instance "Zemel'nye nadely dlia uchastnikov voiny," *MV,* no. 148 (1916): 1; "Zemel'nyi fond dlia Georgevskikh Kavalerov," *Russkoe slovo,* no. 187 (1916): 3; I. Iordanskii, "Golosa iz derevni," *Russkie vedomosti,* no. 78 (1915): 7. The best study of the far-reaching impact of conscription is Joshua Sanborn's, *Drafting the Russian Nation: Military Conscription, Total War, and Mass Politics, 1905–1925* (DeKalb, IL, 2003).

91. RGIA, f. 1344, op. 200 (1907), d. 928, ll. 7–8, 21, 34–38; quotation is from 13ob. The continuation of the case is in op. 217 (1909), d. 393. Unfortunately, the Senate's final ruling is not included in these files. Administrative slowness had seriously complicated the case. In 1901, the Senate had confirmed that there were 24 households in Volynkino and that women householders had the right to participate. In 1902 and 1904, the Senate further confirmed resolutions from 1900 stipulating that income was to be distributed according to revision souls (thus with participation of women). But in 1906, an appeal to the MVD reopened the case, and the General Assembly of the Senate confirmed the 1898 resolution that had established a restricted assembly. But by that time, the commune had been acting according to the Senate's 1901 ruling for five years, and the local land captain had to forward the case once again up the administrative ladder because it was impossible to implement. The MVD, which commented on the situation in 1908, voiced considerable irritation with the provincial board for not having worked harder to find a solution, and with the Senate for having produced two conflicting rulings. The Senate was still collecting testimony at the end of 1909.

92. RGIA, f. 1344, op. 200 (1907), d. 928, l. 20ob. The village in fact no longer farmed its arable land but rented it out and distributed the income among its households.

93. RGIA, f. 1291, op. 121 (1915), d. 35, ll. 17ob.–18ob.

94. GARO, f. 694, op. 22 (1882) d. 318, l. 1ob.; d. 260, l. 6.

95. Ibid., op. 26 (1886), d. 148, ll. 1ob.–2. The tone of the "unanimous" resolution was no less combative. It opened with a statement that the opponents to redistribution (who held extra land "unfairly") had brought the village great harm as land had been exhausted (it was common for households to cease manuring their strips on the eve of redistribution) during the four-year dispute.

96. Burds, 221–22; Anfimov, *Ekonomicheskoe polozhenie*, 54–72.

97. Prugavin, *Russkaia zemel'naia obshchina*, 16–18, 23–30, 46–51; V. P. Vorontsov, *Progressivnaia techeniia v krest'ianskom khoziaistve* (St. Petersburg, 1892), 119–21, 146ff.; Christine Worobec, "The Post-Emancipation Russian Peasant Commune in Orel Province, 1861–90," in Bartlett, ed., *Land Commune*, 86–105; Judith Pallot, "The Commune in the 1870s," in *Landscape and Settlement in Romanov Russia, 1613–1917*, ed. Judith Pallot and Denis Shaw (Oxford, 1990), 136–63. On the relation of tax payments to productivity, see Druzhinin, *Russkaia derevniia*, 124–33. David Darrow has convincingly argued that the perceived crisis caused by the discrepancy between agricultural earnings and tax burdens was much exaggerated, and that the framers of the Emancipation settlement had not intended such a correspondence in any case. This useful reminder, however, does not change the fact that tax burdens did affect peasant perceptions of the relative desirability of holding more allotment land. "The Politics of Numbers," 145–59.

98. Khauke, 89; V. E. Denskii, "Imeiut li vykupnye platezhi pravo na razrushenie obshchiny," *RM*, no. 2 (1883): 151–59; S. M. Blekov, "O formakh krest'ianskogo zemlevladenie v Zubtsovskom uezde Tverskoi gubernii," *Sbornik pravovedeniia i obshchestvennogo znanii* (St. Petersburg, 1893), 1:69–71; Krasnoperov, *Svodnyi sbornik*, 42–43; Markov, 297; Selivanov, 91; Riazanskoe gubernskoe zemstvo, *Sbornik statisticheskikh svedenii po Riazanskoi gubernii*, vol. 1, *Riazanskii uezd* (Moscow, 1882), 20–25; A. Eropkin, "Sel'skaia obshchina i prochnyi pravoporiadok," *Novyi put'*, no. 6 (1903): 114–17.

99. GARO, f. 694, op. 25 (1885), d. 113, l. 1; f. 79, op. 1 (1890), d. 9, l. 1; f. 694, op. 25 (1885) d. 139, l. 13–13ob.; op. 22 (1882), d. 349, l. 2–2ob.

100. "Obshchee polozhenie," *PSZ*, 2nd series, vol. 36, no. 36657, arts. 11, 16; "Polozhenie o vykupe," *PSZ*, no. 36659, arts. 1–4, 165.

101. GARO, f. 721, op. 4 (1890), d. 9, l. 7.

102. Ibid., f. 721, op. 1 (1900), d. 57; f. 694, op. 26 (1886), d. 128, l. 4; f. 694, op. 22 (1882), d. 497, l. 1ob.; f. 721, op. 2 (1903), d. 12, l. 2; f. 81, op. 9 (1903), d. 2, l. 1.

103. Shanin, 2:120–37; Danilova and Danilov, 27–28.

104. Maria Agren, "Asserting One's Rights: Swedish Property Law in the Transition from Community Law to State Law," *Law and History Review* 19, no. 2 (2001): 241–82; Nadine Vivier, *Propriété collective et identité communale. Les Biens communaux en France, 1750–1914* (Paris, 1998); Gerald Strauss, *Law, Resistance, and the State: The Opposition to Roman Law in Reformation Germany* (Princeton, 1986); Thompson.

105. GARO, f. 697, op. 1 (1885), d. 882, l. 7–7ob.

106. "Polozhenie o vykupe," arts. 118, 160; K. Skvortsov, "Nasledovanie v zemle krest'ian," *VP,* no. 2 (1901): 43–44.

107. GARO, f. 721, op. 2 (1890) d. 16b, ll. 5ob.–6. For other examples, see Riazanskoe gubernskoe zemstvo, 1:31–35.

108. Veniaminov, 164–69. See also Prugavin, *Russkaia zemel'naia obshchina,* 40–45; Khauke, 101–2. Judith Pallot has convincingly argued that the purpose of redistributions was not equalization, but "it had the more modest purpose of delivering a minimum amount of land to households." Pallot, "The Commune in the 1870s," 157.

109. In 1866, and again more firmly in 1892, the Senate specified that article 36 did not apply to property still being redeemed, and in 1897 that the article did not apply to land redeemed under article 165. I. Danilov, 183–84; Goremykin, 1:54.

110. Goremykin, 1:566–67, 572.

111. Quotation from Popkins, "Peasant Wills," 12. For the text of the 1881 ruling: I. Danilov, 124–25.

112. Tiutriumov, *Obshchee polozhenie,* 430; Skvortsov, 32–36; "Krest'ianskie spory o zemle," *IuG,* no. 73 (1892): 3.

113. Figes, "Village Commune," 457.

5—The Challenges of Property Reform, 1906–1916

1. Polivanov, no. 7–8: 59.

2. S. M. Dubrovskii, *Stolypinskaia zemel'naia reforma* (Moscow, 1963), 574–76.

3. While estimates of the number of incidents requiring armed intervention vary, they number in the hundreds, not the thousands. G. A. Gerasimenko, *Bor'ba krest'ian protiv stolypinskoi agrarnoi politiki* (Saratov, 1985); Dubrovskii, 514–66; N. A. Mal'tseva, "O kolichestve krest'ianskikh vystuplenii v period stolypinskoi agrarnoi reformy," *Istorii SSSR,* no. 1 (1965): 126–31; A. V. Shapkarin, ed., *Krest'ianskoe dvizheniie v Rossii, iiun 1907 g.–iiul' 1914. Sbornik dokumentov* (Moscow-Leningrad, 1966). For a good summary of this debate, see Zyrianov, *Krest'ianskaia obshchina,* 140–46.

4. Estimates on the proportion of households consolidating range from 8 to 10%, and from 3 to 8% for the central provinces such as Moscow, Riazan, and Tver. The range of estimates for individual titling *(ukprelenie)* is much wider, between 18 and 40%. All depends on whether the number of households in 1905 is used as the denominator or the much higher number of households in 1916, on whether the nominator includes applications for title or only titles received, etc. Too much of the debate over the success or failure of reform has centered on numbers, not only because the statistics regularly published by the MVD are of doubtful accuracy, but also because—as Judith Pallot has best shown—the act of applying for title did not necessarily indicate a rejection of communal tenure. Riazan had the lowest rate of land titling of the central agricultural provinces, with an estimated 18–20% of households in 1916 living under hereditary tenure. "Svedeniia o vykhode iz obshchiny," RGIA, f. 1291, op. 121 (1916), d. 4, ll. 322–27. For discussion of the difficulties of establishing accurate land reform statistics, see Atkinson, "Statistics," 773–87; V. P. Danilov, "Ob istoricheskikh sud'bakh krest'ianskoi obshchiny v Rossii," *Ezhegodnik po agrarnoi istorii,* vol. 6, *Problemy istorii russkoi obshchiny* (Vologda, 1976), 103–6; Adrian Jones, *Late-Imperial Russia, An Interpretation: Three Visions, Two Cultures, One Peasantry* (Bern, 1997). Unfortunately, the latest foray into the debate over numbers is too riddled with errors to be reliable. Tiukavkin.

5. G. A. Krestovnikov, *Mogyt li byt' peredely nadel'noi zemli krest'ian posle okonchaniia vykypnoi operatsii* (Moscow, 1908); Zyrianov, *Krest'ianskaia obshchina*, 77–78.

6. RGIA, f. 408, op. 1, d. 552, l. 24.

7. Some 1.7 million households applied for individual title by the end of 1909. Even after 1910, when the government shifted its attention from individual consolidation to group land reorganization, and when participation in land reorganization automatically conferred title, individual householders continued to file title requests. Thus, title applications filed after 1910 had nothing to do with consolidation of strips, yet over 1.4 million households requested either *ukreplenie* (in repartitional communes) or individual certificates of ownership (these were issued in communes not having conducted repartitions since Emancipation and accounted for 433,000 applications). *IZO*, no. 8 (1916): 218–19; Dubrovskii, 200.

8. Matveev, "V volostnykh starshinakh," no. 5: 172; RGIA-otchety, "Otchet gubernatora Novgorodskoi gubernii za 1908," vol. 128: 190–190ob.; I. V. Mozzhukhin, *Zemleustroistvo v Bogorodskom uezde, Tul'skoi gubernii* (Moscow, 1917), introduction, 153–55.

9. I. V. Chernyshev, *Obshchina posle 9 noiabria po ankete Vol'nogo Ekonomicheskogo Obshchestva*, 2 vols. (Petrograd, 1917), 1:21, 48–49, 77–78, 107, 129, 158. For an overview of the results of other surveys, see Dubrovskii, 213–18.

10. Zyrianov calculates that the average size of titled holdings declined from 7.7 *desiatiny* in 1907 to 6.0 in 1914. *Krest'ianskaia obshchina*, 94; see also N. P. Oganovskii, "Pervye itogi velikoi reformy," *RB*, no. 10 (1911): 146.

11. RGIA, f. 1291, op. 63 (1907), d. 23, ll. 5–7. For an overview of similar findings in other provinces, see Pallot, *Land Reform*, 110–11. Data for Riazan is calculated from N. S. Zuzykina, "Provedenie Stolypinskoi agrarnoi reformy v Riazanskoi gubernii, 1907–1914" (Kand. diss., Moskovskii gor. ped. institut im. Potemkina, 1958), 182; *Statistika zemlevladeniia 1905 g.*, vol. 4, *Riazanskaia guberniia* (St. Petersburg, 1906), 51; Selivanov, 65.

12. Dubrovskii, 199. These frequently cited figures somewhat overstate the discrepancy, however, because titled land is expressed as a share of total communal holdings as reported in the 1905 survey of agricultural lands. The survey included all allotment land—pasture, forest, and wasteland used in common and to which titled households had access—while the data on titled land apparently included only the household plot and arable land. Application forms for titles (used by governors' offices to compile data forwarded to the MVD) did not note the area of lands in common use but registered the number of shares to which proprietors were entitled. Even when the 1905 numbers are adjusted to exclude commons, however, a discrepancy remains (as in the example of Riazan cited above). When historians discuss such average holdings, it is sometimes impossible to know if they are in fact comparing comparable figures. See for instance Vronskii, *Gosudarstvennaia vlast'*, 307–8. The only contemporary commentator I have found who even noted this statistical difficulty is A. E. Lositskii, *Raspadenie obshchiny* (St. Petersburg, 1912), 54. The problem is noted by Anfimov and Tiukavkin, but they offer no alternative data. Anfimov, P. A. *Stolypin i rossiiskoe krest'ianstvo* (Moscow, 2002), 120; Tiukavkin, 196.

13. Both Zyrianov and Vronskii have concluded that the desire to protect land against redistribution was not the most common motive for taking out title. According to article 3 of the 1906 decree, in any commune where there had been a redistribution within the last 24 years, a household titling more than its share of land had to pay the commune the equivalent of the original redemption price on the extra land *(izlichki)*. In spite of the fact that this meant land could be acquired at below-market prices, only 3.5% of those obtaining title by September 1909 received such extra land. A. Manuilov, "Noveishee zakonodatel'stvo o zemel'noi obshine," *VE*, no. 11 (1912): 255; Vronskii, *Gosudarstvennaia vlast'*, 321–22; Zyrianov, *Krest'ianskaia obshchina*, 112–15.

14. The figure for European Russia includes sales through 1915 and encompassed 22% of the land area titled. *IZO*, no. 1 (1916): 32; Dubrovskii, 361. For Riazan, see Zuzykina, 160–61; Vronskii, *Gosudarstvennaia vlast'*, 362–65.

15. Sales by absentees represented 16.4% of all those receiving land titles that year. M. S. Simonova, "Mobilizatsiia krest'ianskoi nadel'noi zemli v period Stolypin-skoi agrarnoi reformy," *Materialy po istorii sel'skogo khoziaistva i krest'ianstvo SSSR* (Moscow, 1962), 5:443–49.

16. The eight provinces are Kaluga, Kostroma, Pskov, Samara, Nizhgorod, Sim-birsk, Tver, and Tambov. *IZO* (1915), no. 3: 109; no. 6: 217; no.7: 246, 328. Data on Tula is cited in L. M. Ivanov, "Preemstvennost' fabrichno-zavodskogo truda i formirovanie proletariata v Rossii," in *Rabochii klass i rabochee dvizhenie v Rossii, 1861–1917* (Moscow, 1966), 117. On Simbirsk and Novgorod: Mozzhukhin, 138. Other data can be found in Vronskii, *Gosudarstvennaia vlast'*, 118, 121–22, 235.

17. Vs. N., "Zakon 9-go noiabria," *VE*, no. 8 (1910): 298. The issue examined here is separate from the question of the economic impact of the reforms. As Vronskii has argued, sale of titled land may very well have been progressive (or at least neutral) in terms of agricultural production, as marginal households sold out to those better able to exploit the land. But this is not the same as evaluating the impact on internal village relations. Economically, it may not have mattered whether an absentee sold to Petrov, or whether his land was allotted to Ivanov. But to Petrov and Ivanov, the out-come was of vital importance.

18. Chernyshev, 1:107.

19. V. P. Drozdov, *Okolo zemli. Ocherki po zemleustroistvu* (Moscow, 1909), 66.

20. *IZO*, no. 9 (1912): 402. Tiukavkin is incorrect in assuming that sales did not cover common use shares, and that therefore communes would gain from sales that allegedly gave them extra common land for free. Tiukavkin, 191.

21. "Bor'ba obshchiny s obezzemeleniem svoikh chlenov," *Vestnik Riazanskogo gubernskogo zemstva*, no. 1 (1914): 101–4. Izhevskoe had already tried to limit sales in the 1890s. See Eropkin, 125–33; GARO, f. 721, op. 1 (1894), d. 19, l. 3.

22. Compiled from RGIA, f. 1290, op. 7, dd. 464 and 474.

23. See also: GARO, f. 695, op. 24 (1914), d. 49; Simonova, "Mobilizatsiia," 425–26.

24. Chernyshev, 1:29, 83, 85; Simonova, "Mobilizatsiia," 425–26; Zyrianov, *Krest'ianskaia obshchina*, 209–16; Vronskii, *Gosudarstvennaia vlast'*, 367–68.

25. RGIA, f. 1291, op. 120 (1911), d. 17, l. 112; Vs. N., 300; Chernyshev, 1:81, 106, 127; *IZO*, no. 9 (1911): 411–12. Zyrianov has gone so far as to call this aspect of the reform a "wager on the old." *Krest'ianskaia obshchina*, 113–14. Obviously not all these sales were undertaken to the detriment of household members. Elderly or de-parting peasants could use this mechanism to keep within a clan an allotment that might otherwise have escheated to the commune.

26. TsIAM, f. 62, op. 2, d. 3274. One absentee son expressed his dissatisfaction with the requirement that he must prove his father to be a drunkard and of "general bad behavior." "I do not consider my father a squanderer. I only want to protect our property from sale without my approval." Ibid., f. 749, op. 1, d. 34, l. 2. "Krest'ian-skaia opeka," *Sel'skii vestnik*, no. 71 (1910): 1–2.

27. Chernyshev, 1:71, 48, 105, 128.

28. Ibid., 76; *Krest'ianskoe delo*, no. 10 (1911): 201. On the ambivalence of peas-ant attitudes toward migrant workers, see especially Barbara Engel, "Russian Peasant Views of City Life, 1861–1914," *SR* 52, no. 3 (1993): 446–53.

29. Vs. N., 299.

30. GARO, f. 695, op. 22 (1912), d. 23, l. 13ob.

31. Quotation from TsIAM, f. 749, op. 1 (1909), d. 13, decision 63. GATO, f. 589, op. 1 (1910), d. 1432; GATO f. 998, op. 1 (1914), dd. 44, 53; TsIAM, d. 749, op. 1 (1914), d. 20, decisions 29, 43, 58, 113; dd. 32–34.

32. "Kartinki derevenskoi zhizni," *RZh*, no. 280 (1913): 3.

33. GARO, f. 695, op. 24 (1914), d. 49 and d. 48.

34. RGIA, f. 1291, op. 120 (1910), d. 6, ll. 30, 189.

35. A. Peshekhonov, "Sotsial'nye posledstviia zemleustroistva," *RB*, no. 11 (1909): 86; Burds, 119–31. On peasant circular migration, see Bradley, 27–34, 347; James Bater, "Transience, Residential Persistence, and Mobility in Moscow and St. Petersburg, 1900–1914," *SR* 39, no. 2 (1980), 239–54.

36. "Nishchentsvo," *Statisticheskii ezhegodnik Moskovskoi gubernii za 1910 god* (Moscow, 1911), 89. Thanks to Jeffrey Burds for drawing my attention to this article.

37. Peshekhonov, no. 10: 113–14. Sergei Semenov likewise noted that migrant workers were among the most vocal supporters of the commune, because it freed them from worrying about their land while they were away. S. T. Semenov, 316–18.

38. Peshekhonov, no. 10: 112–13. See also V. Iakushkin, "Kolliziia prava na nadelenie s pravami ukrepivshikhsia chlenov obshchestva," *VPiN*, no. 45 (1912): 1417–18.

39. GARO, f. 695, op. 22 (1912), d. 240, l. 3; *IZO*, no. 9 (1911): 412 (Novgorod). The 29 May 1911 law on land settlement also reduced the number of individual title applications as households involved in land reorganization were automatically registered under hereditary tenure.

40. By 1916, the northern, nonagricultural districts of Spassk, Kasimov, and Egorevsk, which each had approximately 40% of its male population engaged in outside work in the late 1880s, had 9%, 13%, and 16% of their households with land titles, respectively. Meanwhile, the southern agricultural districts of Riazhsk and Ranenburg, with lower migration rates of 12% and 20%, had the highest rates of titling in the province (25.5% and 27.5%). Calculated from RGIA, f. 1291, op. 121 (1916), d. 4, ll. 322–25; "Otkhozhie promysly v Riazanskoi gubernii," *Vestnik Riazanskogo gubernskogo zemstva*, no. 4–5 (1916): 40.

41. Chernyshev, 1:80; "Meshcherskii krai (Etnograficheskii ocherk)," *Vestnik Riazanskogo gubernskogo zemstva*, no. 4 (1914): 22.

42. Moskovskaia gubernskaia zemleustroitel'naia komissiia, *Lichnoe krest'ianskoe zemlevladenie v Moskovskoi gubernii v 1907–1912 gg.* (Moscow, 1913), 39; Vs. N., 295; TsIAM, f. 748, op. 1 (1910–13), d. 62, ll. 179–80.

43. Koz'modem'ianskoe volost was chosen simply because it was the only village-level data that I could find. Such data are largely missing from the archives, a fact deplored even by reform officials. On the value of data on leases as a surrogate measure for long-term migration, see V. V., "Bezzemel'nye krest'iane v Moskovskom gubernii," *IuV*, no. 9 (1885): 93–123.

44. S. L. Maslov, *Obshchinnoe zemlevladenie i kak ego okhraniat'* (Moscow, 1916), 11–12; RGIA-otchety, "Otchet gubernatora Novgorodskoi gubernii za 1908," vol. 128: 190ob.–191ob.; Chernyshev, 1:xx–xxi; Vronskii, *Gosudarstvennaia vlast'*, 253; Zyrianov, *Krest'ianskaia obshchina*, 176–88.

45. Tiukavkin, 171–74; Mironov, *Sotsial'naia istoriia*, 1:479–81. A provincial breakdown of the MVD survey is available in *Rossiia 1913 god. Statistiko-dokumental'nyi spravochnik*, ed. A. M. Anfimov and A. P. Korelin (St. Petersburg, 1995), 67–68.

46. The report also added up all communes that had not conducted redistributions within the previous ten years, concluding that 45% of communes had not used their right to conduct a *peredel* "for a long period of time." It is this number that was subsequently most often cited. *IZO*, no. 3 (1905): 108–9.

47. Kachorovskii, "Biurokraticheskii zakon i krest'ianskaia obshchina," *RB*, no. 7 (1910): 134; Veniaminov, 86–90. For Tver, see Krasnoperov, *Svodnyi sbornik*, 1:43. Data covered 11 of 12 districts: 51.5% of communes conducted general repartitions, 7.4% partial repartitions *(skidki-nakidki)*.

48. GARO, f. 694, op. 22 (1882), d. 497, l. 1ob.

49. Yaney, *Urge*, 381; David Macey, "A Wager on History: The Stolypin Agrarian Reforms as Process," in *Transforming Peasants: Society, State, and the Peasantry, 1861–1930*, ed. Judith Pallot (New York, 1998), 157, 162. The 24-year limit had been set in 1906 to determine which households would have to pay *izlichki*. The MVD

specified that the phrase "since land was allotted" referred to the date land charters were issued to former serfs (early 1860s), and to 1866 in the case of state peasants. *IZO*, no. 9 (1912): 390–91.

50. Kachorovskii, "Biurokraticheskii zakon," no. 8: 53–55. Land captain registers in Riazan show that individual reallocations were common even in communes that had never officially repartitioned.

51. Ibid., 55–56; TsIAM, f. 748, op. 1, d. 62, l. 166.

52. GARO, f. 695, op. 18 (1907), d. 60, ll. 2–2ob.; Riazanskoe gubernskoe zemstvo, 1:4–6. For examples of other such communes discovered after 1910: f. 695, op. 22 (1912), d. 242; f. 695, op. 25 (1915), d. 108.

53. *IZO*, no. 11 (1910): 496; no. 11 (1911): 497. The MVD even added that a *peredel* that had occurred without the support of law and administration was testimony to vitality of communal principles. Partial redistributions, however, were not to be recognized. *IZO*, no. 12 (1910): 518–19.

54. Matveev, "V volostnykh starshinakh," no. 5: 169–77.

55. Only in 1908, with 32 redistribution resolutions, did the number of repartitions reach the potential, pre-reform yearly average of 29. There were only 12 in each of 1913 and 1914. Zyrianov further argues that a second, smaller wave of repartitions picked up in 1912–1913, after the firmest opponents of redistribution had left. Zyrianov, *Krest'ianskaia obshchina*, 180–85. For data on communes falling under article 1: RGIA, f. 1291, op. 121, d. 4, ll. 168ob.–69.

56. Moskovskoe gubernskoe zemstvo, *Sbornik statisticheskikh svedenii*, 4: 150–52, 160. A recent study of resolutions submitted to the Bogorodsk district congress between 1893 and 1906 also suggests that the slowdown in repartitioning began earlier. The author found only 103 *peredely* submitted to the board. But as the author notes, the unlikely absence of any resolutions for six of the years covered suggests that illegal repartitions were not uncommon. In addition, the data does not cover partial redistributions, quite common in this district. Iu. V. Kurkova, "Zemel'no-raspredelitel'naia deiatel'nost' krest'ianskoi obshchiny na rubezhe XIX–XX vekov," *Otechestvennaia istoriia*, no. 1 (2003): 154–62.

57. Eropkin, 120. The average number of years between redistributions is calculated on the basis of 301 redistributions reported in "Spiski sel'skikh obshestv sovershaiushchikh obshchie peredely zemli," GARO, f. 695, op. 18-1 (1908), d. 15.

58. "Svedenii o peredelakh zemli po zakonu 8 iiunia 1893," GARO, f. 695, op. 24 (1914), d. 9; op. 26 (1916), d. 8; RGIA, f. 1291, op. 121 (1915), d. 132; op. 120 (1913), d. 146, ll. 4–6.

59. If they did not use it more frequently, it was probably because titling did entail some risk. Not all households requesting titles wanted to consolidate their parcels, yet during a repartition the commune could force a household under personal ownership to do so. After 1910, a vote by one-half of communal households sufficed to force consolidation, an action that could give rise to desperate pleas from those pushed out of the village fields. GARO, f. 695, op. 25 (1915) d. 109; op. 24 (1914), d. 80. Inspectors of Penza province reported that fear of obligatory consolidation was slowing applications for title in that province. *IZO*, no. 11 (1909): 365.

60. On governors' instructions: Sidel'nikov, 133–34; *IZO*, no. 3 (1909): 90. MVD reprimands: *IZO*, no. 10 (1909): 320; no. 6 (1908): 307. Quotation from *IZO*, no. 11 (1909): 351.

61. RGIA, f. 1291, op. 120 (1913), d. 146, ll. 4–6. George Yaney rejects the view that the MVD continued to oppose redistributions after 1911, arguing that it understood they were an effective means for introducing agronomic improvements within the constraints of the commune. He also surmises that peasants could bypass land captains by relabeling *peredely* as land reorganization projects and presenting them to more sympathetic district land settlement commissions. This may be true, but it is also true that land captains and commissions could tell the difference between a redistribution that

consolidated parcels or introduced multi-field rotation from one that left agricultural practices unchanged. See for instance GARO, f. 851, op. 1 (1909), dd. 45–47.

62. Numerous observers noted that the 1905 announcement of the cancellation of the remaining redemption debt had as significant an impact on peasant attitudes toward their holdings as did the decree on agrarian reform. P. St-ov, "V derevne," *Krest'ianskoe delo,* no. 10 (1911): 201; "O vykhode iz obshchiny," *Sel'skii vestnik,* no. 10 (1908): 2–3. See also Andrew Verner, "Discursive Strategies in the 1905 Revolution: Peasant Petitions from Vladimir Province," *RR* 54, no. 1 (1995): 65–90.

63. "Obshchina, lichnoe zemlevladenie i peredely nadel'noi zemli," *Sel'skii vestnik,* no. 7 (1908): 2–3.

64. GARO, f. 695, op. 18 (1907), d. 60, l. 2ob.

65. RGIA, f. 1344, op. 264 (1912), d. 229, l. 3ob.

66. GARO, f. 695, op. 18-1 (1908), d. 69, ll. 3, 37ob.

67. Ibid., op. 24 (1914), d. 86, l. 3ob.

68. Quotation from GARO, f. 721, op. 1 (1908), d. 313, l. 22ob.; (1896), d. 30; op. 4 (1909), d. 467; f. 695, op. 18-1 (1908), d. 129; op. 23 (1913), d. 30; f. 81, op. 23 (1915), sv. 25, d. 36.

69. For examples of each of the above scenarios, see GARO, f. 695, op. 18-1 (1908), d. 208; op. 25 (1915), dd. 108–9; op. 24 (1914), d. 80; RGIA, f. 408, op. 1 (1914), d. 547.

70. TsIAM, f. 696, op. 1 (1909), d. 1503.

71. GARO, f. 721, op. 1 (1916), d. 924; (1908), d. 310; TsIAM, f. 808, op. 2 (1915), d. 7, l. 4; GARO, f. 695, op. 24 (1914), d. 92, l. 9.

72. Calculated from GARO, f. 721, op. 1 (1912), d. 777, ll. 5–10; (1903), d. 96, ll. 3–7ob.; f. 80, op. 19 (1914), d. 149, ll. 50–55.

73. TsIAM, f. 696, op. 1 (1915), d. 2933, ll. 5–5ob., 26ob.

74. RGIA, f. 1291, op. 31 (1909), d. 149, ll. 222ob., 245ob. (Riazan); op. 120 (1911), d. 17, ll. 112, 147 (Penza); see also RGIA-otchety, "Otchet Novgorodskogo gubernatora za 1908," vol. 128: 191.

75. *IZO,* no. 5 (1906): 213; no. 7–8 (1907): 301–2; MVD explanation, RGIA, f. 1291, op. 54 (1911), d. 253, l. 3ob.; op. 50 (1911), d. 86.

76. *IZO,* no. 6 (1907): 244; RGIA, op. 54 (1912), d. 29, l. 7; Yaney, *Urge,* 237.

77. Yaney, *Urge,* 238; see also Louis Skyner, "Property as Rhetoric: Land Ownership and Private Law in Pre-Soviet and Post-Soviet Russia," *Europe-Asia Studies* 55, no. 6 (2003): 889–905.

78. Senate decrees 18 May 1910, no. 3569; 10 May 1912, no. 5064; 28 March 1913, no. 3320. *IZO,* no. 5 (1913): 208–9; RGIA, f. 1291, op. 121 (1916), d. 73, ll. 3–4, 5ob.–6. This last case continued to wind its way up the Senate under the Provisional Government, the new minister of interior siding with the opinion of his tsarist predecessor in favor of expiration of claim rights.

79. GARO, f. 695, op. 20 (1910), d. 240, l. 3ob.; RGIA, f. 1291, op. 121 (1910), d. 6, l. 3.

80. GARO, f. 695, op. 20 (1910), d. 57 and d. 56.

81. Ibid., op. 19 (1909), d. 82; op. 18-1 (1908), d. 49, l. 11ob.

82. Ibid., op. 25 (1915), d. 73; op. 16 (1917), d. 64.

83. Two such cases can be found in RGIA, f. 1291, op. 121 (1916), d. 46, ll. 9, 44–45.

84. TsIAM, f. 748, op. 2 (1914), d. 24, ll. 3, 47, 49; op. 1 (1914), d. 68, ll. 22, 65–7, 127; GARO, f. 695, op. 23 (1913), dd. 27, 269.

85. For instance: GARO, f. 695, op. 23 (1913), d. 259.

86. RGIA, f. 1291, op. 54 (1915), d. 67, l. 227. Regulations can be found in *IZO,* no. 9 (1912): 389.

87. *RV,* no. 296 (1907): 3; see also Zuzykina, 102.

88. GARO, f. 695, op. 21 (1911), d. 43, ll. 2–2ob. See also op. 20 (1910), dd. 56, 59.

89. Ibid., op. 26 (1916), d. 33. On the ambivalent attitudes of some rural officials toward the land reforms, see Yaney, *Urge,* 288–95; Macey, "The Peasant Commune," 228–30.

90. David Macey has argued that peasant reactions to the reforms "cannot be equated with principled opposition," because conflicts were between competing interests and not "between two systems of property ownership." In my view, this is too narrow a definition of principles. Conflicts did have an underlying logic, and that logic was decidedly principled. "Government Actions," 160.

91. GARO, f. 695, op. 18-1 (1908), d. 49, ll. 2–2ob.

92. Ibid., op. 18-1 (1908), d. 19, n.p.

93. Ibid., op. 21 (1911), d. 123, l. 2ob.

94. Ibid., op. 18-1 (1908), d. 129, ll. 2–6.

95. B. V. Tikhonov, *Pereselenie v Rossii vo vtoroi polovine XIX v. (po materialam perepisi 1897 g. i pasportnoi statistika)* (Moscow, 1978), 117–21, 128–29.

96. GARO, f. 714, op. 25 (1914), d. 86, l. 11ob.

97. Ibid., f. 80, op. 21 (1916), d. 43, l. 9ob.

98. Engel, *Between the Fields*, 52–53, 85; Tsentral'nyi statisticheskii komitet, *Pervaia vseobshchaia perepis' naseleniia Rossiiskoi imperii, 1897* (St. Petersburg, 1903), 35: 28–35. Household lists from 12 Riazan villages in 1908 show a wide variation from village to village, with women heading from 0–30% of all households (for an average of 12.5%).

99. GARO, f. 695, op. 24 (1914), d. 48, l. 6.

100. Calculated from RGIA, f. 1290, op. 7, d. 464 and d. 474.

101. GARO, f. 1255, op. 1 (1908), sv. 1, d. 13, ll. 2ob.–4; f. 721, op. 1 (1915), d. 924; f. 721, op. 1 (1908), dd. 312–13.

102. The resolution was not approved. The land captain and the provincial board agreed that the stated desire to transfer to hereditary tenure was a sham, as nothing prevented the commune from doing so according to existing holdings. GARO, f. 851, op. 4 (1909), d. 8, n.p.

103. See Senate rulings in *IZO* (1908), no. 1: 7; no. 3: 163; no. 9: 367; (1909), no. 2: 38–39.

104. TsIAM, f. 62, op. 4, d. 1654, l. 2.

105. GARO, f. 695, GO, op. 20 (1909), d. 6, l. 2.

106. *Vtoroi Departament Pravitel'stvuiushchego Senata* (St. Petersburg, 1909), 67–68.

107. RGIA, f. 1344, op. 252 (1911), d. 1158. Yet, in another case, where the widow was listed as head in the household registers, the provincial board chose instead to follow the land redistribution list drawn up by the assembly *after* she filed for title, where her absentee son was listed. GARO, f. 695, op. 22 (1912), d. 169, ll. 5–5ob. On the lack of documentation for household divisions, see Frierson, "Peasant Family Divisions," in Bartlett, ed., *Land Commune*, 303–20.

108. TsIAM, f. 62, op. 4 (1910), d. 1649. Similar examples can be found in RGIA, f. 1344, op. 264 (1912), d. 708; GARO, f. 695, op. 20 (1910), d. 58, l. 7; f. 930, op. 16 (1909), sv. 2, d. 7.

109. RGIA, f. 1291, op. 121 (1916), d. 46, l. 58ob.

110. Ibid., f. 1344, op. 217 (1909), d. 640, ll. 3–4ob.

111. GATO, f. 256, op. 1 (1911), d. 13, l. 18.

112. GARO, f. 714, op. 25 (1914), d. 1.

113. TsIAM, f. 62, op. 1 (1912), d. 4405, l. 3ob.; op. 1 (1908), d. 2809.

114. *IZO*, no. 1 (1907): 19; Sh. M. "Nasledovanie u krest'ian," *VPiN*, no. 38 (1913): 2043.

115. Khauke, 112; Leont'ev, *Krest'ianskoe pravo*, 2nd ed., 336.

116. A. E. Vorms, "Primenenie obychaia k nasledovaniiu v lichnoi sobstvennosti na nadel'nye zemli," *IuZ*, no. 1–2 (1912): 112–13, 137.

117. GARO, f. 695, op. 22 (1912), d. 22; f. 714, op. 26 (1915), d. 10.

118. A. N. Butovskii, "Vdov'i stony," *Pravo*, no. 16 (1911): 979–80; Brzheskii, *Ocherki*, 81–99; Leont'ev, *Krest'ianskoe pravo*, 2nd ed., 330–37.

119. Sh. M., 2039; A. A. Leont'ev, "Priimaki i zakon 14 iiunia 1910g.," *VPiN*, no. 8 (1911): 232–34.

120. TsIAM, f. 62, op. 1 (1908), d. 2796, ll. 2–2ob.

121. RGIA, f. 1291, op. 54 (1915), d. 34, ll. 2–3, 6; op. 54 (1916), d. 36; op. 51 (1916), d. 30b, l. 39. For a description of other war-related problems that the legal system could not address, see A., "Iuridicheskii pomoshch postradavshim ot sobytii voennogo vremeni," *Tverskii listok*, no. 6 (1916): 2.

122. RGIA, f. 1291, op. 51 (1915), d. 151, ll. 12–14.

123. Ibid., d. 150.

CONCLUSION

1. Unless peasants wrote to the Imperial Chancellery for Receipt of Petitions, however, recipients merely funneled the petitions back into the regular system. RGIA, f. 1291, op. 54 (1915), dd. 63, 67.

2. RGIA, f. 1291, op. 51 (1915), dd. 39a and 39b; Emily Pyle, "Village Social Relations and the Reception of Soldiers' Family Aid Policies in Russia, 1912–1921" (Ph.D. diss., University of Chicago, 1997).

3. *IZO*, no. 1 (1915): 17–18. RGIA, f. 1291, op. 31 (1917), d. 57, l. 9; op. 31 (1916), d. 206, ll. 39, 225; op. 54 (1915), d. 65.

4. GARO, f. 695, op. 2 (1915), d. 743b, ll. 57–58; RGIA, f. 1291, op. 121 (1915), d. 76, l. 2ob. For other governors' circulars appealing to land captains' paternal duty, see RGIA, f. 1291, op. 51 (1915), d. 39b, ll. 17–18, 31, 176, 182, 188, 200.

5. RGIA, f. 1291, op. 51 (1915), d. 150, ll. 6–8ob.; op. 54 (1915), d. 34, ll. 9–10.

6. A number of historians have questioned this interpretation of triumph of rural traditionalism, most recently Sanborn; Scott Seregny, "Peasants, Nation, and Local Government in Wartime Russia," *SR* 59, no. 2 (2000): 336–42; Chris Chulos, *Converging Worlds: Religion and Community in Peasant Russia, 1861–1917* (DeKalb, IL, 2003).

7. Andrew Verner has suggested, rightly in my view, that demands for more land and internal conflicts were intimately related: "[T]he only safe means of satisfying the land hunger of the worse-off was to project their grievances onto the outside. . . . In this sense, the unity expressed towards the outside was not so much a reflection of internal cohesion as it was an effort to defuse internal tension." "Discursive Strategies," 80–81.

8. On redistributions of the early Soviet period, see especially V. V. Kabanov, "Oktiabr'skaia revoliutsiia i krest'ianskaia obshchina," *Istoricheskie zapiski* 111 (1984): 100–150. Figes, *Peasant Russia*, chaps. 1–2. Figes has noted (128–31) that even as peasants repartitioned, they grew disillusioned with the commune because of the deleterious impact of repeated repartitions on agriculture. This suggests, as I have argued in this book, that in the Soviet period also one must distinguish between the "commune" as an arena for resolving conflict and the "commune" as an agricultural system.

9. See, for instance, Xavier Rousseaux and René Lavy, eds., *Le pénal dans tous ses états. Justice, Etats et sociétés en Europe (XIIe–XXe siècles)* (Bruxelles, 1997), especially Clive Emsley, "The Nation-State, the Law, and the Peasant in Nineteenth-Century Europe," 153–78.

10. The phrase is borrowed from Paul Warde, "Law, the 'Commune,' and the Distribution of Resources in Early Modern German State Formation," *Continuity and Change*, 17 no. 2 (2002): 183–211.

11. See especially James Heinzen, *Inventing a Soviet Countryside: State Power and the Transformation of Rural Russia, 1917–1929* (Pittsburgh, PA, 2004).

SELECTED BIBLIOGRAPHY

✦ ✦ ✦

ARCHIVAL SOURCES

RGIA (Rossiiskii gosudarstvennyi istoricheskii arkhiv)
  fond 91   Imperial Free Economic Society
  fond 408   Committee for land settlement affairs
  fond 1290   Central statistical committee, Ministry of Internal Affairs
  fond 1291   Land section, Ministry of Internal Affairs
  fond 1344   Second (Peasant) Department of the Governing Senate
  fond 1405   Ministry of Justice

GARF (Gosudarstvennyi arkhiv Rossiiskoi Federatsii)
  fond 586   V. K. Pleve

GARO (Gosudarstvennyi arkhiv Riazanskoi oblasti)
  fond 5   Chancellery of the Governor of Riazan
  fond 7   Riazan statistical committee
  fond 58   Land captain, 2nd precinct, Kasimov district
  fond 60   Land captain, 4th precinct, Kasimov district
  fond 62   Land captain, 6th precinct, Kasimov district
  fond 70   Land captain, 1st precinct, Riazhsk district
  fond 79   Land captain, 1st precinct, Spassk district
  fond 80   Land captain, 2nd precinct, Spassk district
  fond 81   Land captain, 3rd precinct, Spassk district
  fond 640   Riazan circuit court
  fond 694   Riazan provincial board for peasant affairs
  fond 695   Riazan provincial board
  fond 697   Spassk district board for peasant affairs
  fond 714   Kasimov district congress
  fond 717   Riazan district congress
  fond 721   Spassk district congress
  fond 811   Izhevskoe volost court (Spassk district)
  fond 847   Riazhsk district land settlement committee
  fond 851   Spassk district land settlement committee
  fond 929   Land captain, 3rd precinct, Riazhsk district
  fond 930   Land captain, 4th precinct, Riazhsk district
  fond 1255   Land captain, 2nd precinct, Sapozhok district
  fond 1256   Land captain, 4th precinct, Sapozhok district
  fond 1257   Izhevskoe volost administration

GATO (Gosudarstvennyi arkhiv Tverskoi oblasti)
  fond 255   Land captain, 3rd precinct, Tver district
  fond 256   Land captain, 4th precinct, Tver district
  fond 424   Stepanovo volost administration (Kaliazin district)
  fond 488   Tver provincial board
  fond 589   Tver district congress
  fond 709   Antonovo volost court (Ves'egonsk district)
  fond 728   Stepanovo volost court
  fond 984   Land captain, 7th precinct, Ves'egonsk district
  fond 998   Liubegoshchi volost court (Ves'engonsk)
  fond 1012   Liubegoshchi volost administration

GATO-Tambov (Gosudarstvennyi arkhiv Tambovskoi oblasti)
  fond 26   Tambov provinical board
  fond 233   Rybinsk volost court (Morshansk district)
  fond 444   Tambov district congress

TsIAM (Tsentral'nyi istoricheskii arkhiv Moskvy)
  fond 62   Moscow provincial board
  fond 696   Bogorodsk district congress
  fond 705   Ignat'evo volost administration (Bogorodsk district)
  fond 748   Iagunino volost administration (Zvenigorod district)
  fond 749   Iagunino volost court
  fond 808   Chulkovo volost administration (Bronnitsy district)
  fond 1112   Ignat'evo volost court (Bogorodsk district)
  fond 1641   Timonovo volost court (Dmitrov district)
  fond 1891   Sinkovo volost court (Dmitrov district)
  fond 1938   Land captain, 4th precinct (Zaraisk district, Riazan province)
  fond 1943   Verkhne-Beloomut volost administration (Zaraisk)
  fond 1964   Karino volost court (Zaraisk)
  fond 1989   Zaraisk district congress

CONTEMPORARY JOURNALS AND NEWSPAPERS

Delo
Derevenskaia gazeta
Grazhdanin
Iaroslavskie gubernskie vedomosti
Iuridicheskaia gazeta
Iuridicheskie zapiski
Iuridicheskii vestnik
Iuridicheskoe obozrenie
Izvestiia zemskogo otdela
Krest'ianskoe delo
Moskovskie vedomosti
Novoe vremia
Otechestvennye zapiski
Pravitel'stvennyi vestnik
Pravo
Riazanskaia zhizn'
Riazanskii vestnik
Russkaia mysl'
Russkie vedomosti

Russkoe bogatstvo
Russkoe obozrenie
Sankt-Peterburgskie vedomosti
Sel'skii vestnik
Severnyi krai
Severnyi vestnik
Sovremennyi mir
Sudebnaia gazeta
Sudebnaia letopis'
Trudy Imperatorskogo vol'nogo ekonomicheskogo obshchestva
Vestnik Evropy
Vestnik prava
Vestnik prava i notariata
Vestnik Riazanskogo gubernskogo zemstva
Volostnoi pisar'
Vladimirskii zemskii sbornik
Zhurnal grazhdanskogo i ugolovnogo prava
Zhurnal Ministerstva iustitsii
Zhurnal iuridicheskogo obshchestva pri Imperatorskom Sankt-Peterburgskom universitete

PUBLISHED PRIMARY SOURCES

Abramovich, K. G. *Krest'ianskoe pravo po resheniiam Pravitel'stvuiushchego Senata: Alfavitnyi ukazatel'*. 1st ed., St. Petersburg, 1902; 2nd ed., 1912.

Astyrev, N. M. "Mirskie raskhody." *RM*, no. 12 (1886): 73–100.

———. *V volostnykh pisariakh. Ocherki krest'ianskogo samoupravleniia*. 1st ed. Moscow, 1886; 3rd ed., 1904.

B., O. "Sel'skoe obshchestvennoe prizrenie." *VE*, no. 6 (1890): 648–66.

Barykov, F. L., et al., eds. *Sbornik materialov dlia izucheniia sel'skoi pozemel'noi obshchiny*. St. Petersburg, 1880.

Beer, V. A. *Kommentarii novykh provintsial'nykh uchrezhdenii 12 iiulia 1889 goda*. 2 vols. Moscow, 1894–1895.

Briunelli, P. A. *Krest'ianskii advokat. Nastol'naia spravochnaia kniga dlia prisiazhnykh povernnykh, ikh pomoshchnikov i lits, vedushchikh krest'ianskiia dela*. St. Petersburg, 1912.

Brzheskii, N. K. *Natural'nye povinnosti krest'ian i mirskie sbory*. St. Petersburg, 1906.

———. *Nedoimochnost' i krugovaia poruka sel'skikh obshchestv*. St. Petersburg, 1897.

———. *Ocherki iuridicheskogo byta krest'ian*. St. Petersburg, 1902.

———. "Sel'skie i volostnye skhody." *Vestnik finansov, promyshlennosti i torgovli* (1906), no. 10: 384–91; no. 11: 439–44; no. 13: 531–37; no. 14: 5–12; no. 15: 46–57.

Bystrov, N. N. *Sistematicheskii ukazatel' voprosov razreshennykh opredeleniiami obshchogo sobraniia kassatsionnykh i s uchastiem I i II departamentov Senata s 1866 po 1 ianvaria 1900*. St. Petersburg, 1901.

Charushin, A. A. *Sel'skie skhody v bytovom ikh osveshchenii*. Arkhangel'sk, 1911.

———. "Volostnye sudy v bytovom ikh osveshchenii." *Izvestiia Arkhangel'skogo obshchestva izucheniia russkogo severa*, no. 12 (1912): 985–96.

Chepurnyi, N. "K voprosu o iuridicheskikh obychaiakh. Ustroistvo i sostoianie volostnoi iustitsii v Tambovskoi gubernii." *Kievskie universitetskie izvestiia* (1874), no. 9: 497–512; no. 10: 645–54.

Chernyshev, I. V. *Obshchina posle 9 noiabria 1906 po ankete Vol'nogo ekonomicheskogo obshchestva*. 2 vols. Petrograd, 1917.

Danilov, I. *Sbornik reshenii Pravitel'stvuiushchego Senata po krest'ianskim delam, 1890–1898*. St. Petersburg, 1898.

Dashkevich, P. "Grazhdanskii obychai-priimachestvo u krest'ian Kievskoi gubernii." *IuV*, no. 8 (1887): 538–65.

———. "Volostnoi sud i kassatsionnaia instantsiia." *IuV*, no. 12 (1892): 524–88.

Dediulin, S. A. *Krest'ianskoe samoupravlenie v sviazi s dvorianskim voprosom. K voprosu o peresmotre zakonopolozhenii o krest'ianakh.* St. Petersburg, 1902.

Doklady chlenov Riazanskoi gubernskoi zemskoi upravy o revizii volostei uezdov Spasskogo, Sapozhkovskogo, Skopinskogo i Riazhskogo. Moscow, 1875.

Drozdov, V. P. *Okolo zemli. Ocherki po zemleustroistvu.* Moscow, 1909.

Druzhinin, N. "Byvshie svobodnye khlebopashtsy." *Zhizn'* (1898), no. 10: 204–18; no. 12: 363–82.

Druzhinin, N. P. *Iuridicheskoe polozhenie krest'ian. Issledovanie, s prilozheniem statei.* St. Petersburg, 1897.

———. *Pravo i lichnost' krest'ianina.* Iaroslavl', 1912.

Efimenko, P. S. "Narodnye iuridicheskie obychai Arkhangel'skoi gubernii." *Trudy Arkhangel'skogo-statisticheskogo komiteta za 1867 i 1868.* Arkhangel'sk, 1869.

Efimov, V. "Volostnoi sud v vidu reformy mestnoi iustitsii." *VE*, no. 8 (1896): 559–96.

Engelgardt, Aleksandr. *Letters from the Country, 1872–1887.* Translated by Cathy Frierson. New York and Oxford, 1993.

Entsiklopedicheskii slovar'. Edited by F. A. Brokgaus and I. A. Efron. 86 vols. St. Petersburg, 1890–1907.

Ermolov, A. S. *Neurozhai i narodnoe bedstvie.* St. Petersburg, 1892.

Eropkin, A. "Sel'skaia obshchina i prochnyi pravoporiadok." *Novyi put'*, no. 6 (1903): 103–37.

Filatov, B. "Iz deiatel'nosti gubernskikh prisutstvii." *ZhIuO*, no. 10 (1894): 95–108.

Firsov, B. M., and I. G. Kiseleva, eds. *Byt velikorusskikh krest'ian-zemlepashtsev. Opisanie materialov etnograficheskogo biuro kniazia V. N. Tenisheva (na primera Vladimirskoi gubernii).* St. Petersburg, 1993.

Ganeizer, E. "Mirskie sbory v odnom uezde." *RB*, no. 7 (1896): 145–53.

Golike, P., and A. Vil'borg. *O volostnom pisare.* St. Petersburg, 1910.

Gol'msten, A. Kh. "Dvadtsatipiatiletnaia praktika Kemetskogo (Valdaiskogo uezda, Novgorodskoi gubernii) volostnogo suda po voprosam grazhdanskogo prava." In *Iuridicheskiia izsledovaniia i stat'i*, vol. 1:50–91. St. Petersburg, 1894.

Goremykin, I. L., ed. *Svod uzakonenii i rasporiazhenii pravitel'stva ob ustroistve sel'skogo sostoianiia.* 2 vols. St. Petersburg, 1898.

Gorodyskii, Ia. "Praktika sudebno-administrativnykh uchrezhdenii." *ZhIuO*, no. 6 (1895): 51–84.

Iakushkin, E. I. *Obychnoe pravo. Materialy dlia bibliografii obychnogo pravo.* 4 vols. Iaroslavl', 1878–1910.

Ianovich, V. *Itogi shestiletiia (zametki zemskogo nachal'nika).* Perm, 1902.

Ilimskii, D. "Bor'ba za pravo (vpechatleniia derevenskogo advokata)." *RB*, no. 4 (1912): 146–59.

Kachorovskii, K. R. "Biurokraticheskii zakon i krest'ianskaia obshchina." *RB* (1910), no. 7: 121–42; no. 8: 44–62.

———. *Russkaia obshchina. Vozmozhno li, zhelatel'no li ee sokhranenie i razvitie?* 2nd ed. St. Petersburg, 1906.

Kataev, M. M. *Mestnye krest'ianskie uchrezhdenii. 1861, 1874, 1889.* 3 vols. St. Petersburg, 1911–1912.

Khauke, O. A. *Krest'ianskoe zemel'noe pravo.* Moscow, 1914.

Korf, S. A. *Administrativnaia iustitsiia v Rossii.* 2 vols. St. Petersburg, 1910.

Kozhukhar, K. Ia. "Zemskie nachal'niki." *Vestnik prava* (1905), no. 5: 93–132; no. 8: 53–102; no. 9: 42–102.

Krasnoperov, I. *Svodnyi sbornik statisticheskikh svedenii po Tverskoi gubernii.* 2 vols. Tver, 1897.

Kremnev, B. "Proekt ob uporiadochenii sel'skikh skhodov." *IuV*, no. 5 (1885): 143–59.

Krestovnikov, G. A. *Mogyt li byt' peredely nadel'noi zemli krest'ian posle okonchaniia vykypnoi operatsii*. Moscow, 1908.

Kupchinov, Ivan. *Iz dnevnika volostnogo pisaria*. Moscow, 1910.

Leont'ev, A. A. *Krest'ianskoe pravo. Sistematicheskoe izlozhenie osobennostei zakonodatel'stva o krest'ianakh*. St. Petersburg, 1909. 2nd ed., St. Petersburg, 1914.

———. *Volostnoi sud i iuridicheskie obychai krest'ian*. St. Petersburg, 1895.

———. "Volostnoi sud po zakonu o mestnom sude." *Trudy iuridicheskogo obshchestva pri Sankt-Peterburskom universitete*, vol. 2: 183–212. St. Petersburg, 1914.

Lichkov, L. "Krugovaia poruka i obshchinnoe zemlevladenie." *RM*, no. 10 (1886): 21–39.

Lositskii, A. *Raspadenie obshchiny*. St. Petersburg, 1912.

Ludmer, Ia. "Bab'i stony (Iz zametok mirovogo sud'i)." *IuV*, no. 11 (1884): 446–67.

M., Sh. "Nasledovanie u krest'ian." *VPiN*, no. 38 (1913): 2037–44.

Markov, E. "Uezdnoe upravlenie." *Russkaia rech'*, no. 9 (1881): 266–315.

Marychev, F. "Volostnoi pisar' i volost'." *VE*, no. 5 (1902): 240–72.

Maslov, S. *Obshchinnoe zemlepol'zovanie i kak ego okhraniat'*. Moscow, 1916.

Materialy k zakonu o mestnom sude. 2 vols. St. Petersburg, 1912–1913.

Matveev, S. "V volostnykh starshinakh." *RB* (1912), no. 2: 74–95; no. 4: 120–45; no. 5: 156–85.

———. "Iz zhizni sovremennogo krest'ianskogo mira (V volostnykh starshinakh)." *RB* (1913), no. 9: 116–42; no. 10: 148–80.

Mikhailovskii, S. A. "Sudebno-administrativnye uchrezhdenii Tverskoi gubernii za piatiletie, 1892–1897 gg." *Sbornik pravovedeniia i obshchestvennykh znanii*, vol. 8 (1898): 155–71.

Ministerstvo finansov, Departament okladnykh sborov. *Sushchestvuiushchii poriadok vzimaniia okladnykh sborov s krest'ian*. 2 vols. St. Petersburg, 1894–1895.

Moskovskaia gubernskaia zemleustroitel'naia kommissiia. *Lichnoe krest'ianskoe zemlevladenie v Moskovskoi gubernii v 1907–1912 gg*. Moscow, 1913.

Moskovskoe gubernskoe zemstvo. *Siroty, prestarelye i ne trudosposobnye v Moskovskom gubernii*. Moscow, 1915.

———. *Sbornik statisticheskikh svedenii po Moskovskoi gubernii*, ed. V. I. Orlov. Vol. 3, *Materialy dlia opredeleniia tsennosti i dokhodnosti zemel'*. Moscow, 1879. Vol. 4, part 1, *Krest'ianskoe khoziastvo. Formy krest'ianskogo zemlevladeniia v Moskovskoi gubernii*. Moscow, 1879.

Mozzhukhin, I. V. *Zemleustroistvo v Bogorodskom uezde, Tul'skoi gubernii*. Moscow, 1917.

Mukhin, V. F. *Obychnyi poriadok nasledovaniia u krest'ian*. St. Petersburg, 1888.

N., Vs. "Zakon 9-go noiabria." *Vestnik Evropy*, no. 8 (1910): 286–301.

Naumov, A. N. *Iz utselevshikh vospominanii, 1868–1917*. 2 vols. New York, 1954–1955.

Novikov, A. I. *Zapiski zemskogo nachal'nika*. St. Petersburg, 1899.

Oganovskii, N. P. "Pervye itogi velikoi reformy." *RB* (1911), no. 10: 124–62; no. 11: 67–98.

———. *Revoliutsiia naoborot (Razrushenie obshchiny)*. Petrograd, 1917.

Orshanskii, I. G. *Izsledovaniia po russkomu pravu obychnomy*. St. Petersburg, 1879.

P., M. N. "Sud v derevne (Iz dnevnika byvshego mirovogo sud'i)." *Nabliudatel'*, no. 2 (1882): 95–124.

Pazukhin, A. *Sovremennoe sostoianie Rossii i soslovnii vopros*. Moscow, 1886.

Peshekhonov, A. "Sotsial'nye posledstviia zemleustroistva." *RB* (1909), no. 7: 139–160; no. 10: 105–13; no. 11: 78–107.

Pogorelov, G. *Chto takoe volostnoi pisar'?* Moscow, 1907.

Polivanov, Vladimir. "Zapiski zemskogo nachal'nika." *RM* (1917), no. 3–4: 102–29; no. 5–6: 53–75; no. 7–8: 59–89; no. 9–10: 17–46.

Polnoe sobranie zakonov Rossiiskoi imperii. 2nd series. 55 vols. St. Petersburg, 1825–1884. 3rd series. 33 vols. 1885–1916.

Postnikov, V. E. *Iuzhno-russkoe krest'ianskoe khoziaistvo*. Moscow, 1891.

Pravitel'stvuiushchii Senat. *Istoriia pravitel'stvuiushchego senata za dvesti let',*
1711–1911. 5 vols. St. Petersburg, 1911.

Preobrazhenskii, F. A. *Voprosy krest'ianskago samoupravlenii. Sel'skie uchrezhdeniia i*
dolzhnostnye litsa. Moscow, 1893.

Prugavin, V. S. *Russkaia zemel'naia obshchina v trudakh ee mestnykh issledovatelei.*
Moscow, 1888.

Riazanskoe gubernskoe zemstvo. *Sbornik statisticheskikh svedenii po Riazanskoi gubernii.*
Vol. 1, part 1, *Riazanskii uezd.* Moscow, 1882.

Vol. 3, part. 1, *Zaraiskii uezd.* Riazan, 1885.

Vol. 6, *Pronskii uezd.* Riazan, 1886.

Vol. 7, *Kasimovskii uezd.* Riazan, 1887.

Vol. 8, parts 1–2, *Spasskii uezd.* Riazan, 1887–1890.

Vol. 9, parts 1–2, *Sapozhkovskii uezd.* Riazan, 1888–1890.

Vol. 10, *Riazhskii uezd.* Riazan, 1888.

Rittikh, A. A. *Krest'ianskii pravoporiadok.* St. Petersburg, 1904.

———. *Krestianskoe zemlepol'zovanie.* St. Petersburg, 1903.

———. *Zavisimost' krest'ian ot obshchiny i mira.* St. Petersburg, 1903.

Sankt-Peterburgskoe gubernskoe zemstvo. *Statisticheskii sbornik po Sankt-Peterburgskoi*
gubernii za 1897. Vol. 5, *Materialy po nekotorym voprosam, kasaiushchimsia*
krest'ianskikh uchrezhdenii. St. Petersburg, 1898.

Selivanov, A. *Svod dannykh ob ekonomicheskom polozhenii krest'ian Riazanskoi gubernii.*
Riazan, 1892.

Semenov, S. T. *Dvadtsat' piat' let v derevne.* Petrograd, 1915.

Shapkarin, A. V., ed. *Krest'ianskoe dvizhenie v Rossii v 1890–1900 gg. Sbornik dokumentov.*
Moscow, 1959.

Shrag, Il'ia. "Krest'ianskie sudy Vladimirskoi i Moskovskoi gubernii." *IuV,* no. 3–4
(1877): 11–48; no. 5–6: 52–101; no. 7–8: 58–86; no. 9–10: 61–99.

Shustikov, A. A. "Na mirskom peredele zemli." *Severnyi krai,* no. 32 (1899): 2; no. 35:
2; no. 36: 2–3.

Skalon, V. Iu. *Zemskie vzgliady na reformy mestnogo upravleniia. Obzor zemskikh otzyvov i*
proektov. Moscow, 1884.

Skorobogatyi, P. "Dokazatel'stvo v volostnom sude." *IuV,* no. 2 (1883): 239–53; no. 5:
132–45.

———. "Ustroistvo krest'ianskikh sudov." *IuV,* no. 6 (1880): 309–46; no. 7: 486–516.

Skvortsov, K. "Nasledovanie v zemle krest'ian." *Vestnik prava,* no. 2 (1901): 27–69.

Sokolovskii, N. "Derevenskaia konsul'tatsiia. Ocherki i nabliudeniia." *RB,* no. 3 (1900):
110–38; no. 1 (1901): 25–51.

Stashko, P. *Po sledam istiny. Razskazy iz zhini pisarei.* 2nd ed. St. Petersburg, 1913.

Stoliaroff, Ivan. *Un village russe. Récit d'un paysan de la région de Voronej, 1880–1906.*
Translated by Valérie Stoliaroff and Irène Rovère-Sova. Paris, 1992.

Strakhovskii, I. M. "Krest'ianskii vopros." In *Nuzhdy derevni po rabotam komitetov o*
nuzhdakh sel'sko-khoziaistvennykh promyshlennosti. Vol. 1. St. Petersburg, 1904.

———. "Sovremennoe polozhenie i znachenie krest'ianskikh volostei." *VP,* no. 9
(1901): 1–40; no. 1 (1902): 51–80.

Tabashnikov, I. "Zhelatel'noe otnoshenie budushego grazhdanskogo ulozheniia k
nashemu obychnomu pravu." *ZhGiUP,* no. 3 (1885): 67–107.

Tagantsev, N. S. *Ustav o nakazaniiakh, nalagaemykh mirovymi sudiami. Dopolneniiami po*
svodnomu prodolzheniiu 1912 goda, s prilozheniem motivov i izvlechenii iz reshenii
kassatsionnykh departamentov Senata. St. Petersburg, 1913.

Tenishev, V. V. *Administrativnoe polozhenie russkogo krest'ianina.* St. Petersburg, 1908.

———. *Pravosudie v russkom krest'ianskom bytu.* Briansk, 1907.

Tiutriumov, A. "Grazhdanskoe sudoproizvodstvo volostnykh sudov." *IuV,* no. 5–6
(1892): 185–91.

Tiutriumov, I. M., ed. *Obshchee polozhenie o krest'ianakh s raziasneniiami*

Pravitel'stvuiushchego Senata. 3rd ed. St. Petersburg, 1915.

——. *Praktika Pravitel'stvuiushchego Senata po krest'ianskim delam, 1882 po 1 marta 1914.* St. Petersburg, 1915.

Trirogov, V. G. *Obshchina i podat'.* St. Petersburg, 1882.

Tsentral'nyi statisticheskii komitet. *Statistika pozemel'noi sobstvennosti i naselennikh mest Evropeiskoi Rossii.* Vols. 1–7. St. Petersburg, 1880–1885.

——. *Statistika zemlevladeniia 1905 g. Svod dannykh po 50 guberniiam Evropeiskoi Rossii.* Vol. 4, *Riazanskaia guberniia.* St. Petersburg, 1906.

Tsytovich, I. *Sel'skoe obshchestvo, kak organ mestnogo upravleniia.* Kiev, 1911.

Tur, K. I. *Golos zhizni o krest'ianskom neustroistve.* St. Petersburg, 1898.

Tverskoe gubernskoe zemstvo. *Sbornik statisticheskikh svedenii po Tverskoi gubernii.* Vol. 8, parts 1–2, *Tverskoi uezd.* Tver, 1892–1893.

Vol. 11, *Ves'egonskii uezd.* Tver, 1894.

——. *Sel'sko-khoziastvennyi obzor Tverskoi gubernii za 1896 god.* Tver, 1896.

——. *Statisticheskii ezhegodnik Tverskoi gubernii (1909–1910).* Tver, 1911.

——. *Statisticheskii ezhegodnik Tverskoi gubernii (1913–1914).* Tver, 1916.

Veniaminov, P. *Krest'ianskaia obshchina. Chto ona takoe, k chemu daet i chto mozhet dat' Rossii?* St. Petersburg, 1908.

Volkov, N. T., ed. *Nakaz zemskim nachal'nikam po administrativnym delam.* Moscow, 1907.

Volzhin, V. "Revizionnyi poriadok otmeny i izmeneniia postanovlenii, prigovorov i reshenii volostnoi iustitsii." *ZhIuO,* no. 4 (1897): 89–104.

Vorms, A. E. "Primenenie obychaia k nasledovaniiu v lichnoi sobstvennosti na nadel'nye zemli." *IuZ,* no. 1–2 (1912): 112–39.

——. "Zakon i obychai v nasledovanii u krest'ian." *IuV,* no. 1 (1913): 97–125.

Vorontsov, V. P. *Progressivnaia techeniia v krest'ianskom khoziaistve.* St. Petersburg, 1892.

Zarudnyi, M. I. *Zakony i zhizn'. Itogi izsledovaniia krest'ianskikh sudov.* St. Petersburg, 1874.

Zhdanov, V. "O neobkhodimosti dopolneniia st.31 vremmenykh pravil." *ZhGiUP,* no. 4 (1892): 23–33.

SECONDARY SOURCES

Agren, Maria. "Asserting One's Rights: Swedish Property Law in the Transition from Community Law to State Law." *Law and History Review* 19, no. 2 (2001): 241–82.

Alavi, Hamza. "Peasant Classes and Primordial Priorities." *Journal of Peasant Studies* 1, no. 1 (1973): 23–62.

Aleksandrov, V. A. *Sel'skaia obshchina v Rossii (XVII–nachalo XIX v.).* Moscow, 1976.

Anfimov, A. M. *Ekonomicheskoe polozhenie i klassovaia bor'ba krest'ian Evropeiskoi Rossii (1881–1904).* Moscow, 1984.

——. *P. A. Stolypin i rossiiskoe krest'ianstvo.* Moscow, 2002.

Atkinson, Dorothy. *The End of the Russian Land Commune, 1905–1930.* Stanford, 1985.

——. "The Statistics on the Russian Land Commune, 1905–1917." *SR* 32, no. 4 (1973): 773–87.

Baberowski, Jörg. *Autokratie und Justiz. Zum Verhältnis von Rechtsstaatlichkeit und Rückständigkeit im ausgehenden Zarenreich, 1864–1914.* Frankfurt am Main, 1996.

Bartlett, Roger, ed. *Land Commune and Peasant Community in Russia: Communal Forms in Imperial and Early Soviet Society.* London, 1990.

Behar, Ruth. *Santa Maria del Monte: The Presence of the Past in a Spanish Village.* Princeton, 1986.

Bensidoun, Sylvain. *L'agitation paysanne en Russie de 1881 à 1902.* Paris, 1975.

Bradley, Joseph. *Muzhik and Muscovite: Urbanization in Late Imperial Russia.* Berkeley, 1985.

Brooks, Jeffrey. *When Russia Learned to Read: Literacy and Popular Literature, 1861–1917.* Princeton, 1985.

Bukhovets, O. G. *Sotsial'nye konflikty i krest'ianskaia mental'nost' v Rossiiskoi imperii nachala XX veka. Novye materialy, metody, resul'taty.* Moscow, 1996.

Burbank, Jane. *Russian Peasants Go to Court: Legal Culture in the Countryside, 1905–1917.* Bloomington, IN, 2004.

Burds, Jeffrey. *Peasant Dreams and Market Politics: Labor Migration and the Russian Village, 1861–1905.* Pittsburgh, 1998.

Bushnell, John. "Peasants in Uniform: The Tsarist Army as a Peasant Society." *Journal of Social History* 13, no. 4 (1980): 565–76.

Channon, John. "The Peasantry in the Revolutions of 1917." In *Revolution in Russia: Reassessments of 1917,* edited by E. R. Frankel, Jonathan Frankel, and Baruch Knei-Paz, 105–30. Cambridge, 1992.

Chernukha, V. G. *Krest'ianskii vopros v pravitel'stvennoi politike Rossii (60–70 gody XIX v.).* Leningrad, 1972.

Clements, Barbara, Barbara Engel, and Christine Worobec, eds. *Russia's Women: Accomodation, Resistance, Transformation.* Berkeley, 1991.

Crisp, Olga. "Peasant Land Tenure and Civil Rights Implications before 1906." In *Civil Rights in Imperial Russia,* edited by Olga Crisp and Linda Edmondson, 33–65. Oxford, 1989.

Crubaugh, Anthony. *Balancing the Scales of Justice: Local Courts and Rural Society in Southwest France, 1750–1800.* University Park, PA, 2001.

Czap, Peter. "Peasant-Class Courts and Peasant Customary Justice in Russia, 1861–1912." *Journal of Social History* 1, no. 2 (1967): 149–78.

Danilov, V. P. "Ob istoricheskikh sud'bakh krest'ianskoi obshchiny v Rossii." *Ezhegodnik po agrarnoi istorii.* Vol. 6, *Problemy istorii russkoi obshchiny.* Vologda, 1976.

Danilova, L. V., and V. P. Danilov. "Krest'ianskaia mental'nost' i obshchina." In *Mentalitet i agrarnoe razvitie Rossii XIX–XX vv.,* 22–39. Moscow, 1995.

Darrow, David. "The Politics of Numbers: Statistics and the Search for a Theory of Peasant Economy in Russia." Ph.D. diss., University of Iowa, 1996.

De Moor, Marina, et al., eds. *The Management of Common Land in North-West Europe, c.1500–1850.* Turnhout, Belgium, 2002.

Druzhinin, N. M. *Gosudarstvennye krest'iane i reforma P. D. Kiseleva.* 2 vols. Moscow-Leningrad, 1946, 1958.

———. *Russkaia derevnia na perelome, 1861–1880.* Moscow, 1978.

Dubrovskii, S. M. *Stolypinskaia zemel'naia reforma.* Moscow, 1963.

Eklof, Ben. *Russian Peasant Schools: Officialdom, Village Culture, and Popular Pedagogy, 1861–1914.* Berkeley, 1986.

Engel, Barbara. *Between the Fields and the City: Women, Work, and Family in Russia, 1861–1914.* Cambridge, 1994.

———. "Russian Peasant Views of City Life, 1861–1914." *SR,* 52, no. 3 (1993): 446–53.

———. "The Woman's Side: Male Out-Migration and the Family Economy in Kostroma Province." *SR* 45, no. 2 (1986): 257–71.

Falk-Moore, Sally. "Treating Law as Knowledge: Telling Colonial Officers What to Say to Africans about Running 'Their Own' Native Courts." *Law and Society Review* 26, no. 1 (1992): 11–45.

Farnsworth, Beatrice. "The Litigious Daughter-in-Law: Family Relations in Rural Russia in the Second Half of the Nineteenth Century." *SR* 45, no. 1 (1986): 49–64.

Field, Daniel. *The End of Serfdom: Nobility and Bureaucracy in Russia, 1855–1861.* Cambridge, MA, 1976.

Figes, Orlando. *Peasant Russia, Civil War: The Volga Countryside in Revolution, 1917–1921.* Oxford, 1991.

———. *A People's Tragedy: The Russian Revolution, 1891–1924.* London, 1996.

———. "The Village Commune and Rural Government." In *Critical Companion to the Russian Revolution, 1914–1921,* edited by Edward Action, Vladimir Cherniaev, and William Rosenberg, 457–67. Bloomington, IN, 1997.

Frank, Stephen. "Confronting the Domestic Other: Rural Popular Culture and Its Enemies in *Fin-de Siècle* Russia." In *Cultures in Flux: Lower-Class Values, Practices, and Resistance in Late Imperial Russia,* edited by Stephen Frank and Mark Steinberg, 74–107. Princeton, 1994.

———. *Crime, Cultural Conflict, and Justice in Rural Russia, 1856–1914.* Berkeley, 1999.

Frierson, Cathy. "Crime and Punishment in the Russian Village: Rural Concepts of Criminality at the End of the Nineteenth Century." *SR* 46, no. 1 (1987): 55–69.

———. "I Must Always Answer to the Law: Rules and Responses in the Reformed Volost' Court." *SEER,* 75 no. 2 (1997): 308–34.

———. *Peasant Icons: Representations of Rural People in Late Nineteenth-Century Russia.* Oxford, 1993.

———. "Rural Justice in Public Opinion: The Volost Court Debate, 1861–1912." *SEER* 64, no. 4 (October 1986): 326–45.

Garnot, Benoit, ed. *L'infrajudiciaire du Moyen Age à l'époque contemporaine.* Paris, 1996.

Geertz, Clifford. "Local Knowledge: Fact and Law in Comparative Perspective." In *Local Knowledge: Further Essays in Interpretive Anthropology.* New York, 1983.

Gerasimenko, G. A. *Bor'ba krest'ian protiv stolypinskoi agrarnoi politiki.* Saratov, 1985.

Gluckman, Max. "Gossip and Scandal." *Current Anthropology* 5, no. 4 (1963): 307–16.

Gromyko, M. M. "Mesto sel'skoi (territorial'noi, sosedskoi) obshchiny v sotsial'nom mekhanizme formirovaniia, khraneniia i izmeneniia traditsii." *Sovetskaia etnografiia,* no. 5 (1984): 70–80.

———. *Mir russkoi derevni.* Moscow, 1991.

———. *Traditsionnye normy povedeniia i formy obshcheniia russkikh krest'ian XIX v.* Moscow, 1986.

Herrup, Cynthia. "Crime, Law, and Society." *Comparative Studies in Society and History,* 27, no. 1 (1985): 159–70.

Hoch, Steven. "On Good Numbers and Bad: Malthus, Population Trends, and Peasant Standard of Living in Late Imperial Russia." *SR* 53, no. 1 (1994): 41–75.

———. *Serfdom and Social Control in Russia: Petrovskoe, a Village in Tambov.* Chicago, 1986.

Hoffman, Philip. *Growth in a Traditional Society: The French Countryside, 1450–1815.* Princeton, 1996.

Hosking, Geoffrey. *The Russian Constitutional Experiment: Government and Duma, 1907–1914.* Cambridge, 1973.

Jones, Adrian. *Late-Imperial Russia, an Interpretation: Three Visions, Two Cultures, One Peasantry.* Bern, 1997.

———. "The Peasants of Late Imperial Russia: Economy and Society in the Era of the Stolypin Land Reform." Ph.D. diss., Harvard University, 1988.

Joseph, Gilbert, and Daniel Nugent, eds. *Everyday Forms of State Formation: Revolution and the Negotiation of Rule in Modern Mexico.* Durham, NC, 1994.

Kabanov, V. V. "Oktiabr'skaia revoliutsiia i krest'ianskaia obshchina." *IZ* 111 (1984): 100–150.

Kingston-Mann, Esther, and Timothy Mixter, eds. *Peasant Economy, Culture, and Politics of European Russia, 1800–1921.* Princeton, 1991.

Konovalov, V. S. *Krest'ianstvo i reformy. Rossiiskaia derevnia v nachale XX veka. Analiticheskii obzor.* Moscow, 2000.

Korelin, A. P. *Dvorianstvo v poreformennoi Rossii, 1861–1904.* Moscow, 1979.

Kotsonis, Yanni. *Making Peasants Backward: Agricultural Cooperatives and the Agrarian Question in Russia, 1861–1914.* New York, 1999.

Kuchumova, L. I. "Sel'skaia pozemel'naia obshchina evropeiskoi Rossii v 60–70e gody XIX v." *IZ* 106 (1981): 115–27.

Kurkova, Iu. V. "Zemel'no-raspredelitel'naia deiatel'nost' krestianskoi obshchiny na rubezhe XIX–XX vekov." *Otechestvennaia istoriia,* no. 1 (2003): 154–62.

Lenman, Bruce, and Geoffrey Parker. "The State, the Community, and the Criminal Law in Early Modern Europe." In *Crime and the Law: The Social History of Crime in Western Europe since 1500,* edited by V. A. C. Gatrell, Bruce Lenman, and Geoffrey Parker, 11–48. London, 1980.

Levy, René, and Xavier Rousseaux. "Etats, justice pénale et histoire: Bilan et perspectives." *Droit et société,* no. 20/21 (1992): 249–77.

Liessem, Peter. *Verwaltungsgerichtsbarkeit im späten Zarenreich. Der Dirigierende Senat und seine Entscheidungen zur russischen Selbstverwaltung, 1864–1917.* Frankfurt am Main, 1996.

Lincoln, Bruce. *In the Vanguard of Reform: Russia's Enlightened Bureaucrats, 1825–1861.* DeKalb, IL, 1982.

Luebke, David. *His Majesty's Rebels: Communities, Factions, and Rural Revolt in the Black Forest, 1725–1745.* Ithaca, NY, 1997.

Macey, David. *Government and Peasant in Russia, 1861–1906: The Prehistory of the Stolypin Reforms.* DeKalb, IL, 1987.

———. "Government Actions and Peasant Reactions during the Stolypin Reforms." In *New Perspectives in Modern Russian History: Selected Papers from the Fourth World Congress for Soviet and East European Studies,* edited by Robert McKean, 133–73. New York, 1992.

———. "The Land Captains: A Note on Their Social Composition." *Russian History* 16, nos. 2–4 (1989): 327–51.

Mallon, Florencia. "The Promise and Dilemma of Subaltern Studies." *American Historical Review* 89, no. 5 (1994): 1491–515.

Mandel, James. "Paternalistic Authority in the Russian Countryside, 1856–1906." Ph.D. diss., Columbia University, 1978.

Melton, Edgar. "Household Economies and Communal Conflicts on a Russian Serf Estate, 1800–1817." *Journal of Social History,* 22, no. 3 (Spring, 1993): 559–85.

Merry, Sally. "Legal Pluralism." *Law and Society Review* 22, no. 5 (1988): 869–96.

Mironov, Boris. "The Russian Peasant Commune after the Reforms of the 1860s." *SR* 44, no. 3 (1985): 438–67.

———. *Sotsial'naia istoriia Rossii perioda imperii XVIII–nachalo XX v. Genezis lichnosti, demokraticheskoi sem'i, grazhdanskogo obshchestva i pravovogo gosudarstva.* 2 vols. St. Petersburg, 1999.

Mitchell, Timothy. "Everyday Metaphors of Power." *Theory and Society* 19, no. 5 (1990): 545–77.

Moon, David. "Peasants into Russian Citizens? A Comparative Perspective." *Revolutionary Russia* 9, no. 1 (1996): 43–81.

———. *Russian Peasants and Tsarist Legislation on the Eve of Reform: Interaction between Peasants and Officialdom, 1825–1855.* Basingstoke, 1992.

Neuberger, Joan. "Popular Legal Cultures: The Saint Petersburg *Mirovoi Sud.*" In *Russia's Great Reforms, 1855–1881,* edited by Ben Eklof, John Bushnell, Larissa Zakharova, 231–46. Bloomington, IN, 1994.

Orlovsky, Daniel. *The Limits of Reform: The Ministry of Internal Affairs in Imperial Russia, 1802–1881.* Cambridge, MA, 1981.

Palat, Madhavan. "Regulating Conflict through the Petition." In *Social Identities in Revolutionary Russia,* edited by M. Palat, 86–112. New York, 2001.

Pallot, Judith. *Land Reform in Russia, 1906–1917: Peasant Responses to Stolypin's Project of Rural Transformation.* Oxford, 1999.

Pallot, Judith, and Denis Shaw. *Landscape and Settlement in Romanov Russia, 1613–1917.* Oxford, 1999.

Pearson, Thomas. "Russian Law and Russian Justice: Activity and Problems of the Russian Justices of the Peace." *JfGO* 32, no. 1 (1984): 52–71.

———. *Russian Officialdom in Crisis: Autocracy and Local Self-Government, 1861–1900.* Cambridge, 1989.

Pomeranz, William. "Justice from Underground: The History of the Underground Advokatura." *RR* 52, no. 3 (1993): 321–40.

Popkins, Gareth. "Code vs. Custom? Norms and Tactics in Peasant Volost Court Appeals, 1889–1917." *RR* 59, no. 3 (2000): 408–24.

———. "Peasant Experiences of the Late Tsarist State: District Congresses of Land Captains, Provincial Boards and the Legal Appeals Process, 1891–1917." *SEER* 78, no. 1 (2000): 90–114.

———. "The Russian Peasant Volost Court and Customary Law, 1861–1917." Ph.D. diss., Oxford University, 1995.

———. "Russian Peasant Wills in the Decisions of the Ruling Senate, 1861–1906." *Legal History* 68, no. 2 (1999): 1–23.

"Porter plainte. Stratégies villageoises et institutions judiciaires en Ile-de-France (XVIIe–XVIIIe siècles)." *Droits et cultures*, v. 19 (1990): 7–118.

Prokof'eva, L. S. *Krest'ianskaia obshchina v Rossii vo vtoroi polovine XVIII–pervoi polovine XIX veka.* Leningrad, 1981.

Raskin, D. I. "Ispol'zovanie zakonodatel'nykh aktov v krest'ianskikh chelobitnykh serediny XVIII v." *Istoriia SSSR*, no. 4 (1979): 179–92.

Rieber, Alfred. "The Sedimentary Society." *Russian History* 16, nos. 2–4 (1989): 353–76.

Robbins, Richard. *Famine in Russia, 1891–1892: The Imperial Government Responds to a Crisis.* New York, 1975.

———. *The Tsar's Viceroys: Russian Provincial Governors in the Last Years of the Empire.* Ithaca, 1987.

Robinson, Geroid. *Rural Russia under the Old Regime: A History of the Landlord-Peasant World and a Prologue to the Peasant Revolution of 1917.* Berkeley, 1968.

Root, Hilton. *Peasants and Kings in Burgundy: Agrarian Foundation of French Absolutism.* Berkeley, 1987.

Rouland, Norbert. *Introduction historique au droit.* Paris, 1998.

Sabean, David. *Power in the Blood: Popular Culture and Village Discourse in Early Modern Germany.* Cambridge, 1984.

Sanborn, Joshua. *Drafting the Russian Nation: Military Conscription, Total War, and Mass Politics, 1905–1925.* DeKalb, IL, 2003.

Scott, James. *Domination and the Arts of Resistance: Hidden Transcripts.* New Haven, 1990.

———. *Weapons of the Weak: Everyday Forms of Peasant Resistance.* New Haven, 1985.

Seregny, Scott. "Peasants, Nation, and Local Government in Wartime Russia." *SR* 59, no. 2 (2000), 290–315, 336–42.

Shadle, Brett. "'Changing Traditions to Meet Current Altering Conditions': Customary Law, African Courts and the Rejection of Codification in Kenya, 1930–60." *Journal of African History* 40, no. 3 (1999): 411–31.

Shanin, Teodor. *The Roots of Otherness: Russia's Turn of Century.* Vol. 1, *Russia as a "Developing Society."* Vol. 2, *Russia, 1905–07: Revolution as Moment of Truth.* New Haven, 1985.

Sharpe, J. A. *Defamation and Sexual Slander in Early Modern England.* Oxford, 1988.

Shoemaker, Robert. "The Decline of Public Insult in London, 1600–1800." *Past and Present*, no. 169 (2000): 97–131.

Sidel'nikov, S. M., ed. *Agrarnaia reforma Stolypina.* Moscow, 1973.

Simonova, M. S. *Krizis agrarnoi politiki tsarizma nakanune pervoi Rossiiskoi revoliutsii.* Moscow, 1987.

———. "Mobilizatsiia krest'ianskoi nadel'noi zemli v period Stolypinskoi agrarnoi reformy." *Materialy po istorii sel'skogo khoziaistva i krest'ianstvo SSSR*, vol. 5 (Moscow, 1962): 398–458.

———. "Otmena krugovoi poruki." *Istoricheskie zapiski* 83 (1969): 159–95.

Skyner, Louis. "Property as Rhetoric: Land Ownership and Private Law in Pre-Soviet and Post-Soviet Russia." *Europe-Asia Studies* 55, no. 6 (2003): 889–905.

Stanziani, Allesandro. *L'économie en révolution. Le cas russe, 1870–1930.* Paris, 1998.

———. "Statisticiens, zemstva et Etat dans la Russia des années 1880." *CMRS* 32, no. 4 (1991): 445–68.

Tamanaha, Brian. "A Non-Essentialist Version of Legal Pluralism." *Journal of Law and Society* 27, no. 2 (2000): 296–321.

Tarabanova, T. A. "Volostnoi sud v Rossii v pervoe poreformennoe desiatiletie." Avtoreferat Kand. diss., MGU, 1993.

Taranovski, Theodore. "Alexander III and His Bureaucracy: The Limitations on Autocratic Power." *Canadian Slavonic Papers* 26, nos. 2–3 (1984): 207–19.

———. *Reform in Modern Russian History: Progress or Cycle?* New York, 1995.

Thompson, E. P. *Customs in Common: Studies in Traditional Popular Culture.* New York, 1991.

Tiukavkin, V. G. *Velikorusskoe krest'ianstvo i stolypinskaia agrarnaia reforma.* Moscow, 2001.

Verner, Andrew. *The Crisis of Russian Autocracy: Nicholas II and the 1905 Revolution.* Princeton, 1990.

———. "Discursive Strategies in the 1905 Revolution: Peasant Petitions from Vladimir Province." *RR* 54, no. 1 (1995): 65–90.

Vivier, Nadine. *Propriété collective et identité communale. Les Biens Communaux en France, 1750–1914.* Paris, 1998.

Vronskii, O. G. *Gosudarstvennaia vlast' Rossii i krest'ianskaia obshchina v gody "velikikh potriasenii" (1905–1917).* Tula, 2000.

———. *Krest'ianskaia obshchina na rubazhe XIX–XX vv. Struktura upravleniia, pozemel'nye otnosheniia, pravoporiadok.* Moscow, 1999.

Wagner, William. *Marriage, Property, and Law in Late Imperial Russia.* Oxford, 1994.

Waldron, Peter. *Between Two Revolutions: Stolypin and the Politics of Renewal in Russia.* DeKalb, IL, 1998.

Wcislo, Frank. *Reforming Rural Russia: State, Local Society, and National Politics, 1855–1914.* Princeton, 1990.

Weissman, Neil. *Reform in Tsarist Russia: The State Bureaucracy and Local Government, 1900–1914.* New Bruswick, NJ, 1981.

Whelan, Heidi. *Alexander III and the State Council: Bureaucracy and Counterreform in Late Imperial Russia.* New Brunswick, NJ, 1981.

Wirtschafter, Elise. "Legal Identity and the Possession of Serfs in Imperial Russia." *Journal of Modern History* 70, no. 3 (1998): 561–87.

———. *Social Identity in Imperial Russia.* DeKalb, IL, 1997.

Woodman, Gordon. "Ideological Combat and Social Observation: Recent Debate about Legal Pluralism." *Journal of Legal Pluralism,* no. 42 (1998): 21–59.

Worobec, Christine. *Peasant Russia: Family and Community in the Post-Emancipation Period.* Princeton, 1991.

Wortman, Richard. *The Development of Russian Legal Consciousness.* Chicago, 1976.

———. *Scenarios of Power: Myth and Ceremony in Russian Monarchy.* Vol. 2, *From Alexander II to the Abdication of Nicholas II.* Princeton, 1995.

Yaney, George. *The Systematization of Russian Government.* Urbana, IL, 1973.

———. *The Urge to Mobilize: Agrarian Reform in Russia, 1861–1930.* Urbana, IL, 1982.

Zaionchkovskii, P. A. *Pravitel'stvennyi apparat samoderzhavnoi Rossii.* Moscow, 1979.

———. *Rossiiskoe samoderzhavie v kontse XIX stoletiia.* Moscow, 1970.

Zakharova, L. G. *Samoderzhavie i otmena krepostnogo prava v Rossii, 1856–1861.* Moscow, 1984.

Zemtsov, L. I., ed. *Volostnoi sud v Rossii 60x–pervoi poloviny 70x godov XIX veka.* Voronezh, 2002.

Zuzykina, N. S. "Provedenie Stolypinskoi agrarnoi reformy v Riazanskoi gubernii, 1907–1914." Kand. diss., Moskovskii gor. ped. institut im. Potemkina, 1958.

Zyrianov, P. N. *Krest'ianskaia obshchina Evropeiskoi Rossii, 1907–1914.* Moscow, 1992.

———. "Obychnoe grazhdanskoe pravo v poreformennoi Rossii." *Ezhegodnik po agrarnoi istorii.* Vol. 6: 91–101. Vologda, 1976.

———. "Sotsial'naia struktura mestnogo upravleniia kapitalisticheskoi Rossii (1861–1914gg)." *IZ* 107 (1982): 226–303.

———. "Tret'ia Duma i vopros o reforme mestnogo suda i volostnogo upravleniia." *Istoriia SSSR,* no. 6 (1969): 45–62.

INDEX

◆ ◆ ◆